Who's Who in Shakespeare

Who's Who in Shakespeare

**Peter Quennell
and Hamish Johnson**

CHANCELLOR
PRESS

First published in Great Britain by Weidenfeld and Nicolson Ltd

This edition published by Chancellor Press
59 Grosvenor Street
London W1

© 1973 Peter Quennell and Hamish Johnson

ISBN 0 907486 14 2

The quotations from Shakespeare in this volume are taken
from the C. J. Sisson edition.

Printed in Hong Kong

Contents

List of abbreviations

The following abbreviations for
Shakespeare's plays are used:

All'sW.	All's Well that Ends Well
Ant.	Antony and Cleopatra
AYL.	As You Like It
Err.	The Comedy of Errors
Cor.	Coriolanus
Cym.	Cymbeline
Ham.	Hamlet
1H.IV	I Henry IV
2H.IV	2 Henry IV
H.V	Henry V
1H.VI	1 Henry VI
2H.VI	2 Henry VI
3H.VI	3 Henry VI
H.VIII	Henry VIII
Caes.	Julius Caesar
John	King John
Lr.	King Lear
LLL.	Love's Labour's Lost
Mac.	Macbeth
Meas.	Measure for Measure
Mer.V.	The Merchant of Venice
Wiv.	The Merry Wives of Windsor
MND.	A Midsummer Night's Dream
Ado	Much Ado About Nothing
Oth.	Othello
Per.	Pericles
R.II	Richard II
R.III	Richard III
Rom.	Romeo and Juliet
Shr.	The Taming of the Shrew
Tp.	The Tempest
Tim.	Timon of Athens
Tit.	Titus Andronicus
Troil.	Troilus and Cressida
Tw.N.	Twelfth Night
Gent.	The Two Gentlemen of Verona
Wint.	The Winter's Tale

Authors' acknowledgements

The authors would like to acknowledge their indebtedness to the following sources:

Barber, C.L., *Shakespeare's Festive Comedy*, 1959.

Bradbrook, M.C., *Shakespeare the Craftsman*, 1969.

Bradbrook, M.C., *Shakespeare and Elizabethan Poetry*, 1951.

Brockbank, J.P., 'History and Histrionics in *Cymbeline*', *Shakespeare Survey*, 11, 1958.

Brooke, Nicholas, *Shakespeare's Early Plays*, 1968.

Brown, J.R., *Shakespeare and his Comedies*, 1957.

Brown, J.R., *Shakespeare's Dramatic Style*, 1970.

Bullough, Geoffrey B., *Narrative and Dramatic Sources of Shakespeare*, 5 vols, 1957–65.

Dickens, Charles, 'The Restoration of Shakespeare's *Lear* to the stage', *The Examiner*, 4 February 1838.

Dickinson, H., 'The Reformation of Prince Hal', *Shakespeare Quarterly*, 12, 1961.

Draper, J.W., *The Humours of Shakespeare's Characters*, 1945.

Dunkel, W., 'Law and Equity in *Measure for Measure*', *Shakespeare Quarterly*, 13, 1962.

Duthie, G.I., *Shakespeare*, 1951.

Ettin, A.V., 'Shakespeare's first Roman Tragedy', *English Literary History*, 37, 1970.

Foakes, R.A., *Shakespeare: the Dark Comedies to the Last Plays*, 1971.

Heilbrun, C., 'The Character of Hamlet's Mother', *Shakespeare Quarterly*, 8, 1957.

Huntley, F.L., 'Macbeth and the Background of Jesuitical Equivocation', *Publications of the Modern Language Association*, LXXIX, 1964.

Jorgensen, P.A., *Shakespeare's Military World*, 1956.

Kermode, Frank, 'The Mature Comedies' in *Early Shakespeare, Stratford-upon-Avon Studies*, 3, 1961.

Kermode, Frank, 'What is Shakespeare's *Henry VIII* about?', *Durham University Journal*, new series ix, 1948.

Kirshbaum, L., 'Hamlet and Ophelia', *Philological Quarterly*, 35, 1956.

Knights, L.C., *William Shakespeare: the Histories*, 1962.

Manner and Meaning in Shakespeare. Stratford Papers 1965–7, ed. B.A.W. Jackson, 1969.

Marsh, D.R.C., *The Recurring Miracle*, 1964.

Matthews, H., *Character and Symbol in Shakespeare's Plays*, 1962.

Morris, Ivor, 'Cordelia and Lear', *Shakespeare Quarterly*, 13, 1957.

Muir, K., *Shakespeare's Tragic Sequence*, 1972.

Nosworthy, J.M., *Shakespeare's Occasional Plays*, 1965.

Othello, a casebook, ed. J. Wain, 1971.

Palmer, J.L., *Political and Comic Characters of Shakespeare*, 1962.

Pettigrew, H.P., 'Bassanio, the Elizabethan Lover', *Philological Quarterly*, 16, 1937.

Prosser, E., *Hamlet's Revenge*, 1968.

Ranold, M.R., 'The Indiscretions of Desdemona', *Shakespeare Quarterly*, 14, 1958.

Ribner, I., 'Bolingbroke, a True Machiavellian', *Modern Language Quarterly*, 9, 1948.

Richard II, new Arden edition, ed. P. Ure, 1956.

Schanzer, E., 'The Marriage-Contracts in *Measure for Measure*', *Shakespeare Survey*, 13, 1960.

Shakespeare 400, ed. J. Macmanaway, 1964.

Sisson, C.J., *The Mythical Sorrows of Shakespeare*, 1934.

Spencer, T.J.B., 'Greeks and Merrygreeks', in *Essays on Shakespeare*, ed. R. Hosley, 1962.

Spencer, T.J.B., 'Shakespeare and the Elizabethan Romans', *Shakespeare Survey*, 10, 1957.

Spivack, B., *Shakespeare and the Allegory of Evil*, 1958.

Studies in English Renaissance Literature, ed. W.F. McNeir, 1962.

Stokes, F.G., *A Dictionary of Characters in Shakespeare*, 1924.

The Tempest, new Arden edition, ed. F. Kermode, 1954.

Thomson, W.H., *Shakespeare's Characters, a Historical Dictionary*, 1951.

Trienew, R.J., 'The Inception of Leontes' Jealousy in *The Winter's Tale*', *Shakespeare Quarterly*, 4, 1953.

Ure, Peter, *Shakespeare: The Problem Plays*, 1961.

Waith, E.M., 'The Metamorphosis of Violence in *Titus Andronicus*', *Shakespeare Survey*, 10, 1957.

Wilson, J.D., *Shakespeare's Happy Comedies*, 1962.

Weiss, Theodore, *The Breath of Clowns and Kings*, 1967.

Photographic acknowledgements

The authors and publishers would like to thank the following museums, institutions and photographers for supplying the illustrations reproduced on the pages listed below:

Gordon Anthony 270 (top left); City of Manchester Art Galleries 52, 204 (top left); City Museum & Art Gallery, Birmingham 134 (left), 156, 222-3, 276-7; Anthony Crickmay 141, 257; Dominic 37, 148, 217 (right), 248; Eye International 32, 140, 191, 249; David Farrell 231; J. Freeman 33, 51, 93, 94, 101, 104, 153, 157 (right), 177 (right), 230, 240, 249, 273; Holte Photographics 118, 210, 217; Kunsthaus, Zurich 49, 102; Angus McBean 76, 106, 158, 160, 176 (left), 176 (right), 218 (right), 265, 288; Mansell Collection 78, 175 (top), 199, 202-3, 213, 236, 244 (right), 272 (top right), 284, 285 (top); Mary Evans Picture Library 36, 55 (left), 70, 80 (bottom), 136, 138 (top), 161 (left), 177 (left), 185, 255 (left), 256 (top), 269 (top left); National Film Archive Stills Library 27, 35, 59, 117, 125 (right), 151, 154, 155, 173 (top), 205, 246, 266; National Galleries of Scotland 207; National Theatre, London 35, 45 (top), 112, 132, 140, 141, 151, 152, 191, 217 (right), 243 (bottom left), 248, 249, 257, 288; Old Vic Archives 45 (bottom), 80 (top), 159 (left), 195; Radio Times Hulton Picture Library 28, 29, 31 (left), 31 (right), 32 (top), 32 (bottom), 36 (top right), 36 (bottom right), 38, 39, 41, 43, 44, 47, 50, 55 (right), 56, 58, 60, 67 (left), 67 (top right), 67 (bottom right), 71 (top), 73, 75, 89, 90, 91, 92, 98, 107, 111, 113, 114, 115, 116, 119, 121 (left), 121 (right), 122, 123, 124, 125 (left), 126 (top), 126 (bottom), 127, 128, 129 (top), 131 (left), 131 (right), 134 (right), 137, 139 (top), 139 (bottom), 142 (right), 143 (top), 143 (bottom), 149, 150 (left), 150 (right), 153, 157 (left), 159 (right), 161 (right), 162 (bottom), 163, 164 (right), 165, 171, 180, 181, 183, 188, 192, 193, 194, 197, 198 (bottom), 200, 201, 204 (bottom right), 208, 209, 214, 216, 218 (left), 219, 221, 224 (left), 225, 226 (left), 226 (right), 234, 239 (left), 239 (right), 241, 242, 243 (top), 244 (left), 245, 247 (bottom left), 247 (bottom right), 253, 255 (right), 258, 259, 260, 268 (top left), 268 (top right), 269 (top right), 270 (top left), 270 (top right), 270 (bottom), 271 (top), 271 (bottom), 279, 280 (top), 280 (bottom left), 280 (bottom right), 283, 285 (bottom left), 285 (bottom right); Raymond Mander and Joe Mitchenson Theatre Collection 138 (bottom); Royal Shakespeare Theatre, Stratford-upon-Avon 47, 101, 186, 187, 206, 235; Shakespeare Memorial Library, Stratford-upon-Avon 27, 76, 160, 176 (left), 176 (right), 218 (right), 265; Stratford Picture Gallery 148, 187 (top); Tate Gallery, London 52, 53, 71 (bottom), 96, 175 (bottom), 178, 179, 229, 232; Victoria & Albert Museum, London 26, 30, 33, 34, 42, 46, 48, 51, 66, 97, 100, 104, 129 (bottom), 135, 145, 157 (right) (Harry Beard Collection), 164 (left), 172 (top), 172 (bottom), 173 (bottom), 177 (right), 189, 193, 204 (top right), 211, 212, 215 (right), 224 (right), 227, 228, 230, 232, 233, 243 (bottom left), 256 (bottom), 268 (bottom), 272 (top left), 273, 278 (right), 286; Walker Art Gallery, Liverpool 122 (Sir J. Gilbert), 146-7, 187 (bottom) (F. R. Pickersgill), 198 (top), 240 (James T. Eglinton), 247 (top right) (Millais); Reg Wilson 25, 64, 68, 72, 174, 206, 215 (left), 231, 281.

Picture research by Pat Hodgson.

Introduction

Shakespeare's creative life began about 1590 and had ended before 1614; and during that period he wrote the thirty-seven plays that contain the material of the present volume. Over a thousand personages are listed here, ranging from characters who deserve only the briefest reference to such extraordinary creations of dramatic art as Othello, Falstaff, Lear and Hamlet. Like other great artists, besides sharpening and enlarging our vision of the world that we already know, Shakespeare opens our eyes to a whole new world, peopled by the creatures of his own mind; and, once we have encountered them, they seem often far more real and solid – since the traits they exhibit have been condensed by imaginative genius – than the majority of men and women we meet every day.

While Shakespeare was still active, at least one of his characters would appear almost to have crossed the dividing-line between the 'real' world and the world of fancy. Thus, in July 1599, Lady Southampton writes a gossiping letter to her husband, Shakespeare's early patron and beloved friend, then abroad on military service, where she remarks that 'all the news I can send you that I think will make you merry is that . . . Sir John Falstaff is by his dame, Mistress Pintpot, made father of a goodly miller's thumb, a boy that's all head and very little body . . . .' A miller's thumb is a small freshwater fish; and the nobleman she nicknames 'Falstaff' is thought to have been a one-time Lord Chamberlain, Lord Cobham. Similarly, a year later, Sir Charles Percy, when 'pestered with country business' at his secluded manor house in Gloucestershire, laments that, 'if I stay here long, you will find me so dull, that I shall be taken as a . . . Justice Shallow'. Evidently, Falstaff and his acquaintances and hangers-on had assumed just the kind of reality for a cultivated Elizabethan that Dickens' dramatis personae would later possess for the Victorian reading public. They were part of the background of daily existence, to be discussed and criticized, admired or hated; they had stepped off the dramatist's stage and found their way into the streets of London.

In what sense did Shakespeare 'create' his characters? Well, it was he, certainly, who endowed them with life, and lent them their distinctive form. Yet he never hesitated to borrow; and Falstaff himself, strangely enough, was a composite production, built up of three disreputable knights, Ned, Tom and Sir John Oldcastle, who figure in an early historical play, *The Famous Victories of Henry V,* written about 1586. Falstaff's accomplices, too, bear a strong resemblance to some of the comic personages presented there; and the carrier Derick's behaviour towards his hostess, Mistress Cobbler, recalls Falstaff's high-handed exploitation of the warm-hearted Mistress Quickly. Yet *The Famous Victories* is an inferior work, which modern critics have dismissed as nonsensically 'crude' and 'ribald'; while Shakespeare's portrait of the fat knight is one of his masterpieces, a character so surely and subtly drawn that we feel that it discloses only a fraction of Falstaff's monumental personality; that there is far more to him than the dramatist chooses to tell us, lurking, like the hidden bulk of an iceberg, immediately beyond our range.

We must always beware, however, of adopting a twentieth-century approach towards a sixteenth-century work of literature, and crediting Shakespeare with a degree of 'psychological' expertise that no Elizabethan playwright would either have appreciated or understood. Shakespeare's plays embody many of the traditions he had inherited from the learning of the Middle Ages. He seems to have believed, for example, not only that the Sun revolved around the Earth, and above the Earth rose a series of crystalline spheres, but that the human organism was compounded of four elements, Earth, Water, Fire and Air, each corresponding to a separate bodily 'humour' – Earth to melancholy, Water to phlegm, Fire to choler, Air to blood. A man's temperament was determined by the proportions in which they circulated through his body.

The noblest men had the most finely balanced systems, as Antony clearly shows when he delivers his splendid speech above the fallen Brutus:

> His life was gentle, and the elements
> So mixed in him that Nature might stand up
> And say to all the world 'This was a man!'

Nor does Cleopatra, on the point of committing suicide, forget this curiously persuasive theory. During the supreme crisis of her headstrong career, she thinks that she detects a sudden change in her spiritual metabolism, as the finest elements prevail over their less delicate, more earth-bound fellows:

> I am air and fire; my other elements
> I give to baser life. . . .

So far as we can judge, Shakespeare, at all events in his scientific and philosophic beliefs, remained a staunch conservative; but his conservatism was counterbalanced by a wonderfully acute insight into the working of the human spirit. He was an empirical realist; no other English poet has equalled him in observation. Who else could have reproduced so perfectly the accents of a devoted father speaking to a little boy, whose nose is smudged?

> I'fecks!
> Why, that's my bawcock. What, hast smutcht thy nose? –
> They say it is a copy out of mine. Come, captain,
> We must be neat; – not neat, but cleanly, captain. . . .

Shakespeare was never a man who studied life at a distance. Undoubtedly, he was very much attached to the social world in which he lived. He enjoyed life; and all the surviving descriptions of the dramatist dwell on his friendliness and amiability, his wit, civility and social charm. He had 'loved the man', wrote Ben Jonson, who might have been expected to dislike his brilliant rival. Shakespeare, he declared, 'was, indeed, honest, and of an open and free nature: had an excellent Fancy, brave notions and gentle expressions: wherein he flowed with that facility that sometimes it was necessary he should be stopped'.

There is a peculiar fairness – a kind of open-minded generosity – about Shakespeare's treatment of his main characters that makes them all the more impressive. Even his villains, from Richard III to Iago, are examined and illuminated – Richard, for instance, is the victim of self-hatred, mixed with solipsistic self-love – rather than written off as mere monstrosities. Not that his general view of life was sanguine. During his closing period, when he produced his darkest tragedies and his bitter tragi-comedies, he would appear to have passed through a phase of black depression, from which he did not finally emerge until, in 1611, he wrote *The Tempest*; and his last comedy, despite its exquisitely romantic atmosphere, ends on a peculiarly uncheerful note. Human life, announces Prospero, is an 'insubstantial pageant', a dream that will one day fade and dissolve, leaving 'not a wrack behind'.

This volume, however, is largely confined to facts. It is intended as a guide-book for the reader of the huge Shakespearian canon who wishes to recollect where such-and-such a character occurs, and the function he or she performs. The text employed throughout is that of *William Shakespeare: the Complete Works,* edited by C. J. Sisson, a convenient and reliable edition, based on the findings of modern textual scholarship, which incorporates some useful historical essays and an Index of Characters, compiled by Terence Spencer. Characters from *Pericles* and *Henry VIII* are included in the present volume, since both plays are now usually held to have been, for the most part, Shakespeare's work. None has been taken, on the other hand, from *Sir Thomas More* or *The Two Noble Kinsmen*, where his contribution – if indeed he contributed scenes – is thought to have been relatively small. Each entry summarizes a character, and establishes that character's importance in the action of the play; and quotations from famous early critics, Johnson, Coleridge, and Hazlitt, have been added to detailed accounts of the more imposing personages. How vividly Shakespeare's characters still live is shown by the multitude of different responses that they have evoked during the last three hundred years. We continue to discuss them as we discuss our friends and enemies; and it is often no less difficult to reach a definite conclusion about their virtues or their vices. Was Hamlet an heroic visionary or a murderous paranoiac? Wherever the truth may lie, Hamlet still exists; and his existence has had a profound effect on the English literary imagination.

A

AARON *(Tit.)*: a Moor, loved by Tamora, who is brought to Rome with her and other prisoners after the Goths have been defeated by Titus Andronicus (I.i). He checks a quarrel between Tamora's sons over Lavinia, and incites them both to rape and mutilate her. He organizes the murder of Bassianus, and fixes the blame on Titus' sons Quintus and Martius, who are executed for the crime. He then tells Titus that he can save his sons by sacrificing his right hand, and cuts it off for him (III.i). Tamora bears an illegitimate child by Aaron which threatens to expose his treachery, but he refuses to have it killed (IV.ii). He is captured by Lucius' army while trying to smuggle the child out of Rome, and confesses when Lucius agrees to spare the child (v.i). He is condemned to be set 'breast deep' in the earth and starved to death.

Aaron is essentially a mixture of three theatrical types: like Barabas in Marlowe's *The Jew of Malta* he is a heartless Machiavel, an advocate of 'policy and stratagem', and 'chief architect and plotter' of the tragic events; like the fiendish Muly Hamet in Peele's *The Battle of Alcazar* he is the evil Moor of Christian tradition, a figure distinguished by his eroticism and cruelty; above all, he is a stage devil, the direct descendant of the figure of Vice in the medieval morality plays. Shakespeare gives him a superficial rationale for his villainy in ambition and a vague desire for revenge, but it is not adequate to account for his behaviour. The need to adapt the allegorical figure of Vice to the more naturalistic Elizabethan stage lies behind Aaron's extraordinary combination of utter villainy and paternal affection: he is given a motive for his final confession in his desire to save his bastard son, whom he has previously fiercely defended in what Hazlitt saw as the best scene (IV.i) in the play – 'the only one worthy of Shakespeare'. After confessing his crimes, Aaron reverts to his role of the personification of evil as he scornfully dismisses any notion of repentance for his deeds:

Ay that I had not done a thousand more,

Anthony Quayle as Aaron, the Moor brought to Rome by Titus with Tamora who bears him a child, the incriminating evidence of his treachery against the Romans.

Even now I curse the day and yet I think
Few come within the compass of my curse,
Wherein I did not some notorious ill.
As kill a man, or else devise his death,
Ravish a maid, or plot the way to do it,
Accuse some innocent, and forswear myself,
Set deadly enmity between two friends,
Make poor men's cattle break their necks,
Set fire on barns and haystacks in the night,
And bid the owners quench them with their tears:
Oft have I digg'd up dead men from their graves,
And set them upright at their dear friends' door,
Even when their sorrows almost was forgot,
And on their skins as on the bark of trees,
Have with my knife carved in Roman letters,
Let not your sorrow die though I am dead.
But I have done a thousand dreadful things,
As willingly as one would kill a fly,
And nothing grieves me heartily indeed,
But that I cannot do ten thousand more. (v.i)

This is villainy for the sake of homiletic display: here, as frequently throughout the play, Aaron speaks according to the convention of self-revelation that was requisite for a figure such as Vice in the abstract and didactic morality plays.

For all his obvious ancestry, Aaron is a peculiarly Shakespearian figure – although there is a Moor in the story in the Folger Library chap-book that is the probable major source of the play, he is always subservient to the queen. In *Titus Andronicus* Aaron is at the centre of the play, the controlling intelligence who plots monstrous deeds and leads others to commit them. He is a forebear of other Shakespearian villains, notably Richard III and Iago, whose scorn for 'honest men' he shares.

ABBESS, THE *(Err.)*, *see* AEMILIA.

ABBOT OF WESTMINSTER, THE *(R.II)*, *see* WESTMINSTER.

ABERGAVENNY, LORD *(H.VIII)*: George Neville, son-in-law to Buckingham. He is arrested and sent to the Tower at the same time as his father-in-law (I.i).

Historically, George Neville (c.1471–1535), eldest son of George, 2nd Baron Abergavenny, and grandson of Edward Neville, sixth and youngest son of the 1st Earl of Westmorland. He was a favourite of Henry VIII's until he became involved with the troubles which overtook Buckingham. He was arrested in 1521, and though he was pardoned after a year, he was never fully trusted again.

ABHORSON *(Meas.)*: an executioner who reluctantly agrees to take on the bawd Pompey as his apprentice (IV.ii). He and Pompey come for Barnadine who insists that he is too hung-over to die (IV.iii).

ABRAHAM *(Rom.)*: servant to Montague. He quarrels with two of Capulet's servants and a fight breaks out which is the first dramatic indication of the hostility between the two families (I.i).

ACHILLES *(Troil.)*: son of Peleus and Thetis, the Greeks' most illustrious warrior. The war is reduced to stalemate by his refusal to fight; he remains in his tent enjoying Patroclus' mimicry of the other Greek leaders. He disdains Hector's challenge (II.i). Ulysses instigates a plot to use Achilles' pride to rouse him to action: Ajax is selected to meet Hector in combat, and is made the centre of attention, while Achilles is treated with ostentatious indifference. As Ajax prepares to fight Hector, Achilles watches with amusement (IV.v); after meeting Hector, he agrees to fight with him on the following day. A letter from Hecuba in Troy reminding him of his 'major vow' to her daughter Polyxena causes him to withdraw. He is finally roused to action when Hector kills Patroclus. On the battlefield Hector finds Achilles tired and resting, and courteously avoids a fight (V.vi); Achilles then instructs his Myrmidons to find Hector and kill him. They murder him while he is unarmed, and proclaim Achilles as his conqueror.

The character of Achilles shares the problematic quality of *Troilus and Cressida* as a whole. Before he appears he is called a 'drayman' (by Pandarus) and

... great Achilles, whom opinion crowns
The sinew, and the fore-hand of our host, (I.iii)

(by Ulysses); and much is made of his overweening pride. Yet we first see him laughing and joking with Thersites, who is a surprising companion for a proud man. Indeed, Achilles is the only character in the play who finds Thersites amusing, and who is not so proud as to be offended by his insults. It is not pride, but rather confidence, that allows Achilles to disdain Hector's challenge: as Ajax prepares to fight Hector, Achilles simply watches with amusement, and passes sardonic comments. He has earlier seen through

Achilles, the disdainful warrior who refuses to fight Hector and is only roused to action by a plot devised by Ulysses.

Ulysses' attempt to trick him by appealing to his pride:

> I see my reputation is at stake,
> My fame is shrewdly gor'd. (III.iii).

The final murder of Hector by the Myrmidons, for which Achilles claims the credit, is heavily ironic: when Achilles finally does act, it is dishonourably. He has learnt from Ulysses to equate honour with reputation: the murder is the logical outcome of the translation of Ulysses' cynical intellectual exercise into action.

The Achilles who orders the murder of Hector is a different, less complex figure than that of the earlier scenes: the distinctively Shakespearian character becomes a near burlesque version of the wrathful Achilles of legend. The shift of emphasis is marked by a change in his style of speech – his final speeches are rhetorical, almost incantatory:

> Look now Hector how the sun begins to set;
> How ugly night comes breathing at his heels,
> Even with the vail and darking of the sun,
> To close the day up, Hector's life is done. (v.viii)

This Achilles is not the epic hero of Homer's *Iliad*, but the tainted figure of medieval tradition which took Hector as the model chivalric hero. During the Renaissance the Greeks were generally denigrated – the word 'Greek' itself was common slang for a voluptuary or crook. The 'Greek vice' was common slang for homosexuality, but we should beware of making too much of Thersites' suggestion that Patroclus is Achilles' 'masculine whore', since it comes from a very unreliable source. Shakespeare's most likely sources for his version of Achilles in the later scenes were Caxton's *Recuyell of the Historyes of Troy* (c. 1474) and Lydgate's *Troy-Booke* (1513). From these he took the story of the

murder of Troilus by the Myrmidons and adapted it to Hector. Both Caxton and Lydgate mention Achilles' love for Polyxena, but they have it starting a year after Hector's death; Shakespeare brings it forward to provide Achilles with an excuse for not meeting Hector, and to draw a parallel with the situation of Troilus.

It has been suggested that there is a parallel between Achilles and Patroclus sitting in their tent deriding their fellow commanders and the situation at Essex House in the winter of 1600–01: from there the dissident Earl of Essex and his followers railed at the Queen's Privy Councillors. Chapman had already identified Achilles with Essex in the dedication to his translation of the *Seven Books of the Iliads of Homer* (1598). Shakespeare was an admirer of Essex, and this perhaps accounts for the sympathetic treatment that Achilles receives in the first half of the play – he is, in his perverse way, a man of some integrity and honesty. His sudden transformation into a mindless murderer is one of the many inconsistencies in the play which have given rise to prolonged and unresolved critical debate (*see* PANDARUS).

ADAM *(AYL.)*: an old servant of Sir Rowland de Boys, now serving Orlando, whom he warns of Oliver's plans against his life. He offers Orlando all his savings, and follows him into exile; he drops out of the play after the second act.

The corresponding character in Lodge's *Rosalynde* is Adam Spencer (i.e. Adam the Spencer). Legend has it that this part was played by Shakespeare.

ADAM *(Shr.)*: one of the servants at Petruchio's country house (IV.i).

ADRIAN *(Cor.)*: a Volscian, sent to Rome to find Nicanor, a Roman spy for the Volscians. He meets him

Arthur Hughes' painting showing Touchstone and Audrey, Orlando and his old servant Adam, and Rosalind in scenes from *As You Like It*.

on the road, and learns from him that Coriolanus has been banished (IV.iii).

ADRIAN *(Tp.)*: a lord, attendant to Alonso, King of Naples, who is shipwrecked with him (II.i).

ADRIANA *(Err.)*: the jealous wife of Antipholus of Ephesus, who mistakes his twin brother Antipholus of Syracuse for her husband. When she hears that her 'husband' has been making love to her sister Luciana she reproaches him, and forgives him, but fears that he is mad. Her impression is confirmed when she is accused of having locked her husband out of his own house. She has Antipholus of Ephesus bound as a lunatic, and then encounters Antipholus of Syracuse with drawn rapier. She pursues him to an abbey, where she is told that if her husband is mad it is due to her shrewishness.

A scene from *The Comedy of Errors*. Left to right: Pinch, Adriana (Diana Rigg), her husband Antipholus of Ephesus, and Dromio of Ephesus.

Finally both twins appear and the errors are resolved, and she is reconciled with her husband.

In the source, the *Menaechmi* of Plautus, the corresponding figure is the Wife, a conventional jealous shrew. Adriana is more complex: her grief when she thinks herself abandoned, and her loyalty to her husband, are genuinely moving. There is nothing farcical about her jealousy:

Ah do not tear away thyself from me;
For know, my love, as easy may'st thou fall
A drop of water in the breaking gulf,
And take unmingled thence that drop again,
Without addition or diminishing,
As take from me thyself, and not me too.
Shouldst thou but hear I were licentious,
And that this body, consecrate to thee,
By ruffian lust should be contaminate?
Wouldst thou not spit at me, and spurn at me,
And hurl the name of husband in my face,
And tear the stained skin off my harlot brow,

And from my false hand cut the wedding ring,
And break it with a deep-divorcing vow? (II.ii)

It seems that Shakespeare could not entirely withhold sympathy from Adriana, and gave her several poignant speeches that are out of key with the general light-hearted tone of the play. But it is in these speeches that we see signs of the great poet to come.

ADRIANO, DON *(LLL.)*, *see* ARMADO.

AEDILES *(Cor.)*: Roman municipal officers, in charge of public buildings, policing, etc. Brutus calls aediles to arrest Coriolanus (III.i), but they are driven off in the ensuing brawl. An aedile collects the votes when Coriolanus is tried (III.iii).

AEGEON *(Err.)*, *see* EGEON.

AEMILIA, THE ABBESS *(Err.)*: wife to Egeon, and mother of the Antipholus twins. Separated from her family during a shipwreck, and thinking them dead, she has become an abbess at Ephesus. She gives sanctuary to Antipholus of Syracuse, and when she takes him before the Duke to seek justice she recognizes her husband, who is on his way to execution. The errors are resolved, and the family reunited (v.i).

The domestic drama of Aemilia and Egeon that frames the main comedy derives from the popular romance *Apollonius of Tyre,* which was available to Shakespeare in Gower's *Confessio Amantis.*

AEMILIUS *(Tit.)*: a 'noble Roman', who announces that Lucius and the Goths are marching on Rome, and is sent as envoy to them (IV.iv). At the end, he recognizes Lucius as emperor, and presents him to the people (v.iii).

Aemilius is a representative figure, associated with Lucius and the new regenerate order, a somewhat unnecessary supplementary to Marcus Andronicus *(q.v.)*.

AEMILIUS LEPIDUS *(Caes; Ant.)*, *see* LEPIDUS.

AENEAS *(Ham.)*: part assumed by the First Player (II.ii).

AENEAS *(Troil.)*: a Trojan warrior who accompanies Troilus to the battlefield (I.i). He arrives at the Greek camp, where he fails to recognize 'great Agamemnon', and delivers Hector's challenge to single combat with the Greek champion (I.iii). He informs Troilus that Cressida is to be given up to the Greeks (IV.ii). He is present at the end when Hector's death is announced.

According to Pandarus, Aeneas is 'one of the flowers of Troy' (I.ii). His ceremonial manner is in sharp contrast

to the bluntness of the Greek generals.

He was the son of Anchises and Venus; his wanderings after the fall of Troy form the subject of Virgil's *Aeneid.* According to Holinshed, the name 'Britain' derived from Aeneas' grandson Brutus; thus during the Middle Ages and the Renaissance the Trojans and not the Greeks were seen by the English as the heroes of the Troy legend.

AGAMEMNON *(Troil.)*: brother of Menelaus; King of the Mycenaeans and commander of the Greeks at Troy. He says a lot, but does little, and has hardly any influence on the plot. He seems barely involved in the battle he is supposedly directing. His appearance and bearing are also apparently undistinguished, since Aeneas fails to recognize him as 'the high and mighty Agamemnon' (I.iii).

The eighteenth-century actress Mrs Inchbald as the Abbess Aemilia, mother of the Antipholus twins, who has entered a convent at Ephesus.

Despite his office, Agamemnon is not a figure of great importance in either the Homeric or the medieval versions of the Troy legend; nor is he in *Troilus and Cressida.* He is notable chiefly for his large vocabulary and his convoluted, Latinate style. For a general, he is surprisingly impractical and fatalistic – are not the Greek misfortunes simply

. . . the protractive trials of great Jove,

To find persistive constancy in men? (I.iii)

he complacently asks.

AGRIPPA *(Ant.)*: friend of Octavius, who suggests that Antony should marry Octavia (II.ii). He has a short speech extolling the memory of Antony (V.i).

Agrippa is not strongly characterized, but in his one important scene (II.ii) he comes over as a slick politician, a cynic with a sharp eye for public appearances rather than the truth. Despite his stress on Octavia's grace and beauty, his real interest is in the political consequences of the marriage.

Historically, he was Marcus Vipsanius Agrippa, the commander of Octavius' fleet at Actium. He later married Octavius' daughter.

AGRIPPA, MENENIUS *(Cor.), see* MENENIUS.

AGUECHEEK, SIR ANDREW *(Tw.N.)*: a foolish knight, suitor to Olivia. He is gulled by Sir Toby Belch into composing a challenge to Cesario (the disguised Viola), but is then terrified by Sir Toby's fictitious accounts of his valour and fencing skill. The duel is interrupted by Antonio, and Cesario withdraws. Sir Andrew sees this as an indication of cowardice, and follows him; he meets Sebastian, and strikes him, mistaking him for Cesario, and is soundly beaten as a result.

Sir Andrew is a caricature, a lean 'thin faced' figure with hair that 'hangs like flax on a distaff', who imagines that he is a gallant. He is easily gulled – Fabian calls him Sir Toby's 'manakin'. He has his own peculiar kind of insight into his condition:

Methinks sometimes I have no more wit than a Christian or an ordinary man has. But I am a great

An engraving by J. Swain showing, from left to right, Sir Andrew Aguecheek, Feste and Sir Toby Belch.

eater of beef, and I believe that does harm to my wit (I.iii)

AJAX *(Troil.)*: a Greek commander who is also a lord of Trojan blood since he is Hector's nephew. Lumbering and slow-witted, he is easily persuaded by Ulysses' flattery into replacing Achilles in single combat with Hector (II.iii). The fight is broken off when Hector remembers their kinship (IV.v). In the battle at the end, he overcomes Aeneas (V.vi).

Shakespeare's Ajax is probably a combination of Homer's slow but stalwart Ajax Telamon and the boastful, stupid Ajax described in Ovid's *Metamorphoses*. He is characterized early on by Alexander:

This man, Lady, hath robb'd many beasts of their particular additions, he is as valiant as the lion, churlish as the bear, slow as the elephant: a man into whom nature hath so crowded humours, that his valour is crushed into folly, his folly sauced with discretion: there is no man hath a virtue, that he hath not a glimpse of, nor any man an attaint, but he carries some stain of it. He is melancholy without cause, and merry against the hair, he hath the joints of everything, but everything so out of joint, that he is a gouty Briareus, many hands and no use; or purblinded Argus, all eyes and no sight. (I.i)

It has been suggested that an Elizabethan audience would recognize Ajax as a caricature of Ben Jonson, and that this is Shakespeare's 'purge' referred to in the third of the anonymous *Parnassus* plays as a reply to the 'pill' of Jonson's *Poetaster*. The scatological pun that results from the Elizabethan pronunciation of Ajax as 'a jakes' (a privy) perhaps relates to the 'purge'; it also must have made it impossible to present Ajax as other than a comic butt.

ALARBUS *(Tit.)*: eldest son of Tamora, queen of the Goths. He is brought to Rome as a prisoner with his mother and brothers where he is dismembered and burnt as a sacrifice to appease the 'groaning shadows' of Titus' sons who have been killed in the war against the Goths (I.i).

The incident is probably adapted from Seneca's *Troades*, in which Hecuba's daughter Polyxena and Andromache's son Astyanax have to be sacrificed to appease the shade of Achilles.

ALBANY, DUKE OF *(Lr.)*: the husband of Goneril, who scorns him for his 'milky gentleness' (I.iv). His rebukes to her turn to hatred and rage as he discovers more of her machinations and cruelties. He is distressed by the blinding of Gloucester, and vows to 'revenge his eyes'. He has to choose between opposing the foreign-backed rebels following Cordelia and supporting Goneril and Regan, rulers that he knows to be wicked. He is irresolute, but duty leads him to oppose Cordelia. On the death of Lear he becomes King of

Britain, and asks Kent and Edmund to rule with him.

Albany's character is largely a function of the plot: he has to be in love with Goneril at first until he sees her as she is, and he has to be prepared to fight a foreign invader. He is the representative of common sense and outraged decency.

ALCIBIADES *(Tim.)*: 'an Athenian Captaine' who asks the Athenian senate to pardon a friend who has been condemned to death for manslaughter. His request is refused, and his defiant and angry retort results in his immediate banishment (III.v). He meets Timon in the wood and offers him gold, although he has very little; Timon spurns the offer, and gives him more gold to finance an attack on Athens. Alcibiades enters Athens with an army, but magnanimously restricts his vengeance to the proven enemies of Timon and himself. He speaks Timon's epitaph (v.iv), and also the final words of reconciliation.

It seems as though Shakespeare intended Alcibiades as a contrast to Timon: Alcibiades is a pragmatist, Timon an idealist. Alcibiades is a victim of injustice and ingratitude, but his response is quite different from that of Timon – he takes positive action, like the practical soldier he is, and gathers an army with which to take his revenge. But Alcibiades is not a fully rounded character; the part is only roughly shaped, and he is certainly not acceptable as a standard by which Timon can be judged.

Shakespeare based his character on the account of Alcibiades in Plutarch's *Life of Marcus Antonius*; he does not seem to have made very extensive use of Plutarch's *Life of Alcibiades*. In the latter Alcibiades is a prodigal womanizer, distinguished by his chameleon-like adaptability. Historically, Alcibiades was an Athenian general and politician (*c*.450–04 BC) who changed sides twice.

ALENCON, DUKE OF *(H.V)*: John, 1st Duke of Alençon. He is mentioned as being with the French army before Agincourt (III.v). We hear that Henry has fought with Alençon during the battle, and taken his glove, which he gives to Fluellen (IV.vii). Alençon is killed in the battle, having previously killed the Duke of York.

According to Holinshed, Henry was 'almost felled by the Duke of Alençon; yet with plain strength he slue two of the Dukes companie, and felled the duke himself; whome, when he would have yielded, the king's gard (contrarie to his mind) slue out of hand'.

ALENCON, DUKE OF *(1H.VI)*: John, 2nd Duke of Alençon. He joins Charles against the English, and marvels at their courage (I.ii). He advises Charles to make a truce, and 'break it when his pleasure serves'.

ALEXANDER *(Troil.)*: servant to Cressida. He characterizes Ajax to her, and tells of Hector's anger and shame since Ajax 'struck him down' in battle (I.ii).

ALEXANDER THE GREAT *(LLL.)*: role assumed by Nathaniel in the pageant (v.ii).

ALEXAS *(Ant.)*: eunuch, an attendant to Cleopatra. He is sent as an envoy to Herod; it is later revealed (IV.vi) that he treacherously tried to turn him against Antony. Enobarbus reports that he was hanged on Caesar's orders (IV.vi).

ALICE *(H.V)*: one of the Princess Katharine's waiting-women, who teaches her mistress a little English (III.iv). She acts as interpreter when Henry tries to woo Katharine (v.ii).

ALIENA *(AYL.)*: name assumed by Celia *(q.v.)*.

ALONSO *(Tp.)*: King of Naples, father of Ferdinand and brother of Sebastian, who had helped Antonio usurp Prospero's dukedom on condition that it was held as a fief of Naples. He is returning from Tunis, where he has seen his daughter married to the king, when he is shipwrecked on Prospero's island. He thinks his son Ferdinand drowned, and when reminded of his misdeeds by the spirit Ariel he is filled with remorse, and contemplates suicide (III.iii). He asks for, and is granted, Prospero's pardon; he restores his dukedom, and joyfully assents to the marriage of Ferdinand and Miranda (v.i).

AMAZONS *(Tim.)*: a mythical race of female warriors. Women in this guise are led in by a boy dressed as Cupid to perform a masque for Timon and his guests at a banquet (I.ii).

AMAZONS, QUEEN OF THE *(MND.)*, *see* HIPPOLYTA.

AMBASSADOR, ANTONY'S *(Ant.)*, *see* SCHOOLMASTER.

AMBASSADORS, ENGLISH *(Ham.)*: they arrive bringing word to Hamlet that Rosencrantz and Guildenstern have been executed in accordance with his instructions; but they are too late, as Hamlet is already dead (v.ii).

AMBASSADORS OF FRANCE *(H.V)*: they bring a contemptuous message from the Dauphin to Henry, and present him with tennis balls. They are angrily dismissed by Henry with his declaration of war on France (I.ii).

AMBASSADORS, PAPAL *(1H.VI)*: two are sent by the Pope to Henry VI with a letter asking him to make peace with France. Henry tells them that he agrees to their request, and also to the condition that he marry the daughter of the Earl of Armagnac (v.i).

AMIENS *(AYL.)*: a lord attending the banished Duke in the Forest of Arden. It is a musical part. Amiens sings 'Under the greenwood tree' (II.v) and 'Blow, blow, thou winter wind' (II.vii).

ANDREW, SIR *(Tw.N.), see* AGUECHEEK.

ANDROMACHE *(Troil.)*: Hector's wife. Because of her ominous dreams, she tries to dissuade him from joining the battle; he ignores her warnings, and is killed (v.iii).

ANDRONICUS, MARCUS *(Tit.)*: a Roman tribune, brother to Titus Andronicus. He announces that the Roman people have adopted Titus as candidate for the vacant throne. He welcomes the victorious Titus, who declines the offer; Marcus proclaims Saturninus emperor (I.i). He supports Bassianus when he claims Lavinia for his bride; he persuades Titus to allow the unfortunate Mutius *(q.v.)* to be buried in the family vault. It is he who discovers the raped and mutilated Lavinia, and brings her to Titus; he later teaches her to write in the sand (IV.i). He remains close to Titus, and humours him in his insanity. At the end he explains to the people the reasons for Titus' revenge, and hails Lucius as emperor.

Marcus is the representative of goodness and normality, which disappear as Rome degenerates into 'a wilderness of tigers'. Unlike his brother Titus, age has brought him wisdom and maturity: when he explains the tragic events to the people at the end, he reminds them of his

> . . . frosty signs and chaps of age
> Grave witnesses of true experience. (v.iii)

(Some editors give these lines to Aemilius.) Marcus is the representative of the old imperial order which is contrasted with the decadence associated with Saturninus; and he is a link with the new order under Lucius. Thus at the end it is he who presents Lucius to the people, and stresses the need for internal order and the restoration of 'degree', one of the most important Elizabethan political tenets:

> You sad-fac'd men, people and sons of Rome,
> By uproars sever'd like a flight of fowl
> Scatter'd by winds and high tempestuous gusts,
> O, let me teach you how to knit again
> This scatter'd corn into one mutual sheaf,
> These broken limbs again into one body;
> Lest Rome herself be bane unto herself,

> And she whom mighty kingdoms court'sy to,
> Like a forlorn and desperate castaway,
> Do shameful execution on herself. (v.iii)

ANDRONICUS, TITUS *(Tit.)*: an ageing Roman general who returns to Rome in triumph after his sixth victory over the Goths. He brings their queen, Tamora, as captive. He has her son Alarbus sacrificed on behalf of his own dead sons; this last campaign has left him with only four out of twenty-five. He waives the offer of the imperial crown in favour of the late emperor's son Saturninus, and consents to the marriage of his daughter Lavinia to him. Lavinia is claimed by Bassianus, and carried off by him. Titus' son Mutius tries to stop him pursuing the couple, and is killed by him. But Saturninus scorns Titus, and chooses Tamora as his bride. She is determined to have revenge on Titus, and her lover Aaron arranges a trap for two of his sons, Quintus and Martius. They are accused of the murder of Bassianus, and condemned to death. While Titus is grieving over their deed, the mutilated Lavinia is brought before him; he is told by Aaron that if he sacrifices a hand his sons will be spared. The severed hand is returned to him along with the heads of his sons. Titus urges Lucius, who decides to flee to the Goths, to return with an avenging army; and he shoots arrows towards heaven with messages for the gods. Tamora, Demetrius and Chiron, disguised as 'Revenge', 'Murder' and 'Rapine', try to get Titus to invite Lucius to a banquet; recognizing them, he agrees. He summons help, and ritually kills Demetrius and Chiron, cutting their throats while Lavinia catches the blood in a basin. He bakes their flesh in pies, and dressed as a cook serves them to Tamora and Saturninus at a banquet. He kills Lavinia, tells his guests what they have eaten, and then stabs Tamora; he is killed by Saturninus, who in turn is killed by Lucius.

Titus is introduced as a traditional 'noble Roman' – he is 'renowned Titus' and 'Patron of virtue, Rome's best champion' (I.i). He is devoted to authority and tradition: the sacrifice of Alarbus, an indication of his 'cruel, irreligious piety', is just the kind of behaviour an Elizabethan audience would have expected from a stern 'Roman'. Likewise they would have approved of his choice of Saturninus, the dead emperor's eldest son, to succeed to the throne; in their terms it was the right choice, though in the play it turns out to be fatal. Titus' killing of Mutius, however, shows the danger inherent in his blind devotion to a rigid code of morality: although Roman fathers had unlimited powers of life and death over their sons, Mutius' only crime was disobedience, and Titus' response reveals that age has not brought him wisdom and magnanimity.

As his sufferings increase, we see another aspect of Titus – that of the impotent and pathetic old man. He

Colin Blakely as Titus in the Royal Shakespeare
Company's 1972 production of *Titus Andronicus*.

wavers between stoic nobility and frenzied anguish.
His distraction produces one marvellous dramatic
surprise that foreshadows the madness of Lear – Titus
sees Marcus kill a fly:

Titus: Out on thee, murderer: thou kill'st my
          heart,
          Mine eyes cloy'd with view of tyranny:
          A deed of death done on the innocent
          Becomes not Titus' brother: get thee gone,
          I see thou art not for my company.
Marcus: Alas, my Lord, I have but kill'd a fly.
Titus: But how, if that fly had a father and
          mother?
          How would he hang his slender gilded
          wings
          And buzz lamenting doings in the air, ·
          Poor harmless fly,
          That with his pretty buzzing melody
          Came here to make us merry,
          And thou hast kill'd him. (III.ii)

In the last act, all trace of the 'noble Roman'
disappears as Titus becomes an absurd demonic
avenger, who is seemingly determined to be even more
barbaric than his enemies. Even so, he still appeals to
authority – a classical precedent – before he murders
his daughter. Virginius' murder of his daughter
provides for him

A reason mighty, strong, and effectual;
A pattern, precedent, and lively warrant
For me, most wretched, to perform the like.
Die, die, Lavinia, and thy shame with thee. (V.iii)

The character of Titus has many elements that
Shakespeare was to develop more fully in his great
tragic heroes. The closest parallel is with Lear, another
old man who is forced to suffer the consequences of his
own folly. And like Coriolanus, Titus' tragedy proceeds
from the very quality that has made him great – his
rigorous devotion to a stern Roman code of honour.

The most likely source of *Titus Andronicus* is a prose
story which is preserved in an eighteenth-century

Titus Andronicus (v.ii): Titus ritually kills Tamora's sons with the aid of Lavinia. The frontispiece to Rowe's 1709 edition of Shakespeare.

chap-book now in the Folger Library. The dominant influence on the play, and the source of several of its incidents, is Ovid's *Metamorphoses*.

Titus Andronicus is one of Shakespeare's earliest plays, possibly the earliest: it was certainly written before 1594, possibly as early as 1589. Critics have until recently been offended by the violence and horror in the play, and have sought to relieve Shakespeare of responsibility for it. It has been attributed to a variety of other authors; it has been suggested that it is the product of a collaboration, or a hasty revision of an old play. However, modern scholars accept that the play is from Shakespeare's hand, and have found in it much that prefigures his later development. There is solid external evidence too: Francis Meres listed the play as Shakespeare's in 1598, and Heminge and Condell printed it in the First Folio in 1623.

ANGELICA *(Rom.)*, *see* Nurse.

ANGELO *(Err.)*: a goldsmith. He makes a necklace for Antipholus of Ephesus, and when ordered to take it to him he meets Antipholus of Syracuse: he denies ordering it, but Angelo insists that he has it (III.ii). Angelo needs money to pay a debt: Antipholus of Ephesus tells him to take the necklace to his wife Adriana and ask for payment. Angelo insists that he has already given him the chain, and has him arrested for debt (IV.i).

He is amazed when Antipholus of Syracuse enters wearing the golden chain. At the end he helps clear up the various mysteries.

ANGELO *(Meas.)*: the deputy who is given full authority in the Duke's absence, and who is told to enforce the lapsed laws against immorality. He commits Claudio to prison for the seduction of Juliet before marriage, and condemns him to death. Isabella appeals for mercy for her brother: he rejects her pleas, but finds himself tempted, and offers to save Claudio in return for her chastity. When the assignation takes place Mariana, his rejected fiancée, takes Isabella's place in bed. Angelo is unaware of the deception, and fearing Claudio's revenge, orders his death. When Angelo greets the returning Duke at the city gates, he is confronted by Mariana, who accuses him before the Duke of being a murderer and a violator. He is exposed: he confesses and begs immediate death. He is made to marry Mariana, and then sent to execution. When Claudio is brought on unharmed, Angelo is spared.

Early on we hear from the Duke that:

> . . . Lord Angelo is precise,
> Stands at a guard with envy; scarce confesses
> That his blood flows, or that his appetite
> Is more to bread than stone. (I.iii)

From Lucio we hear that Angelo has been living like a monk:

> . . . Lord Angelo, a man whose blood
> Is very snow-broth; one who never feels
> The wanton stings and motions of the sense,
> But doth rebate and blunt his natural edge
> With profits of the mind, study and fast. (I.iv)

Ascetic retirement has left him ignorant of himself, and of the actual conditions of living: he confesses that he rejected Mariana

> . . . in chief,
> For that her reputation was disvalued
> In levity. (v.i)

She was not up to the standards of his severe morality. It is thus appropriate that Angelo is brought down by the saintly purity of Isabella. The sexuality that he had denied suddenly overwhelms him, and transforms him into a ruthless seducer. He is not a hypocrite – he is amazed and horrified by what he feels happening to him, and yet is quite unable to resist it. He seems almost relieved by his final exposure, and asks only for death.

Most critics and directors have found Angelo a highly unsympathetic character. Coleridge was indignant at his reprieve: 'the pardon and marriage of Angelo not merely baffles the strong indignant claim of justice – (for cruelty, with lust and damnable baseness, cannot be forgiven, because we cannot conceive them as being morally repented of) but it is likewise degrading to the character of woman'. In Angelo's defence it can be said that he is to some extent a victim of the Duke's manipulations; and that the audience, once they are aware of the controlling presence of the Duke, knows that no real crime will be committed.

Measure for Measure was probably written not long before its first recorded performance at court on 26 December 1604. There are several possible sources for it; the most immediate one would appear to be George Whetstone's play *Promos and Cassandra* (1578).

ANGIERS, CITIZEN OF *(John)*: a spokesman for the citizens of Angiers who will not open the gates of the city to John or Arthur until the claim to the throne has been settled by war; he then suggests that a marriage between Blanch of Spain and Lewis the Dauphin might settle the matter peacefully (II.i).

ANGUS *(Mac.)*: a Scottish nobleman who supports Malcolm against Macbeth (v.ii; v.viii).

ANJOU, DUKE OF *(1H.VI)*, see REIGNIER.

ANNE, LADY (NEVILLE) *(R.III)*: the Princess of Wales, who is chief mourner at Henry VI's funeral, where she is accosted by Richard, Duke of Gloucester.

below Isabella (Barbara Jefford) appeals to Angelo (John Gielgud) for her brother's life; a scene from the 1950 production of *Measure for Measure (left)*; Claire

She hates him, but is won over by his violent and persistent wooing, and become Duchess of Gloucester. When Richard becomes king, she is crowned queen. She dies mysteriously, and her ghost confronts Richard at Bosworth (v.iii).

On her first appearance, she curses Richard:
O cursed be the hand that made these holes,
Cursed the heart that had the heart to do it,
Cursed the blood that let this blood from hence.
More direful hap betide that hated wretch
That makes us wretched by the death of thee,
Than I can wish to wolves, to spiders, toads,
Or any creeping venomed thing that lives.
If ever he have child, abortive be it,
Prodigious, and untimely brought to light,
Whose ugly and unnatural aspect
May fright the hopeful mother at the view,
And that be heir to his unhappiness.
If ever he have wife, let her be made
More miserable by the death of him
Than I am made by my young lord, and thee. (I.ii)
This is grimly ironic, as Anne later realizes: within a few moments she has been wooed, and won, by Richard, the man she has cursed. The wooing scene is one of the most dramatic in Shakespeare, and it is too frequently played as a *tour de force* for the actor playing Richard, with little regard for dramatic probability. For the scene to have its full effect, it is necessary for Anne to be won by Richard's real charm and brilliant persuasion, and not hypnotized by his evil spell. To show him as a villain in this part of the scene, as in the Olivier film, ruins the dramatic effect of his sudden revelation when she leaves the stage.

Bloom as Lady Anne and Laurence Olivier as Richard in Olivier's 1955 film of *Richard III (right).*

The Winter's Tale (II.iii): Leontes commands Antigonus *(left)* to dispose of his infant daughter. After a painting by John Opie.

Anne Neville (1452–85) was betrothed to Edward, Prince of Wales, in 1470. In 1471, when the funeral of Henry VI took place, Anne was in the country, hidden there by Clarence to keep her from the attentions of Richard Plantagenet. He eventually found her disguised as a kitchen-maid; he married her in 1473, and she was crowned with him in 1483. Their only son (*b.*1474) died in 1484. Anne's grief aggravated her consumption and she died in 1485. Shakespeare's version of her relationship with Richard is almost pure fiction: it seems very likely that he was sincerely attached to her.

ANTENOR *(Troil.)* : a Trojan warrior captured by the Greeks. At the request of Calchas, Cressida's father, he is exchanged for Cressida (IV.i).

Pandarus calls Antenor 'one o' th' soundest judgement in Troy whosoever' (I.ii) – and he is certainly highly valued by the Trojans. The fact that he never utters a word in the play is a subtle stroke of irony. In the *Iliad* Antenor was also one of the wisest of the Trojans, who advised the return of Helen.

ANTHONY *(Rom.)* : a servant at the house of Capulet. He and Potpan are the only two named when another calls them (I.v).

ANTIGONUS *(Wint.)* : a Sicilian lord and husband of Paulina. He says he will do anything to save the life of Hermione's child Perdita, but he is forced by Leontes to take it and leave it exposed in some 'remote and desert place'. He leaves Perdita on the shore of Bohemia (III.iii), and is chased off by a bear, which eats him.

ANTIOCH, KING OF *(Per.)*, *see* ANTIOCHUS.

ANTIOCHUS *(Per.)* : King of Antioch, who presents Pericles with a riddle that he must solve before he can marry his daughter. The key to the riddle is Antiochus' incestuous relationship with his daughter. When Pericles solves the riddle, Antiochus fears that he will reveal his secret, and he pays Thaliard to poison him. Thaliard fails, and we hear later from Helicanus (II.iv) that Antiochus and his daughter have been killed by the gods with a lightning bolt.

ANTIOCHUS, DAUGHTER OF *(Per.)* : the beautiful daughter of the King of Antioch, with whom Pericles is enraptured until he solves the riddle and discovers that she is having an incestuous relationship with her father (I.i).

ANTIPHOLUS OF EPHESUS *(Err.)* : one of the identical twin sons of Egeon and Aemilia, separated from his family by a shipwreck. For twenty years he has been under the patronage of Solinus, and is now serving him as a soldier in Ephesus. The arrival of his twin brother, unknown to him, causes a series of misunderstandings and mistaken identities. He thinks he has been locked out of his own house by his wife Adriana, and decides to give a gold chain that he has ordered for her from a goldsmith to another woman; it gets given to Antipholus of Syracuse, and Antipholus of Ephesus is arrested for debt when he refuses to pay for it. He is carried off as a lunatic, along with his servant Dromio. All is made clear at the end – he is reconciled with his wife, and restored to his family.

Although the twins are physically identical, Antipholus is the stronger character of the two. He is determined and rather aggressive, especially when he thinks that he alone is sane, and desperately tries to assert his identity in a world that suddenly seems to have gone mad.

ANTIPHOLUS OF SYRACUSE *(Err.)*: one of the identical twin sons of Egeon and Aemilia who has lived with his father in Syracuse until he was eighteen, when he set off in search of his lost brother. After seven years he arrives at Ephesus, already suspicious of it as a place full of

William Haviland as Antonio and Alexandra Carlisle as Portia in a production of *The Merchant of Venice* early this century.

Dark-working sorcerers that change the mind,
  Soul-killing witches that deform the body. (I.ii)
His fears are soon confirmed: his own servant (his twin, Antipholus of Ephesus) does not know him; a strange woman (Adriana) attacks him for deserting her; he is amazed to find that the townspeople know him. He falls in love with Luciana, though he fears that he has been bewitched. He finally concludes that the whole city is in the grip of an evil power, and seeks safety in an abbey. He is brought before the Duke, and all the errors are resolved when he is reunited with his family.

In Ephesus, Antipholus of Syracuse is at first apprehensive, then bewildered, and finally convinced that he is lost in a world of illusions, and that his long search for his brother has caused him to lose his identity.

ANTIUM, CITIZEN OF *(Cor.)*: Coriolanus, in disguise, meets the citizen in the street and asks him where Aufidius lives (IV.iv).

ANTONIO *(Mer.V.)*: the merchant of the title. When his beloved friend Bassanio reveals that he needs money in order to present a suitable appearance as a suitor to the wealthy Portia, Antonio agrees to help him. He looks for credit in Venice, and is finally forced to accept three thousand ducats from Shylock, pledging his ships and merchandise, or, failing that, 'a pound of flesh'. His ships are reported lost, and he is unable to repay the debt. Before the court, he expresses his willingness to suffer and die as Shylock demands his bond. Portia (in disguise as a lawyer) turns the tables on Shylock, who is convicted for plotting against the life of a citizen, and is made to forfeit his fortune. Antonio requests that he should retain half of it as long as he becomes a Christian. At the end he hears that his ships have arrived safely after all, but he remains isolated amid the gaiety at Belmont.

Antonio is a rich, sophisticated gentleman of Venice, the city which for Elizabethan London provided a model of wealth, power and polished society. He is confident, careless and above all generous – Salarino declares that 'A kinder gentleman treads not the earth' (II.viii). His generosity causes Shylock to hate him, because

               . . . in low simplicity
He lends out money gratis, and brings down
  The rate of usance here with us in Venice. (I.iii)
Antonio shares the medieval Christian attitude to usury, which required loans to be free of interest, and acts of pure Christian charity.

The very first line of the play reveals that Antonio suffers from a mysterious sadness which has no apparent cause. It has frequently been suggested that he is a repressed, *unconscious* homosexual, and that his depression is caused by his friend Bassanio's sudden interest in marriage. Certainly his love for Bassanio is all-absorbing ('I thinks he only loves the world for him', comments Solanio (II.viii)); he shows no interest in women. He faces death stoically, and makes no real attempt to fight Shylock's claim. All he wants is Bassanio's presence:

> Pray God Bassanio come
> To see me pay his debt, and then I care not. (III.iii)

At the trial, he seems almost eager for death:

> I am a tainted wether of the flock,
> Meetest for death, the weakest kind of fruit
> Drops earliest to the ground, and so let me;
> You cannot better be employ'd, Bassanio,
> Than to live still, and write mine epitaph (IV.i)

A watercolour by J. Grieve of *The Tempest* (I.i), Kean's production at the Princess Theatre in 1857.

All he seems to desire is one last great gesture of love.

In the last act, Antonio is as much an outcast in the world of love and marriage as Shylock was in the world of finance. At Belmont he is alone, strangely obtrusive in the atmosphere of lyrical romance. For the director in the theatre his presence among the happy couples is a problem: it is perhaps most appropriate for him to be left alone on stage at the end after they have entered the house.

ANTONIO *(Ado)*: brother of Leonato, and Hero's uncle. He advises Leonato, who is grieving over the supposed loss of his daughter, to 'make those that do offend you suffer too', and offers a violent challenge to Claudio himself, despite his age. In the end, when he finds that all is in fact well, he presents his masked 'daughter' (in fact Hero) in marriage to Claudio.

ANTONIO *(Tp.)*: the usurping Duke of Milan, Prospero's brother. Twelve years previously he had Prospero and the child Miranda set adrift in a rotting boat, expecting them to drown. Now he is shipwrecked on Prospero's island, where his continuing villainy is revealed when he suggests to Sebastian that they murder Gonzalo and Alonso (II.i). He is foiled by Ariel, who wakes Gonzalo. He is denounced, along with Sebastian, by Ariel in the form of a harpy, but he shows no sign of repentance. Ariel leads him and Sebastian into a magic circle, where they are confronted by Prospero (v.i). They remain silent when he rebukes them; even when he forgives them, they show no sign of contrition.

Antonio, usurper and would-be murderer, is a degenerate nobleman. His noble birth should have given him a predisposition to virtue; in rejecting it, and in using his rationality in the cause of evil, he sinks below the level of even Caliban, the 'natural' brute. Antonio remains unrepentant and unregenerate at the end – an indication of the limitations of Prospero's power, and, perhaps, an embodiment of the defiant will on which freedom of choice depends.

ANTONIO *(Tw.N.)*: a sea captain and friend of Sebastian. He follows Sebastian to Orsino's court, where he is in danger of arrest because of an earlier offence in Illyria. In the city he lends Sebastian his purse (III.iii). He enters when Cesario (the disguised Viola) is about to fight Aguecheek, and, mistaking 'him' for Sebastian, offers to take his place; he is amazed when the supposed Sebastian denies all knowledge of the purse. He is arrested 'at the suit of Count Orsino'; he is brought before him, and recognized as an enemy (v.i). He again mistakes Cesario for Sebastian, but is saved when the real Sebastian appears and all is explained.

ANTONIO *(Gent.)*: the father of Proteus. He accepts the advice of his servant Panthino and sends his son to serve the Duke in Milan in order to give him experience of the world (I.iii).

ANTONY *(Ant.)*: the historical Antony, Marcus Antonius, one of Caesar's most distinguished allies, was born about 83 BC and died in 30 BC. Having aroused the Roman mob against Brutus and Cassius after Caesar's tragic death, he first formed an alliance with Octavian, his friend's adopted son and heir (later the Emperor Augustus); but the coalition gradually dissolved. Under the Second Triumvirate, Antony was allotted Asia as his province; and in 42 BC he encountered Cleopatra, the Ptolemaic Queen of Egypt, a Greek-speaking lady of great intelligence and charm, who had previously been Caesar's mistress. At this point, Shakespeare picks up the story that he drew from Plutarch's *Lives*, translated by Sir Thomas North. Antony, now the Queen's lover, is reluctant to abandon the voluptuous pleasures of Egypt; but, as the political situation grows more and more threatening, he at length returns to Rome, where, since his wife Fulvia has recently died, he marries Octavia, Octavian's sister, and organizes an uneasy truce. Octavian, however, has decided to achieve supreme control; and Antony sails back to Egypt. From that moment we know that he is a doomed man. Though he prepares to fight – 'my sword, made weak by my affection' – he has lost his taste for warfare; and at the Battle of Actium the Egyptian fleet suddenly deserts its Roman allies. Antony is defeated, and suffers a second yet more

crushing reverse when Octavian attacks Egypt. Brought to bay at Alexandria, he receives a false report of Cleopatra's death, stabs himself and is lifted into the palatial 'monument', where the Queen has taken refuge. He dies, and, rather than be carried off to Rome and paraded in Octavian's triumph, Cleopatra follows her lover's example, dying of the bite of a poisonous snake, 'the pretty worm of Nilus', that, with the help of an unsuspicious peasant, she has provided as her executioner.

Written after *King Lear* and *Macbeth*, between 1606 and 1607, *Antony and Cleopatra* is an unevenly constructed but extraordinarily romantic play. The text contains some of Shakespeare's most magnificent verse; yet he did not hesitate to paraphrase North's

below The bust of Marcus Antonius (83–30 BC) in the Vatican *(left)*; F. R. Benson as Mark Antony *(right)*.

above Mark Antony's oration over Caesar's body, *Julius Caesar* (III.ii). After the painting by Benjamin West.

translation of Plutarch whenever it might suit his purpose. Here, for example, is North's account of the lovers' famous meeting:

> She disdained to set forward otherwise, but to take her barge in the river of Cydnus, the poop whereof was of gold, the sails of purple, and the oars of silver, which kept stroke in rowing after the sound of flutes, haut-boys, cithern, viols. . . . She was laid under a pavilion of cloth of gold tissue. . . . Her ladies and gentlewoman . . . were apparelled like the nymphs Nereides . . . some steering the helm, others tending the tackle and ropes of the barge, out of which there came a wonderful passing sweet of perfumes, that perfumed the wharf's side . . .

In Shakespeare's hands this comparatively prosaic passage undergoes a miraculous transformation:

> The barge she sat in, like a burnish'd throne,
> Burn'd on the water, the poop was beaten gold;
> Purple the sails, and so perfumed that
> The winds were love-sick with them . . .
> Her gentlewomen, like the Nereides,
> So many mermaids, tended her i' th' eyes,
> And made their bends adornings: at the helm
> A seeming mermaid steers: the silken tackle
> Swell with the touches of those flower-soft hands,
> That yarely frame the office. From the barge
> A strange invisible perfume hits the sense
> Of the adjacent wharfs.

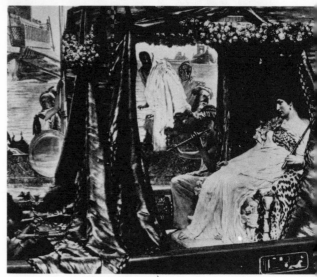

above Antony and Cleopatra, after a painting by Alma Tadema (1836–1912).

Similarly, Plutarch having observed that, as a dolphin shows its back above the water, Antony rose superior to the worldly pleasure he indulged in, Shakespeare produces a particularly arresting simile:

>   . . . His delights
> Were dolphin-like, they showed his back above
> The element they lived in . . .

As a study of amorous infatuation, *Antony and Cleo-*

right Charles Buchel's poster for the production of *As You Like It* at His Majesty's Theatre, 1907.

HIS MAJESTY'S THEATRE

Propr. H. Beerbohm Tree

CHAS. A. BUCHEL

OSCAR ASCHE & LILY BRAYTON
IN SHAKESPEARE'S COMEDY
"AS YOU LIKE IT"

MILES & C°
WARDOUR S^T

patra may be compared with *Othello* and *Troilus and Cressida*. But, while Othello is a man surprised by love, and betrayed by his own native innocence, and Troilus merely the victim of a ravening sexual appetite, the love to which Antony and Cleopatra succumb is at once physical and spiritual, a passion that both includes and transcends the ordinary experiences of sexual pleasure:

> Eternity was in our lips and eyes,
> Bliss in our brows' bent; none our parts so poor
> But was a race of heaven . . .

Yet Shakespeare sets out to idealize neither his hero nor his heroine. Antony is still a coarse-grained soldier; Cleopatra, a woman no longer young and not regularly beautiful. Shakespeare dwells on her bodily defects. At their first meeting, Cleopatra was twenty-seven; she died at the age of thirty-nine; and the dramatist makes her describe her own sun-burnt, already wrinkled face:

> . . . Think on me,
> That am with Phoebus' amorous pinches black
> And wrinkled deep in time . . .

He also emphasizes the hoydenish side of her character,

Marlon Brando as Mark Antony in Makiewicz's 1953 film of *Julius Caesar*.

her bravado and her insolence. Such is her disregard for her feminine and royal dignity that, on one occasion, in a mood of wild abandon, she hops 'forty paces through the public street'. Yet, even then, dishevelled and sweating, she continues to make 'defect perfection', and remains 'a most triumphant lady'. In 1677, some seven decades after the production of Shakespeare's play, John Dryden would take up the same theme. His

All for Love is his dramatic masterpiece, better constructed than the Jacobean tragedy, and, in some passages at least, nearly as eloquent and moving; but his portrait of the great Egyptian Queen lacks Shakespeare's realistic touches. He pays his tribute to Cleopatra's charm and magnificence, but generally ignores the deep Shakespearian wrinkles.

APEMANTUS *(Tim.)*: 'a churlish philosopher' who foresees Timon's ruin, and warns him of false friends (I.ii). He later meets Timon in the woods, and the two revile each other and compete in misanthropic bitterness; the slanging match ends when Timon drives Apemantus off with stones (IV.iii).

Early on in the play Apemantus is described as one 'that few things loves better than to abhor himself' (I.i). His comments are cynical and misanthropic, but he has true insight into the nature of Timon's prodigality, and Timon ignores his warnings at his peril. When he later meets Timon in the wood he offers no sympathy or advice, only raillery. He appears to be a kind of mirror-image of Timon, but Timon distinguishes Apemantus' natural misanthropy from his own which is the result of experience:

> Thou art a slave whom Fortune's tender arm
> With favour never clasp'd, but bred a dog.
> Hadst thou, like us from our first swath, proceeded
> The sweet degrees that this brief world affords
> To such as may the passive drugs of it
> Freely command, thou woulds't have plung'd thyself
> In general riot, melted down thy youth
> In different beds of lust, and never learn'd
> The icy precepts of respect, but followed
> The sug'red game before thee. (IV.iii)

Hazlitt's comment on Apemantus is apt: 'His lurking selfishness does not pass undetected amidst the grossness of his sarcasms and his contempt for the pretensions of others.'

Apemantus represents the general Elizabethan notion of the Cynic philosophy; Shakespeare was possibly influenced by the character of the Cynic philosopher Diogenes in John Lyly's *Campaspe* (1584). Apemantus is mentioned by Plutarch as a companion whom Timon liked 'because he was much like of his nature and conditions, and also followed after him in manner of life'.

APOTHECARY *(Rom.)*: he is forced by desperate poverty into risking death by breaking Mantua's law and selling a dram of deadly poison to Romeo (V.i).

APPARITIONS, THREE *(Mac.)*: when Macbeth goes to question the witches in their cavern, they present for him their 'masters', these three apparitions. The first is an armed head, which warns him to 'beware

left Duke Frederick in *As You Like It* — a costume design by Domenico Groli.

35

above Romeo buys the fatal poison: an eighteenth-century engraving of *Romeo and Juliet* (v.i).

Macduff'. The second is a bloody child which tells him that 'none of woman born' will harm him. The third, a child crowned and carrying a tree tells him that he

   . . . shall never vanquished be, until
  Great Birnam wood to high Dunsinane Hill
  Shall come against him. (IV.i)

ARC, JOAN OF *(1H.VI)*, *see* JOAN PUCELLE.

ARCHBISHOPS, *see* CANTERBURY, YORK.

ARCHIDAMUS *(Wint.)* : a lord of Bohemia attending Polixenes at Leontes' court. In the first scene he converses with Camillo, and invites him to Bohemia. He does not reappear.

ARIEL *(Tp.)* : 'an ayrie sprite' who had been confined in a cloven pine for twelve years by the witch Sycorax

for refusing to obey her. He was freed by Prospero, who he now obeys. He relates how he raised the tempest, dispersed the fleet, and brought the King's ship in safely (I.ii). He demands his freedom, but Prospero rebukes him and promises him it in two days. He assumes the form of a sea-nymph and leads Ferdinand to Prospero's cell with his music and the song 'Full fathom five thy father lies'. He lulls the King's party (though not Antonio and Sebastian) to sleep, and awakes Gonzalo in time to save his life (II, i). While invisible he sets Caliban, Trinculo and Stephano at each other's throats, and lures them into a 'filthy-mantled pool'. In the form of a harpy he denounces the 'three men of sin' – Alonso, Antonio and Sebastian – for their treachery to Prospero (III.iii). He organizes

below Ariel, in an engraving by C. W. Sharpe from a painting by H. J. Townsend *(top)*; *The Tempest* (I.i), the storm, after an engraving by Gustave Doré *(bottom)*.

and directs a masque of spirits for Miranda and Ferdinand. He baits Stephano, Trinculo and Caliban with 'glistering apparel' and sets spirit hounds on them. As he helps Prospero put on his ducal robes he sings 'Where the bee sucks, there suck I' in anticipation of his freedom. He awakes the ship's crew from their entranced sleep and leads them to Prospero's cell. His last task, before he is 'released to the elements', is to ensure a calm homeward voyage.

Ariel has been identified as elemental Air in opposition to Caliban's Earth; he has been seen as the embodiment of Fancy, or of Imagination. In Cornelius Agrippa's *Occult Philosophy* (translated 1651), Ariel is the presiding spirit of the element of earth. Shakespeare's Ariel appears to suffer no such limitations: he seems able to handle all the elements. He is able

> . . . to fly,
> To swim, to dive into the fire: to ride
> On the curl'd clouds . . . (I.ii)

and even to do Prospero's business 'in the veins o' th' earth'. He is not human, and he is potentially dangerous, since he can manipulate both natural forces and the will of human beings. His pneumatological status is ambiguous, perhaps deliberately so, for fairies were often equated with demons, or fallen angels. Prospero is frequently harsh to Ariel – he calls him 'malignant thing' – and needs to keep his will subdued. While Ariel is grateful to Prospero for his release from the cloven pine, he is essentially his slave, and chafes at his restriction.

ARMADO, DON ADRIANO DE *(LLL.)*: a pompous, verbose, 'fantastical' Spaniard, Costard's rival for the love of Jacquenetta. He resolves to write to her, and is 'for whole volumes in folio' (I.ii). He takes the part of Hector in the pageant of the 'Nine Worthies' (v.ii) and is jeered, and then shamed and humbled: it is revealed that he cannot afford to wear a shirt beneath his magnificent doublet.

In the Folio stage directions he is termed 'braggart' – a stock figure in Italian comedy, usually an offensive soldier. The King refers to this 'refin'd traveller of Spain' as one

> That hath a mint of phrases in his brain:
> One who the music of his own vain tongue
> Doth ravish like enchanting harmony. (I.i)

Armado lives in a world of illusion, separated from reality by the smoke-screen of his fantastic rhetoric and bizarre vocabulary. He is a caricature figure, but beneath the absurd pose there is a real man, and his final predicament is not without pathos, as he feebly tries to pass off his lack of a shirt as due to some mysterious and romantic penance.

ARRAGON, PRINCE OF *(Mer.V.)*: a suitor to Portia, the second to undergo the test of the caskets. He chooses the silver one, and finds in it a picture of a 'blinking idiot' and an insulting rhyme (II.ix).

ARTEMIDORUS *(Caes.)*: a teacher of rhetoric who writes a paper to Caesar warning him of the conspiracy (II.iii), which Caesar refuses to accept (III.i).

In Plutarch's account, Caesar was prevented from reading Artemidorus' scroll by the crowd of people around him; Shakespeare's Caesar is too preoccupied with his public persona to read it: 'What touches us ourself shall last be served'. He was 'born in the isle of Gnidos, a doctor of rhetoric in the Greek tongue'.

Ronald Pickup as Don Armado in *Love's Labour's Lost.*

ARTHUR (PLANTAGENET), DUKE OF BRITAIN *(John)*: nephew to King John, with a claim to the throne. John takes him prisoner, and orders Hubert de Burgh to blind him. Hubert is moved by Arthur's pleas for mercy, and hides him; he tells the king the boy is dead. Arthur is killed when he tries to escape by jumping from the castle walls (IV.iii).

Historically, he was the posthumous son of Geoffrey, third son of Henry II of England, and Constance,

A Victorian production of *King John*, with Charles Sefton as Prince Arthur and Franklin McLeary as Hubert.

daughter and heiress of Conan le Petit, Count of Brittainy. Born in 1187, he was declared heir to the English throne by his uncle Richard I three years later. Shakespeare has him assert this claim, which he never did; he did claim to be ruler of all English possessions in France. He lived in Paris under the care of Philip II, but was captured by John at the siege of the castle of Mirabeau. He was probably put to death on John's orders.

Shakespeare makes Arthur a child, presumably to give his scene with his would-be executioner more pathos; but Arthur was seventeen at the time of his death.

ARVIRAGUS *(Cym.)*: the younger son of Cymbeline, and brother of Imogen. Arviragus and his brother Guiderius have been living in a 'pinching cave' with Morgan (the assumed name of Belarius) in the belief that they are his sons Cadwal and Polydore. In fact they were kidnapped as infants by Belarius as an act of revenge for his banishment. Imogen, disguised as a boy, takes refuge in their cave; Arviragus finds her apparently dead, and he and Guiderius sing 'Fear no more the heat o' the sun' over her body. The brothers and Belarius join the British forces fighting the Romans, and they inspire them by their courage. At the end Arviragus is identified as Cymbeline's son by the 'curious mantle' in which he had been wrapped as an infant, and he is restored to his father and sister.

ASMATH *(2H.VI)*: the spirit invoked by Roger Bolingbroke the sorcerer. It prophesies that Henry will be deposed by a duke, that Suffolk will die by water, and warns that Somerset should avoid castles (I.iv).

ASTRINGER, AN *(All's W.)*: a keeper of goshawks. He delivers Diana's petition to the King of France (v.iii). At this, his second entry, he is described in the stage directions only as a 'gentleman', which suggests that 'astringer' may be a mistake.

ATHENIAN, AN OLD *(Tim.)*: he appears before Timon and asks him to stop Lucilius wooing his only daughter, since he considers him too poor for her. Timon offers to give Lucilius as much money as his daughter receives as dowry if he will consent to the marriage, and the old man agrees (I.i).

ATHENS, DUKE AND DUCHESS OF *(MND.)*, *see* THESEUS, HIPPOLYTA.

AUDREY *(AYL.)*: a stolid country girl living in the forest of Arden, who is wooed by Touchstone. She rejects him at first but finally agrees to marry him. When he presents her to the Duke, he calls her 'a poor virgin, sir, an ill-favoured thing sir, but mine own', and adds that it is 'a poor humour of mine sir, to take that that no man else will' (v.iv).

AUFIDIUS, TULLUS *(Cor.)*: the Volscian leader, defeated opponent of Coriolanus. The banished Coriolanus seeks him as an ally when he wants to revenge himself by destroying Rome. Aufidius accuses Coriolanus of ingratitude and treachery when he is persuaded to spare Rome, and joins the conspirators in killing him. He stands in triumph on the body of his old enemy, but is suddenly touched by sorrow, and helps carry the corpse away with martial honours.

Before Aufidius appears, Coriolanus refers to him as 'the man of my soul's hate'. Aufidius has fought Coriolanus five times, and each time has been defeated: he is now embittered and resentful, and determined to defeat his enemy by any means:

> . . . My valour's poison'd,
> With only suffering stain by him: for him
> Shall fly out of itself, nor sleep, nor sanctuary,
> Being naked, sick; nor fane, nor Capitol,
> The prayers of priests, nor times of sacrifice:
> Embarquements all of fury, shall lift up
> Their rotten privilege, and custom 'gainst
> My hate to Martius. Where I find him, were it
> At home, upon my brother's guard, even there
> Against the hospitable canon, would I
> Wash my fierce hand in 's heart. (I.x)

Yet when Aufidius is confronted with the banished Coriolanus he greets him warmly; his respect and admiration for his enemy overcome his hatred and jealousy. But when he finds that Coriolanus has begun to overshadow him even among his own people the obsessive hatred returns. When Coriolanus is faced with his wife and his mother pleading with him to spare Rome, Aufidius stands silently by, watching for the slightest sign of weakness that will give him the chance to discredit his enemy. Before the assassination, Aufidius infuriates Coriolanus by calling him first 'traitor' and then 'boy' – he destroys him before killing him.

Shakespeare follows Plutarch's account of the 'marvellous private hate' that existed between Aufidius and Coriolanus.

AUMERLE, DUKE OF (Plantagenet, Edward, later Duke of York) *(R.II; H.V)*: son of Edmund, Duke of York, and cousin of Richard II, who he supports against his other cousin Bolingbroke. At Bolingbroke's first parliament he is accused of murdering his uncle, the Duke of Gloucester. He is punished mildly when he declares that he took part in the proceedings under constraint. His father finds him with a treasonable paper, but he is pardoned when he exposes the plot against Henry to him (v.iii).

In *Henry V,* as Duke of York, he dies bravely at Agincourt.

Historically, he was Edward of Norwich, afterwards 2nd Duke of York, eldest son of Edmund of Langley, 1st Duke of York. He was born *c.*1373, and knighted by Richard II at his coronation. He was awarded the title Aumerle (or Albemarle) after he arrested Gloucester,

Autolycus, after a painting by C. R. Leslie.

Arundel and Warwick. He appears to have deserted Richard at the very last moment in 1399. There is no historical evidence for his complicity in the conspiracy of Christmas 1399 against Henry IV: the story of his ride to Windsor to forestall his father in disclosing his part in the plot to the King is taken from the very unreliable contemporary source *Chronique de la Traison et Mort du Roy Richard.* In 1401 he was appointed Lieutenant of Aquitaine; when the King did not pay him, he joined the abortive attempt to carry off the young Mortimer from Windsor. He commanded the right wing at Agincourt, where he was killed.

AUSTRIA, DUKE OF *(John), see* LYMOGES.

AUTOLYCUS *(Wint.)*: 'a rogue'. He pretends to the Clown that he has been robbed by a thief called Autolycus, and picks his pockets while telling his tale of misfortune (IV.iii). He visits the rustics' merrymaking as a singing pedlar, and fleeces them. He meets Camillo and Florizel, and is made to change clothes with the latter. He overhears the shepherd and his son talking of the real identity of Perdita, and after terrifying them into keeping their secret, he resolves to go to Sicily himself and reinstate himself with Prince Florizel, whom he claims he once served (IV.iv). When he arrives, he finds that he had been pre-empted, and that the secret has been revealed.

Autolycus enters singing, and then characterizes himself:

> My father named me Autolycus, who being (as I am) litter'd under Mercury, was likewise a snapper-up of unconsidered trifles: with die and drab, I purchased this caparison, and my revenue is the silly cheat. Gallows, and knock, are too powerful on the highway. Beating and hanging are terrors to me: for the life to come, I sleep out the thought of it. (IV.iii)

He is a coney-catcher (confidence trickster) like those described in Greene's pamphlets, who battens on unsuspecting innocents. He is happy, carefree and amoral, and he feels that the time is ripe for him to prosper:

> I understand the business, I hear it: to have an open ear, a quick eye, and a nimble hand, is necessary for a cut-purse; a good nose is requisite also, to smell out work for th' other senses. I see this is the time that the unjust man doth thrive. What an exchange had this been, without boot! What a boot is here, with this exchange. Sure the Gods do this year connive at us, and we may do anything extempore. (IV.iv)

AUVERGNE, COUNTESS OF *(1H.VI)*: a French noblewoman who invites Lord Talbot to her castle, intending to trap him. He foils her by arriving with his soldiers; she is impressed by him, and gives a banquet in his honour (II.iii).

B

BAGOT *(R.II)*: a minister to Richard, who with Bushy and Greene *(q.v)* makes up the group of flatterers that Bolingbroke calls 'the caterpillars of the commonwealth'. He is imprisoned, and accuses Aumerle of the murder of Gloucester (IV.i). Unlike his fellow sycophants, he survives.

BALTHASAR *(Rom.)*: Romeo's servant, who announces Juliet's supposed death to him (V.iii). He accompanies his master to the Capulet tomb; he is caught outside by the guards, and tells them all that he knows.

BALTHAZAR *(Err.)*: a merchant, friend to Antipholus of Ephesus. When Antipholus finds himself locked out of his own house, Balthazar persuades him not to break down the door, but instead to be patient and look for an explanation for his wife's strange behaviour (III.i).

BALTHAZAR *(Mer.V.)*: servant to Portia, who is sent to fetch 'notes and garments' from her cousin Doctor Bellario in Padua (III.iv).

BALTHAZAR *(Mer.V.)*: name assumed by Portia.

BALTHAZAR *(Ado)*: attendant to Don Pedro, who sings 'Sigh no more, ladies' (II.iii), though he complains that he is an 'ill singer'.

BANDITS, THREE *(Tim.)*: they hear that Timon has gold, and go to his cave to beg or steal it from him. But Timon gives them gold, and urges them to continue their thieving in Athens. They are amazed, and the third bandit remarks that he 'has almost charmed me from my profession by persuading me to it' (IV.iii).

BANQUO *(Mac.)*: a Scottish nobleman who is returning with Macbeth from a successful battle against the Norwegians when they encounter the witches. They prophesy that Banquo will be the ancestor of kings; it is this that causes Macbeth to have him murdered. His ghost appears at Macbeth's feast, and it is Macbeth's

horrified response that first arouses the suspicion of the other thanes.

Banquo, Thane of Lochaber, an apparently fictitious character, is first mentioned in Hector Boece's *Scotorum Historiae* (1527). Shakespeare's source for the story was Holinshed's *Chronicles,* which told how Macbeth murdered Duncan with the aid of Banquo and others. But James I, whom the play was probably written to please, claimed Banquo as an ancestor, so Shakespeare tactfully makes him a noble counterpart to Macbeth. Macbeth fears him because of his virtues:

Our fears in Banquo stick deep,
And in his royalty of Nature reigns that
Which would be fear'd. 'Tis much he dares,
And to that dauntless temper of his mind,
He hath a wisdom, that doth guide his valour,
To act in safety. There is none but he,
Whose being I do fear: and under him,
My genius is rebuk'd, as it is said
Mark Antony's was by Caesar. (III.i)

BAPTISTA MINOLA *(Shr.)*: a rich Paduan gentleman, father of Katharina and Bianca. He will not consent to the much courted Bianca's marriage until Katharina, the shrew, is married. He is amazed at the end to find that Petruchio has effectively tamed the shrew.

BARDOLPH, LIEUTENANT (or Corporal) *(1 & 2 H.IV)*: an associate of Falstaff, who describes his face as 'all bubukles, and whelks, and knobs, and flames of fire'. He is one of Falstaff's band of robbers at Gadshill. In Part II he assists in the recruitment of Feeble, Shallow and Wart. He is taken to the Fleet prison along with Falstaff at the end of the play.

In *The Merry Wives of Windsor* Falstaff finds him the ideal occupation, that of tapster at the Garter Inn – 'a life that he has desired'.

In *Henry V* he is hanged for looting French churches; as Pistol says 'his vital thread is cut with edge of penny cord and vile reproach'.

BARDOLPH, LORD *(2H.IV)*: he brings the false

Bardolph *(right)* and Falstaff.

news that Hotspur has won the battle at Shrewsbury (I.i). At the council of war he urges prudence.

Thomas, Lord Bardolph (*b.*1368), was implicated in the Hotspur rebellion of 1401, but appears to have been fully pardoned and restored to royal favour. From 1405 onwards he was in rebellion with Northumberland; in 1408 they were defeated by Sir Thomas Rokesby at Bramham Moor. Bardolph was taken prisoner, but died of his wounds. As a traitor, his body was quartered, and the pieces exhibited around the country; the head was put on display at Lincoln.

BARNADINE *(Meas.)*: 'a Bohemian', who is permanently drunk while awaiting sentence after pleading guilty to murder. He has been in prison for nine years. When summoned to execution he refuses to go, as he has 'been drinking all night' and 'is not fitted for it'. The Duke pardons him at the end, and entrusts him to the care of a friar.

His indifference to both life and death baffles the Duke; his lack of fear of death is combined with an obstinate assertion of life that rejects the attitude expressed in the Duke's exhortation to Claudio. 'He is a fine antithesis to the morality and the hypocrisy of the other characters of the play.' (Hazlitt)

BARNADO *(Ham.)*: a sentry at Elsinore who, with Marcellus, was the first to see the ghost of Hamlet's father. Horatio joins them on the third night, and the ghost appears again (I.i). They all go to tell Hamlet (I.ii).

BARTHOL'MEW, A PAGE *(Shr.)*: a page who, disguised as a woman, is ordered to pretend to be the wife of the 'noble lord' who is in reality Christopher Sly *(q.v.)* (Induction).

BASSANIO *(Mer.V.)*: friend of Antonio, and suitor to Portia. He is short of money, and Antonio lends him three thousand ducats that he borrows from Shylock. As a suitor at Portia's Belmont, Bassanio has to pass the test of the three caskets: he chooses the leaden casket, and finds a picture of Portia that proclaims his success. She gives him a ring which he swears never to part with, on pain of his life. When he hears that Antonio's bond is forfeit to Shylock, he hurries to help him. After the trial, Portia, disguised as Balthazar, gets the ring from Bassanio as payment for her services. Later at Belmont she asks him for it, and after his confusion amazes him by producing it.

Bassanio has had many moralistic detractors: they object to him on the grounds that he is a fortune hunter, a 'worldly chooser' who hopes to pay off his debts by marrying Portia. He is also accused of deceit, since he does not tell Antonio that he has to succeed in the trial of the caskets before he can win Portia. However, it is clear that he does not know of the trial when he asks Antonio for money; and his behaviour would appear quite ordinary to an Elizabethan audience, who would accept that a dowry was the chief inducement for a young gentleman to marry. They would have seen in him a realistic hero – adventurous, high-spirited, and noble hearted – for whom the motto on the lead casket, 'Who chooseth me must give and hazard all he hath', would provide an irresistible challenge.

BASSET *(1H.VI)*: one of the Lancastrian faction, who quarrels with the Yorkist Vernon (IV.i).

BASSIANUS *(Tit.)*: brother to Saturninus. He offers

Bassanio – a nineteenth-century costume design for a German production of *The Merchant of Venice*.

himself as a candidate for the vacant throne; he seeks the support of Titus, who rejects him in favour of Saturninus. He carries off Lavinia, who is betrothed to him, but who is claimed by Saturninus, and marries her. He is murdered in the forest by Tamora's sons, and his body is thrown into a pit. (II.iv).

His dignified bearing at the outset suggests that he would have been a better choice as emperor than Saturninus.

BATES, JOHN *(H.V)*: an English soldier who with Williams and Court meets the disguised King on the night before Agincourt. He says that he wishes the King were to be ransomed, but then declares that even so he will 'fight lustily for him' (IV.i).

BAWD, A *(Per.)*: the wife of the Pandar, and manager of his brothel. Trade is bad, and she is delighted when the pirates bring her Marina; she immediately tells

Boult to advertize the new arrival in the marketplace (IV.ii). Later she expresses disappointment when she finds that Marina is ruining trade, since 'she would make a Puritan of the devil' (IV.vi).

Victorian commentators were revolted by this unhappy lady, and most refused to admit her as a creation of Shakespeare.

BEAD *(Wiv.)*: the name assumed by one of the boys disguised as fairies. 'Puck' tells him to seek out the girls who have not said their prayers before going to sleep and to pinch them as a punishment (V.v).

BEAR, A *(Wint.)*: this animal appears before Antigonus after he has left Perdita on the shore of Bohemia, pursues him, and, as we hear later from the Clown, eats him (III.iii).

BEATRICE *(Ado)*: daughter to Leonato. She is continually engaged in a witty war of words with Benedick *(q.v.)*. She recognizes him when he is masked, and cheerfully slanders him to his face (II.i). She is tricked into overhearing Hero and Ursula discussing her and her disdain for Benedick, who, they reveal, loves her. She is amazed, but she drops her misogamistic pose and vows to requite his love. She is present when Hero is slandered by Claudio, and she defends her angrily. She tells Benedick that to prove his love for her he must kill Claudio (IV.i). He agrees, but the duel never takes place, for the repentant Claudio is restored to Hero. Beatrice and Benedick declare their intention to marry.

Beatrice and Benedick are not essential to the main plot, but on stage they dominate the play, and are usually treated as hero and heroine. A performance of *'Benedicte and Betteris'* is recorded in the Lord Treasurer's account for 1613; and in his *Commendatory Verses to Shakespeare's Poems* (1640) Leonard Digges wrote

> . . . let but Beatrice
> And Benedicke be seene, loe in a trice
> The Cockpit Galleries, Boxes, all are full.

Beatrice is aggressive, almost shrewish; she has a low opinion of the mental capacities of men, and loves to better them in 'a skirmish of wit'. 'She speaks poniards, and every word stabs,' complains Benedick, after one such encounter. What Hero says of her is essentially true:

> But Nature never framed a woman's heart
> Of prouder stuff than that of Beatrice.
> Disdain and scorn ride sparkling in her eyes,
> Misprising what they look on, and her wit
> Values itself so highly, that to her
> All matters else seems weak. She cannot love,
> Nor take no shape nor project of affection,

She is so self-endeared. (III.i)

When she hears of Benedick's love for her, Beatrice reveals that her sharp witted disdain is only superficial:

> Stand I condemned for pride and scorn so much?
> Contempt, farewell; and maiden pride, adieu.
> No glory lives behind the back of such.
> And Benedick, love on; I will requite thee,
> Taming my wild heart to thy loving hand. (III.i)

Ellen Terry as Beatrice in *Much Ado About Nothing*.

Her resolution does not prevent her from resuming her banter when she next encounters Benedick. He finally finds an effective way to silence 'My Lady Tongue' – with a kiss.

There is no specific source for the Beatrice–Benedick plot: it is Shakespeare's invention.

BEAUCHAMP *(2H.IV; H.V; 1H.IV)*, *see* WARWICK.

BEAUFORT, EDMUND, DUKE OF SOMERSET *(1, 2 & 3 H.VI)*, *see* SOMERSET.

BEAUFORT, HENRY, BISHOP OF WINCHESTER (later Cardinal) *(1H.VI)*: the great-uncle of the King. He is denounced by the protector Gloucester, who accuses him of having 'murdered' Henry V. He crowns Henry VI in Paris. In V.i he appears as a cardinal.

In *2 Henry VI* he arranges the disgrace of the Duchess of Gloucester, and has the Duke of Gloucester arrested on a false charge, and murdered. He dies in terror in the most powerful scene in the play:

Bring me unto my trial when you will.
Died he not in his bed? Where should he die?
Can I make men live whe'r they will or no?
O torture me no more, I will confess.
Alive again? Then show me where he is.
I'll give a thousand pound to look upon him.
He hath no eyes, the dust hath blinded them.
Comb down his hair; look, look, it stands upright,
Like lime-twigs set to catch my winged soul. (III.iii)

BEAUFORT, HENRY, DUKE OF SOMERSET
(3H.VI), *see* SOMERSET.

BEAUFORT, JOHN, EARL OF SOMERSET
(afterwards Duke) *(1H.VI)*, *see* SOMERSET.

BEAUFORT, THOMAS *(H.V; 1H.VI) see*
EXETER, DUKE OF.

BEDE *(Wiv.)*, *see* BEAD.

BEDFORD, DUKE OF *(1 & 2H.IV; H.V; 1H.VI)*, *see* JOHN (OF LANCASTER).

BEDLAM, TOM O' *(Lr.)*: character assumed by Edgar *(q.v)*.

BELARIUS *(Cym.)*: a banished lord, living in a cave in Wales under the name Morgan. As revenge for his unjust banishment, he stole the two sons of Cymbeline, and brought them up as his own. He joins with his 'sons' in fighting with the British against the Romans: their valour turns the battle, and Belarius is knighted after the battle by Cymbeline. He declares his true identity when Cymbeline condemns Guiderius to death for slaying Cloten, and is condemned to death himself. He reveals all, and is forgiven and greeted as a brother by Cymbeline.

The courageous feat of Belarius and his sons is probably based on Holinshed's account of the battle of Loncarty (AD 976), in which the advance of the Danes was checked in a lane by 'an husbandman . . . named Haie' and his two sons, and defeat turned into victory.

BELCH, SIR TOBY *(Tw.N.)*: the drunken uncle of

Sir Toby Belch, Feste and Sir Andrew Aguecheek carouse before the disgusted Malvolio. An engraving based on the production of *Twelfth Night* at Stratford in 1864.

Olivia who seems to be a more or less permanent part of her household. He establishes himself as mentor to Sir Andrew Aguecheek, who sees him as an ideal gentleman. He gulls him into believing that Olivia loves him, and then into challenging 'Cesario', his supposed rival for her hand. With Maria, he contrives the humiliation of Malvolio, by means of 'some obscure epistles', as revenge for the night when the steward arrogantly interrupted their carousing. He treats the deluded Malvolio as a lunatic, and suggests that he should be locked up (III.iv). At the end, Sir Toby is better off to the extent of two thousand pounds, acquired from Sir Andrew, and a wife, Maria.

Sir Toby brings the atmosphere of Revels Night to the play – he is Lord of Misrule, always surrounded by laughter, song and drinking. He is a theatrical cousin to Falstaff: he has much of Sir John's joviality, but little of his venality. He is essentially genial, and gets uneasy when the gulling of Malvolio becomes spiteful; he feels that 'we were well rid of this knavery'.

BENEDICK *(Ado)*: a young lord of Padua. He is mercilessly bantered by Beatrice, and vows to remain a bachelor. He overhears, as he is intended to, a conver-

above Robert Stephens as Benedick and Maggie Smith as Beatrice in the 1965 production of *Much Ado About Nothing* at the National Theatre.

below Benedick (Keith Michell) and Beatrice (Barbara Jefford) in the 1956 Old Vic production of *Much Ado About Nothing*.

J. Forbes-Robertson's painting of *Much Ado About Nothing* at the Lyceum Theatre in 1882, with Ellen Terry as Beatrice and Henry Irving as Benedick.

sation on the subject of Beatrice's supposed passion for him, and he vows to return her love. At her insistence he agrees to challenge his friend Claudio to redress his insults to Hero, but is not required to fulfil his promise. He obtains Leonato's consent to marry Beatrice, and finally silences her with a kiss.

Benedick is a bluff young soldier who is hard put to hold his own with Beatrice. He is less able to conceal his feelings behind a screen of wit than she is, and he frequently takes her jibes to heart.

BENVOLIO *(Rom.)* : nephew to Montague, friend to Romeo and Mercutio, and innocent cause of the tragedy. His fight with Tybalt (I.i) leads to street brawls being declared capital offences; it is he who persuades Romeo to go to the Capulets' ball where he falls in love with Juliet.

BERKELEY *(R.III)* : a gentleman attending Lady Anne (I.ii). He does not speak.

BERKELEY, LORD *(R.II)* : he is sent by the Duke of York to ask Bolingbroke why he has mounted an armed invasion (II.iii). He is later appointed one of the commissioners who pronounce sentence of deposition on Richard.

BEROWNE *(LLL.)* : one of the three lords attending the King of Navarre. He accepts the oath of asceticism, though he is sceptical, and predicts that 'these oaths and laws will prove an idle scorn' (I.i). He secretly falls in love with Rosaline, and denounces the oath as 'flat treason against the kingly state of youth'. He hides up in a tree, and secretly observes that the King and the other lords have also fallen in love; he confronts them, and claims that he alone has kept the oath, but is exposed when the King is given the letter he had sent to Rosaline (IV.iii). While masked, Berowne woos the Princess, mistaking her for Rosaline. Rosaline rebukes him for his casual use of fine words and phrases, and he says that he will abandon them, and declares his love for her in plain words. She sentences him to spend a year visiting hospitals cheering up the sick before their marriage.

Of all the lords, Berowne is the most brilliant word-spinner:

Berowne, they call him – but a merrier man,
Within the limit of becoming mirth,
I never spent an hour's talk withal.
His eye begets occasion for his wit,
For every object that the one doth catch
The other turns to a mirth-moving jest,
Which his fair tongue (conceit's expositor)

Delivers in such apt and gracious words,
That aged ears play truant at his tales,
And younger hearings are quite ravished,
So sweet and voluble is his discourse. (II.i)

Later Rosaline derides him for his attitude to language, which is self-indulgent: he throws magnificent phrases around without any concern for their connection to reality. He agrees that

Taffeta phrases, silken terms precise,
Three-pil'd hyperboles, spruce affectation;
Figures pedantical, these summer flies,
Have blown me full of maggot ostentation, (v.ii)

and promises to woo her only in 'russet yeas and honest kersey noes'. The sentence that Rosaline pronounces on him is appropriate: she requires him to adjust his language to harsh reality:

You shall this twelvemonth term from day to day,
Visit the speechless sick, and still converse
With groaning wretches: and your task shall be,
With all the fierce endeavour of your wit,
To enforce the painted impotent to smile. (v.ii)

Berowne is the dominant figure in the play. He is the only one of the lords who appreciates the comedy of his predicament. Pater saw in Berowne 'a reflex of Shakespeare himself, when he has just become able to stand aside and estimate the first period of his poetry'.

The first recorded performance of *Love's Labour's Lost* was during the Christmas season of 1597, when it was played before the Queen and court. There are many topical allusions and unexplained references which have been taken to imply that the play was first written for a coterie audience, and that it was perhaps first performed at a private house. This remains speculation however, as the play cannot be related to any specific occasion. The story of the play is Shakespeare's invention.

BERRI, DUKE OF *(H.V)*: he is mentioned as being present at the French council before Agincourt (III.v), and so is presumably among the miscellaneous lords of the dramatis personae.

Historically, he was uncle to Charles VI of France.

BERTRAM *(All's W.)*: the young Count of Rousillon, who is forced into marriage with Helena by the King, after she has been given the choice of any of the nobles at the court. He does not love her, and goes off to the wars in order to get away from her. As he leaves, he tells her disdainfully that he will only accept her if she can get a ring from off his finger, and produce his child – the latter a seemingly impossible task, since he has refused to consummate the marriage. In Florence he seduces Diana Capilet, but unknown to him Helena takes her place in bed, thus securing both ring and child. When Helena's supposed death is reported to

Bertram confronted by Helena: *All's Well that Ends Well* (v.iii). From the painting by Francis Wheatley.

him, he is undisturbed. In the end, after some stern threats from the king, he recants, and when Helena reappears, he accepts her and begs forgiveness.

Nobody except Helena, who sees him as a model courtier, has much to say for Bertram. In the play the wise elder figures condemn him as deceitful, dishonourable and a disgrace to his nobility. His inveterate lying alone makes him an unworthy gentleman. Critics have been virtually unanimous in condemning him. Samuel Johnson's comment is typical: 'I cannot reconcile my heart to Bertram; a man noble without generosity, and young without truth; who marries Helen as a coward, and leaves her as a profligate: when she is dead by his unkindness, sneaks home to a second marriage, is accused by the woman whom he has wronged, defends himself by falsehood, and is dismissed to happiness.'

It is difficult to find much in Bertram's favour. The key to his character is his youth: he is 'an unseason'd courtier'; his petulance and callousness are aspects of his immaturity. To some extent his progress through the play is an education, not unlike that of the morality play hero torn between good and evil. Bertram becomes embroiled with the evil Parolles, but is finally saved by the goodness of Helena.

All's Well That Ends Well was probably written

sometime between 1600 and 1603; it has been suggested that the play is a revised version of the *Love's Labour's Won* that Meres listed as being by Shakespeare in 1598. Shakespeare's source was Boccaccio's *Decameron* (Day III, Story 9), which he could have read in William Painter's *The Palace of Pleasure* (1566–7, 1575).

BEVIS, GEORGE *(2H.VI)*: a follower of Jack Cade.

BIANCA *(Oth.)*: a courtesan, mistress of Cassio, who is made the unwitting instrument of Iago's plot against Othello. She is asked by Cassio to copy the needlework on a handkerchief he has found in his chamber(III.iv). In Othello's sight she returns the handkerchief to Cassio (IV.i). She finds Cassio lying wounded in the street, and admits that he supped with her that night (V.i).

    Although she is frequently accused of being a whore (mostly by Iago), Bianca seems to be Cassio's mistress. He treats her flippantly, but she appears to love him.

All's Well that Ends Well: frontispiece to Rowe's 1709 edition of Shakespeare's plays.

She is witty and shrewd, and quick to defend her reputation:

    I am no strumpet; but of life as honest
    As you that thus abuse me. (v.i)

Bianca has no counterpart in Cinthio's tale (see *Othello*), but she does bear some relationship to the conventional courtesan of the Italian stage, whose function was to make intrigues yet more complicated.

BIANCA MINOLA *(Shr.)*: daughter to Baptista and sister to Katharina. She is forbidden to marry before her shrewish sister. When she marries Lucentio without her father's consent, she ironically proves to be less tractable than Katharina.

BIGOT, LORD *(John)*: Robert, Earl of Norfolk. He is the representative of the nobles who join the Dauphin when they discover the body of Arthur and conclude that he was murdered by John. He later returns to his allegiance to the throne.

BIONDELLO *(Shr.)*: servant to Lucentio. When his master assumes the identity of Tranio in order to gain access to Bianca, he assumes the identity of Tranio's servant.

BIRON *(LLL.)*, *see* BEROWNE.

BISHOPS, *see* CARLISLE, ELY, LINCOLN, LONDON, ROCHESTER, ST. ASAPH, WINCHESTER.

BISHOPS, TWO *(R.III)*: these are the 'two deep divines' with whom Richard is seen 'meditating' while Buckingham persuades the Mayor and the citizens that his holiness and virtue will make him an ideal monarch. They are not named (III.vii).

BLACK CHILD *(Tit.)*: the illegitimate son of Aaron and Tamora. He is brought to Aaron to be killed on Tamora's command, but he defends the child fiercely. Aaron is captured while trying to smuggle the child out of Rome, and agrees to confess only when Lucius promises 'to nourish and bring him up' (v.i).

BLANCH OF SPAIN, LADY *(John)*: in response to the suggestion of the citizens of Angiers, John and Philip of France form an alliance by marrying Blanch to the Dauphin, Lewis (II.i). The alliance is broken by Pandulph, the papal legate, and Blanch is unhappily drawn into the war between her husband and her uncle (III.i).

BLUNT, SIR JAMES *(R.III)*: a captain in Richmond's army (v.ii; v.iii).

    He was the third son of Sir Walter Blunt, 1st Baron

Mountjoy, and grandson of Sir Walter Blunt in *1 Henry IV*.

BLUNT, SIR JOHN *(2H.IV)*: son of Sir Walter Blunt. He is falsely reported killed at Shrewsbury. The rebel Coleville is given into his custody.

He was the eldest son of Sir Walter Blunt, and at some time Governor of Calais. In 1482 he was besieged in a castle in Aquitaine by a large French army, but repelled them with a much inferior force. He served under Henry v at the siege of Harfleur, and died at the siege of Rouen in 1418.

BLUNT, SIR WALTER *(1H.IV)*: a supporter of the King, who tries to mediate between him and Hotspur. He wears the King's surcoat at the battle of Shrewsbury, and is killed by Douglas in mistake for him.

BOATSWAIN *(Tp.)*: duty officer on Alonso's ship. When the storm breaks he orders Alonso and his party to stay below decks, and then when all seems lost and the others turn to prayer, he turns to drink.

A cheerful, competent sailor who is more worried by the interfering panic-stricken nobles than by the storm. His presence comforts Gonzalo, who thinks 'he hath no drowning mark upon him, his complexion is perfect gallows' (I.i).

BOHEMIA, KING OF *(Wint.)*, *see* POLIXENES.

BOHEMIA, PRINCE OF *(Wint.)*, *see* FLORIZEL.

BOHUN, EDWARD *(H.VIII)*, *see* BUCKINGHAM, DUKE OF.

BOLEYN, ANNE *(H.VIII)*, *see* BULLEN, ANNE.

BOLINGBROKE (afterwards Henry IV) *(R.II; 1&2 H.IV)*, *see* **HENRY (BOLINGBROKE).**

BOLINGBROKE, ROGER *(2H.VI)*: a sorcerer, who with the witch Margery Jourdain and the priests Southwell and Hum invokes a spirit, Asmath, to foretell the future for the Duchess of Gloucester. They are all arrested, and Bolingbroke is hanged (I.iv).

BONA, LADY *(3H.VI)*: agrees to Warwick's suggestion that she should marry Edward IV, and when she hears that he has married Lady Jane Grey she urges Lewis to supply Margaret with troops to depose Edward and reinstate Henry (III.iii).

She was third daughter to Louis, 1st Duke of Savoy. Her eldest sister Charlotte was the queen of Lewis XI.

BORACHIO *(Ado)*: a follower of Don John, who initiates the scheme to 'misuse the Prince, to vex Claudio, to undo Hero and kill Leonato' (II.ii). He deceives Claudio into thinking the disguised Margaret is Hero, and woos her in front of him, thus 'proving' her faithlessness. He is found out, arrested and cross-examined by Dogberry; he confesses, and clears Margaret of all blame. He asks for 'nothing but the reward of a villain'.

BOTTOM, NICK *(MND.)*: a weaver of Athens. He is allotted the part of Pyramus in the Interlude, though he would have liked to play all the parts. Puck gives him an ass's head, and makes Titania fall in love with him. He remains unperturbed, and accepts both her and her fairy servants with complete equanimity. When Puck releases him from the spell, he thinks he has dreamed it all. He performs his part in the Interlude before Theseus and the lovers.

Bottom is the one character in the play who moves cheerfully through all its worlds; he holds the comedy

Bottom and Titania. A painting by the Swiss artist Henry Fuseli.

together, being equally at home among the fairies, the nobles, or his own rude mechanicals. Nothing surprises him – he is ready for anything. He delights in the world as he finds it. Even his conceit is endearing; it springs from his boundless energy, which makes him dissatisfied with merely one phrase, one qualification, or even one role. The only thing that worries him slightly is his dream, which has been too wondrous for his verbal capacity:

I have had a most rare vision. I have had a dream,

past the wit of man to say what dream it was. Man is but an ass, if he go about to expound this dream. Methought I was – there is no man can tell what. Methought I was, and methought I had – but man is but a patched fool, if he will offer to say, what methought I had. The eye of man hath not heard, the ear of man hath not seen, man's hand is not able to taste, his tongue to conceive, nor his heart to report, what my dream was. I will get Peter Quince to write a ballet of this dream; it shall be called Bottom's Dream, because it hath no bottom; and I will sing it in the latter end of our play, before the Duke. (IV.i)

Bottom triumphs over his confusion regardless of the damage he inflicts on the language; as soon as he finds a way of rendering his dream into some form of self-expression, he is satisfied.

Bottom has suffered in the theatre by being over-played; his role in the Interlude, in particular, is usually handled in a spirit of burlesque. This does him less than justice: he is an ass perhaps, but not a bumpkin; he is simple, but he is not stupid.

BOULT *(Per.)*: servant to the Pandar. He is sent out to find new inmates for the brothel and meets the pirates with their captive, Marina. He arranges for her purchase (IV.ii). She offers him money to find her some other employment (IV.iv).

BOURBON, ADMIRAL *(3H.VI)*: the King of France orders him to set sail for England with troops in support of Queen Margaret (III.iii).

He was Louis, Count of Rousillon, natural son to Charles, Duke of Bourbon.

BOURBON, JOHN, DUKE OF *(H.V)*: uncle of Charles VI of France, who we hear has been captured at Agincourt (IV.viii).

Bottom surprises his fellow 'rude mechanicals' by appearing with an ass's head. A nineteenth-century impression of a performance at the Globe.

right R. J. Hamerton's song cover for the *Falstaff Polka* from Otto Nikolai's opera *The Merry Wives of Windsor*.

THE FALSTAFF POLKA,

ON AIRS IN OTTO NICOLAI'S OPERA

"THE MERRY WIVES OF WINDSOR."
BY
A. MANNS.

T.PACKER CHROMO

STANNARD & DIXON. IMP.

Pr. 3/-

Ent Sta Hall

He was in fact taken to England after his capture, and died there in 1433. He was buried at Christ-Church, Newgate Street, London.

BOURCHIER, CARDINAL *(R.III)*: he is persuaded by Buckingham that the privilege of sanctuary does not extend to children, and agrees to go with Hastings to seize the Duke of York (III.i).

He was Thomas Bourchier (1404–86), Archbishop of Canterbury and a Cardinal.

BOYET *(LLL.)*: a lord attending the Princess of France. It is he who discovers that the Moscovites are in fact the King and his friends. Otherwise his role is that of messenger.

It has been suggested that Boyet is a portrait of the poet George Chapman, since when he first enters the Princess rebukes him with the lines:

Beauty is bought by judgement of the eye,

Not uttered by base sale of chapmen's tongues. (II.i)

BRABANT, ANTHONY, DUKE OF, *(H.V)*: one of the French nobles addressed by Charles VI of France before Agincourt. He is killed in the battle. He does not speak.

BRABANTIO *(Oth.)*: Desdemona's father, and a Venetian senator. He is outraged by her secret marriage to a Moor, and brings Othello before the Duke, since he is convinced that his daughter has been won by some foul means. He is persuaded to pardon his daughter, and to accept Othello – but he warns him that 'she has deceived her father, and may thee'. At the end we hear of his death, for Desdemona's marriage

    . . . was mortal to him, and pure grief

    Shore his old thread in twain. (v.ii)

Brabantio's outrage at his daughter's deceit, and his horror at her marrying a Moor, would probably have evoked a sympathetic response in an Elizabethan audience.

BRAKENBURY, SIR ROBERT *(R.III)*: 'Lieutenant of the Tower'. He surrenders the sleeping Clarence to the two murderers when they present Richard's warrant and 'will not reason what is meant hereby'. Presumably it is also he who gives up the princes to Tyrrel.

BRANDON *(H.VIII)*: the name of an officer who is sent to arrest Buckingham and Abergavenny (I.i).

The arrest was in fact made by Sir Henry Marne (or Marney), the captain of the King's guard.

BRANDON, CHARLES *(H.VIII)*, *see* SUFFOLK, DUKE OF.

BRANDON, SIR WILLIAM *(R.III)*: Richmond's standard-bearer at Bosworth. After the battle Stanley (Derby) reports his death (v.v). His son Charles became the Duke of Suffolk who appears in *Henry VIII*.

BRITAINE, DUKE OF *(H.V)*: a French nobleman, one of those sent to reinforce towns against the advancing English (II.iv).

BROOK *(Wiv.)*: name assumed by Ford (q.v.).

BRUTUS, DECIUS *(Caes.)*: one of the conspirators, who is responsible for making sure that Caesar gets to the Capitol. He finds that Caesar is unwilling to leave his home because of his ominous dream, but he reinterprets it favourably, and adds incentive by mentioning that the senate has resolved to offer him a crown. He takes part in the murder, and is seen no more afterwards; though we hear that the citizens intend to burn his house.

Bottom in Titania's bower. A painting by Henry Fuseli.

Shakespeare follows North's *Plutarch*: he was Decimus Junius Brutus (84–43 BC), whom Caesar had named as one of his heirs. He was later captured and killed by Antony.

BRUTUS, JUNIUS *(Cor.)*: 'a tribune of the people'. He talks of Coriolanus' arrogance (I.i), and inveighs against his pride (II.i). With Sicinius, he rouses the people against Coriolanus, and urges them to make their voices heard (II.iii). They have Coriolanus arrested, and order him to be thrown from the Tarpeian rock; they are driven off, but they return 'with the rabble' and pursue Coriolanus. They are worried when they hear of the banished Coriolanus' march on Rome with the Volscian army, and ask Menenius to seek mercy for Rome (v.i).

The two tribunes, Brutus and Sicinius, are clever politicians who eventually overreach themselves, but they are not villains. Dr Johnson saw them as representatives of 'plebeian malignity, and tribunitian insolence' – but he was a conservative. They are unscrupulous, but then so are the patricians. They have a case against Coriolanus: he attacks the constitution when he declares tribunes unnecessary, and he strikes them, officers of the state. For this the punishment is death, but they commute the sentence to one of banishment because of his services to the state.

Once Coriolanus is banished, the tribunes become ludicrous. For once Coriolanus is quite right when he says that they

> . . . do prank them in authority
> Against all noble sufferance. (III.i)

They become complacent and vain, and glory in their power. But when they hear of the approach of Coriolanus on his mission of vengeance they fear for themselves, but they also have some concern for their fellow citizens (which Cominius and Menenius do not), and ask Menenius to intercede.

BRUTUS, MARCUS *(Caes.)*: alarmed by Caesar's rapid rise to power, yet also jealous of his greatness, Shakespeare's Cassius (in history, Caius Cassius Longinus) urges his friend Brutus (Marcus Junius Brutus) to join the opposition against Caesar before he can overthrow the Roman republic by accepting the royal crown that Mark Antony has pressed on him. Brutus, though he loves and admires Caesar, is even more devoted to the idea of the republic. He and Cassius resolve to eliminate the future tyrant and, with a band of fellow conspirators, stab Caesar to death in the Senate House during the Ides of March, 44 BC. Mark Antony, however, having delivered a brilliant speech over Caesar's corpse, manages to drive them from the city. A triumvirate is formed, consisting of Antony, Lepidus and Octavius (otherwise Octavian, later destined to rule as the Emperor Augustus); and Brutus and Cassius flee to Asia Minor, where they pitch their camp at Sardis. In Brutus' tent a fierce quarrel suddenly blazes up between the two conspirators. Each is exhausted and has begun to lose hope; but, when Cassius draws his dagger and bids his old friend plunge it in his heart, their antagonism as quickly subsides,

and they prepare to meet the enemy. Soon afterwards, Brutus learns of the death of his beloved wife, Portia, and receives the news with Roman fortitude. At the Battle of Philippi in Eastern Macedonia (42 BC) Brutus and Cassius are defeated. Cassius orders an attendant to kill him; Brutus runs upon his sword; and Antony, surveying the dead man, pays him a superbly eloquent tribute:

> This was the noblest Roman of them all:
> All the conspirators, save only he,
> Did that they did in envy of great Caesar:
> He, only in a general honest thought,
> And common good to all, made one of them.
> His life was gentle, and the elements
> So mix'd in him, that Nature might stand up,
> And say to all the world, 'This was a man!' (v.v)

In September 1599, a Swiss traveller records that he had seen, at a theatre on the Bankside, a 'tragedy about Julius Caesar', which no doubt was Shakespeare's play. As usual, when he dealt with a Roman subject, he made full use of Plutarch's *Lives*, translated by Sir Thomas North. But the dramatist's treatment of his theme is peculiarly Elizabethan. According to the medieval theory of 'degree', which the Elizabethans had adopted, a 'Chain of Being' ran through the universe from the highest to the lowest creatures. The animal realm had its natural sovereigns, the lion, the eagle and the dolphin. The stag, too, was a lord in his own field; and Antony, looking on the fallen Caesar, compares him to a stricken hart:

> Here wast thou bayed, brave hart:
> Here didst thou fall, and here thy hunters stand . . .
> How like a deer strucken by many princes
> Dost thou lie here! (III.i)

The huntsmen themselves are noble. Though Cassius harbours a keen resentment against his victim's overwhelming grandeur –

> Why, man, he doth bestride the petty world
> Like a Colossus, and we petty men
> Walk under his huge legs, and peep about
> To find ourselves dishonourable grave (I.ii)

– he is also inspired by sternly unselfish motives; while Brutus, who had really loved Caesar, is a patriotic politician and a disinterested legalist. Each has done what he believes to be right; and each accepts his fate with the stoical dignity that the Romans named *'gravitas'*. Of the scene that presents their quarrel at Sardis, and the reconciliation that succeeds it, Coleridge wrote that he knew 'no part of Shakespeare that more impresses on me the belief of his genius being superhuman . . .'. They separate as firm friends, their deep affection re-established, well knowing they may have said goodbye for ever:

> Bru. . . . But this same day
>   Must end that work the ides of March began.

above An eighteenth-century engraving showing Mr Thomas Sheridan as Brutus in *Julius Caesar (left)*;

Caesar's ghost appears before Brutus in his tent near Sardis. An engraving after Richard Westall *(right)*.

And whether we shall meet again, I know not:
Therefore our everlasting farewell take:
For ever, and for ever, farewell, Cassius!
If we do meet again, why, we shall smile;
If not, why then this parting was well made.
Cas. For ever, and for ever, farewell, Brutus!
If we do meet again, we'll smile indeed;
If not, 'tis true, this parting was well made.
Bru. Why then, lead on. O, that a man might know
The end of this day's business, ere it come!
But it sufficeth, that the day will end,
And then the end is known. Come, ho! away!
(v.ii)

BUCKINGHAM, DUKE OF (Edward Stafford or 'Bohun') *(H.VIII)*: an enemy of Wolsey, whom he accuses of arrogance, and of selling the King's honour. He is arrested for treason, and sentenced to death (II.i). On his way to execution he proclaims his innocence to the people; he speaks of himself as 'Edward Bohun' (II.i).

Edward Stafford (1478–1521) incurred the enmity of Wolsey, who was powerful enough to dispose of him. There is little evidence that he was a traitor, but he was foolish and loud-mouthed. In Shakespeare's play he is condemned on the evidence of his surveyor, who he had dismissed from his service, and who then reported that he had threatened to assassinate the King. He was most probably betrayed by his Chancellor, Robert Gilbert, in an anonymous letter written to Wolsey in 1520.

BUCKINGHAM, DUKE OF (Henry Stafford) *(R.III)*: a confidant and supporter of Richard. He suggests that the young Edward V should be brought to London (II.ii); he commits Rivers and Grey to prison (II.iv); he persuades the Archbishop of Rotherham to get the young Duke of York out of sanctuary (III.i). He tells Richard how he persuaded the citizens of Richard's legitimate claim to the throne; he tells the Mayor that Richard is 'meditating with two deep divines', and when Richard appears with the two bishops he begs him to

accept the crown (III.vii). Richard resolves to dispose of Buckingham when he shows qualms over the murder of the princes. He tries to escape, but is executed (v.i). His ghost confronts Richard at Bosworth (v.iii).

Henry Stafford (c. 1454–83), was grandson of Humphrey Stafford (q.v.); he became the 2nd Duke of Buckingham on the death of his grandfather in 1460. He became prominent politically after his marriage to Elizabeth Woodville, the sister of the Queen – but he was distrusted by both the Queen's party and by Richard of Gloucester. But he helped the Protector to arrest Rivers and Grey, and was instrumental in getting Edward v into the Tower. It was largely through Buckingham's help that Richard got the crown; he appeared publicly and harangued the citizens on the illegitimacy of Edward IV's children. A month or two after Richard became King he and Buckingham inexplicably became enemies – possibly Buckingham was dissatisfied with the reward he received for his services. He decided to join Richmond, but he became trapped behind the flooded rivers Severn and Wye, and his army dispersed. He went into hiding, but was betrayed by one of his servants, and delivered to Richard. He was beheaded on All Souls' Day, 1483. Shakespeare has his execution take place at the same time as Richmond's landing, which was not in fact until 1485.

BUCKINGHAM, DUKE OF (Humphrey Stafford) *(2H.VI)*: the 1st Duke of Buckingham. He upbraids Gloucester before the King for his 'cruelty' (I.iii); he arrests the Duchess of Gloucester while she is listening to incantations, and is present at Gloucester's examination and arrest (III.i). He offers to pardon all of Cade's rebels who surrender (IV.viii); he supports the King against York, and accepts the submission of York (v.i).

In *3 Henry VI* his death at St Albans is reported in the first scene.

Humphrey Stafford (1402–60) served in France under Henry v, and became a member of Henry VI's council in 1424. In 1430 he was made Constable of France, and spent two years fighting there. On his return to England, he joined a group of nobles in opposition to Richard Duke of Gloucester. In 1450 he made a vain attempt to make terms with Cade's rebels; he later sat at Rochester when they were tried. He supported the Queen against the Duke of York, but also did his best to patch up the quarrels and keep peace in the realm. In 1460 he was killed beside the King's tent, on the eve of the battle of Northampton; his killers were the followers of the bishops who had

appeared with an armed retinue to demand an audience for the Yorkist lords. Shakespeare has him die at the battle of St Albans, which was in 1455.

BULLCALF, PETER *(2H.IV)*: one of the potential recruits rounded up for Falstaff's inspection by Justice Shallow. Bullcalf retains his freedom by bribing Bardolph (III.ii).

BULLEN, ANNE, MARCHIONESS OF PEMBROKE (afterwards Queen) *(H.VIII)*: the King meets her at Wolsey's masque, and is struck by her beauty (I.iv). Wolsey's downfall is precipitated when his letter to the Pope attempting to thwart Henry's marriage to Anne is intercepted. They are married secretly.

Anne is not seen much in the play; Shakespeare concentrates on the birth of Elizabeth. Historically, she was a maid of honour to Queen Katharine and became Henry's mistress after 1527. They were secretly married in 1533, and in the same year Anne gave birth to Elizabeth. She was executed for adultery in 1536.

The scene in which Anne meets Henry was being performed when the Globe Theatre caught fire in 1613.

BUM *(Meas.)*, *see* POMPEY.

BURGH, HUBERT DE *(John)*, *see* HUBERT.

BURGUNDY, DUKE OF *(Lr.)*: a suitor to Cordelia. He refuses to marry her when she has been dispossessed by her father, and she is taken by the King of France (I.i).

BURGUNDY, DUKE OF *(H.V)*: 'Philip the Good'. He brings together Henry v and Charles VI, and arranges the Treaty of Troyes and Henry's marriage to Katharine. He appears only in the last scene (v.ii), in which he makes a plea for peace, and banters with Henry for marrying Katharine.

In *1 Henry VI* he is at first an ally of the English (he is Regent of France), but Joan of Arc changes his mind with her 'sugar'd words' and he rejoins the French.

BUSHY *(R.II)*: one of Richard's sycophantic favourites. He tries to escape to Bristol with Bagot and Greene, but is captured and executed by Bolingbroke.

BUTTS, DOCTOR *(H.VIII)*: physician to Henry. He sees Cranmer kept waiting outside the council-chamber and hurries to tell the King how contemptuously his archbishop is being treated.

left Merle Oberon as Anne Boleyn in the 1933 film *The Private Life of Henry VIII*.

CADE, JACK *(2H.VI)*: the rebel leader, 'a headstrong Kentishman', who is persuaded by York to claim the throne in the name of John Mortimer. He marches on London with a mob, looting and killing. Buckingham and Clifford persuade his followers to desert him. He escapes, but is killed by Iden in his garden in Kent.

CADWAL *(Cym.)*: name given to Arviragus *(q.v.)* by Belarius *(q.v.)*.

CAESAR, JULIUS *(Caes.)*: the dictator of Rome, who returns in triumph after defeating the sons of Pompey. On arrival he is warned to beware of the Ides of March. We hear that he has three times refused a crown. He is undismayed by the portents on the night before his assassination, but he is persuaded by his wife Calphurnia not to go to the Capitol; Decius Brutus persuades him to change his mind (II.ii). At the Capitol he ignores the soothsayer's warning, and refuses to read Artemidorus' scroll; he refuses to hear Metellus Cimber's petition, and is stabbed by the conspirators, and is astonished to find Brutus among them (III.i). His ghost appears to Brutus at Philippi (IV.iii).

Shakespeare's Caesar is an ambiguous figure. He reflects the two views of him that coexisted during the Renaissance: one saw him as a tyrant, the other as the model of the great man and ruler. Shakespeare's Caesar is great; this much is taken for granted even by Cassius, who derides him as a weakling and a man of 'feeble temper', but admits that

　　. . . he doth bestride the narrow world
Like a Colossus, and we petty men
Walk under his huge legs, and peep about
To find ourselves dishonourable graves. (I.ii)
To Antony, Caesar was
　　. . . the noblest man
That ever lived in the tide of times. (III.i)
We see Caesar the ruler mainly through the eyes of the conspirators, who can only produce his ambition as a reason for killing him. This seems somewhat specious, since we are told that Caesar has already refused the crown three times, and his power is already almost total (historically, he was an absolute ruler at the time of his death). It is a fine irony that the assassination leads to the kind of autocratic rule that it was supposed to prevent.

Caesar is very much a public figure. Indeed he always speaks as though he were addressing a public meeting,

The statue of Julius Caesar in the Capitol in Rome.

and his continual self-assertion, though inseparable from his greatness, is at times almost absurd. He seems almost in awe of his own public persona: as the Victorian critic Edward Dowden noted, 'The real man Caesar disappears for himself under the myth.' In this, Shakespeare picked up a hint from Plutarch, who said that Caesar's whole life was 'an emulation with himself as with another man'.

Caesar is a demi-god, but he is also an infirm old man. Shakespeare lays some stress on his physical weaknesses: his deafness, his poor swimming (according to Plutarch he was a very good swimmer) and his epileptic fit (there was a tradition, beginning in the New Testament, of allegorizing the symptoms of epilepsy as the signs of obdurate pride). He overcomes his frailties by exerting his powerful will, and he

Caesar (John Gielgud) is stabbed by Casca (Robert Vaughn) in Stuart Burges' 1970 film of *Julius Caesar*.

achieves his peculiar but undeniable greatness by making himself beyond humanity, a true colossus apart from other men:

> These couchings and these lowly courtesies
> Might fire the blood of ordinary men
> And turn pre-ordinance and first decree
> Into the law of children. Be not fond
> To think that Caesar bears such rebel blood
> That will be thaw'd from the true quality
> With that which melteth fools – I mean, sweet words,
> Low-crooked curtsies, and base spaniel fawning.
>
> (III.i)

Julius Caesar was written and first performed in 1599. It was not among the plays by Shakespeare listed by Francis Meres in 1598, and it was seen at the Globe in the autumn of 1599 by a Swiss traveller, Thomas Platter. Shakespeare's main source was Plutarch's *Lives of the Noble Grecians and Romans*.

CAESAR, OCTAVIUS *(Caes.; Ant.)*, *see* OCTAVIUS.

CAITHNESS *(Mac.)*: a Scottish nobleman who brings an army to reinforce Malcolm's English troops at Birnam (V.ii).

CAIUS *(Lr.)*: name assumed by Kent *(q.v.)*.

CAIUS *(Tit.)*: a kinsman of the Andronici. He helps Titus shoot arrows bearing messages to the gods (IV.iii), and with Publius and Valentine binds and gags Chiron and Demetrius before Titus kills them (V.ii).

CAIUS, DOCTOR *(Wiv.)*: an irascible Frenchman in love with Anne Page. When he finds that Evans favours Slender's suit to her, he challenges him to a duel. The Host of the Garter sends the combatants to different places – they discover his trick and unite against him, and cozen him of three horses. Mistress Page approves of Caius, and arranges for him to take Anne away and marry her while Falstaff is being baited in Windsor Park; but as a result of the plot hatched by Fenton and the Host, he finds that he has married 'oon garsoon, a boy!'

CAIUS CASSIUS *(Caes.)*, *see* CASSIUS.

CAIUS LIGARIUS *(Caes.)*, *see* LIGARIUS.

CAIUS LUCIUS *(Cym.)*, *see* LUCIUS.

CAIUS MARCIUS *(Cor.)*, *see* CORIOLANUS.

CALCHAS *(Troil.)*: a Trojan priest who has joined the Greeks. He successfully requests that the Trojan prisoner Antenor be exchanged for his daughter Cressida. He makes no objection to Diomedes' seduction of her when she arrives in the Greek camp.

According to Homer, Calchas was the son of Thestor, and the wisest soothsayer among the Greeks. In the spurious *De Excidio Trojae Historia* of 'Dares Phrygius' we first see him as a Trojan who goes over to the Greeks because he foresees the outcome of the war. He is first found as the father of Cressida in Benoît de Saint-More's *Le Roman de Troie*.

CALIBAN *(Tp.)*: 'a savage and deformed slave', the offspring of the witch Sycorax and an evil spirit. Prospero finds him on the island, teaches him to speak, and makes him his servant. We hear that at first Prospero had treated him kindly, but he tried to rape Miranda. Thereafter he has been treated harshly, and

Caliban and Prospero, with Miranda and Ariel, by
Henry Fuseli.

cowed by threats, he now obeys his master sullenly. He
becomes the devoted admirer of Stephano when he is
introduced to drink by him; he suggests that they attack
Prospero and take control of the island. They are
easily thwarted by Prospero. At the end Caliban humbles
himself before Prospero; he is left alone on his island
when the other characters sail for Naples.

Caliban is central to the complex scheme of the play:
he is the representative and manifestation of wild,
untamed nature. He is natural man, a standard against
which civilized man can be measured, and, in the case
of the debased nobles Antonio and Sebastian, found
wanting; the corruption of civilized men is worse than
his natural bestiality. He is ugly because he is a product
of evil natural magic.

Shakespeare probably based Caliban on accounts of
West Indian savages; he certainly used Montaigne's
essay 'Of Cannibals'. It is possible that the name
Caliban is simply an anagram of 'Cannibal'.

CALPHURNIA *(Caes.)*: the wife of Julius Caesar.
She is haunted by ominous dreams of a statue spouting
blood, and urges Caesar not to go to the Capitol.
Decius Brutus changes his mind.

She was the daughter of Lucius Calpurnius Piso. Her
ominous dreams come from Plutarch, where it is
related that she dreamed that 'Caesar was slain, and
that she had him in her arms'.

CAMBIO *(Shr.)*: name assumed by Lucentio *(q.v.)*.

**CAMBRIDGE, RICHARD (PLANTAGENET),
EARL OF** *(H.V)*: he is bribed by the French, and
conspires with Sir Thomas Grey and Lord Scroop to
assassinate Henry at Southampton as he is about to set
sail for France. The plot is discovered, and the traitors
are arrested on the quay and later executed (II.ii).

CAMILLO *(Wint.)*: one of four lords of Sicilia.
Leontes makes him promise to poison Polixenes,

whom he suspects of being the lover of his wife Hermione. Camillo decides he cannot do it, and tells Polixenes. Together they escape to Bohemia. After sixteen years Polixenes discovers, with Camillo's help, that his son Florizel is in love with a shepherd's daughter, Perdita. Polixenes forbids their union, but Camillo helps the lovers escape to Sicilia. Camillo follows them to Sicily, where he learns the real identity of Perdita. At Leontes' request, he is betrothed to Paulina.

CAMPEIUS, CARDINAL *(H.VIII)*: the papal legate who, with Wolsey, is commissioned by the Pope to consider the divorce of Katharine of Aragon. He urges the postponement of her trial, and advises her to withdraw her appeal to the Pope. At the end he is said to be 'Stol'n away to Rome'.

He was Lorenzo Campeggio, Bishop of Salisbury 1524–34. He was deprived of his post by the King, but his departure from England was not clandestine.

CANIDIUS *(Ant.)*: lieutenant-general to Antony. He considers that Antony's foolish insistence on a sea battle is due to Cleopatra's influence, and after Antony's defeat he yields his legions to Caesar (III.vii, III.x).

CANTERBURY, ARCHBISHOP OF *(R.III), see* BOURCHIER.

CANTERBURY, ARCHBISHOP OF *(H.V)*: Henry Chicheley. He prepares for an audience with the regenerate Henry, and expatiates on his amazing reformation. In order to avoid a threatened confiscation of church property, he cynically urges Henry to assert his title to the throne in France; he explains his right to it in a long speech (I.ii – taken almost intact from Holinshed), and promises financial aid from the church.

CANTERBURY, ARCHBISHOP OF *(H.VIII), see* CRANMER.

CANTERBURY, ARCHBISHOP OF *(H.VIII)*: he is present at the divorce proceedings at Blackfriars (II.iv). He was William Warham (1450–1532).

CAPHIS *(Tim.)*: the servant to a senator who is one of Timon's creditors. He is sent to collect his master's money, but is diverted by Flavius who has not yet revealed to Timon the true state of his finances. He and the other servants bait Apemantus and the Fool while waiting for their reply (II.ii).

CAPTAIN, A *(Ham.)*: a soldier in the Norwegian army who meets Hamlet, Rosencrantz and Guildenstern on their way to the port where they are to embark for England. He tells Hamlet that the army, under Fortinbras, is marching against Poland (IV.iv).

CAPTAIN, A *(Tit.)*: he announces Titus' victorious return from the war against the Goths, and describes him as 'Patron of virtue, Rome's best champion' (I.i).

CAPTAIN, ROMAN *(Cym.)*: he tells Lucius that his legions have arrived at Milford Haven. He uncovers the body of 'Fidele' (Imogen), and reports that he lives (IV.ii).

CAPTAIN, SEA *(2 H.VI)*: he captures Suffolk. At first he is inclined to seek ransom, but on finding out who his captive is, he sentences him to death.

According to Holinshed, Suffolk was captured by the captain of the *Nicholas of the Tower*, a ship of war, who 'on the one side of a cock bote, caused his head to be struck off'.

CAPTAIN, SEA *(Tw.N.)*: captain of the ship wrecked off the coast of Illyria, who is washed ashore with Viola. He tells her of Orsino and his love for Olivia, which gives her the idea of disguising herself as a boy. She entrusts him with her clothes (I.ii).

CAPUCIUS *(H.VIII)*: a Spaniard, ambassador from the Emperor Charles V, Katharine's nephew. Henry sends him to see Katharine when she is dying, and she asks him to take a last letter from her to the King (IV.ii).

CAPULET *(Rom.)*: Juliet's father, and head of the family that is opposed to the Montagues. He wants Juliet to marry Paris, and is furious when she refuses. He is reconciled to Montague at the end, and promises to build a rich tomb for Romeo.

CAPULET, COUSIN *(Rom.)*: an elderly kinsman to Capulet. The two sit out the dance and reckon how many years have passed since they last took part in a masque (I.v).

CAPULET, LADY *(Rom.)*: wife to Capulet. She supports her husband over the proposed marriage of Juliet to Paris; she says she will have Romeo poisoned, and shows no pity for her daughter's anguish.

CARRIERS, TWO *(1H.IV)*: they meet Gadshill at the inn at Rochester, where they are waiting for Tom, the ostler, to prepare their horses. Gadshill asks them what time they intend to leave, but they are evasive (II.i). After the robbery, one of the carriers comes to the inn at Eastcheap with the sheriff, searching for Falstaff (II.iv).

CARLISLE, BISHOP OF *(R.II)*: a faithful supporter of Richard, who protests against Bolingbroke's usurpation, and predicts civil war. He is involved in an abortive plot against Bolingbroke, but is pardoned by him for the 'high sparks of honour' seen in him.

He was Thomas Merke; he died shortly after being pardoned, in 1409.

CASCA *(Caes.)* : Publius Servilius. He is persuaded by Cassius to join the conspirators, and is the first to stab Caesar. He disappears from the play after the assassination.

Brutus calls him a 'blunt fellow', and recalls his 'quick mettle' as a schoolboy; Cassius explains that he has not changed:

So is he now, in execution

Of any bold or noble enterprise,

However he puts on this tardy form.

This rudeness is a sauce to his good wit,

Which gives men stomach to digest his words

With better appetite. (I.ii.)

Antony calls him 'envious Casca'. He is the first to stab Caesar. The character is almost wholly Shakespeare's invention – there are only a few references to him in Plutarch.

CASSANDRA *(Troil.)* : a prophetess, daughter of King Priam of Troy. She enters 'raving' (II.ii), crying out that Troy must fall if Helen is not returned. Hector is impressed, though Troilus scorns her as 'brainsick'. She foresees Hector's death, and vainly urges him not to fight that day.

She had offended Apollo, who caused her prophecies, though true, never to be believed. She is found both in the medieval and Homeric versions of the legend.

CASSIO, MICHAEL *(Oth.)* : a Florentine, an 'Honourable Lieutenant', newly appointed. Iago uses him in his plot against Othello – he gets him drunk, and he assaults Roderigo. Othello regretfully dismisses him. Iago persuades him to seek Desdemona's help in reinstating himself, having planted the suspicion in Othello's mind that she is Cassio's lover. He admits in Othello's hearing that 'she loves me' – but he is referring to Bianca, not Desdemona. He is attacked in the street by Roderigo, who he wounds; he is himself wounded by Iago. He is carried into the chamber where Desdemona lies dead, and proves Iago's guilt. He assumes Othello's command after his death.

Cassio is a charming, but guileless, soldier-gallant. In Cinthio's tale, where he is simply '*un capo di squadra*', his leg is severed in the fight, and he has to have a wooden replacement.

CASSIUS *(Caes.)* : a high-minded politician, whose character does not lack a certain touch of spite and envy, Cassius first suggests to Brutus that Julius Caesar should be removed before he can assume royal powers. Caesar already mistrusts him:

Yond Cassius has a lean and hungry look,

He thinks too much: such men are dangerous.

But the great soldier, a proudly self-confident man, pays as little heed to these vague suspicions as to the warnings of the Soothsayer, and is murdered in the Senate House. Driven from Rome, Cassius and Brutus then retire to Asia Minor. They are defeated at Philippi by the combined forces of Antony, Lepidus and Octavius; and both conspirators die a Roman death. (*See* BRUTUS.)

CATESBY, SIR WILLIAM *(R.III)* : a faithful supporter of Richard. He is sent to sound out Hastings, and if possible win him over to Gloucester's side. He assists in the performance that Richard stages to convince the Lord Mayor and citizens of London that he is a humble religious figure. Catesby remains faithful to Richard until the end.

He was a lawyer, made Chancellor of the Exchequer for life by Richard in 1483. He was taken prisoner at Bosworth and beheaded.

CATLIN, SIMON *(Rom.)* : one of the musicians engaged to play at Juliet's wedding to Paris. A catling is a small lute string.

CATO, YOUNG *(Caes.)* : the son of Marcus Cato, and friend to Brutus and Cassius. He fights bravely for them at Phillipi, where he is killed (v.iv).

CELIA *(AYL.)* : the only child of Frederick, the usurping Duke, and devoted friend to her cousin Rosalind *(q.v.)*. As 'Aliena' she shares Rosalind's exile and hardships in the Forest of Arden. She discovers Orlando in the forest, and also meets Oliver, whom she marries at the end. Their courtship is peripheral to the plot, and mostly takes place offstage.

She is Alinda in Lodge's *Rosalynde*.

CERES *(Tp.)* : goddess of corn, earth and fertility, who appears in the masque staged by Ariel before Miranda and Ferdinand. She and Juno bless the proposed marriage.

After the masque, Ariel says to Prospero

. . . when I presented Ceres

I thought to have told thee of it; but I fear'd

Lest I might anger thee. (v.i)

Presumably he 'represented', i.e. he played, the part of Ceres.

CERIMON *(Per.)* : 'a lord of Ephesus', and a famous physician. The apparently dead Thaisa is brought to his house, and he revives her with infusions, warmth and music. He gives her the jewels and the letter that were found with her, and helps her become a vestal at the temple of Diana. At the end he tells Pericles the story of her recovery (v.iii).

CESARIO *(Tw.N.)* : name assumed by Viola *(q.v.)* when disguised as a man.

CHAMBERLAIN, A *(H.V)* : the chamberlain (manager) of the inn at Rochester, who is in league with Falstaff and Gadshill. He tells the latter that 'there's a franklin in the weald of Kent hath brought three hundred marks with him in gold' (ii.i). Gadshill calls him a 'muddy knave', but promises him a share of the loot.

CHAMBERLAIN, LORD *(H.VIII)* : he acts as controller at Wolsey's feast, where he presents Anne Bullen to the King. He is one of the council that tries Cranmer. He superintends the arrangements for the christening of Elizabeth.

There were two Lord Chamberlains during the period covered by the play : Charles Somerset, Earl of Worcester, from 1509 until 1526, and Lord Sands, from 1526 until 1543.

CHANCELLOR, LORD *(H.VIII)* : he is president of the council that tries Cranmer. When the King intervenes, he explains that the imprisonment of Cranmer is not malicious (v.iii).

There were three in the period covered by the play : Sir Thomas More, from 1529 to 1532; Sir Thomas Audley, from 1532 (though he was not formally appointed until 1533) until his death in 1544; and Sir Thomas Wriothesley, who succeeded him, and was Chancellor at the time of the attack on Cranmer, his bitter enemy. Shakespeare possibly intended Wolsey throughout, though he was beheaded in 1535.

CHARLES VI, KING OF FRANCE *(H.V)* : the French monarch opposed to Henry. He sends a herald to bid defiance to Henry before Agincourt (iii.v). After his defeat, he makes the Treaty of Troyes with Henry, and gives him his daughter in marriage.

Charles VI of France (1368–1422) was known as 'le bien-aimé'. He was subject to periodic fits of insanity. The Treaty of Troyes provided that Henry should succeed to the throne of France after Charles' death, but Henry died first.

CHARLES, THE WRESTLER *(AYL.)* : a wrestler employed by Duke Frederick. Orlando plans to challenge him, but Charles is afraid of harming him, and asks Oliver to dissuade his brother. Oliver sees a chance to get rid of Orlando, and tells Charles to be

quite ruthless, since 'there is not one so young and so villainous this day living' as Orlando (i.i). In the bout, Orlando defeats Charles (i.ii).

The bout would have been performed with great realism, and at some length, in the Elizabethan theatre, and would have been advertized as one of the play's great attractions.

CHARMIAN *(Ant.)* : waiting woman to Cleopatra, who is usually in attendance. She advises Cleopatra to go to the monument and pretend she is dead (iv.xiii). She is present at Cleopatra's death, and applies the asp to her own breast as the guards enter (v.ii).

CHATILLON *(John)* : a French lord, ambassador to John from Philip II of France, who brings John Philip's challenge in support of Arthur's claim to the throne of England (i.i), and returns with John's answer (ii.i).

There was a Hugh de Chatillon among the grand peers of France who assembled in parliament in 1223; and a Gervais de Chatillon is mentioned in the treaty between Philip Augustus and Richard I in 1194. The family is an important one in French history.

CHIRON *(Tit.)* : the youngest son of Tamora. In response to the promptings of Aaron he stabs Bassianus, and he and his brother Demetrius rape and mutilate Lavinia (ii.i). Two of Titus' sons are blamed for the murder. Chiron and Demetrius are killed by Titus; their flesh is baked in pies and served up to their mother (v.iii).

CHORUS *(H.V.)* : in this play the chorus is used as a device for explanation and exposition, in the form of a prologue to each act. It is used to describe moments in the action that cannot be shown on stage :

> . . . Suppose that you have seen
> The well-appointed King at Hampton pier
> Embark his royalty; and his brave fleet
> With silken streamers the young Phoebus fanning.
> Play with your fancies; and in them behold,
> Upon the hempen tackle, ship-boys climbing;
> Hear the shrill whistle, which doth order give
> To sounds confused; behold the threaden sails
> Borne with th' invisible and creeping wind,
> Draw the huge bottoms through the furrowed sea;
> Breasting the lofty surge. (Prol., iii)

CHORUS *(Rom.)* : the chorus appears as a prologue before Act i to set the scene and explain the story of the play, and again before Act ii to explain the enforced separation of the lovers.

CICERO *(Caes.)* : a senator. Casca describes the

portents he has seen to him (I.iii). Metellus wants him as a figurehead for the conspiracy:

> O let us have him, for his silver hairs
> Will purchase us a good opinion,
> And buy men's voices to commend our deeds.
> It shall be said, his judgement ruled our hands;
> Our youths and wildness shall no whit appear,
> But all be buried in his gravity. (II.i)

Brutus rejects him, on the grounds that he is too independent-minded to join a conspiracy that he has not initiated. We hear that Mark Antony has had him put to death (IV.iii).

He was a Roman philosopher, orator and statesman (106–43 BC). He was at the height of his fame and popularity in the year after Caesar's assassination, but was proscribed by the Triumvirate, and murdered.

CIMBER, METELLUS *(Caes.)*: one of the conspirators. He suggests sounding out Cicero *(q.v.)* and Caius Ligarius *(q.v.)*. His petition to Caesar for the return of his 'banish'd brother' is the signal for the assassination.

He was Lucius Tillius Cimber, who was at first a firm supporter of Caesar. It is not known why he joined the conspiracy. When his petition was refused, he grabbed Caesar's gown and dragged him forward, thus giving the signal for the assassination.

CINNA, THE CONSPIRATOR *(Caes.)*: he places anonymous letters, which purport to come from citizens who fear Caesar's ambition, where Brutus will find them (II.iii). He is present at the assassination.

He was Lucius Cornelius Cinna the younger. He had been made a praetor by Caesar.

CINNA, A POET *(Caes.)*: he is mistaken by the mob for Cinna the conspirator, and is torn to pieces (III.iii).

This apparently random murder is an ironic comment on Antony's use of rhetoric and emotional trickery in his famous speech to the people: the result is farcical bestiality.

This was not Gaius Helvius Cinna, the poet and friend of Catullus, but Helvius Cinna, a tribune friendly to Caesar who was mistaken by the mob for L. Cornelius Cinna, a known antagonist of Caesar. That both North and Shakespeare should confuse the two is understandable.

CLARENCE, GEORGE, DUKE OF *(3 H.VI)*: he is created Duke by his brother Edward IV after the Yorkist victory at Towton, but deserts him (with Warwick) when Edward marries Lady Grey (III.iii). He is made joint Protector, with Warwick, by Henry (IV.vi), but rejoins Edward and opposes Warwick at Coventry. He joins in the murder of the young Prince Edward (V.vi).

The murder of Cinna the poet by the mob. A scene from the Royal Shakespeare Company's 1972 production of *Julius Caesar*.

In *Richard III* he is committed to the Tower (I.i), but Richard assures him of his safety. He has a terrible dream; after an eloquent plea for mercy, he is murdered by two men paid by Richard (I.iv). His ghost appears before Richard at Bosworth (V.iii).

Margaret calls him 'a quicksand of deceit'; and in *Richard III* he is referred to as 'false, fleeting, perjur'd Clarence'.

He was the sixth son of Richard Duke of York and Cicely Neville. After the death of his father he was sent with his younger brother Richard to Utrecht for safety; they returned on the accession of Edward IV in 1461. George was now created Duke of Clarence. At Calais in 1469 he married Isabella, daughter of the Earl of Warwick, and at once joined his father-in-law's invasion of England. They took Edward prisoner at the battle of Edgecote, but public discontent forced them to release him. They fled to France after an unsuccessful Lancastrian rising. In 1470 Clarence and Warwick returned, Edward fled, and Henry VI was restored to the throne. Clarence was secretly reconciled to his brother Edward; he did not like the Lancastrian restoration, since he wanted the throne himself. He rejoined Edward when he invaded in 1471, siding with him at Coventry, and later at Barnet and Tewkesbury, and helped restore the Yorkist dynasty. There is little evidence for the story that he took part in the murder of

the young Edward after Tewkesbury. He became involved in a violent quarrel with his brother Richard
Duke of Gloucester, but they were reconciled in 1474.
He was charged with seeking the death of the King by
necromancy, and sent to the Tower, where he was
secretly executed in 1478. The story about the butt of
malmsey was probably the result of rumour.

CLARENCE, THOMAS *(2 H.IV)* : the second son of
Henry IV. His father appeals to him to guide Prince
Henry, his brother, when he becomes Henry V (IV.iv).

In *Henry V* he is at Troyes, and is addressed by Henry
V (v.ii), but he is not included in the dramatis personae
of any edition.

CLAUDIO *(Meas.)* : 'a young gentleman', brother to
Isabella. He is arrested for fornication with the now
pregnant Juliet, though he claims his betrothal contract made his act legal. He asks Isabella to intercede
with Angelo. His execution is ordered; Isabella tells
him that his life can only be saved at the price of her
honour. He at first agrees with her that the proposition
is unthinkable, but fear of death changes his mind.
Isabella is repelled by his weakness. He is kept hidden,
while the head of a pirate who has been executed is
brought before Angelo. He is produced at the end,
restored to Juliet, and pardoned by the Duke.

Claudio claims in his defence that

. . . upon a true contract

I got possession of Julietta's bed : (I.ii)
this would be a betrothal contract, surrounded by a
mass of complex legal technicalities during the Renaissance, but legally binding. However, it is made clear
that Angelo has reactivated an old law, under which
Claudio is technically guilty of fornication.

After he is committed to prison, Claudio is on the
receiving end of much moral advice from both Isabella
and the Duke : he becomes the centre of a debate on
attitudes to death. He expresses his own fear in a memorable outburst as the reality of his situation suddenly
strikes him:

Ay, but to die, and go we know not where,
To lie in cold obstruction and to rot,
This sensible warm motion to become
A kneaded clod; and the delighted spirit
To bathe in fiery floods, or to reside
In thrilling region of thick-ribbed ice;
To be imprisoned in the viewless winds,
And blown with restless violence round about
The pendent world; or to be worse than worst
Of those that lawless and incertain thought
Imagine howling – 'tis too horrible!
The weariest and most loathed worldly life
That age, ache, penury, and imprisonment
Can lay on nature is a paradise

To what we fear of death. (III.i)
After this scene Claudio is no more than a part of the
play's plot mechanism.

Pater thought Claudio 'a flowerlike young man'; but
Angelo has him killed (as he thinks) despite his promise to Isabella because he fears his revenge.

In Cinthio's tale (in his *Hecatommithi*, 1565) the
equivalent character, Vico, is actually executed. In
Whetstone's *Promos and Cassandra* the heroine's
brother, Andrugio, is saved from death.

CLAUDIO *(Ado)* : a young Florentine lord in the
service of Don Pedro, who has just returned from the
wars. He falls in love with Hero. Don John, who is
jealous, arranges for Claudio to see Hero receiving
Borachio *(q.v.)* in her chamber with apparent affection
(in fact it is not Hero but Margaret, who has been
duped). Before the wedding ceremony in the church
next day, Claudio denounces Hero violently, and
rejects her; she apparently dies as a result of his
onslaught. Claudio learns the truth about Don John's
trick, but not that Hero is still alive; he tells Leonato
that he will marry his niece. At the ceremony, the niece
turns out to be Hero.

Claudio is a young soldier, a gallant with a strong
sense of honour; but he is credulous and easily led.
His love for Hero is romantic, and based on little more
than her attractive appearance. He says very little to
her (they have been called the silent lovers), and since
he only knows her by appearance, he is thrown into
confusion by the shock of her apparent faithlessness.
Like Troilus *(q.v.)*, he cannot believe his eyes, and yet
must: 'Is this face Hero's? are our eyes our own?' is
his agonized question to Leonato.

Claudio is overshadowed by his antithesis Benedick.
It has been suggested that Claudio's whole character is
conditioned by the dramatic necessities of the Beatrice–
Benedick plot : he has to behave ignobly so that Beatrice
can reveal her fundamental good nature and Benedick
can show his love by being prepared to challenge his
friend. Claudio's readiness to take another wife so
quickly has been seen as a problem, but at this point
in the play the audience is already aware of the happy
outcome, so we should not look for psychological
consistency in what is only a convenient fiction.

CLAUDIUS *(Caes.)* : one of Brutus' servants. He is
ordered to sleep in Brutus' tent the night before
Philippi (IV.iii).

CLAUDIUS, KING OF DENMARK *(Ham.)* : uncle
and now stepfather to Hamlet. The Ghost tells Hamlet
that Claudius has murdered his father, seduced his
mother, and usurped the throne. Claudius is worried
by Hamlet's 'transformation' since his father's death,

and instructs Rosencrantz and Guildenstern to find out the cause. He attends the play arranged by Hamlet, and is terror-stricken at the representation of his own crime. He realizes that Hamlet knows his secret, and sends him to England, ostensibly for his own safety, but really to be murdered. Filled with remorse, he tries to pray, but cannot. When Hamlet returns safely from England, Claudius contrives a way to use the enraged Laertes to dispose of him. They arrange a duel with a poisoned rapier, and Claudius adds a poisoned cup to make sure. During the duel, he offers Hamlet the cup, but he refuses it, and the Queen takes it and drinks. Claudius' treachery is revealed, and Hamlet stabs him.

From his first confident and orderly speech, Claudius seems a moderate, efficient ruler. But there is something a little too smooth, almost glib, in his words – 'wisest sorrow', 'defeated joy' 'with mirth in funeral, and with dirge in marriage' – that makes us uneasy. The doubt about the veracity of the ghost's story remains for some time: Claudius does not reveal his guilt until the third act, when he does so in a brief aside:

> Polonius: 'Tis too much prov'd, that with Devotion's
> visage,
> And pious action, we do sugar o'er
> The devil himself.
> Claudius: O 'tis too true!
> How smart a lash that speech doth give
> my conscience!
> The harlot's cheek beautied with
> plastering art
> Is not more ugly to the thing that helps it,
> Than is my deed, to my most painted word.
> O heavy burthen! (III.i)

We see more of the complexity beneath the smooth surface when Claudius, tortured by guilt, struggles to pray:

> Pray can I not,
> Though inclination be as sharp as will:
> My stronger guilt defeats my strong intent,
> And like a man to double business bound,
> I stand in pause where I shall first begin,

Hamlet (III.iii): Claudius and Hamlet. A woodcut by Gordon Craig.

And both neglect. What if this cursed hand
Were thicker than itself with brother's blood,
Is there not rain enough in the sweet heavens
To wash it white as snow? Whereto serves mercy
But to confront the visage of offence?
And what's in prayer but this twofold force,
To be forestalled ere we come to fall,
Or pardoned being down? Then I'll look up;
My fault is past. But oh, what form of prayer
Can serve my turn? 'Forgive me my foul murder'?
That cannot be since I am still possessed
Of those effects for which I did the murder,
My crown, mine own ambition, and my queen. (III.iii)

This whole complex, tortuous speech is remarkable for a villain: it is the kind of agonized struggle with conscience that is more usually associated with tragic heroes (e.g. Macbeth). Claudius is Shakespeare's most complex, and subtly rendered, villain.

The corresponding character in the *Historica Danica* of Saxo Grammaticus is Fengo. The Roman Emperor Claudius incestuously married Agrippina, and she murdered him so that Nero could become emperor. This story may lie behind the change of name (though it was not necessarily first changed by Shakespeare: *see* HAMLET).

CLEOMENES *(Wint.)*: a Sicilian lord. Leontes sends him with Dion to the Apollo at Delphos to find out from it if Hermione is chaste. They return with the answer that she is.

CLEON *(Per.)*: Governor of Tarsus, where famine is relieved by the arrival of Pericles' ships (I.iv). Marina is entrusted to the care of Cleon and his wife Dionyza; he fulfils his vow to 'give her princely training', but discovers that his wife has plotted her murder. He is filled with remorse, thinking Marina dead, but his wife calls him a coward, and he gives in to her and takes part in the display of mourning that is put on for the benefit of Pericles. His death is described in the final chorus:

> For wicked Cleon and his wife, when Fame
> Had spread his cursed deed, the honour'd name
> Of Pericles, to rage the City turn,
> That him and his they in his Palace burn:
> The gods for murder seemed so content,
> To punish, although not done, but meant.

CLEOPATRA *(Ant.)*: Queen of Egypt and mistress of the triumvir Antony, she ensnares her lover in a 'strong toil of grace' and, by gradually sapping his resolution, at length brings about his total ruin. When, during the Battle of Actium, her ships desert the Roman fleet, he is worsted and obliged to fall back on Egypt. There he commits suicide and dies in his mistress'

above Cleopatra, Queen of Egypt (69–30 BC), in a bas-relief at Dendera *(left)*; Cleopatra and Julius Caesar, from the painting by Jean Léon Gérôme (1824–1904) *(top right)*; Lillie Langtry as Cleopatra *(bottom right)*.

Janet Suzman as Cleopatra in the Royal Shakespeare
Company's 1972 production of *Antony and Cleopatra*.

arms. Cleopatra, reluctant to be exhibited as the
prisoner of his arch-enemy, Octavian, allows herself to
be poisoned by a deadly snake. *See* ANTONY.

CLERK OF CHATHAM *(2 H.VI), see* EMANUEL.

CLERK, LAWYER'S *(Mer.V.)*: part assumed by
Nerissa *(q.v.)*.

CLIFFORD, JOHN (YOUNG CLIFFORD) (later
Lord) *(2 H.VI)*: at St Albans, he enters to find his

father slain, and vows revenge on the house of York
(v.ii).

In *3 Henry VI* he takes his revenge by ruthlessly
killing the young Duke of Rutland; he is the first to
stab the captive York. He dies of wounds he receives at
Ferrybridge (II.vi). His head is sent to be placed over the
gates at York.

He is called 'butcher', 'cruel child killer', and 'treacherous coward'; and in *Richard III* we hear of

. . . the piteous moan that Rutland made
When black-faced Clifford shook his sword at him.
(I.ii)

According to Holinshed, he was 'a deadly bloud-supper'. He was the ninth son of Thomas Clifford (see below).

CLIFFORD, THOMAS, LORD (OLD CLIFFORD) *(2H.VI)*: a supporter of the King, who successfully appeals to the rebels to forsake Jack Cade. He denounces York as a traitor, and refuses to pay homage to him. He is killed at St Albans in a fight with York (v.ii).

He was the eighth Baron Clifford (1414–55), a powerful supporter of Henry VI during the Wars of the Roses.

CLITUS *(Caes.)*: one of Brutus' servants. After the defeat at Philippi he refuses to kill his master, and runs away to escape capture by Octavius and Antony (v.v).

CLOTEN *(Cym.)*: Cymbeline's stepson, a lecherous, bullying coward, who is 'too bad for report' (I.i). He loves his stepsister Imogen: his advances are 'as fearful as a siege', and consist mainly of insults to her banished husband Posthumus. She tells him she loves Posthumus' 'meanest garment' more than him. He remains unsuccessful when, on the Queen's advice, he tries wooing her with music. He shows a kind of brute courage when he refuses to pay tribute to the Romans, and tells Lucius that war must decide all (III.i). He finds that Imogen has gone to Milford Haven to meet her husband, and resolves to follow and kill Posthumus before her eyes, and then rape her while wearing Posthumus' clothes (which he has stolen from Pisanio [*q.v.*]). He is recognized by Belarius, and is killed and beheaded by Guiderius. Imogen mistakes his headless body for that of Posthumus.

CLOWN, A *(Ant.)*: he is a rustic who brings in a basket of figs which conceal the asp with which Cleopatra kills herself. He lingers with her, joking bawdily; she finds it hard to get rid of him. His innocent presence raises the dramatic tension to an almost unbearable level.

CLOWN, A *(Oth.)*: he enters and jokes bawdily with Cassio and the musicians. Cassio sends him to tell Desdemona that he wants to see her (III.i). He riddles with Desdemona, and she sends him to fetch Cassio (III.iv).

CLOWN, A *(Tit.)*: he enters with a basket of pigeons. As he is on his way to the emperor with a petition, Titus gives him a letter to take, one that is wrapped round a dagger (IX.iii). He reads the letter to Saturninus and Tamora, and they order him to be hanged (IX.iv).

CLOWN, A *(Wint.)*: he is the old shepherd's son. He

buries the remains of Antigonus. He has his pockets picked by Autolycus, who overhears him explaining to his father that he should tell Leontes how Perdita was found in Bohemia. At the end he is made a gentleman, and feels he knows exactly how to behave:

> ... I'll swear to the Prince, thou art a tall fellow of thy hands, and that thou wilt not be drunk: but I know thou art no tall fellow of thy hands, and that thou wilt be drunk: but I'll swear it, and I would thou wouldst be a tall fellow of thy hands. (v.ii)

Lying and oaths are for him the attributes of a gentleman. He is a cheerful gull, whose chief function is as a foil to Autolycus.

COBWEB *(MND.)*: one of Titania's fairy servants. She is chosen to wait upon Bottom (III.i; IV.i).

COLEVILE, SIR JOHN *(2 H.IV)*: he surrenders to Falstaff in Gaultree Forest, and is sent to York for execution (IV.iii).

It is probable that his life was in fact spared, and that he was the same Sir John Colvyl, knight, who was with Henry V in France in 1415.

COMINIUS *(Cor.)*: consul and commander-in-chief of the Roman army against the Volscians. He eulogizes Caius Marcius before the Senate, and bestows on him the name of 'Coriolanus' (II.ii). He tries to prevent Coriolanus' banishment, and warns the Romans of the danger when he hears that Coriolanus is preparing to attack Rome. He tries to prevent the attack; but he is pleased to be able to tell the tribunes that Coriolanus is coming 'to shake your Rome about your ears' (IV.vi).

According to Plutarch he was the Roman consul who led the siege at Corioli; the victory was largely due to the valour of Caius Marcius, who Cominius rewarded with a tenth part of the spoils, a 'goodly horse', and the name Coriolanus.

CONRADE *(Ado)*: a follower of Don John, who promises to aid him 'to the death' when the time comes to cross Claudio. He is not present at the plot, but Borachio tells him of it, and they are both arrested as he is doing so. During the interrogation he calls Dogberry an ass.

CONSTABLE OF FRANCE, THE *(H.V)*: one of the leaders of the French army at Agincourt, where he is killed. He warns the French King of Henry's new reputation, but jokes and boasts confidently before Agincourt, where he anticipates an easy victory over 'yon poor and starved band'.

He was Charles de la Bret, the illegitimate son of Charles le Mauvais, King of Navarre.

King John: an eighteenth-century engraving showing Mrs Barry as Constance.

CONSTANCE, LADY *(John)*: the mother of Arthur, who asserts his legitimacy and claim to the throne. When Austria and France stop supporting the claim, she becomes distracted; when John defeats her allies and captures Arthur, she goes mad. We hear of her death 'in a frenzy'.

She was Constance, Duchess of Brittany (d. 1201). Arthur was her son by her first husband, Geoffrey Plantagenet. She was not a widow as she describes herself in the play; at the time she was married to her third husband, Guy, Viscount of Tours. She died in Nantes in 1201, long before the death of Elinor; in Shakespeare's play the two events occur close together.

CORDELIA *(Lr.)*: the youngest, and best loved, daughter of King Lear. He decides to divide his kingdom between his three daughters, who are expected to make a public declaration of their love as they receive their portion. Cordelia is unable to flatter like her hypocritical sisters, and when asked what she can say to bring her 'A third more opulent than your sisters', she replies simply 'Nothing, my lord' (I.i). Lear is furious;

he dispossesses her, and banishes her. Of her two suitors, Burgundy and France, only France is willing to accept her without a dowry. She leaves with him for France, and only returns much later in the play, when she comes at the head of a French army intent upon avenging the wrongs that have been done to her father (IV.iv). She is reunited with her deranged father, who is regenerated by her presence. Her forces are defeated, and she and Lear are captured and imprisoned. Cordelia is hung on Edmund's orders, and Lear enters with her dead in his arms. He dies thinking that she still lives.

Cordelia's part in the play is relatively small, yet it is of enormous significance. She is the embodiment of natural virtue, love and loyalty in a world where evil is rampant. If we follow Coleridge, as many critics have done, and see 'some little admixture of pride and sullenness' in her 'Nothing', we undercut the central conception of the play. Her behaviour in the opening scene is a norm by which the attitudes and motives of the other characters can be judged. It is her hatred of hypocrisy that lies behind her plain statement:

> . . . I love your Majesty
> According to my bond; no more nor less. (I.i)

Her filial duty and affection are natural, and need no rhetorical embellishment; her love is beyond the scope of materialistic analogies. There is much about her that is symbolic – she is saintlike, she

> . . . redeems Nature from the general curse
> Which twain have brought her to (IV.vi)

– that is, she redeems original sin. In a beautiful emblematic description she is presented as a perfectly integrated person, a personification of harmony in Nature:

> . . . You have seen
> Sunshine and rain at once; her smile and tears
> Were like a better way; those happy smilets
> That play'd on her ripe lip seem'd not to know
> What guests were in her eyes; which parted thence,
> As pearls from diamonds dropp'd. (IV.iii).

And yet she dies, as Johnson put it, 'contrary to the natural ideas of justice'.

In Nahum Tate's eighteenth-century revision of *King Lear* (which held the stage for 150 years), Cordelia is given a lover, Edgar, and they both live happily ever after. Even Johnson found this alteration satisfactory:

> Cordelia, from the time of Tate, has always retired with victory and felicity. And, if my sensations could add any thing to the general suffrage, I might relate, that I was many years ago so shocked by

right 'Cordelia's Portion'; a painting by Ford Madox Brown *(above)*; Lear and Cordelia in prison, from a watercolour by William Blake *(below)*.

Cordelia's death, that I know not whether I ever endured to read again the last scenes of the play till I undertook to revise them as an editor.
Her death is shocking, but it is the final proof of her love and constancy, as she sees:

... We are not the first
Who, with best meaning, have incurr'd the worst.
For thee, oppressed King, I am cast down;
Myself could else out-frown false Fortune's frown.
(V.iii)

In *The True Chronicle History of King Leir* Cordella does not die. In Holinshed's account Cordeilla stabs herself, and in Spenser's *Fairie Queene* Cordelia hangs herself; in both these cases the suicide takes place some years after the death of Lear.

CORIN *(AYL.)*: an old shepherd, who buys a cottage and pasture on behalf of Rosalind and Celia. He has a lively discussion on the relative merits of life in the country and life in the court with Touchstone (III.ii).

CORIOLANUS, CAIUS MARCIUS *(Cor.)*: the historical character described in Sir Thomas North's translation of Plutarch's *Lives of the Noble Grecians and Romans* (1579), from which Shakespeare derived the raw materials of his drama, is thought to have flourished about the beginning of the fifth century BC. A renowned general, entitled 'Coriolanus' after his triumphant campaign against the Volscian city of Corioli, he is offered the honour of a consulship by his grateful fellow Romans, but treats the populace with such proud contempt that he is banished and then joins the Volscians, whose army he leads in an attack they plan on Rome. His mother, Volumnia, his patient, submissive wife, Virgilia, their mettlesome little boy, and his Falstaffian old friend, the senator Menenius – 'one that loves a cup of hot wine with not a drop of allaying Tiber in't ... one that converses more with the buttock of the night than with the forehead of the morning' – go out to meet him while he advances, and plead that he will turn back. He repulses Menenius, and breaks the old man's heart, just as Prince Hal, once he had ascended the throne, was to break Falstaff's. But Volumnia, an imperious matriarch, eventually undermines his resolution. He returns to Corioli, having secured an honourable peace. Coriolanus, however, is always his own worst enemy; his reputation soon exasperates the Volscian leader, Aufidius; and he is murdered by his hosts.

Written between 1607 and 1608 – no record can be found of its first performance – *Coriolanus* is a monolithic play. It introduces few personages; the outlines of the plot are singularly uncomplicated; it moves at a rapid pace towards its climax. The hero is a victim of his overweening personal pride; he has a sense of

Ian Hogg as Coriolanus in the Royal Shakespeare Company's 1972 production of *Coriolanus*.

superiority that he cannot control or curb; he remains a 'lonely dragon'. Volumnia herself, who shares her son's pride, has grasped the imperfections of his character:

You might have been enough the man you are,
With striving less to be so ...

while his enemy Aufidius pays him a reluctant tribute that explains the causes of his downfall:

... I think he'll be to Rome
As is the osprey to the fish, who takes it
By sovreignty of nature. First he was
A noble servant to them, but he could not
Carry his honours even. Whether 'twas pride,
Which out of daily fortune ever taints
The happy man; whether defect of judgement,
To fail in the disposing of those chances
Which he was lord of ... (IV.vi)

Coriolanus is moved by his mother's pleas and agrees
to spare Rome. From a painting by Benjamin West.

Though the construction of the play is stark and plain,
it includes some vivid naturalistic touches. The fierce
soldier can, now and then, be merciful; but, having
begged Cominius to spare a poor man's life, he finds
that the prisoner's name has escaped his memory:

> ... By Jupiter, forgot!
> I am weary; yea, my memory is tired.
> Have we no wine here?
> Cominius: Go we to our tent:
>> The blood upon your visage dries; 'tis
>> time
>> It should be looked to ... (I.ix)

Despite his solitariness, the hero loves his wife; while
his mother is loudly congratulating him on a victory he
has just won, he turns towards the mute Virgilia:

> ... My gracious silence, hail!

Wouldst thou have laughed had I come coffined
home,
That weeps't to see me triumph? (II.i)

All the pathos of Virgilia's affection for her husband is
expressed in those brief and simple phrases.

CORNELIUS *(Cym.)*: the physician from whom the
Queen orders poisonous drugs. He suspects her intentions, and supplies instead a potent but harmless
soporific (I.vi). He reports her death at the end (V.v).

CORNELIUS *(Ham.)*: a courtier at Elsinore who
Claudius sends, with Voltemand, as ambassador to the
King of Norway (I.ii).

CORNWALL, DUCHESS OF *(Lr.)*, *see* REGAN.

CORNWALL, DUKE OF *(Lr.)*: husband to Regan. He has Lear's messenger Kent put in the stocks, and agrees when his wife suggests that they close the castle gates and leave Lear out on the heath in the storm. Finding that Gloucester has been helping Lear, he blinds him; he is himself attacked by one of the servants, and dies of his wounds.

His sadistic cruelty ideally complements that of his wife; it is he who initiates the blinding of Gloucester. His death is a dramatic necessity; it brings into the open the sexual rivalry between Regan and Goneril that leads to their, and Edmund's, destruction. His ducal title probably derives from Holinshed, where Cornwall is the husband of Goneril.

COSTARD *(LLL.)*: 'a clown', the rival of Don Armado for Jaquenetta. He is jailed when it is discovered that he has been consorting with her contrary to the King's proclamation. He acts as a messenger, and muddles the letter from Berowne to Rosaline with that from Don Armado to Jaquenetta. He plays Pompey in the 'Pageant of the Nine Worthies'.

A 'costard' is a large apple – hence, jocularly, the head. Moth plays on this (III.i). Granville-Barker saw in Costard a stage fool who plays a role throughout the play, and only slips out of it when he commends Nathaniel in response to the jeers of the lords and ladies (v.ii).

COURT, ALEXANDER *(H.V)*: an English soldier who with Williams and Bates meets the disguised King Henry on the night before Agincourt (IV.i).

COURTEZAN, A *(Err.)*: she meets Antipholus of Syracuse (who she mistakes for Antipholus of Ephesus) and demands the chain he wears, or the ring he had had from her at dinner. She resolves to tell Adriana about her husband's behaviour (IV.iii). At the end she discovers that she has accused the wrong Antipholus, and receives her ring back from Antipholus of Ephesus.

She is described by Antipholus of Ephesus as 'of excellent discourse; pretty and witty; wild, and, yet too, gentle' (II.i). The corresponding character in Plautus' *Menaechmi* is Erotium.

CRAB, A DOG *(Gent.)*: Launce's dog, 'the sourest-natured dog that lives' (II.iii). This unfortunate animal is the recipient of numerous other insults from its master.

CRANMER, THOMAS, ARCHBISHOP OF CANTERBURY *(H.VIII)*: at the outset he is away from England on an embassy; the King anxiously awaits the return of his 'learn'd and well-beloved servant Cranmer' (II.iv). On his return he is installed as Archbishop of Canterbury (III.ii). He crowns Anne Bullen (IV.i). He confides his fears to Henry who reassures him and gives him a ring as a token of good faith. He is refused admission to the council chamber (V.ii), before being brought before the council and charged with heresy (V.iii). He is ordered to the Tower, but is released when he produces the King's ring. The King rebukes the council, and tells the members to embrace Cranmer. Cranmer is godfather to the infant Elizabeth, and speaks a prophetic oration at the christening (V.v).

To Norfolk Cranmer is 'a worthy fellow'; to Wolsey he is an arch heretic who 'hath crawled into the favour of the King'.

Thomas Cranmer (1489–1556) was appointed chaplain to Henry VIII because of the support he gave him over the divorce of Katharine. He suggested that the question 'Do the laws of God allow a man to marry his brother's widow?' be put to the universities, both English and foreign. He was on this mission at the beginning of Shakespeare's play. The answer he brought back was negative, and having been appointed Archbishop of Canterbury during his absence, it was he who pronounced the marriage of Katharine and Henry null and void in 1533. He later pronounced Henry's marriage to Anne Boleyn lawful. In 1534 he authorized the production of the *Great Bible*, and after Henry's death he was largely instrumental in drawing up the first and second *Books of Common Prayer*. He reluctantly joined those opposed to the succession of Mary, and when she came to the throne he was deprived of his position and put in the Tower. He was condemned for heresy, publicly degraded, and burnt at the stake in 1556.

CRESSIDA *(Troil.)*: the daughter of Chalchas, who, during the siege of Troy, has defected to the Greek camp. Cressida is beloved by Troilus, one of King Priam's younger sons. Her uncle, Pandarus, with whom she lodges, a super-subtle and naturally mischievous character, decides that he will become their go-between; but, meanwhile, Chalchas has persuaded the Grecian generalissimo, Agamemnon, to authorize an exchange of certain prisoners; and Diomedes arrives as the emissary who escorts Cressida back through the Greek lines. A truce follows, which enables Troilus to revisit Cressida. But now he finds her embracing Diomedes; and next day, when the truce is broken, though Achilles kills the noble Hector, Diomedes eludes Troilus' vengeance. Throughout the drama, Thersites, cynic *par excellence*, provides a spiteful commentary upon the action.

Though the play appears to have been written before 1603, the preface to a quarto edition of *Troilus and Cressida*, published in 1609, describes it as a completely new work, 'never staled with the stage, never clapper-clawed with the palms of the vulgar'. Derived from a number of different sources, including Chaucer's splendid narrative poem, *Troilus and Criseyde* (itself largely based on Boccaccio's *Filostrato*), *Troilus and Cressida* is one of Shakespeare's most curious and most disconcerting tragi-comedies. Not only does chivalric heroism go by the board: Achilles is a stupid, self-satisfied braggart, the conceited 'idol of idiot idol-worshippers', lounging in his tent beside Patroclus, his homosexual crony; but Troilus, the great romantic lover, is also thoroughly dismembered and debased. Cressida, the romantic heroine, fares even worse. She is, after all, Ulysses points out, a mere 'daughter of the game', an amatory opportunist who casually exploits her attractions; for whom her own beauty (writes a modern critic) 'is at once a weapon and a plaything, which she handles with half-amused indifference'. She has no real heart, no genuine strength of feeling. What Shakespeare exhibits is not Cressida's beauty and charm, but the wildly excessive passion that she awakes in Troilus.

Cressida herself has comparatively little to say. She is obliged to admit that she cannot resist her feelings, and that her emotions are inevitably disturbed by the presence of a handsome man:

Ah, poor our sex! this fault in us I find

The error of our eye directs our mind . . . (v.ii)

She is a passive character, always the emotional patient rather than the agent; and Troilus' miseries are derived from his unwise belief that he and the young woman he loves are capable of experiencing the same emotion at the same moment, and in the same degree. Even before she has proved herself a 'daughter of the game', Troilus has summed up their common plight: 'This is the monstruosity in love, lady, that the will is infinite and the execution confined, that the desire is boundless and the act a slave to limit'. (*See* TROILUS).

CRICKET, A FAIRY *(Wiv.)*: the name assumed by one of the boys disguised as a fairy. 'Puck' tells him to fly to Windsor and wherever he finds unswept chimneys to pinch the women for their sluttishness (v.v).

CRIER, A *(H.VIII)*: he summons Henry and Katharine before the court at Blackfriars (II.iv).

CROMER, SIR JAMES *(2 H.VI)*: son-in-law to Lord Say. Only his head appears, carried on a pole through the streets of London by Jack Cade's rebels, who have removed it (IV.vii).

Shakespeare follows Hall in calling Sir John Cromer the son-in-law of his fellow victim Lord Say. There are many discrepancies in the various accounts of who Sir John really was: possibly he can be identified with Sir

Troilus and Cressida. An engraving by P. Lightfoot from the painting by John Opie.

William Cromer, Sheriff of Kent in the years of Cade's rebellion.

CROMWELL, THOMAS *(H.VIII)*: a servant of Wolsey 'in much esteem with the King' (IV.i). He acts as secretary to the council and defends Cranmer against the Bishop of Winchester's attack.

Thomas Cromwell (*c.* 1485–1540) rose from being a small merchant to become Earl of Essex. He lost favour with Henry VIII when he arranged his marriage to the ugly Anne of Cleves. He helped to dissolve the smaller

Cymbeline (Robert Harris) with his page (Michael Saunders) in Peter Hall's 1957 production of *Cymbeline* at Stratford-upon-Avon.

monasteries. He was executed for treason in 1450.

CUPID *(Tim.)*: the god of love. A boy in this guise introduces the masque of the Amazons at Timon's first banquet in the play (I.ii).

CURAN *(Lr.)*: a courtier who is sent by Regan and Cornwall to advise Gloucester of their imminent arrival at his castle. He meets Edmund in the castle and tells him of his mission, and hints at the possibility of war between Cornwall and Albany (II.i).

CURIO *(Tw. N.)*: attendant to Duke Orsino.

CURTIS *(Shr.)*: an old servant who is caretaker at Petruchio's house in the country. Grumio arrives to warn Curtis that his master and Kate will arrive shortly, and describes to him their journey. When Petruchio arrives he finds fault with everything, even though Curtis and the other servants are skilful and attentive (IV.i).

CYMBELINE, KING OF BRITAIN *(Cym.)*: he is reported to be violently angry because his daughter Imogen has married a poor gentleman (Posthumus) instead of his stepson Cloten for whom she was intended (I.i). He banishes Posthumus, reviles Imogen, and chides the Queen for allowing them to meet (I.ii). He receives the Roman emissary courteously, but is persuaded by the Queen to refuse tribute to Rome, and to go to war. During the preparations for war he discovers that Imogen is missing, and flies into a rage (III.v). His distraction approaches madness as he hears of his wife's 'madness', of Cloten's absence, and that the Roman legions have landed (IV.iii). He is taken prisoner, and rescued by Belarius and his 'sons'; and after the victory over the Romans he honours them. He is told of the Queen's death-bed confession. The identity of 'Fidele' is revealed, and Iachimo is forced to confess. When Cymbeline discovers that Guiderius has killed Cloten, he orders his execution. Belarius explains all: Cymbeline reclaims his sons, and pardons all the prisoners he had condemned, and agrees to pay tribute to Rome (V.v).

Although he gives his name to the play, Cymbeline is not the centre of dramatic interest. He is a passive figure for most of the play, though much of the action stems from him. He is like Lear when he is enraged by Imogen's resolute honesty; and like Leontes (*q.v.*) he lacks self-knowledge, and the ability to achieve it. At the end, he remains obdurately cruel and impulsive: the restoration of his daughter does not move him to show sympathy for Guiderius, who has saved his life. It is only when Guiderius is revealed as his son, and his virtue thrust under his nose by Belarius, that he forgives him. He is not a very engaging character: he is perhaps best seen as a symbolic, fairy-tale king rather than a realistic character.

The historical Cymbeline is usually assumed to be Cunobelinus, about whom very little is known. He appears to have been the son of Cassivelaunus, who died in AD 43. The Roman expedition against Britain was not until after his death, and was resisted by his sons Caractacus and Togodumnus.

Cymbeline was probably written in 1608–09, though we only know for certain that it was written between 1606 and 1611. Shakespeare's sources were probably varied: Holinshed's confused account, a pamphlet *Frederyke of Jennen* (for the wager plot, derived from Boccaccio), and a romantic drama *The Rare Triumphs of Love and Fortune*. The conception of the play owes little to any known source, and seems to have been Shakespeare's own. The flaws in the play have led critics to suspect collaboration, but they are perhaps better explained as a result of the experimental nature of the romance form which Shakespeare was using.

D

DANCER, A *(2 H.IV)*: he speaks the Epilogue, which contains an apology and the promise of another play to continue the story. After his speech he dances; Elizabethan plays frequently ended with a jig.

DARDANIUS *(Caes.)*: one of Brutus' servants. After the defeat at Philippi he refuses to kill his master, and runs away to avoid capture by Octavius and Antony (v.v).

DAUPHIN *(1 H.VI; John; H.V)*, *see* CHARLES; LEWIS.

DAVY *(2 H.IV)*: servant to Justice Shallow. Falstaff observes (v.iii) that he serves him very well.

DE BURGH, HUBERT *(John)*, *see* HUBERT.

DECIUS BRUTUS *(Caes.)*, *see* BRUTUS.

DEIPHOBUS *(Troil.)*: a Trojan lord, one of the sons of Priam, and brother to Troilus. He only speaks once, when he announces the arrival of Aeneas (IV.i).

In the Homeric tradition, Deiphobus married Helen after the death of Paris, and was killed and mutilated by Menelaus.

DEMETRIUS *(Ant.)*: a Roman soldier and friend to Antony. He is astonished when he hears Antony refuse to grant an audience to Caesar's ambassadors, and sadly comments that in doing so 'he approves the common liar who thus speaks of him at Rome' (i.i).

DEMETRIUS *(MND.)*: an Athenian youth who is loved by Helena but who loves Hermia. Hermia's father favours him above Lysander, who she loves. Demetrius argues with Lysander over Hermia, who accuses him of having won her soul (i.i). He hears that Hermia and Lysander have fled into the woods, and follows them; he is followed by Helena, who he rejects harshly, saying he will leave her 'to the mercy of the wild beasts' (II.ii). When he meets Hermia she accuses him of having killed Lysander in his sleep; he denies it, and lies down to sleep. Oberon touches his eyes with magic love-juice: he awakes, sees Helena, and is enraptured. He looks for a place to fight the jealous Lysander, but is led astray by Puck (III.ii). He sleeps again and awakes still under the charm, and vows to be true to Helena. He joins the nobles in ridiculing the Interlude at the end.

DEMETRIUS *(Tit.)*: the eldest son of Tamora, Queen of the Goths. He and his brother Chiron *(q.v.)* are rivals for Lavinia, who has married Bassianus. Aaron prompts them to kill Bassianus, and to rape and mutilate her, while he ensures that the blame falls on two of Titus' sons (II.i). They are exposed when Lavinia manages to scrawl Demetrius' name in the sand. He and Chiron are killed by Titus, and their flesh is served up in a pie for their mother and Saturninus.

DENMARK, KING OF *(Ham.)*, *see* CLAUDIUS; HAMLET.

DENMARK, PRINCE OF *(Ham.)*, *see* HAMLET.

DENMARK, QUEEN OF *(Ham.)*, *see* GERTRUDE.

DENNIS *(AYL.)*: a servant to Oliver. Oliver summons him and asks if Charles the wrestler is waiting to see him, and asks him to show him in (i.i).

DENNY, SIR ANTHONY *(H.VIII)*: he is commanded to bring Cranmer before the King, and does so (v.i).

Sir Anthony Denny (1500–49) was a favourite and constant companion of Henry VIII.

DERBY, EARL OF, THOMAS, LORD STANLEY *(R.III)*: he professes friendship for Richard, but the king does not trust him, and holds his son hostage to ensure that his forces fight on his side against Richmond. Stanley visits Richmond on the night before Bosworth and wishes him success, and explains why he cannot help him. During the battle he refuses to help Richard, and after it he 'crowns' Richmond king.

The title is inaccurate, since Stanley was not created Earl of Derby until the accession of Henry VII.

DERCETAS *(Ant.)*: a friend to Antony. He discovers Antony dying, and taking his bloody sword, hurries to Caesar to tell him and to offer his services to him (IV.xiv; V.i).

Shakespeare follows Plutarch, where the name is Dercetaeus.

DESDEMONA *(Oth.)*: the wife of Othello, who she has married secretly without her father's consent. She is summoned to the council chamber to explain, and to prove that Othello has not seduced her with magic. She proclaims her love for him, and her father accepts the marriage reluctantly. She is escorted to Cyprus by Iago. When Cassio has been disgraced as a result of Iago's stratagem, he asks Desdemona to intercede for him with Othello; Iago uses this to suggest to Othello that Cassio and Desdemona are lovers. Othello, spurred on by Iago, becomes increasingly jealous and brutal, until he finally smothers her in their bed. She remains faithful to her dying breath; her last words are 'Commend me to my Lord'.

We first hear of Desdemona when her father enters raging at her 'treason of the blood'. To him her marriage to the Moor is quite out of character:

> ...A maiden never bold;
> Of spirit so still and quiet that her motion
> Blush'd at herself; and she, in spite of nature,
> Of years, of country, credit, every thing,
> To fall in love with what she fear'd to look on!
> It is judgment maim'd and most imperfect,
> That will confess perfection so could err
> Against all rules of nature; and must be driven
> To find out practices of cunning hell,
> Why this should be. (I.iii).

Othello denies that he has bewitched Desdemona, and explains at some length how he won Desdemona with stories of his military exploits; he concludes that 'She loved me for the dangers I had pass'd'. Desdemona herself is much more forthright:

> That I did love the Moor to live with him,
> My downright violence and storm of fortunes
> May trumpet to the world. (I.iii)

This boldness must have seemed surprising, if not shocking, to an Elizabethan audience: especially as she had already violated the normal precept by which a young woman of good family was betrothed by her father. In taking her marriage into her own hands she disregards the conventions of filial obligation, and in doing so she brings on the death of her father (*see* BRABANTIO).

Desdemona is not a meek and passive beauty, which is how she is too frequently presented on stage. She is a sophisticated, witty woman of the world; we see this in her flippant banter with Iago and Cassio on the quayside (II.i). She is a Venetian lady, and Iago carefully reminds the socially naive Othello of his ignorance of Venetian women (who had a very poor reputation in early seventeenth-century Europe). She loves Othello for his military glamour, but she does not fully understand his nature: she thinks of Cassio's suit as another social game, and is very slow to catch the jealous Othello's tone (III.iv). Her chastity is undeniable, but her background and her independent wilfulness make her act in a manner that Iago is able to exploit. She is essentially blameless, but her small faults and indiscretions do contribute to the tragedy. In the last acts these are set aside, and the focus is on her virtue and love, on her as 'the true and loyal wife'. Emilia speaks her epitaph:

> O she was heavenly true!

DIANA CAPILET *(All's W.)*: the daughter of a widow in Florence. She is warned against the advances of Bertram; she admires him, but wishes 'he were honester' (III.v). He finds her 'wondrous cold'. She knows of Helena's unhappiness and, after scolding him for neglecting his wife, and obtaining a ring from him as a loan, she consents to be visited by him that night (IV.ii). She has arranged a 'bed-trick' by which Helena takes her place unknown to Bertram. She says she is ready to endure much on Helena's behalf. She presents herself before the King, and declares that Bertram has seduced her. Bertram calls her 'a fond and desperate

Desdemona, by Dante Gabriel Rossetti.

creature'. She produces his ring, and mentions that the ring she gave him resembles that on the King's finger (it had come from Helena, who had it from the King). She is committed to prison for refusing to explain where she got the ring. She is saved by the appearance of Helena, and is awarded a dowry by the King.

DIANA, THE GODDESS *(Per.)*: the Roman goddess of chastity and celibacy, and of the chase. Marina appeals to her when she is sold into the brothel (IV.ii), and it is to her temple that Thaisa retires when she believes that Pericles is dead. After Pericles is reunited with Marina, Diana appears to him in a vision, and commands him to sail to her temple at Ephesus, where he discovers Thaisa (v.iii).

Shakespeare obviously intended the Roman goddess, for the Diana actually worshipped at Ephesus was not at all appropriate. She was notably unchaste, being one form of the oriental mother-goddess, normally represented as multi-breasted, and associated with fertility.

DICK, THE BUTCHER OF ASHFORD *(2 H.VI)*: a follower of Jack Cade. He is sceptical of Cade's claims to the throne (IV.ii), but is eager for violence; he wants to 'kill all the lawyers' and break open the gaols. He deals with his enemies as though he was still in his slaughterhouse (IV.iii).

DIGHTON *(R.III)*: with Forrest he murders the princes in the Tower. The murderers do not appear, but we hear from Tyrrel that he suborned them 'to do this piece of ruthfull butchery', and that they were almost dissuaded from the deed by the sight of the sleeping princes. Afterwards they are shattered with 'conscience and remorse' (IV.iii).

DIOMEDES *(Ant.)*: an attendant to Cleopatra, who is sent to tell Antony that she is not dead but hiding in the monument. He finds Antony dying and he and Antony's guard carry him to Cleopatra (IV.xiv; IV.xv).

DIOMEDES *(Troil.)*: a Greek general who is sent to bring back Cressida from Troy. He presents her to the Greeks, and she is given into his care. He finds that she is easily seduced; an assignation between them, during which she gives him Troilus' sleeve, is witnessed by Troilus. In the battle he fights with Troilus, and when he has 'chastis'd the amorous Trojan' he sends Cressida his horse. In his down-to-earth way, he is the most positive and effective of the Greeks.

In Homer's *Iliad* Diomedes is second only to Achilles among the Greek warriors. Shakespeare's Diomedes is a cynic whose complete lack of illusions allows him to see clearly: he is contemptuous of Helen (q.v.), and of both the Greeks and Trojans for fighting for a whore.

He has an appropriate answer to Troilus' jealous outburst as he hands over Cressida:

Let me be privileged by my place and message,
To be a speaker free. When I am hence,
I'll answer to my lust; and know you, lord,
I'll nothing do on charge; to her own worth
She shall be prized. (IV.iv).

And she is: within a short time he has contrived to get *her* wooing *him*. He sees her weaknesses at once, and exploits them. His easy seduction of Cressida provides an ironic answer to Troilus' question in the debate on Helen: 'What's aught but as 'tis valued?'

DION *(Wint.)*: a lord of Sicilia. Leontes sends him, with Cleomenes (q.v.), to consult the oracle at Delphi.

DIONYZA *(Per.)*: the wife of Cleon and mother of Philoten. She accepts the charge of the infant Marina, but grows increasingly jealous as she sees her beauty and talents eclipse those of her own daughter. She instructs Leonine to murder Marina, and poisons him when she thinks he has done so. She confronts Cleon with her crimes; he compares her to a harpy with 'an angel's face' and 'eagle's talons'. She and Cleon are burned to death in their palace by the enraged citizenry when their deeds are exposed.

DOCTOR BUTTS *(H.VIII)*, *see* BUTTS.

DOCTOR OF PHYSIC *(Lr.)*: he gives the deranged King Lear sleep inducing drugs (IV.iv), and watches over his reawakening; he advises that his mind should be kept at rest. He is simply a 'Gentleman' in the Folio.

DOCTOR OF PHYSIC, ENGLISH *(Mac.)*: 'A Scotch Doctor'. He sees the queen sleepwalking, and suspects her secret (v.i). He tells Macbeth that his wife's illness is mental, and that she must cure herself; he longs to get away from Dunsinane (v.iii).

DOCTOR OF PHYSIC, SCOTTISH *(Mac.)*: he announces that the English King is about to touch and cure those afflicted with 'the evil' (IV.iii). This was probably a compliment to James I, who prided himself on having similar healing powers. According to Holinshed, Edward used to help those troubled with 'the king's evil, and left that virtue as it were a portion of the inheritance unto his successors'.

DOGBERRY *(Ado)*: the head constable of Messina, in charge of the watch. He arrests Borachio and Conrade, and conducts a long and laborious examination of them; he accuses them of the wrong crimes, but succeeds in exposing the plot against Hero. He is outraged when Conrade says that he needs the Sexton to 'write him down an ass'; he asks Leonato to take this into consideration when punishing him.

Dogberry shows an extraordinary combination of slow-mindedness and prolixity that leads him into numerous silly circumlocutions and diversions. Nevertheless, this absurd constable obstinately persists until he has uncovered the truth; though a 'shallow fool', he succeeds where others fail. His speeches are spiced with memorable malapropisms:

> One word sir. Our watch sir, have indeed comprehended two aspicious persons, and we would have them examined this morning before your worship.
>
> (III.v)

DOLABELLA *(Ant.)*: a friend to Caesar who is sent by him to persuade Antony to surrender (v.i). He finds Antony dead. He tells Cleopatra of Caesar's plans to lead her in triumph through Rome, and in doing so precipitates her suicide.

DOLL TEARSHEET *(2 H.IV)*, *see* TEARSHEET.

DONALBAIN *(Mac.)*: the younger son of Duncan. He escapes to Ireland after Duncan's murder, while his brother Malcolm goes to England; they both agree that 'our separated fortune shall keep us both the safer' (II.iii). This is his only appearance.

DORCAS *(Wint.)*: a shepherdess, in love with the Clown. In the sheep-shearing scene she joins in the dancing, and sings a song with Mopsa and Autolycus (IV.iii).

DORICLES *(Wint.)*: name assumed by Florizel *(q.v.)* when he is pretending that he is of humble birth.

DORSET, MARCHIONESS OF *(H.VIII)*: mother to the Marquess of Dorset. She is one of the godmothers at the christening of Queen Elizabeth (v.v).

DORSET, MARQUESS OF *(H.VIII)*: he carries the sceptre at the coronation of Anne Bullen (IV.i).

He was Henry Grey, third Marquess of Dorset, the father of Lady Jane Grey.

DORSET, MARQUESS OF *(R.III)*: after Richard's execution of his brother Lord Grey he joins Richmond in Brittany. He is not present at Bosworth.

He was Thomas Grey (1451–1501), the elder son of Sir John Grey by Elizabeth Woodville (later queen of Edward IV). He was created 1st Marquess of Dorset in 1475. In 1483 he took up arms against Richard, and in 1484 he joined Buckingham's rebellion. When this failed he fled to Richmond in Brittany. He did not join the expedition to England because Richmond distrusted him, a result of his attempts, under his mother's influence, to be reconciled to Richard in 1485.

DOUGLAS, EARL OF, ARCHIBALD *(1 H.IV)*: an ally of Hotspur. He gives brave advice before the battle of Shrewsbury (IV.iii), and suggests an attack by night. In the battle he kills Blunt, believing him to be the King. He fights with the King and overpowers him, but is driven off by the intervention of Hal. He fights with Falstaff, who feigns death. After the battle he is set free, ransomless, because of his valour.

Falstaff talks of 'that sprightly Scot of Scots, Douglas, that runs a horseback up a hill perpendicular'; Henry praises Hotspur because he has three times defeated

> . . . renowned Douglas, whose high deeds,
> Whose hot incursions, and great name in arms,
> Holds from all soldiers chief majority,
> And military title capital,

below Dogberry (Dudley Jones) in the 1956 production of *Much Ado About Nothing* at the Old Vic Theatre *(top)*; an eighteenth-century engraving showing Mr Brunsdon as Dromio of Syracuse in *The Comedy of Errors (bottom)*.

Through all the kingdoms that acknowledge Christ.
(III.ii)

He was Archibald, 4th Earl of Douglas (1369–1424), known as Black Douglas. He was taken prisoner by Hotspur at Hamildon Hill in 1402, and joined his captor at Shrewsbury against Henry IV. He later fought in France, and was created Duke of Touraine by Charles VII shortly before his death at the Battle of Verneuil. Despite his bravery and prowess on the battlefield, he seems to have been an ineffective commander: he was on the losing side in all his engagements.

DROMIO OF EPHESUS *(Err.)* : the twin brother of Dromio of Syracuse, and servant to Antipholus of Ephesus. He meets Antipholus of Syracuse, and mistakes him for his master: when he tells him he is to go home for dinner, he is cuffed (I.ii). He tells Adriana that his master must be mad, since he demands money from him, and denies having either a wife or a house (II.i). He helps his master in his attempt to get into his own house (III.i). He is again beaten by his master, who has sent Dromio of Syracuse to fetch some money, when he appears without it. He is certified mad along with his master, and they are carried bound to a 'dark room' (IV.iv). When they are released, and the errors resolved, he is reunited with his brother.

DROMIO OF SYRACUSE *(Err.)* : the twin brother of Dromio of Ephesus, and servant to Antipholus of Syracuse. He is sent to the Centaur with his master's money (I.ii); he is amazed when he is beaten for faults he has not committed (II.ii). He keeps the gate at Adriana's house, and keeps Dromio and Antipholus of Ephesus out of their own home (III.i). He mistakes Antipholus of Ephesus for his master, and tells him that a ship is waiting; he is sent to fetch a purse from Adriana; he gives it to Antipholus of Syracuse, who thinks him mad. He is impressed when they are given a gold chain for nothing, and decides that they should stay in Ephesus after all (IV.iv). He seeks refuge in the priory with his master, and is relieved when the mysteries are unravelled and he meets his lost brother.

The Dromios are treated more lightheartedly than their masters, though Dromio of Syracuse echoes his master's loss of identity: 'I am an ass, I am a woman's man, and besides myself' (III.ii). There is only one slave, Messenio, in the *Menaechmi* of Plautus; by doubling the twins, Shakespeare doubles the comic confusions. The name Dromio may be a variant of Dromo, the type name for a slave in several of Terence's comedies; or it may be borrowed from Lyly's *Mother Bombie* (printed 1594).

DUKE (SENIOR), THE *(AYL.)* : Rosalind's father. He has been banished by his usurping younger brother,

and has gone to the Forest of Arden with a few 'loving lords' and 'a many merry men'; there they 'fleet the time carelessly, as they did in the golden world'. When at the end he hears that his title has been restored, he prefers to defer 'this new-fall'n dignity' in favour of 'rustic revelry' to celebrate the various weddings.

DULL, ANTHONY *(LLL.)* : a constable. He brings Costard before the King, and hands him over to Armado. He agrees to dance and play the tabor in the 'Pageant of the Nine Worthies'.

He is as his name suggests. Sir Nathaniel apologizes for his unlettered ignorance:

Sir, he hath never fed of the dainties that are bred in a book. He hath not eat paper, as it were; he hath not drunk ink. His intellect is not replenished; he is only an animal, only sensible in the duller parts. (IV.ii)

He is confused and led into misunderstanding by the wealth of words which pours from the book-men, but his rustic instinct is sound: he doggedly insists on calling a pricket a pricket, because he knows that is what it is. In this he echoes the ladies' insistence on an economical use of words.

DUMAIN, CAPTAIN *(All'sW.)*, *see* FRENCH LORDS, TWO.

DUMAINE *(LLL.)* : 'A lord attending upon the King in his retirement'. He accepts the vow of asceticism enthusiastically (I.i). He falls in love with Katharine, and is rebuked for it by Longaville before it is revealed that all the lords have broken their oath. As a 'Muscovite' he addresses Maria by mistake. He promises to serve Katharine 'true and faithfully' in the year he has to wait before their marriage.

DUNCAN, KING OF SCOTLAND *(Mac.)* : he confers the thaneship of Cawdor on Macbeth for his part in the defeat of Macdonwald and the Norwegians. He accepts an invitation to Macbeth's castle, where he is murdered in his sleep.

Shakespeare drew on Holinshed's account of how Macbeth, urged on by his wife and aided by Banquo, killed Duncan. The details of the murder are taken from another episode in Holinshed, that of an earlier king, King Duff, who was murdered by four servants of Donwald in AD 972.

Duncan 'the meek' came to the throne of Scotland in 1033; his reign was notably peaceful. He was killed not in his castle, but on the battlefield, by his cousin Thorfinn (or possibly by Macbeth).

DUTCH GENTLEMAN, A *(Cym.)* : a silent observer in the scene in which Iachimo and Posthumus make their wager. (I.v).

E

EDGAR *(Lr.)* : the legitimate son of the Earl of Gloucester, and brother to the illegitimate Edmund. Edmund tells his father that Edgar has designs on his life, and then tells Edmund to flee from his father's anger. When he realizes that he has been duped, Edgar adopts the disguise of a 'Bedlam beggar', and takes the name 'Tom O'Bedlam'. As 'Poor Tom' he is joined in a hovel on the heath by Lear and the Fool; while they are sheltering from the storm, Lear finds Tom's mad chatter both intelligible and congenial. Later, Edgar meets his blind father wandering alone, and consents to take him to Dover, without revealing his identity. He stages a 'miracle' by which his father is preserved from suicide: he pretends that they are on the edge of Dover cliff, and convinces Gloucester that he has thrown himself over and been miraculously preserved. He kills Goneril's steward, and takes from him a letter from Goneril to Edmund. As an unknown champion he kills Edmund in single combat. He is made joint ruler, with Kent, by Albany.

Edmund sees that his brother is vulnerable because of his virtue:

> . . . a brother noble,
> Whose nature's so far from doing harms
> That he suspects none; on whose foolish honesty
> My practices ride easy! (I.ii)

He is forced to reduce himself to the lowest level of humanity, to conceal his nobility in rags:

> . . . Whiles I may 'scape,
> I will preserve myself; and am bethought
> To take the basest and most poorest shape
> That ever penury, in contempt of man,
> Brought near to beast; my face I'll grime with filth,
> Blanket my loins, elf all my hairs in knots,
> And with presented nakedness outface
> The winds and persecutions of the sky.
> The country gives me proof and precedent
> Of Bedlam beggars, who, with roaring voices,
> Strike in their numb'd and mortified bare arms
> Pins, wooden pricks, nails, sprigs of rosemary;
> And with this horrible object, from low farms,
> Poor pelting villages, sheep-cotes, and mills,
> Sometime with lunatic bans, sometime with prayers,
> Enforce their charity. (II.iii)

In this role, with his feigned madness, he acts as a counterpoint to Lear's crumbling sanity: his random babblings make perfect sense to Lear, who sees in him an interesting 'philosopher'. Edgar has a practical dramatic role in the scenes of Lear's madness: his asides in his own character guide the audience's response; this was probably important with an Elizabethan audience who were used to being entertained by madness.

Edgar's faith in divine justice is increasingly challenged as the play develops; it is shaken when he meets his blinded father, but he quickly recovers his stoic acceptance:

> And worse I may be yet; the worst is not
> So long as we can say 'This is the worst'. (IV.i)

He moves from impotence to almost providential authority as he transforms his father's suicidal despair into hope. He creates a steep cliff for his blind father:

> . . . How fearful
> And dizzy 'tis to cast one's eyes so low!
> The crows and choughs that wing the midway air
> Show scarce as gross as beetles; half way down
> Hangs one that gathers samphire, dreadful trade!
> Methinks he seems no bigger than his head.
> The fishermen that walk upon the beach
> Appear like mice, and yond tall anchoring bark
> Diminish'd to her cock, her cock a buoy
> Almost too small for sight. The murmuring sirge,
> That on th'unnumber'd pebble chafes,
> Cannot be heard so high. (IV.vi)

Edgar assures Gloucester that he has been preserved by 'the clearest Gods' when he thinks he has fallen from this great height. His final role is that of champion of right and justice, when he confronts and defeats Edmund. He is, simply in terms of the plot, 'a superfluous character' (Orwell); his symbolic function, however, is vital to the play.

EDMUND *(Lr.)* : the illegitimate son of the Earl of Gloucester. He is jealous of his legitimate brother Edgar, and successfully devises a scheme to discredit him. He wounds himself after a mock fight with Edgar, and tells his father that he has been attacked by Edgar, and that Edgar had tried to persuade him to kill him; Edgar is banished, and Edmund becomes his father's favourite. He tells Cornwall that Gloucester had intended to assist Lear; he is sent from the castle with Goneril while Gloucester is blinded. He admits that 'to both sisters have I sworn my love'. He captures Lear and Cordelia, and commits them to prison, with orders that they should be hanged. He is arrested by Albany 'on capital treason'; he claims judicial combat, and is defeated and mortally wounded by an unknown champion, who is Edgar in his final disguise. As he is dying he repents, and sends a token of reprieve for Cordelia; but he is too late.

We find in Edmund the self-awareness and delight in his own villainy that marks him as a descendant of the Vice of the morality plays. As Gloucester's 'natural' son, he decides that he will act 'naturally':

> Thou, Nature, art my goddess; to thy law
> My services are bound. Wherefore should I
> Stand in the plague of custom, and permit
> The curiosity of nations to deprive me,
> For that I am some twelve of fourteen moonshines
> Lag of a brother? Why bastard? Wherefore base?
> When my dimensions are as well compact,
> My mind as generous, and my shape as true,
> As honest madam's issue? Why brand they us
> With base? with baseness? bastardy? base, base?
> Who in the lusty stealth of nature take
> More composition and fierce quality
> Than doth, within a dull, stale, tired bed,
> Go to th' creating a whole tribe of fops,
> Got 'tween asleep and awake? Well then,
> Legitimate Edgar, I must have your land:
> Our father's love is to the bastard Edmund
> As honest madam's issue? Why brand they us
> Well, my legitimate, if this letter speed,
> And my invention thrive, Edmund the base
> Shall top th' legitimate – :I grow, I prosper;
> Now, gods, stand up for bastards! (I.ii)

He believes in himself, and entrusts himself to Fortune, which he frequently invokes, and which he sees as the cause of his downfall: 'The wheel is come full circle; I am here' (v.iii) – this is Fortune's wheel, which has lifted him up, and brought him down.

Edmund is a witty and attractive villain – Shakespeare makes him less guilty than Plexirtus in Sidney's *Arcadia* who he is derived from. Plexirtus tears out his own father's eyes, but Edmund seeks to make amends at the end, by trying to save Cordelia.

EDMUND, EARL OF RUTLAND *(3 H.VI)*, *see* RUTLAND.

EDMUND OF LANGLEY, DUKE OF YORK

(R.II) : the uncle of Richard and Bolingbroke. He tries ineffectively to keep peace between them. He is left as Regent while Richard is in Ireland. He rebukes Bolingbroke, but joins him and acknowledges him as Henry IV. He tells the King of the plot against him, even though it involves Aumerle, his son.

Edmund de Langley (1341–1402) was the fifth son of Edward III by Philippa of Hainault. He became the 1st Duke of York. He was Regent from September 1394 until September 1396.

EDWARD, EARL OF MARCH (afterwards Edward IV) *(2 H.VI; 3 H.VI; R.III)* : in *2 Henry VI* he and his brother the Duke of Gloucester are called to stand bail for their father, the Duke of York, when he is arrested for treason.

In *3 Henry VI* as the Earl of March he claims to have killed, or seriously wounded, Buckingham (I.i). He sees three suns in the sky shortly before he hears of the death of his father; Warwick acclaims him as the Duke of York, and tells him to raise an army in Wales. Edward reviles Queen Margaret, and demands the crown (II.ii). After his victory over Margaret and the Lancastrians at Towton, Edward creates his brother Richard the Duke of Gloucester, and his brother George the Duke of Clarence (II.vi). He orders Henry VI to the Tower. He marries Lady Grey, and learns that as a consequence Warwick has sworn to dethrone him (IV.i). He is seized in his tent near Warwick by Warwick and Clarence, and his crown taken from him. He is imprisoned in Middleham Castle, but escapes easily with the help of Hastings. He raises an army in Burgundy, and returns to England; he gains admission to York through his title Duke of York, but as soon as he is inside he proclaims himself king (IV.vii). After his victory at Barnet, he leads in the mortally wounded Warwick (v.ii), he then marches against Margaret, and meets her army at Tewkesbury. On the battlefield he is the first to stab the young Prince Edward, but after the victory he orders Margaret's life spared (v.v). From the throne, Edward orders his brothers to salute his infant son, and orders Margaret deported to France.

In *Richard III* he is 'led in sick', and tries to mediate between factions at court; he laments the death of Clarence (II.i). We hear of his death from Queen Elizabeth (II.ii).

Edward (1442–83) was the son of Richard, Duke of York, and Cicely Neville. He was attainted a Yorkist in 1459. In 1460 he returned from Calais with Warwick and Salisbury and assisted in the defeat of Henry VI at Northampton; subsequently they governed in the King's name. After the death of his father, Edward gathered an army and defeated Margaret at Mortimer's Cross, and was proclaimed king in London in 1461. In the same year he defeated the Lancastrians at Towton.

In 1464 he was privately married to Elizabeth Woodville, which offended Warwick, who supported his projected marriage to the French Lady Bona of Savoy; Warwick swore to dethrone him. In 1469 Edward was defeated by Clarence and committed to the custody of George Neville, Archbishop of York, but he escaped and defeated the rebels. Warwick and Clarence fled to France, where they were reconciled with Queen Margaret. They attacked England in 1470. and Edward had to seek refuge in Holland. He enlisted the aid of the Duke of Burgundy, and on his return to England he was reconciled to his brother Clarence; he took King Henry prisoner, and defeated and killed Warwick at the Battle of Barnet on Easter Day 1471. He defeated Margaret at Tewkesbury shortly afterwards, and killed her son, the young Prince Edward; he was at last secure on the throne. In 1478 he imprisoned and put to death his brother Clarence for his apparent treason. Edward died in 1483: on his deathbed, as in *Richard III*, he tried to reconcile the supporters of Gloucester with his wife's relations.

Holinshed cites More's account of Edward:

He was a goodlie personage, and princelie to behold, of heart couragious, politike in counsell, in adversitie nothing abashed, in prosperitie rather joifull than proud, in peace just and mercifull, in warre sharpe and fierce, in the field bold and hardie, and natheless no further (than wisdome would) adventurous; whose warres who so well considered, he shall no less commend his wisdome where he voided, than his man hood where he vanquished. He was of visage lovelie, of bodie mightie, strong, and cleane made: howbeit, in his latter daies, with over liberall diet, somewhat corpulent and boorlie, and natheless not uncomlie. He was of youth greatlie given to fleshlie wantonness.

EDWARD, PRINCE OF WALES *(3 H.VI)*: the only son of Henry VI. He protests at being disinherited by his father, and leaves with Queen Margaret (I.i). He is knighted by Henry before York. At the French court he pledges himself to marry Warwick's daughter (III.iii). He is summoned from France by Henry; he joins Warwick's attack on Edward, but is taken prisoner at Tewkesbury, where he is stabbed to death by Edward, Gloucester and Clarence (v.v).

Edward Plantagenet (1453–71) was the last legitimate male of the house of Lancaster. He was present at the second battle of St Albans in 1461, and afterwards he was knighted by his father. Shakespeare follows Hall's account of Edward's death; other sources absolve Gloucester of any part in the killing; the exact circumstances of his death are not clear.

EDWARD, PRINCE OF WALES *(3 H.VI)*:

successor to the above. Buckingham advises the young Prince be brought to London (II.ii). He is welcomed by Buckingham and the Lord Mayor; he objects to being lodged in the Tower, though he is told it is for his safety. Richard, who is preparing for his usurpation, spreads rumours of Edward's illegitimacy (III.v). Richard orders the murder of Edward and his brother Richard Duke of York; Tyrrel describes how they were smothered in the Tower by Dighton and Forrest:

O thus, quoth Dighton, lay the gentle babes.
Thus, thus, quoth Forrest, girdling one another
Within their alabaster innocent arms.
Their lips were four red roses on a stalk,
Which in their summer beauty kissed each other.
A book of prayers on their pillow lay,
Which once, quoth Forrest, almost changed my mind;
But o the devil – there the villain stopped;
When Dighton thus told on, we smothered
The most replenished sweet work of nature,
That from the prime creation e'er she framed. (IV.iii)

The ghost of Edward and his brother appear to Richard before Bosworth (V.iii).

Edward (1470–83) was the eldest son of Edward IV by Elizabeth Woodville. He became Prince of Wales in 1471, and succeeded to the throne in 1483, at the age of thirteen. During his two months reign he was an impotent spectator as Gloucester and the Woodvilles struggled for power. He was deposed on the grounds of the invalidity of his mother's marriage by an assembly of Lords and Commons under the control of Gloucester. Shortly afterwards he and his brother were murdered in the Tower, probably on Richard's orders. In 1674 two skeletons were discovered at the foot of a staircase in the White Tower and were buried as those of the princes.

EGEON *(Err.)*: a merchant from Syracuse, father of the Antipholus twins. He comes to Ephesus in search of his lost son, and is arrested and condemned to death for landing there unlawfully (I.i). He is on his way to execution when he recognizes his sons and his lost wife Aemilia *(q.v.)*. After all is explained, his life is spared.

Egeon's fate hangs over the whole farce: his story is presented in the style of tragedy until the very end, when the resolution of the errors transforms all to joy. In Plautus' *Menaechmi* the father of the twins dies before the start of the story – the hopeless condition of Egeon adds a serious dimension to Shakespeare's play. There are several possible sources for the story of Egeon and Aemilia, including Plautus' *Pudens* and Nicolo Secchi's *Gl'Inganni*.

EGEUS *(MND.)*: Hermia's father. He brings her before Theseus because she refuses to marry Demetrius (I.i). He is a member of Theseus' hunting party which discovers the young couples in the wood (IV.i).

EGLAMOUR, SIR *(Gent.)*: 'a knight well-spoken, neat and fine' (I.ii), who takes vows of chastity. He helps Silvia to escape from Milan and the attentions of Thurio. He runs away when they are attacked by outlaws.

Sir Eglamour was one of the knights of the Round Table in Arthurian romance, a brave slayer of dragons. This 'nimble-footed' knight is like him only in name.

EGYPTIAN, AN *(Ant.)*: a messenger, who brings a message from Cleopatra to Octavius (v.i).

ELBOW *(Meas.)*: 'a simple constable' who twice arrests Pompey the bawd, and makes incoherent charges against him and Froth, calling them 'notorious benefactors'.

Elbow has trouble with words: 'attest' becomes 'detest', 'carnally' becomes 'cardinally'. His incompetence with the law parallels Angelo's misuse of it, and shows what happens when justice and law are simply equated. Escalus, wearily watching the examination, is driven to ask: 'Which is the wiser here, Justice or Iniquity?' (II.i)

ELINOR, QUEEN *(John)*: mother to King John, who supports his claim to the throne even though she knows it to be spurious. She accepts the bastard Falconbridge as her grandson, and he becomes her devoted follower. She accompanies John on his French campaign, and stays in France. John is told of her death (IV.ii).

ELIZABETH, PRINCESS (afterwards Queen Elizabeth I of England) *(H.VIII)*: the only child of Henry VIII and Anne Bullen. After her christening procession, Cranmer delivers a prophetic panegyric:

This royal infant – heaven still move about her –
Though in her cradle, yet now promises
Upon this land a thousand thousand blessings,
Which time shall bring to ripeness. She shall be –
But few now living can behold that goodness –
A pattern to all princes living with her,
And all that shall succeed. Saba was never
More covetous of wisdom and fair virtue
Than this pure soul shall be. All princely graces
That mould up such a mighty piece as this is,
With all the virtues that attend the good,
Shall still be doubled on her. Truth shall nurse her,
Holy and heavenly thoughts still counsel her.
She shall be loved and feared. Her own shall bless her;
Her foes shake like a field of beaten corn,
And hang their heads with sorrow. Good grows with her. (v.v)

ELIZABETH WOODVILLE *(3 H.VI; R.III)*: in *3 Henry VI* the daughter of Earl Rivers and Lady Grey. She appears before Edward IV as a supplicant for the lost estates of her husband, Sir Richard Grey, who was killed at St Albans (III.ii). Edward falls in love with her and marries her, and in doing so he loses the support of Warwick. She appears as queen with her son, the future Edward V.

In *Richard III* she has a passive role – she is the 'poor painted queen'. She tries to take her sons into sanctuary. After they are killed, this 'shallow, changing woman' is persuaded by Richard into promising him her daughter as his queen (IV.iv).

Elizabeth Woodville (*c*.1431–92) was the daughter of Sir Richard Woodville, afterwards Earl Rivers. Her husband, Sir John Grey, left her with two sons when he was killed at St Albans in 1461. These were Thomas, later Marquess of Dorset, and Richard, later Duke of York. The Woodvilles were supporters of the Lancastrians, and Elizabeth was deprived of her inheritance on the accession of the Yorkist Edward IV. But Edward was fascinated by her when they met, and married her secretly in 1464. She was crowned queen in 1465, and at once caused dissent among the older nobles by advancing her relatives. On the death of Edward in 1483 she took sanctuary from Gloucester and Buckingham; she was persuaded to give up her son Richard by Cardinal Bourchier, and he was sent to the Tower to join his brother Edward. After her marriage to Edward had been declared invalid by Parliament, Richard induced her to leave sanctuary by promising to provide for herself and her daughters; his aim was to prevent the marriage of her daughter Elizabeth to Richmond. On the accession of Richmond as Henry VII her full rights were restored, though a year later her lands were forfeit because of her cooperation with Richard in handing over her daughter. She retired to the abbey at Bermondsey, where she lived, ignored by Henry, until her death in 1492. She appears to have had an unfortunate talent for making personal enemies.

ELY, BISHOP OF *(H.V)*: John Fordham. The Archbishop of Canterbury explains to him the economic necessity (for the church) of a war with France (I.i), and together they convince Henry that under the Salic law his claim to the throne of France is just (I.ii).

ELY, BISHOP OF *(H.VIII)*: Nicholas West (1461–1533). He is one of the clergy present at the divorce proceedings at Blackfriars (II.iv).

As Katharine's chaplain he was opposed to the divorce, but in Shakespeare's scene he says nothing.

ELY, BISHOP OF *(R.III)*: John Morton (1410–1500). Richard sends him for strawberries from his garden (III.iv). Richard is disturbed when Ratcliffe reports that Ely has joined Richmond (IV.iii).

EMANUEL, CLERK OF CHATHAM *(2 H.VI)*: when Jack Cade declares that he intends to kill all the lawyers, some of his band seize the Clerk. Cade questions him and finds him guilty of being able to write his name; he is hanged 'with his pen and ink-horn about his neck' (IV.ii).

EMILIA *(Oth.)*: Iago's wife and Desdemona's servant. She innocently helps to bring about the tragedy by retaining the handkerchief that Desdemona drops, and by assisting Cassio to 'some brief discourse with Desdemona alone.' Iago professes to doubt her faithfulness. When she discovers Desdemona dead she rails at Othello for his stupidity, and when she discovers her husband's villainy she flies into a rage and exposes him. He kills her to silence her.

She dies in a moment of heroic dignity. She is the *balia,* or servant-confidante, of sixteenth-century Italian drama.

EMILIA *(Wint.)*: a lady attending Hermione who accompanies her to prison. When Paulina is refused access to Hermione, Emilia is allowed to see her and tell her that Hermione has given birth to Perdita (II.ii).

ENOBARBUS, DOMITIUS *(Ant.)*: a Roman soldier, and the trusted friend of Antony. He is worried by Antony's involvement with Cleopatra, although he admires her. He speaks the famous description of her in her barge (II.ii). He advises Antony to fight on land rather than on the sea; he blames him for the defeat, and resolves to desert to Octavius. Antony sends all his treasure after him 'with his bounty over-plus'. Enobarbus dies of a broken heart, with Antony's name on his lips.

Enobarbus has the role of choric commentator: from him we get our impression of Antony the soldier, and from him we hear how his fine Roman qualities are being undermined in Egypt. He remains steadfastly loyal, determined to

 . . . follow
The wounded chance of Antony, though my reason
Sits in the wind against me. (III.i)

As he sees Antony increasingly give way to his will and deny his reason, Enobarbus begins to waver:

Mine honesty, and I, begin to square.
The loyalty well held to fools, does make
Our faith mere folly: yet he that can endure
To follow with allegiance a fall'n Lord,
Does conquer him that did his master conquer,
And earns a place in th' story. (III.xiii)

When he does leave Antony, he feels that he is the 'villain of the earth' when faced by Antony's generosity. He dies filled with remorse, of a broken heart:

 . . . Throw my heart
Against the flint and hardness of my fault
Which being so dried with grief, will break to powder,
And finish all foul thoughts. Oh Antony,
Nobler than my revolt is infamous,
Forgive me in thine own particular,
But let the world rank me in register
A master-leaver, and a fugitive:
Oh Antony! Oh Antony! (IV.ix)

Just as Antony's military fortunes are declining, Shakespeare gives him this remarkable endorsement as a man. Enobarbus is almost wholly his creation; there is only a brief account of Domitius Ahenobarbus in Plutarch.

EPHESUS, DUKE OF *(Err.)*, *see* SOLINUS.

EROS *(Ant.)*: Antony's servant. He is sworn to kill his master if commanded, but when after Cleopatra's 'death' Antony tells him to, he turns his back and kills himself.

ERPINGHAM, SIR THOMAS *(H.V)*: an officer in the English army, a 'good old knight' who lends Henry his cloak (IV.i).

ESCALUS *(Meas.)*: an 'ancient lord' who is appointed by the Duke as 'secondary' to Angelo. He publicly supports Angelo but in private he deprecates his severity to Claudio. He is lenient to Froth and Pompey when they are brought before him. He orders the disguised Duke to prison on the testimony of Lucio for slandering the state. The Duke thanks him for his 'much goodness' at the end.

ESCALUS *(Rom.)*: Prince of Verona, who intervenes in the brawl between the Capulets and Montagues and threatens death to the heads of both houses 'If ever you disturb our streets again' (I.i). He banishes Romeo for killing Tybalt. He investigates the tragedy at the end, declaring that 'Some shall be pardon'd, and some punish'd' (V.iii).

He represents order and reason, which have been violated.

ESCANES *(Per.)*: a lord of Tyre. Helicanus tells him how Antiochus and his daughter were killed by a lightning bolt as punishment for their incest (I.iii).

ESSEX, EARL OF *(John)*: he presents the Faulconbridge brothers to the King (I.i). He was Geffrey Fitzpeter (*d.*1213).

EUPHRONIUS *(Ant.)*, *see* SCHOOLMASTER.

EVANS, SIR HUGH *(Wiv.)* : a Welsh parson who, according to Falstaff, 'makes fritters of English' (v.v). Because he favours Slender's suit to Anne Page he is challenged to a duel by Dr Caius; he awaits the encounter with much 'trempling of mind' (III.ii). The host tricks the two combatants by sending them to different places; they unite against him and cozen him of two horses. Evans joins in the plan to bait Falstaff, and instructs the children. He takes part in the guise of a satyr.

Evans sings 'To shallow rivers', a sophisticated song for lute and voice, of which a setting survives in William Corbine's *Second Book of Ayres* (1612).

EXETER, DUKE OF *(H.V; 1 H.VI)* : Thomas Beaufort. In *Henry V* tells the King to rouse himself against the French; he announces that the Dauphin's 'tun of treasure' contains tennis balls (I.ii). He arrests the conspirators Scroop, Cambridge and Grey. As Henry's ambassador, he presents an ultimatum to Charles VI (II.iv). He is ordered to remain at Harfleur after it is taken and fortify it (III.iii). He describes the death of Suffolk and York at Agincourt, and enumerates the prisoners. He is at the council at Troyes.

In *1 Henry VI* he laments Henry's death at the lying-in-state. At the coronation of Henry VI in Paris he deprecates the strife between Somerset and York, and foresees disaster (IV.i). He objects to Henry's betrothal to Margaret of Anjou (v.v).

Thomas Beaufort (*d.*1427) was the third and youngest son of John of Gaunt by Catherine Swynford. He was appointed Governor of Harfleur and was probably still there at the time of Agincourt. In 1416 he was appointed Lieutenant of Normandy, and he was created Duke of Exeter in the same year. He went with Henry to Rouen in 1418, and in 1419 he was appointed Captain of that city. He helped negotiate the Treaty of Troyes, and was a member of the Council of the Regency on Henry's death. He died in 1427, some five years before the coronation of Henry VI, which Shakespeare has him attend.

EXETER, DUKE OF *(3 H.VI)* : he appears briefly, and admits that Henry is the 'lawful king'. At Towton he persuades Henry to escape with him. He is present when Henry is seized (IV.viii).

He was Henry Holland, 2nd Duke of Exeter (1447–73). He married Anne Plantagenet, the sister of Edward IV, but remained faithful to Henry VI. He was left for dead after the Lancastrian defeat at Barnet, but was found by a servant, and recovered from his severe wounds. He was attainted by Edward and reduced to penury.

EXTON *(R.II)*, *see* PIERCE OF EXTON.

F

FABIAN *(Tw.N.)* : servant to Olivia. He has fallen out of favour with her since Malvolio told her of his involvement in a bear-baiting. He wants to see Malvolio humiliated, and eagerly joins the plot against him. He reads Malvolio's letter appealing to Olivia at the end, and explains to her how he has been gulled (v.i).

FAIRIES, QUEEN OF *(Wiv.)* : character assumed by Anne Page *(q.v.)*.

FAIRY, A *(MND.)* : one of Titania's attendants. He meets Puck, and from their conversation we learn of the quarrel between Titania and Oberon, and that both of them will be in the wood that night (ii.i).

FALSTAFF, SIR JOHN *(1 & 2 H.IV; H.V; Wiv.)* : the offspring of a family of country gentlemen, Sir John Falstaff – 'Jack Falstaff with my familiars, John with my brothers and sisters, and Sir John with all Europe' – appears to have been born about 1346, the year when King Edward III defeated the French at Crécy; for in 1402 he announces that he is between fifty and sixty years old. Of his youth we know comparatively little, except that his friend Shallow, a somewhat credulous witness, asserts that he had once served as page in the household of Thomas Mowbray, Duke of Norfolk, and describes the cheerful beginnings of their friendship when both were studying law at the London Inns of Court. There, we learn, the young Falstaff had been a famous 'swinge-buckler', had broken heads and courted every attractive girl around their lodgings. 'I may say to you, we knew where the bona robas were, and had the best of them all at commandment.' Once they had rambled so far into the country that they had found the City's gates already shut against them on their return, and had been obliged to spend the night 'in the windmill in Saint George's field'. Falstaff is pleased to corroborate Shallow's stories: 'We have heard the chimes at midnight, Master Shallow.'

In Shakespeare's dramas, Falstaff re-emerges, after a neglected education and an ill-spent youth, as the dissolute crony of the hard-living Prince of Wales, the future King Henry V, and the leader of a thievish London gang who have made their headquarters at the Boar's Head, Eastcheap. During his earlier years, he himself informs us, Falstaff had had a slight and graceful figure: 'I was not an eagle's talon in the waist; I could have crept into an alderman's thumb-ring . . .' But heavy drinking and compulsive eating have now caused him to develop an enormous paunch – 'how long is't ago, Jack', demands the Prince, 'since thou sawest thine own knee?' – and all that remains of his youthful charm is his unfailing gaiety and good humour. Meanwhile, he has become the Prince's favourite buffoon, and is proud to share his rowdiest pastimes. 'Hal' is his substitute son; and for the unruly Prince himself Falstaff is a kind of second father, a parent he need neither fear nor respect, on whom he exercises all his whims, even persuading Falstaff to play a parental role, while he himself kneels at his feet and pretends to listen to his admonitions. Among their cronies are Poins, Bardolph, Peto, Gadshill, a professional cut-purse, and Mistress Nell Quickly, the warm-hearted hostess of the Eastcheap tavern. Committing 'the oldest sins the newest kinds of ways' is the Prince's chief amusement; and in 1402 he helps to organize an entertaining piece of highway robbery. But the Prince and Poins, under cover of darkness, fall upon their fellow gangsters; and Falstaff is worsted and driven from the field, larding 'the lean earth with sweat'.

Meanwhile, news arrives that Hotspur, a leader of the turbulent Percy clan, has joined the Welsh rebel, Owen Glendower, and is swiftly marching southwards. Falstaff, as the Prince's favourite, is entrusted with 'a charge of foot'. While recruiting troops, he seizes the opportunity of enlisting none but the most prosperous and unwarlike citizens, then allowing them to purchase an immediate discharge, a stratagem that earns him some 'three hundred and odd pounds', and substituting a motley collection of half-starved yokels. At the Battle of Shrewsbury, on 21 July 1403, they are nearly wiped out; and Falstaff, who has ventured to engage

right A nineteenth-century Falstaff: Herbert Beerbohm Tree in *1 Henry IV*.

1 Henry IV (II.v): Falstaff plays the role of Hal's father, the King. An etching by George Cruickshank.

Douglas, soon decides that he has seen enough of action and saves his skin by feigning death.

On his return to London, he has a brush with the Lord Chief Justice, but carries off this alarming encounter in his usual gay, high-handed style. He is also arrested for debt at the instigation of his old acquaintance, Mistress Quickly, but escapes by a fine display of gentlemanly bluff. That same summer, when a new revolt is mounted under the command of Northumberland and other rebellious lords, he is again appointed a recruiting officer and, at a Gloucestershire manor house, meets his ancient crony Shallow, now a placid Justice of the Peace. From Gloucestershire he leads his men to Yorkshire, and during an engagement between the King's enemies and the assembled royal forces, captures a knight named Colville of the Dale. Falstaff reappears in 1413 on another visit to the admiring Justice Shallow; and one afternoon, when the company have eaten their dinner and retired to the orchard to taste 'a last year's pippen, with a dish of caraways', his ensign Pistol, a boastful, down-at-heels soldier, abruptly stalks across the garden. He brings welcome news of the old King's death. 'Sweet knight,' he announces triumphantly, 'thou are now one of the great men in this realm'; at which Falstaff hastens back to London,

but not before, on the strength of the honours he expects to receive, he has obtained the loan of a thousand pounds from Shallow, promising him any royal post that he may choose.

He never repays the loan. Once he has reached London and, from the crowd that surrounds the Abbey, paid affectionate homage to the new soverign – 'God save thy Grace, King Hal! My royal Hal . . . God save thee, my sweet boy!' – he receives a quick and crushing snub:

I know thee not, old man: fall to thy prayers . . .

Reply not to me with a fool-born jest . . .

For God doth know, so shall the world perceive,

That I have turned away my former self . . . (v.v)

Although Falstaff's response is courageous and dignified, thereafter his decline is rapid. Yet he can still command affection, and, indeed, a measure of respect, among his raffish Eastcheap friends; and, when Henry v is about to invade France, and they learn from Falstaff's page that his master now lies dying, they express a general sense of sorrow. It remains for Mistress Quickly, whom he has so often beguiled and defrauded, to narrate the pathetic circumstances of the old man's death:

A' made a finer end and went away an it had been

any christom child; a' parted even just between twelve and one, even at the turning o' the tide; for after I saw him fumble with the sheets, and play with flowers, and smile upon his fingers' ends, I knew there was but one way . . . 'How now, Sir John!' quoth I: 'what, man, be o' good cheer.' So a' cried out, 'God, God, God!' three or four times. Now I, to comfort him, bid him, a' should not think of God; I hoped there was no need to trouble himself with any such thoughts yet. So a' bade me lay more clothes on his feet: I put my hand into the bed and felt them, and they were as cold as any stone, and so upward and upward, and all was as cold as any stone. (II.iii)

Henry IV Part I, was written in 1597, *Part II* in 1598. They were succeeded, probably soon afterwards, by *The Merry Wives of Windsor,* said to have been produced at the request of the Queen herself, who wished to see Falstaff enacting the role of lover. Despite some amusing scenes and admirable speeches, it adds little to the hero's portrait. Here Falstaff pays simultaneous court to Mistress Ford and Mistress Page; and, learning of his schemes through the treachery of Pistol and Nym, they resolve to punish his presumption, persuade him to take refuge in a basket of dirty linen from Mistress Page's vengeful husband, then have him thrown 'hissing hot' into the waters of the Thames. Other humiliations follow. The play has all the air of being a hurriedly executed work. It is in *Henry IV* (both Parts) and *Henry V* that Falstaff achieves his true dimensions as a human being far more genuinely great than the callous sovereign who renounces him. Yet Falstaff was originally a composite personage, built up from a trio of different characters, Ned, Tom and Sir John Oldcastle, each presented in an old play, *The Famous Victories of Henry V*, thought to have been staged about 1586. Shakespeare combined the three into a splendidly living whole. Samuel Johnson wrote in a famous tribute:

Falstaff, unimitated, inimitable, how shall I describe thee! Thou compound of sense and vice; of sense which may be admired, but not esteemed; of vice which may be despised, but hardly detested. Falstaff is a character loaded with faults . . . Yet the man thus corrupt, thus despicable, makes himself necessary to the prince that despises him by the most pleasing of all qualities, perpetual gaiety.

It was Falstaff's composure, his natural grasp of life, that enchanted William Hazlitt. 'His body is like a good estate to his mind, from which he receives rents and revenues of profit and pleasure . . . Falstaff's wit is the emanation of a fine constitution'; and he is endowed with a masterly presence of mind, that nothing mortal can disturb. Falstaff is human throughout; and he is glad to accept the limitations of ordinary flesh-and-blood. Though he may brag and

Falstaff and Doll Tearsheet, with Prince Henry and Poins disguised as drawers, in the Boar's Head Tavern at Eastcheap. A painting by Henry Fuseli.

boast, he does not aspire to grandeur; whereas the 'iron men' who surrounded him are mail-clad puppets, bent on wielding power and 'making history'. Falstaff is an egotist; but his egotism, though frequently mischievous, is never harsh or self-destructive. If he excites contempt, he also arouses love; and in the women he desires and sometimes cheats – even in the unfortunate Mistress Quickly – he usually inspires a warm affection. For his 'royal Hal' he feels a deep love; and it is the cruel desertion by his cold, vain-glorious idol that suddenly extinguishes his zest for living. 'The King has killed his heart', exclaims poor Mistress Quickly, who had hoped one day to become Lady Falstaff, when she learns that the old man's end is near.

FANG *(2 H.IV)*: a sheriff's officer. With Snare he arrests Falstaff on charges brought against him by Mistress Quickly (II.i).

FASTOLFE, SIR JOHN *(1 H.VI)*: a cowardly knight, who we hear allowed Talbot to be captured at Patay (I.i). He again deserts Talbot before Rouen (III.ii). When Talbot meets him again, he tears the Garter from his leg, and the King banishes him on pain of death (IV.i).

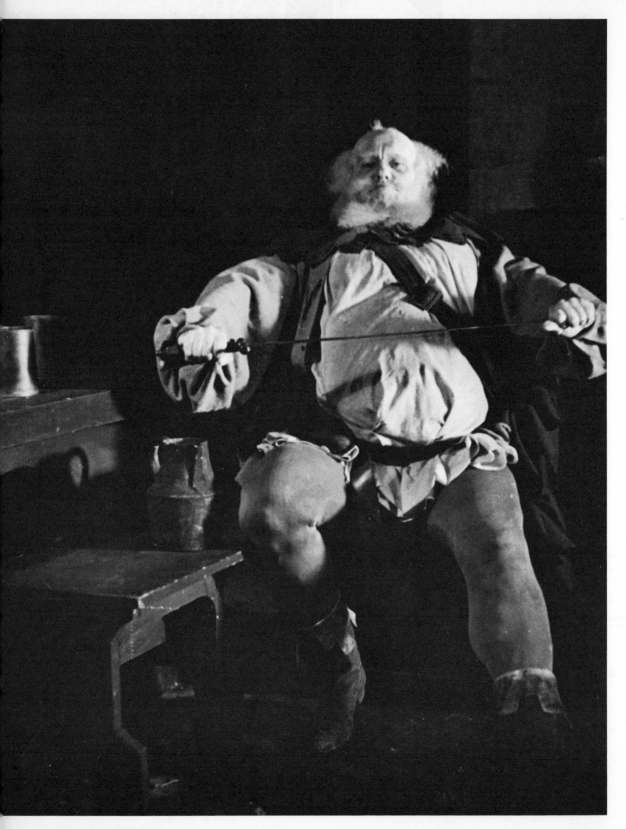

above Sir Ralph Richardson as Falstaff.
right Claudio and Isabella (*Measure for Measure*),
painted by William Holman Hunt.

overleaf William Blake's *Oberon, Titania, and Puck with
Fairies Dancing (A Midsummer Night's Dream).*

Aldwych Theatre

Miss VIOLA TREE'S COMPANY

THE TEMPEST

The real Sir John Fastolfe (c.1378–1459) was a distinguished soldier who fought bravely at Agincourt, and later became Regent of Normandy. He did desert Talbot at Patay, though not ignominiously as Shakespeare suggests. He was deprived of the Garter, but it was later restored; even so, his reputation as a coward and a Lollard clung to him.

FATHER THAT HAS KILLED HIS SON

(3H.VI): as Henry sits on a hill observing the battle at Towton between the forces of Edward and those of Queen Margaret two men drag bodies from the field: one discovers that he has killed his own son, and the other that he has killed his father (II.v).

This small incident is a vivid illustration of the horrific consequences of the Civil War.

FAULCONBRIDGE, LADY *(John)*: mother of

Robert Faulconbridge and his bastard half-brother Philip. When Philip tells her that he has given up his claim to the name of Faulconbridge, she admits to him that he is her illegitimate son by Richard I (I.i).

FAULCONBRIDGE, PHILIP (THE BASTARD)

(John): he claims his inheritance before the King, but is resisted by his brother Robert who claims that Philip is illegitimate. Philip gladly resigns his patrimony, preferring to be 'the reputed son of Coeur-de-Lion'; King John approves, and dubs him 'Sir Richard and Plantagenet'. On the entrance of his mother, he induces her to admit his true parentage (I.i). He presses John and Philip to unite in attacking Angiers; he rails at Lymoges, and later kills him, and enters with his head (III.ii). He is sent on a mission to England 'to shake the bags of hoarding abbots' (III.iii). He warns the King of the disaffection among his nobles. He is present when Arthur's body is discovered, and denounces the supposed murderer; he is convinced of Hubert's innocence, and tells the nobles to refrain from their accusations (IV.iii). He tells John that the Dauphin has landed and that Arthur is dead, and is appalled to find that the King has placed himself in the hands of the papal legate. He presents himself before Pandulph and the Dauphin, and hurls defiant insults at the latter. He is present at the death of John, and does homage to Henry. He closes the play with a soliloquy on the future of England.

Faulconbridge has been seen as the hero of the play, the representative of the spirit of England which is burdened with an unworthy king. He is the son of the last true king. He is also a comic chorus, commenting on the action, a 'crystal glass to gaze upon the follies of the times'. He presents himself as a cynical Machiavel, devoted to expediency, but he is truly concerned for England, unlike John, whose primary concern is for his throne. His final speech is perhaps the main reason why the play was revived at times of threatened invasion (in 1745, and during the Napoleonic scares):

> O let us pay the time but needful woe,
> Since it hath been beforehand with our griefs.
> This England never did, nor never shall
> Lie at the proud foot of a conqueror,
> But when it first did help to wound itself.
> Now these her princes are come home again,
> Come the three corners of the world in arms,
> And we shall shock them. Naught shall make us rue,
> If England to itself do rest but true. (V.vii)

The Bastard appears in *The Troublesome Raigne of King John,* an earlier play that Shakespeare is supposed to have rewritten. However if, as some scholars claim, *The Troublesome Raigne* is a very bad pirated version of Shakespeare's play rather than its source, the only source for Faulconbridge is a brief mention in Holinshed of 'Philip, bastard son to King Richard'. He has been identified with Falcasius de Breauté (d. c.1227), a notably cruel lord under John. There are no recogni-

Mr C. Kemble as Faulconbridge (the Bastard) in *King John.* An engraving published in 1831.

left The Tempest, a poster designed by Charles Buchel and used for the 1921 production.

zable similarities to Shakespeare's Philip, who is essentially the dramatist's own creation.

FAULCONBRIDGE, ROBERT *(John)*: the legitimate son of Lady Faulconbridge. He and his half-brother Philip appear before John to settle their rights to Robert's father's inheritance. Philip is declared to be illegitimate and Robert is awarded the title and the lands (I.i).

FEEBLE, FRANCIS *(2 H.IV)*: one of the potential recruits found by Justice Shallow. Feeble, a woman's tailor, is, as his name suggests, contemptible in appearance; but he suddenly emerges as a brave and patriotic man when he refuses to bribe Bardolph to escape service:

> By my troth, I care not. A man can die but once. We owe God a death. I'll ne'er bear a base mind. An't be my destiny, so. And let it go which way it will, he that dies this year is quit for the next. (III.ii)

These are perhaps the only truly heroic words in *2 Henry IV*. They show up the venality and corruption of Falstaff and his cronies, and they prepare us for their downfall: we remember Hal's rebuke to Falstaff at Shrewsbury, 'Thou owest God a death.'

FENTON *(Wiv.)*: a young gentleman of high birth and a reputation for riotous living. He has been wooing Anne Page for her father's wealth, but has fallen in love with her, and reformed his ways. He bribes the Host, and during the baiting of Falstaff by the 'fairies' he slips away with Anne and marries her. When they return they are forgiven.

FERDINAND *(Tp.)*: the son of the King of Naples. He is separated from his companions after the shipwreck, and roams the island looking for them. He is led by Ariel's music to Prospero's cell, where he meets and falls in love with Miranda. Prospero tests his devotion by setting him to strenuous manual labour. He is rewarded with Prospero's consent to marry Miranda, and the couple are entertained with Ariel's pageant of spirits.

FERDINAND, KING OF NAVARRE *(LLL.)*: the play opens with his decision to turn his court into a monastic academe where the courtiers will foreswear all contact with women and devote themselves to study for three years. He is almost immediately forced to suspend the decree forbidding women when he is reminded that the daughter of the French king is about to arrive 'in embassy' (I.i). He welcomes the Princess and her ladies, and apologizes to them for the trouble they had gaining admittance. Ferdinand is overheard by Berowne reading an ode expressing his love for the

Ferdinand lured to Prospero's cell by Ariel. After a painting by John Everett Millais.

Princess, and himself overhears Dumain and Longaville reading their 'guilty rimes', and accuses them of breaking their oath; he is exposed by Berowne. He is given Berowne's letter to Rosaline, which allows him to expose Berowne (IV.iii). Disguised as a Muscovite, Ferdinand wooes the masked Rosaline in mistake for the Princess. She chides him for his extravagant use of words, and tells him to

> . . . go with speed
> To some forlorn and naked hermitage,
> Remote from all the pleasures of the world:
> There stay, until the twelve celestial signs
> Have brought about their annual reckoning.
> If this austere insociable life,
> Change not your offer made in heat of blood:
> If frosts, and fasts, hard lodging, and thin weeds
> Nip not the gaudy blossoms of your love,
> But that it bear this trial, and last love:
> Then at the expiration of the year,
> Come challenge me, challenge by these deserts,
> And by this virgin palm, now kissing thine,
> I will be thine. (V.II)

Ferdinand's first words indicate that the reason for his withdrawal from the world is based on pride and self-interest:

> Let Fame, that all hunt after in their lives,
> Live registered upon our brazen tombs,

And then grace us in the disgrace of death:
When spite of cormorant devouring Time,
Th' endeavour of this present breath may buy
That honour which shall bate his scythe's keen edge,
And make us heirs of all eternity. (I.i)

He is, in Granville-Barker's words, 'a bundle of phrases'; he speaks in strings of commonplace conceits, and is quite insensitive to the real meanings of words. For him words are a means of imposing his authority on reality. His lack of awareness leads him to crassly suppose that a series of flowery phrases will be enough to dispel 'the cloud of sorrow' caused by the news of death brought by Mercade; he wants to go on with the courtly games (v.ii). His penance appropriately requires him to endure a hard life for a year.

FESTE *(Tw.N.)*: Olivia's fool. Because Malvolio has discredited him with his mistress he joins the plot against him. He pretends to be Sir Topas, a curate; he interrogates Malvolio with a display of great esoteric learning and hair-splitting, and concludes that he is possessed by a devil. He brings Malvolio 'light and paper and ink' when he sees through the deception.

Feste is a wise fool, a mature, sensible wit who is conscious of his superiority to the fools who surround him. He has little to do with the plot before the last act. His function is to indicate to the audience the foolishness of the main characters: he accurately diagnoses Orsino's melancholy and Olivia's obsessive mourning. Olivia characterizes him:

This fellow is wise enough to play the fool,
And to do that well, craves a kind of wit:
He must observe their mood on whom he jests,
The quality of persons, and the time:
And like the haggard, check at every feather
That comes before his eye. This is a practice,
As full of labour as a wise man's art:
For folly that he wisely shows, is fit;
But wise men folly-fall'n, quite taint their wit. (III.i)

Feste sings three songs: 'O mistress mine', 'Come away, come away, death', and 'When that I was and a little tiny boy'. The last is sung by the actor as himself, alone on the empty stage, and signals the return from the dream world of Illyria to the world as it is. The part was written for Robert Armin.

FIDELE *(Cym.)*: name assumed by Imogen *(q.v.)* when disguised as a boy.

FIENDS, JOAN OF ARC'S *(1 H.VI)*: spirits which Joan invokes at Anjou. She asks for their help once more to defeat the English, but they do not speak and disappear (v.iii).

FISHERMAN *(Per.)*: three fishermen find Pericles

on the beach at Pentapolis (II.i). Two are named (*see* PATCH-BREECH and PILCH).

FITZWATER, LORD *(R.II)*: he is the first to challenge Aumerle when Bagot accuses him of murdering the Duke of Gloucester (IV.i).

FLAMINIUS *(Tim.)*: servant to Timon. He is sent to borrow money for Timon from Lucullus, who tries to bribe him into saying that he could not find him. Flaminius throws down the money and curses Lucullus as a false friend (III.i). He later tries to prevent Timon from meeting the messengers from his creditors.

FLAVIUS *(Caes.)*: a tribune who, with Marullus, rebukes the people of Rome for turning Caesar's triumphant return to Rome into a holiday. They remove decorations from the statues of Caesar, and are punished (I.i; I.ii).

FLAVIUS *(Caes.)*: a soldier in Brutus' army. He appears twice during the battle of Philippi, but does not speak (v.iii; v.iv).

FLAVIUS *(Tim.)*: Timon's steward. He is dismayed by his master's extravagance, and tries to restrain him. He explains the desperate state of Timon's finances when creditors beset him, and warns him not to rely on friends. After Timon's ruin he divides the last of his own money among the servants. When he visits Timon in his cave he is acknowledged by him as the 'one honest man'; he is the only visitor that Timon does not abuse.

FLEANCE *(Mac.)*: Banquo's son. Macbeth hires assassins to murder Banquo and Fleance so as to nullify the witches' prophecy that Banquo will father a line of kings. Banquo is killed, but Fleance escapes (III.iii).

FLORENCE, DUKE OF *(All'sW.)*: he justifies the war against Sienna to the two French lords (III.i), and appoints Bertram general of his cavalry (III.iii).

FLORIZEL, PRINCE *(Wint.)*: son of Polixenes, King of Bohemia, who is in love with Perdita, whom he supposes to be the daughter of a shepherd. Polixenes denounces him when he discovers that they intend to marry. With the assistance of Camillo Florizel sails to Sicily with Perdita, where he presents her to Leontes, claiming that she is a Libyan princess. When Perdita's identity is revealed, Polixenes blesses the marriage.

He and Perdita are linked with summer and the flowering of love, in contrast to the barren, wintry atmosphere at Leontes' court. He praises her thus:

. . . What you do
Still betters what is done. When you speak, sweet,
I'd have you do it ever: when you sing,
I'd have you buy and sell, so give alms,
Pray so; and for the ordering of your affairs,
To sing them too: when you do dance, I wish you
A wave o' the sea, that you might ever do
Nothing but that; move still, still so,
And own no other function; each your doing,
So singular in each particular,
Crowns what you are doing in the present deeds
That all your acts are queens. (IV.iv)

FLUELLEN *(H.V)* : a Welsh officer in Henry's army,
He quarrels with Macmorris and Pistol. In the end he
makes Pistol eat the leek he has derided. The King helps
precipitate the quarrel between Fluellen and Williams,
but is careful to ensure that it does not become too
serious,

For I do know Fluellen valiant,
And touch'd with choler, hot as gunpowder,
And quickly will return an injury. (IV.vii)

Fluellen is the most lively character in the play; he
combines absurdity with real courage. He is a stickler
for what he believes to be the protocols of war, as when
Gower calls out his name on the night before Agincourt:

So, in the name of Jesu Christ, speak lower. It is the
greatest admiration in the universal world, when the
true and ancient prerogatifes and laws of the wars is
not kept. If you would take the pains but to examine
the wars of Pompey the Great, you shall find, I
warrant you, that there is no tiddle-taddle nor pibble-
pabble in Pompey's camp. I warrant you, you shall
find the ceremonies of the wars, and the cares of it,
and the forms of it, and the sobriety of it, and the
modesty of it, to be otherwise. (IV.i)

FLUTE, FRANCIS *(MND.)* : a bellows-mender who

Fluellen makes Pistol eat the leek (*Henry V,* v.i). An
engraving published in 1795.

plays Thisbe to Bottom's Pyramus in the Interlude, despite his incipient beard.

FOOL *(Lr.)* : the court fool. He comments ironically on Lear's folly, and tries to avert his madness with jokes. He disappears from the play when Cordelia returns to England.

The Fool is not a comic buffoon, but a professional domestic fool who is 'all-licensed', that is, permitted almost total freedom in his addresses to his master. There was a tradition that the Fool speaks the truth that he knows by intuition: this Fool has that magic wisdom, though he confesses that his brains are 'but a little cracked'. In the scenes of Lear's madness on the heath, he acts as chorus, pointing out the absurdity of the situation to the audience. As Lear shifts his attention from him to the irrational chatter of Poor Tom, the Fool's comments become more serious; he begins to fear that 'This cold night will turn us all to fools and madmen' (III.iv). His devotion to his master is complete – he never thinks of his own suffering.

Nahum Tate's version of *King Lear* dispensed with the Fool, and from 1680 until Macready hesitantly restored him in 1838 he was absent from the English stage. Dickens, reviewing the restored play in the *Examiner,* was quick to see the importance of the Fool:

> Can there be a doubt after this that his love for the *Fool* is associated with Cordelia, who has been kind to the poor boy, and for the loss of whom he pines away? And are we not even then prepared for the sublime pathos of the close, when *Lear*, bending over the dead body of all he had left to love upon earth, connected with her memory of that other gentle, faithful, and loving being who had passed from his side – unites, in that moment of final agony, the two hearts that had been broken in his service – and exclaims – 'And my poor fool is hanged!'

This comment of Lear's has also given rise to the

The Fool (David O'Brien) and Lear (John Gielgud) in the Stratford Memorial Theatre's 1955 touring production of *King Lear.*

suggestion that the reason for the Fool's disappearance from the play at III.vi was because the same boy actor also took the part of Cordelia.

FOOL *(Tim.)* : employed by a courtesan, he enters with Apemantus and cracks jokes with the servants. His part, and this part of the scene, do not seem to be fully developed (II.ii).

FORD, FRANK *(Wiv.)* : a gentleman of Windsor. He is told by Pistol that Falstaff is in love with his wife. He visits Falstaff under the name 'Brooke' and pays him to 'lay an amiable seige' to Mrs Ford on his behalf. He vows revenge on Falstaff, and invites friends to his house to see 'a monster' but fails to find Falstaff there, and is rebuked for his jealousy by his wife. He visits Falstaff again as 'Brooke', and learns of his escape in a laundry basket. For the second time he fails to discover Falstaff at his house, and in frustration he beats 'Mother Prat' (who is Falstaff in disguise). He joins in the baiting of Falstaff in the park, and in the end forgives him, realizing that his jealousy has been excessive.

FORD, MISTRESS ALICE *(Wiv.)* : the wife of Frank Ford. With Mrs Page she decides to discomfit Falstaff, and to punish her husband for his jealousy at the same time. She encourages Falstaff, and then packs him off in a laundry basket when they are interrupted (by Mrs Page, by previous arrangement) (III.iii).

The Merry Wives of Windsor: the wives conceal Falstaff in a laundry basket. A painting by Henry Fuseli.

She receives Falstaff again, and terrifies him before persuading him to escape disguised as the 'fat woman of Brentford'. She helps contrive the baiting of Falstaff in the forest, and takes part (V.v).

Mistress Quickly says that 'the sweet woman leads an ill life' with Ford.

FORESTER, A *(LLL.)* : he points out to the Princess a 'stand' where she may shoot deer; he is perplexed by her verbal elaboration (IV.i).

FORREST *(R.III)* : one of the murderers of the Princes in the Tower (*see* DIGHTON). He does not appear.

FORTINBRAS, PRINCE *(Ham.)* : the son of the King of Norway, who is preparing to regain by force the lands lost by his father to King Hamlet (Hamlet's father, now dead). Claudius diverts him into attacking Poland, and allows him to march his army through Denmark. Hamlet sees him and his army pass through. He arrives at the end to find the whole Danish royal family dead. He hears that Hamlet has given him his 'dying voice', and he becomes king. He orders Hamlet's body to be borne off with full military honours.

Like Hamlet, Fortinbras is out to avenge injury done to his father. He is a man of action, a

         . . . delicate and tender prince,
Whose spirit with divine ambition puff'd
Makes mouths at the invisible event,

Exposing what is mortal and unsure
To all that fortune, death, and danger dare,
Even for an egg-shell. Rightly to be great
Is not to stir without great argument,
But greatly to find quarrel in a straw
When honour's at the stake. (IV.iv)

As Hamlet fully perceives here, Fortinbras has all the qualities necessary for heroic greatness. This description of Fortinbras is sometimes taken to be mock-heroic, but Hamlet's definition of greatness is one that would have been taken seriously by an Elizabethan audience.

FRANCE, KING OF *(All'sW.)*: he is seemingly incurably ill, but is persuaded by Helena to try her father's remedy; he does so on condition that she loses her life if it fails, and that she will be able to choose a husband from the bachelors at court if it succeeds. He is cured, and she chooses the unwilling Bertram. He laments the supposed death of Helena, and speaks the Epilogue.

FRANCE, KING OF *(H.V)*, see CHARLES VI.

FRANCE, KING OF *(1 H.VI)*, see CHARLES VII.

FRANCE, KING OF *(3 H.VI)*, see LEWIS XI.

FRANCE, KING OF *(John)*, see THE DAUPHIN.

FRANCE, KING OF *(John)*, see PHILIP II.

FRANCE, PRINCESS OF *(H.V)*, see KATHARINE.

FRANCE, PRINCESS OF *(LLL.)*: she arrives with her three ladies 'in embassy' at the court of Navarre. She discovers that her ladies have fallen in love with the courtiers. When the 'Muscovites' woo her and her ladies she is wooed by Berowne in mistake for Rosaline. She embarrasses the King and his courtiers by revealing their mistake, and she rebukes them for breaking their vow. During the 'Pageant of the Nine Worthies' she receives news of her father's death. She says that she will lament in solitude for a year, and tells the King to go to 'some forlorn and naked hermitage' for the same period, after which, if he still loves her, she will marry him.

She is the centre of the play, the upholder of truth and reality in a world of meaningless words. She is dominant in the final act, when she directs the King and his lords away from their word games towards values based on reality.

FRANCIS *(1 H.IV)*: a tapster serving his apprenticeship at the tavern in Eastcheap. He is teased into a state of complete bewilderment by Hal and Poins (II.iv).

FRANCIS, FRIAR *(Ado)*: religious adviser to Leonato. He begins the ceremony at the marriage of Claudio and Hero, but is interrupted by Claudio's tirade against Hero. He asserts his belief in her innocence, and advises her to have it given out that she is dead in order to make Claudio remorseful. At the end he officiates at the wedding of Claudio to the masked Hero, and marries Beatrice and Benedick.

FRANCISCA *(Meas.)*: a nun of the convent where Isabella is a novice, who explains to her some of the restrictions that the order imposes (I.iv).

FRANCISCO *(Ham.)*: a sentry at Elsinore who is relieved at midnight by Barnado *(q.v.)* (I.i).

FRANCISCO *(Tp.)*: attendant lord to Alonso, King of Naples, who is shipwrecked on Prospero's island with him. He attempts to reassure Alonso of his son Ferdinand's safety by reminding him of his prowess as a swimmer (III.iii).

FREDERICK, DUKE *(AYL.)*: the father of Celia; he has usurped his elder brother's title. He admires Orlando's defeat of Charles, his court wrestler, but is annoyed when he discovers that Orlando's family is close to the banished Duke. He banishes his niece Rosalind from the court; she goes, and Frederick's daughter Celia goes with her. He suspects Orlando has joined them and orders Oliver to find them within a year or face banishment. Frederick leads an army into the Forest of Arden intent on killing his brother, but he meets an old hermit who converts him to a religious life. He restores his brother's dukedom and lands.

FRENCH GENTLEMAN, A *(Cym.)*: friend to Philario. He reopens an argument that he had once had with Posthumus, who had insisted that Imogen was more virtuous than any lady in France; Iachimo joins the discussion, which leads to the wager between him and Posthumus (I.v).

FRENCH LORDS, TWO *(All'sW.)*: they ask Bertram to accompany them to the wars (II.i). The first lord supervises the seizure of Parolles, who makes scandalous accusations against them when he is blindfolded (IV.iii). It appears that they are the brothers Dumain.

FROTH *(Meas.)*: 'a foolish gentleman' arrested with the bawd Pompey and brought before Escalus and Angelo. Escalus warns him to beware of tapsters like Pompey, and dismisses him (II.i).

G

GABRIEL *(Shr.)* : one of the servants at Petruchio's country house (IV.i).

GADSHILL *(1 H.IV)* : a robber, who plans to rob the travellers with Bardolph, Peto and Falstaff as his accomplices. He feels that his profession is now enhanced by 'nobility, tranquillity, burgomasters and great oneyers' (II.i). He is told by the chamberlain at the inn at Rochester that the travellers are about to leave, and rides on to join his companions at Gadshill (a place) (II.ii; II.iv).

GALLUS *(Ant.)* : one of Octavius' men, who is sent with Proculeius to the monument to capture Cleopatra (v.i).

GANYMEDE *(AYL.)* : name assumed by Rosalind.

GAOLER *(Err.)* : he takes Egeon into custody (I.i).

GAOLER *(Mer.V.)* : he brings Antonio to Shylock, presumably to plead for mercy, but Shylock refuses to listen, and calls him a 'naughty gaoler' for letting Antonio out of confinement (III.iii).

GAOLER *(Wint.)* : Hermione's gaoler, who will not allow Paulina in to visit her, but agrees to bring her companion Emilia out. When Paulina hears from Emilia of the birth of Perdita she persuades the gaoler to let her take the baby to Leontes (II.ii).

GAOLER (MORTIMER'S) *(1 H.VI)* : he is in attendance when Mortimer is brought in from prison.

GAOLERS, TWO *(Cym.)* : they take Posthumus to prison. The first gaoler explains to him the advantages of being hanged:

> But the comfort is you shall be called to no more payments, fear no more tavern bills, which are often the sadness of parting, as the procuring of mirth. You come in faint for want of meat, depart reeling with too much drink; sorry that you have paid too much, and sorry that you are paid too much; purse

and brain both empty; the brain the heavier for being too light, the purse too light being drawn of heaviness. O, of this contradiction you shall now be quit. O the charity of a penny cord, it sums up thousands in a trice; you have no true debitor and creditor but it; of what's part, is, and to come, the discharge. Your neck sir, is pen, book, and counters; so the acquittance follows. (v.iv)

He is amazed at Posthumus' enthusiasm for death.

GARDENER, A *(R.II)* : he is introduced to present a moralized version of the state of England under Richard, which he compares to a garden:

> . . . O what pity is it
> That he had not so trimmed and dressed his land
> As we this garden. We at time of year
> Do wound the bark, the skin of our fruit trees,
> Lest being over-proud in sap and blood,
> With too much riches it confound itself.
> Had he done so to great and growing men,
> They might have lived to bear, and he to taste
> Their fruits of duty. Superfluous branches
> We lop away, that bearing boughs may live.
> Had he done so, himself had borne the crown,
> Which waste of idle hours hath quite thrown down.
> (III.iv)

This elaborate political allegory is essential to the theme of the play, but it presents a great problem on the modern stage, where sententious gardeners are inclined to appear ludicrous.

GARDINER, STEPHEN, BISHOP OF WINCHESTER *(H.VIII)* : at first secretary to the King, and then Bishop of Winchester. He conspires with other nobles to attack Cranmer as 'a most arch-heretic'. The King intervenes and makes the enemies embrace.

He first came to prominence as Wolsey's private secretary. He was made Bishop of Winchester in 1531, and was a member of the court that invalidated Katharine's marriage. He published the famous oration *De vera Obedienta,* in which he maintained the supremacy of secular princes over the Church. He had a strong dislike for Cranmer; his harsh disposition is well caught by Shakespeare. He was out of favour during Edward's reign, but he was appointed Chancellor after the accession of Mary in 1553. He caused Elizabeth to be declared illegitimate by Act of Parliament.

GARGRAVE, SIR THOMAS *(1 H.VI)*: an English officer serving with Talbot and Salisbury at the siege of Orleans. They are discussing where to attack next when Gargrave and Salisbury are killed by one shot from the young son of the Master Gunner of Orleans (I.iv).

GARTER KING-AT-ARMS *(H.VIII)*: he takes part in the ceremonies at the coronation of Anne Bullen, and in those at the christening of Princess Elizabeth.

He was Thomas Wriothesley (1505–50), head of the College of Arms.

GAUNT, JOHN OF, DUKE OF LANCASTER *(R.II)*: an old man, suffering because Richard has banished his son Bolingbroke. On his death-bed he warns Richard against flatterers, and tells him that his reputation is waning; he utters his famous panegyric on England before he dies (II.i). Richard confiscates all his property as soon as he dies.

He was so called because of his birth at Ghent in 1340. He was the fourth son of Edward III. He was on the Black Prince's expedition to Spain, and distinguished himself at Najera in 1367. He spent many years campaigning in France; in 1371 he was made Lieutenant of Aquitaine. In the closing years of his father's reign, because of the illness of the Prince of Wales he became the leading figure in domestic politics. There was a suspicion that he was aiming at the succession. On the accession of his nephew Richard II he retired from the court. He was recalled to his old post of Lieutenant of Aquitaine, and made a disastrous mess of an attempt to take the town of St Malo. He caused a scandal in 1396 when he married his mistress Catherine Swynford. When Gloucester, Warwick and Arundel united against Richard, Gaunt and his son Henry of Hereford raised a force and defended him; Gaunt took a prominent part in the arrest and trial of these rebel lords. In 1398, after a quarrel with Norfolk, his son was banished. Gaunt died soon afterwards, in 1399.

GENERAL, A FRENCH *(1H.VI)*: the commander of the French garrison at Bordeaux. Talbot demands that he surrender the city, but he refuses, and warns Talbot that the Dauphin's forces are approaching (IV.ii).

GERTRUDE, QUEEN OF DENMARK *(Ham.)*: Hamlet's mother, now wife to Claudius. Her marriage to the brother of her former husband took place only a month after the death of Hamlet's father. She chides her son for his excessive display of grief, and asks him to stay in Denmark. She is pleased to hear that Hamlet appears to be in love with Ophelia; she hopes that it will bring him back to normal. After the play within the play she has an interview with Hamlet in her closet: she begins to rebuke him for his strange behaviour at the play, when he turns on her and attacks her bitterly for her lust and deceit. She cries for help, disturbing the hidden Polonius, who is stabbed by Hamlet. The Ghost of Hamlet's father appears: she cannot see it, and is amazed at Hamlet's behaviour. She says Hamlet's words have 'cleft my heart in twain', but she does not appear to act on them. At the end, she drinks from the poisoned cup intended for Hamlet, thus revealing Claudius' treachery in the moment of her death.

Gertrude is frequently described as a weak character because of her passivity and subservience to Claudius; but it should be remembered that the Elizabethan feminine ideal exalted the passive virtues. She appears innocent of the murder of her former husband, and the suggestion that she is 'adulterate' as the Ghost accuses does not necessarily mean that she had committed adultery with Claudius before her husband's death: the word was frequently used to cover any act that was 'lewd' or 'unchaste'. She is always rather formal when she appears with Claudius; we never see them on intimate terms. Even her hasty marriage makes sense in Elizabethan political terms: the threat of Fortinbras' attack provided a pressing reason for haste in settling the succession. But though a political necessity, her marriage was incestuous; until the twentieth century marriage with a deceased husband's brother was regarded as such in law.

Gertrude is the tool, if not the accomplice, of Claudius. She seems almost incapable of independent action. She has only a few lines of self-revelation:

To my sick soul, as sin's true nature is,
Each toy seems prologue, to some great amiss:
So full of artless jealousy is guilt,
It spills itself, in fearing to be spilt. (IV.v)

Even so, there is no sign that her interview with Hamlet changes her attitude: in Belleforest's story, the Queen becomes an active ally of her son. Ironically, it is Gertrude's one independent action in the play, when she insists on drinking from the poisoned cup, that leads to her death.

It has been suggested that the closet scene, in which Gertrude protests her innocence and promises to help Hamlet, shows evidence of revision in the cause of political expediency. When *Hamlet* appeared Anne of Denmark had become (or was about to become) Queen of England, and it is possible that Shakespeare thought that any Danish queen who appeared on the English

stage at this time would need to be innocent, for the sake of appearances.

GLANSDALE, SIR WILLIAM *(1H.VI)* : an officer in the English army at the siege of Orleans. He sees Salisbury and Gargrave shot (I.iv).

Subsequent to taking up his position as described by Shakespeare, he was thrown into the River Loire when a drawbridge was shattered by a cannon; he drowned due to the weight of his armour.

GLENDOWER, OWEN *(R.II; 1H.IV)* : in *Richard II* he is referred to by Bolingbroke (III.i).

In *1 Henry IV* he fights offstage with Mortimer. He boasts of the wondrous portents at his birth, but is derided by Hotspur. He joins Hotspur's rebellion, but is not present at Shrewsbury. After the battle the King and Prince Henry set off to deal with him.

He was the Welsh rebel Owain ab Gruffydd (b. *c.*1359). He claimed descent from Llewelyn, the last Prince of Wales. He served under Bolingbroke, but rebelled against him when he became king. When Henry went to suppress his revolt, he withdrew, and the English army was forced to give up its expedition for lack of provisions. He remained in revolt until the rebellion in 1403; he failed to join them at Shrewsbury – he is said to have watched the battle from a distant tree. He returned to Wales and continued harassing the English border. His influence gradually waned; he was defeated twice by Prince Henry. He held out in North Wales, and refused the general pardon offered by Henry V. He is thought to have died of starvation in the mountains in about 1416.

GLOUCESTER, DUCHESS OF (Eleanor de Bohun) *(R.II)* : her husband Thomas Woodstock, brother to John of Gaunt, has been murdered at Richard's command. She vainly pleads with Gaunt to take revenge (I.ii). Her death is reported to the Duke of York (II.ii).

She was Eleanor de Bohun (d.1399); she died of grief at the death of her son Humphrey from plague.

GLOUCESTER, DUCHESS OF (Eleanor Cobham) *(2H.VI)* : the second wife of Humphrey, Duke of Gloucester. She wants to be queen, and practises sorcery against the King: she is discovered in the act of invoking spirits, and is banished (I.iv). On her way to exile on the Isle of Man she meets her husband and reproaches him for allowing her disgrace, and warns him of his own impending fall.

left Queen Gertrude (Diana Wynyard) and Hamlet (Peter O'Toole) in the 1963 production of *Hamlet* by the National Theatre Company.

The Duchess of Gloucester is forced to do penance before she is imprisoned for witchcraft and treason *(2 Henry VI)*.

Eleanor Cobham (d.1454) was first mistress and then wife to Humphrey of Gloucester. Through the malignancy of her husband's enemies she was arrested and tried on the ludicrous charges of 'necromancy, witchcraft, heresy, and treason', by means of which she was supposed to have attempted the King's life. Her punishment was rigorous confinement in Chester, Kenilworth, and finally on the Isle of Man, where she is said to have died.

GLOUCESTER, RICHARD, DUKE OF *(2 & 3 H.VI; R.III)*, see RICHARD (PLANTAGENET), LATER RICHARD III.

GLOUCESTER, EARL OF *(Lr.)* : the father of Edgar and the illegitimate Edmund. He is deceived by Edmund's plot against Edgar, and believes that Edgar is planning to kill him. He banishes the loyal Edgar, and turns his affection to Edmund. He finds Lear on the heath, and leads him to shelter. He directs Lear to Dover, but Edmund betrays him to Regan and Cornwall, who blind him and throw him out of his own castle. He is being led by an old man when he meets Edgar, who is in the guise of a mad beggar, and asks him to take him to Dover. He wants to kill himself: Edgar tricks him into believing that he has thrown himself off a high cliff, and been miraculously preserved. He attempts to converse with the mad Lear, and longs to be mad with him. Edgar saves him from capture by Oswald. When Edgar explains to his father that it is he who has been his guide and protector, we hear that it was too much for the old man:

> . . . but his flaw'd heart,
> Alack, too weak the conflict to support!
> 'Twixt two extremes of passion, joy and grief,
> Burst smilingly. (v.iii)

Like Lear, Gloucester is the victim of his own folly. At the very outset we hear him bawdily joking about Edmund's wanton mother – in front of him. He does not 'see' clearly until after he has been blinded, just as Lear reaches insight through madness. After all his suffering, and his bouts of despair, he dies in ecstasy. Edgar, addressing the dying Edmund, sees his father's suffering as a result of his irresponsibility:

> The dark and vicious place where thee he got
> Cost him his eyes. (v.iii)

GLOUCESTER, PRINCE HUMPHREY (later Duke of) *(2H.IV; H.V; 1 & 2H.VI)*: in *2 Henry IV* he is questioned by his father, the King, concerning his brother Prince Henry. He is summoned to his father's death-bed; he condoles with the Lord Chief Justice when Henry is dead (v.ii).

In *Henry V* he is in charge of the siege of Harfleur, but according to Gower is 'altogether directed by' Macmorris (III.ii). In the English camp on the eve of Agincourt he worries about a surprise attack by night (III.vi). He is later said to be at Troyes (v.ii).

In *1 Henry VI* at the lying-in-state of Henry v he accuses the Bishop of Winchester (Beaufort) of desiring a weak monarch; he departs to proclaim the young Henry King (I.i). He is refused admittance to the Tower on Beaufort's orders; when Beaufort arrives, the two quarrel, and their supporters start a fight which is only quelled by the intervention of the Mayor (I.iii). Later, another bitter altercation with Beaufort leads to a similar brawl; subsequently Gloucester unwillingly agrees to a truce with him (III.i). He is in Paris as 'Lord Protector' at Henry's coronation when he hears of the Duke of Burgundy's defection (IV.i). He advocates Henry's marriage to the daughter of the Earl of Armagnac, and opposes his projected marriage to Margaret of Anjou (v.v).

In *2 Henry VI* Gloucester breaks down while attempting to read the articles of peace with France: he makes an emotional speech to the peers lamenting the shameful loss of Maine and Anjou (I.i). He is accused of malfeasance as Protector; he suggests that York be made Regent in France (I.iii). He detects that Simpcox is an impostor; he is appalled to hear that the Duchess of Gloucester has been accused of witchcraft. He hears sentence pronounced against her, and is deprived of his office of Protector. He is warned by his wife that he is not safe, but he ignores her warning (II.iv). He is arrested for high treason: he protests his innocence, but is taken into custody. The King laments him when his death is announced; the body shows signs that suggest he was strangled (III.ii).

Gloucester was incongruously known as 'the good Duke Humphrey'; neither his personal qualities nor his ability as a statesman indicate that he warranted the epithet. He is supposed to have ruined his constitution by his dissipation before he was thirty. He fought successfully at Agincourt, and the experience seems to have led him to believe that war was the right solution to political problems. Unfortunately, this belief was combined with an intense personal ambition and desire for self-aggrandisement.

Shakespeare's Gloucester is the figure of contemporary popular tradition, which saw him as a warm-hearted, bluff patriot. History shows him to have been unprincipled, factious and blindly selfish.

Gloucester's death by foul play also belongs only to tradition. In this, Shakespeare modifies Holinshed, who wrote that Gloucester 'was found dead in his bed, and his bodie shewed the lords and commons, as though he had died of a palsie, or of an imposteme'.

GOBBO, LANCELOT *(Mer.V.)*: 'a clown', servant to Shylock. He decides to yield to the promptings of the 'fiend' and leave his master's service for that of Bassanio. He helps Lorenzo abduct Jessica, and accompanies Bassanio to Belmont.

Lancelot Gobbo's role is that of messenger and buffoon. He is a 'wit-snapper'; he is absurdly loquacious, and pours out a stream of word-play mixed with misusages and mispronunciations. For all his words, he has very little to say, as Lorenzo points out:

> The fool hath planted in his memory
> An army of good words, and I do know
> A many fools that stand in better place,
> Garnish'd like him, that for a tricksy word
> Defy the matter. (III.v)

GOBBO, (OLD) *(Mer.V.)*: father to Lancelot Gobbo. He is purblind, he does not even recognize his own son at first. He has prepared a dish of doves for Shylock, but his son persuades him to present it to Bassanio (II.ii).

GONERIL *(Lr.)*: the eldest daughter of King Lear, and wife to the Duke of Albany. She professes her great love for Lear, which she knows is what he wants to hear, and is awarded a third of the kingdom. She orders her steward, Oswald, to see that Lear is treated with disrespect. She sneers at her father, and ignores his curses. Her sister Regan cooperates with her against him; at Gloucester's castle they refuse to allow Lear to enter with his train, and send him out into the storm (III.vii). Goneril suggests that Gloucester be blinded, but leaves with Edmund before it happens. She quarrels with Albany, who she despises as a 'milk-liver'd man'. She now loves Edmund, but fears that her sister may prove a rival when she hears that Cornwall is dead. She writes to Edmund, reminding him of her love, and suggesting that he kill Albany. The letter falls into Edgar's hands. After the battle she quarrels with Regan over Edmund, and has her poisoned. She sees the death of Edmund, and shortly afterwards it is announced that she has stabbed herself.

Goneril is the more sensual of the two evil sisters, and the more unnaturally cold and pitiless in her cruelty. She is indifferent to all other claims than her own self-interest. Her predatory nature is stressed by the frequent application of animal imagery to her.

GONZAGO (DUKE) AND WIFE (BAPTISTA) *(Ham.)* : parts assumed by Players *q.v.* (III.ii).

GONZALO *(Tp.)* : 'an honest old counsellor' who had provided Prospero and Miranda with 'rich garments, linens, stuffs and necessaries' and above all with books (which Prospero prized above his dukedom) when they were cast off to drown. On the island, he is saved from being murdered by Antonio and Sebastian by the intervention of Ariel. At the end he is affectionately greeted by Prospero as 'good Gonzalo/My true preserver'.

Gonzalo is inspired by the island into outlining the kind of ideal commonwealth he would like to build there (II.i): the sketch follows closely a passage in Florio's translation of Montaigne's *Essais*.

'It may be observed of Gonzalo, that, being the only good Man that appears with the King, he is the only Man that preserves his cheerfulness in the wreck, and his Hope on the Island.' (Johnson)

GOODFELLOW, ROBIN *(MND.)*, *see* PUCK.

GOTHS *(Tit.)* : the barbaric German tribe defeated by Titus at the beginning of the play. Ironically it is to them that Titus has to turn when he wishes to be revenged on Saturninus and Tamora: he sends Lucius to them for help, and he returns at the head of their army (v.i; v.iii).

GOUGH, MATTHEW *(2H.VI)* : a soldier, veteran of the many French campaigns. Lord Scales sends him to lead the citizens of London against Cade's rebels; he is killed in the first encounter (4.vii).

GOWER *(2H.IV)* : one of the King's attendants. He tells the Lord Chief Justice of the imminent arrival of the King and Prince Henry (II.i).

GOWER *(H.V)* : an officer in Henry's army. He intervenes in the quarrel between Fluellen and Macmorris (III.ii). His main function is to serve as an audience to Fluellen, and to restrain him. Fluellen tells Henry that 'Gower is a good captain, and is good knowledge and literatured in the wars' (IV.vii).

GOWER, THE POET *(Per.)* : he acts as Chorus, speaking a Prologue to each Act, and an Epilogue to the play.

Presumably the English poet John Gower (c.1325–1408) is intended. His speeches in the play are in the same metre as the poet's *Confessio Amantis*, which also contains the source of much of the story of *Pericles*.

GRANDPRÉ *(H.V)* : a French lord. We hear that he has measured the distance between the two armies (III.vii). He enters and urges the French lords to arms with a description of the sorry state of the English:

Yond island carrions, desperate of their bones,
Ill-favouredly become the morning field;
Their ragged curtains poorly are let loose,
And our air shakes them passing scornfully.
Big Mars seems bankrout in their beggar'd host,
And faintly through a rusty beaver peeps. (IV.ii)

Grandpré is listed among those killed at Agincourt (IV.viii).

GRATIANO *(Mer.V.)* : a garrulous and volatile friend of Bassanio and Antonio. He goes to Belmont with Bassanio, where he meets and courts Nerissa, Portia's maid-servant. He marries her. She deceives him into giving up a ring which he had sworn never to part with when she appears in disguise as a lawyer's clerk; she teases him with accusations of unfaithfulness before revealing the deception.

Bassanio comments that Gratiano 'speaks an infinite deal of nothing'.

GRATIANO *(Oth.)* : brother to Brabantio, and uncle to Desdemona. He appears at the end and finds Cassio and Roderigo wounded, and then discovers that Desdemona has been murdered. He indicates that Brabantio has already died of grief at his daughter's marriage to Othello. He is told by Lodovico to take possession of the Moor's fortune (v.ii). He is generally bewildered by the chaos that surrounds him.

GRAVEDIGGERS *(Ham.)*: they joke earthily while digging Ophelia's grave. Hamlet and Horatio come upon the First Gravedigger just as he has unearthed the skull of Yorick, the old court jester. Hamlet's meditations on mortality and decay are punctuated by the Gravediggers' grim jokes.

GREEN *(R.II)*: with Bagot and Bushy, one of the sycophantic 'creatures to King Richard'.

Sir Henry Green was one of the six commoners appointed by Richard along with twelve peers to act as commissioners in 1398. They were invested with the whole power of the Lords and Commons.

GREGORY *(Rom.)*: servant to Capulet. He and his fellow-servant Sampson quarrel with two of Montague's servants, and a fight breaks out which is joined by Tybalt and Benvolio (I.i). (*See* ABRAHAM.)

GREGORY *(Shr.)*: one of the servants at Petruchio's country house (IV.i).

GREMIO *(Shr.)*: an elderly and wealthy suitor to Bianca. He gets 'Cambio' (the disguised Lucentio) the post of tutor to her, on the understanding that he will woo her on his behalf; Lucentio woos and wins her for himself. He gives a marvellous description of Petruchio's 'mad marriage' to Katharina:

> . . . For why, he stamped and swore,
> As if the vicar meant to cozen him.
> But after many ceremonies done,
> He calls for wine. A health quoth he, as if
> He had been aboard, carousing to his mates
> After a storm; quaffed off the muscadel,
> And threw the sops all in the sexton's face;
> Having no other reason,
> But that his beard grew thin and hungerly,
> And seemed to ask him sops as he was drinking.
> This done, he took the bride about the neck,
> And kissed her lips with such a clamorous smack,
> That at the parting all the church did echo. (III.ii)

In the Folio stage directions he is 'Gremio a Pantelowne'.

GREY, LADY *(3 H.VI; R.III)*, *see* ELIZABETH WOODVILLE.

GREY, LORD *(R.III)*: along with Lord Rivers he is imprisoned at Pomfret Castle and executed on Richard's orders (III.iii). His ghost appears to Richard before Bosworth.

He was the youngest son of Elizabeth, the queen of Edward IV, by her former husband Sir John Grey. He had charge of the young Edward V for a time after the death of Edward IV. He was arrested by Richard after dining with him in apparent friendship; Richard disliked his loyalty to Edward V. He was executed without trial in Pomfret Castle in 1485.

GREY, THOMAS *(R.III)*, *see* DORSET, MARQUESS OF.

GREY, SIR THOMAS *(H.V)*: one of the would-be assassins, along with Richard Cambridge and Lord Scroop, who are bribed by the French to kill the King. The plot is discovered and the three traitors are executed (II.ii).

He was the second son of Sir Thomas Grey of Berwick, the Constable of Norham Castle. His execution for treason was in 1415.

GRIFFITH *(H.VIII)*: Queen Katharine's gentleman-usher. He describes Wolsey's last hours to the dying Katharine. He eulogizes the dead Cardinal, and remains with Katharine while she sleeps and dreams (IV.ii).

GROOM OF THE STABLE, A *(R.II)*: Richard's loyal servant, who visits him in prison in Pontefract Castle. He tells Richard sadly that Bolingbroke rode his favourite horse 'roan Barbary' at the coronation (V.v).

GRUMIO *(Shr.)*: Petruchio's manservant, an 'ancient, trusty, pleasant servant' (I.ii). He gives a humorous description of his tribulations while accompanying Katharina and Petruchio on their journey from Padua to Petruchio's country home (IV.i).

GUIDERIUS *(Cym.)*: the eldest son of Cymbeline, brother of Arviragus and Imogen. He has been stolen from home at the age of three, and is living as the son of Belarius under the name Polydore. He dislikes the quiet life he is leading in their Welsh cave. He meets and fights with Cloten, and returns with his head, which he throws into a stream. He persuades Belarius to fight for the British against the Romans. He is sentenced to death by Cymbeline for the killing of Cloten, but is saved by the birthmark which proves his identity.

Guiderius and Arviragus are conventional romantic princes.

GUILDENSTERN *(Ham.)*: a student acquaintance of Hamlet. Together with his inseparable companion

right Hamlet (V.i): The gravediggers.

Rosencrantz (John Stride) and Guildenstern (Edward
Petherbridge) in Tom Stoppard's play *Rosencrantz
and Guildenstern are Dead* by the National Theatre
Company.

Rosencrantz he is invited by Claudius to spy on
Hamlet. After Hamlet kills Polonius, Claudius sends
him to England accompanied by Guildenstern and
Rosencrantz carrying sealed orders for his death.
Hamlet substitutes their names for his in the orders,
and they meet their deaths in England.

He and Rosencrantz have little existence outside
their function in the plot. Tom Stoppard created
personalities for them in his play *Rosencrantz and
Guildenstern are Dead.*

GUILDFORD, SIR HENRY *(H.VIII)*: as 'comp-
troller' at Wolsey's feast he welcomes the lady guests
(I.iv).

GURNEY, JAMES *(John)*: servant to Lady
Faulconbridge. He accompanies her to court (I.i).

H

HABERDASHER, A *(Shr.)* : he delivers a hat that Petruchio has ordered for Katharina, only to have it rejected :

Why this was moulded on a porringer ;
A velvet dish, Fie, fie, 'tis lewd and filthy,
Why 'tis a cockle or a walnut shell,
A knack, a toy, a trick, a baby's cap.
Away with it, come, let me have a bigger. (IV.iii)

This poor tradesman is quite bemused by his unwitting involvement in Petruchio's stratagems.

HAL, PRINCE *(1&2 H.IV)*, *see* HENRY, PRINCE OF WALES.

HAMLET *(Ham.)* : the Prince of Denmark, son of the recently deceased King Hamlet and his consort, Queen Gertrude, is a studious young man who has been excluded from the Danish throne by his uncle Claudius ; but just how this has happened the dramatist never makes completely clear, since Hamlet, the legitimate successor, has already come of age. Besides usurping his nephew's position, Claudius, after an indecently short interval, has taken his amorous sister-in-law to wife. Hamlet is a lonely figure at court, reluctant to share the drunken festivities that his coarse-minded uncle loves and presently he is informed by Horatio that the ghost of the late King, 'in the dead vast and middle of the night', has appeared upon the battlements of Elsinore. Hamlet himself resolves to encounter the ghost, despite his companions' warning bravely follows it along the ramparts, and learns that, although the dead man is reputed to have been killed by a serpent's bite while he lay sleeping in his orchard, it was his brother who had poisoned him. Hamlet then engages to avenge the crime, though he has promised that he will spare the Queen, and, as a sensitive, irresolute character he cannot yet determine what his course of action ought to be. Earlier, Claudius and Gertrude have reproached him with his surly attitude and intemperate displays of grief. Now he sets out to transform his whole existence :

> . . . from the table of my memory

A female Hamlet: Sarah Bernhardt.

> I'll wipe away all trivial fond records,
> All saws of books, all forms, all pressures past,
> That youth and observation copied there . . . (I.v)

Henceforward Hamlet is a changed man ; and his first move is to cast off Ophelia, child of the ancient courtier, Polonius, a girl whom he had previously wooed. His appearance alarms her ; his doublet, she tells Polonius, was 'all unbraced', his stockings 'down-gyved to his ankle' ; he wore a look of ghastly sorrow ; at which Polonius immediately concludes that the distraught young Prince has lost his wits. This opinion he imparts to Claudius and Gertrude ; and their

113

alarm increases when a troupe of actors arrives, and Hamlet stages a play in which Claudius' murder of the King is represented to the life. 'Frightened with false fire', Claudius betrays his guilt. Conscience-stricken, he retires to pray. But Hamlet, though the moment has come for revenge – 'now I might do it pat, now he is praying' – shrinks from executing him upon his knees. Instead, he enters his mother's closet and, hearing the voice of Polonius behind the arras, draws his sword and runs the old man through. Apparently, the killing causes him no remorse; and, when the Queen protests at his 'rash and bloody deed', his reply is no less brutal:

A bloody deed! almost as bad, good mother,

As kill a king, and marry with his brother. (III.iv)

He then proceeds to excoriate Gertrude by reminding her of all her sins and the adulterous lusts that have inspired them, showing her the miniature portrait that

Hamlet (v.i): 'Alas, poor Yorick!'. From an eighteenth-century engraving.

hangs around his neck of the noble husband she has lost.

Claudius now resolves to send Hamlet to England – 'how dangerous it is this man goes loose' – where he plans to have him slain. The Prince obeys, but outwits his two treacherous travelling-companions, Rosencrantz and Guilderstern, who are themselves assassinated, and presently sails back to Denmark, where he finds that Ophelia has gone mad and, in her pathetic distraction, has committed suicide by drowning. As his last throw, Claudius arranges a trial of swordsmanship between Hamlet and Ophelia's brother, Laertes, in which Laertes' weapon is to be a poisoned and unbuttoned rapier. *'Laertes wounds Hamlet* [the stage-directions read]; *then in scuffling, they change rapiers, and Hamlet wounds Laertes.'* When the poison works, and Laertes falls, his assailant turns upon the King, but not until Gertrude has succumbed to the deadly draught that Claudius has prepared for Hamlet. The Prince himself dies of the wound he has received in the arms of his beloved friend Horatio, murmuring as his last words that 'the rest is silence'.

Like *Lear*, Shakespeare's *Hamlet* was founded on an old play, a typical 'revenge-play', now lost, probably the work of Thomas Kyd, performed in 1594; while an even earlier play concerning the Prince of Denmark was already popular about 1589. There Hamlet evidently pretended to be mad merely to disarm the King's suspicions and enable him to penetrate the royal guard; Shakespeare gives his conduct a far deeper psychological significance. The Prince may at first have feigned madness; but, as when he wantonly kills Polonius, and brutalizes the innocent Ophelia, something akin to madness seems gradually to overtake him. Shakespeare also began by portraying a well-known Elizabethan type, 'the malcontent', a personage often described both in contemporary pamphlets and in learned books on medicine. The malcontent was sometimes a returned traveller, who found nothing English to his taste. He and the unhappy Prince adopt the same garb; he would 'walk melancholy' with his arms folded, his hose ungartered and his hat pulled down, 'not affable in speech, or apt to vulgar compliments, but surly, dull, sad, austere'. This type Shakespeare enlarged and subtilized, making it the basis of an extraordinarily individual portrait. Hamlet is no affected melancholic; the clue to his tragedy is his irresolution; he combines a belief in his own superiority – he is gifted, attractive, a favourite of the Danish people – with a gnawing sense of inward weakness. Again and again he fails to keep the promise

right Edmund Kean (1787–1833) as Hamlet.

above John Gielgud as Hamlet, at the Lyceum
Theatre, 1939.

right Laurence Olivier as Hamlet and Jean Simmons as
Ophelia in Olivier's 1947 film of *Hamlet*.

the he had made to his murdered father's spirit; and it needs the ghost's repeated admonitions to resharpen his 'almost blunted purpose'. *Hamlet*, which followed an equally pessimistic play, *Troilus and Cressida*, was advertised as 'latelie Acted' in the month of July, 1602.

HAMLET, KING OF DENMARK, GHOST OF *(Ham.)*: the ghost of Hamlet's father. It appears before Horatio, but will not speak to him. On the following night Hamlet speaks to it; it tells him that his father was poisoned by Claudius, who had already seduced Gertrude, and enjoins him to revenge. From beneath the stage it reminds Hamlet of his oath. Later it appears before Hamlet when it seems he is about to injure his mother (III.iv).

With its military garb, and its violent language, this is a malevolent ghost. Marcellus' speech when it has 'started, like a guilty thing' at the sound of the cock suggests that in Christian terms it is an evil presence. When it is heard in the cellarage beneath the stage it certainly acts like a devil, though this episode has never been adequately explained. And it could be said that on its second appearance it prevents Hamlet from driving Gertrude to repentance (and thus saving herself from damnation), and urges him to think only of revenge on Claudius. It is unlike the usual ghosts of stage tradition, and is very difficult to stage satisfactorily. We are usually shown either a creaking monster or an eerie-voiced shadow, instead of the terrifying warlike 'thing' that scares Horatio.

HARCOURT *(2 H.IV)*: an officer who brings Henry news of the defeat of Northumberland and Lord Bardolph (IV.iv).

HARFLEUR, GOVERNOR OF *(H.V)*: he sends to the Dauphin for troops to help lift the siege of his

left An outstanding modern Hamlet: David Warner in the Royal Shakespeare Company's 1965 production of *Hamlet* at Stratford.

above A nineteenth-century Hamlet: Henry Irving in the production at the Lyceum Theatre in 1874, confronting the Ghost.

town, but his request is refused because the French army is unprepared, and he surrenders the town to Henry (III.iii).

HASTINGS, LORD *(2 H.IV)*: one of the rebel leaders. He favours accepting Prince John's offer of peace. When the rebel forces have been dispersed, the treacherous nature of John's offer is revealed, and Hastings is sent to execution along with Mowbray and the Archbishop.

He was Sir Ralph Hastings, not Lord. According to some writers he was spared.

HASTINGS, LORD *(3 H.VI; R.III)*: in *3 Henry VI* a loyal supporter of Edward IV. He escapes when Edward is captured by Warwick (IV.iii), and helps Edward escape from Middleham Castle (IV.v).

In *Richard III*, although the Queen and her family are his enemies, he refuses to help Gloucester gain the throne; Richard calls him 'a simple gull'. At the outset (I.i) he has just been released from prison; it is later imputed (by Richard) that the Queen was behind his imprisonment. At the coronation council (III.iv) Richard flatters him, and then denounces him as a traitor and protector of the witch and strumpet Jane Shore, and orders his immediate execution (III.v). His head is brought to Richard. His ghost appears to Richard before Bosworth (V.iii).

He was Sir William Hastings, (*c.* 1430–82), a devoted Yorkist. He was ennobled by Edward IV in 1461. He was with Edward at Barnet, and is said to have taken part in the murder of the young Prince Edward. He was devoted to Edward's children, and refused to help Richard in his attempts to gain the crown. Shakepeare follows history closely in his account of Richard's removal of Hastings.

HECATE *(Mac.)*: the goddess of the moon, earth and underworld (often represented as a three-headed monster), and ruler of all demons and witches. She appears to chide the witches for taking it upon themselves to 'trade and traffic with Macbeth' (III.v).

Two of the songs in the Hecate scenes are from Thomas Middleton's play *The Witch*, which has led to the suggestion that the entire scenes are interpolations by him. However Shakespeare's Hecate is quite unlike Middleton's, and she speaks in a similar manner to other Shakespearian theophanies, so that it is reasonable to argue for Shakespeare as author of her scenes.

HECTOR *(Troil.)*: he advocates restoring Helen to the Greeks, but yields to the majority opinion (II.ii). He meets Ajax in single combat, but stops fighting when he remembers their kinship. He ignores

Cassandra's prophetic vision of his death, and goes out to fight. He encounters Achilles, but they do not fight; he spares Thersites. He pursues a sumptuously armoured Greek; while he is resting he is surrounded by Achilles' Myrmidons and killed.

Hector is the noble hero of the play, the ancient hero equipped with a full set of chivalric virtues. His behaviour in the Trojan council is surprising: he perceives the truth, and presents a carefully reasoned case for returning Helen, but then suddenly endorses the opposite opinion. He appears to put chivalric obligation above the reason and justice he has so tellingly appealed to. In this, and in his insistence on going out to fight in spite of all the warnings, he appears as something of a self-deceiver. On the battlefield he is the mighty warrior of Homeric tradition, with a power that rivals natural forces:

> There is a thousand Hectors in the field:
> Now here he fights on Galathe his horse,
> And there lacks work: anon he's there afoot,
> And there they fly or die, like scaled sculls,
> Before the belching whale; then he is yonder,
> And there the strawy Greeks, ripe for his edge,
> Fall down before him, like the mower's wrath;
> Here, there, and everywhere, he leaves and takes;
> Dexterity so obeying appetite,
> That what he will, he does, and does so much,
> That proof is call'd impossibility. (V.v)

Hector was the eldest son of Priam and Hecuba, and Troy's most illustrious warrior. In the *Iliad*, he is wounded by Ajax and cured by Apollo; the god encourages him to slay Patroclus. Achilles chased him three times round the walls of Troy before killing him and dragging his body behind his chariot. In medieval romance, Hector was the flower of chivalry; his wisdom and moderation were equal to his strength. In Caxton's version of the Troy story, it is Troilus who is surrounded and killed by the Myrmidons. For the Elizabethans, who regarded the Trojans as ancestors, Hector was the hero of the war.

HELEN *(Cym.)*: a lady attending Imogen (II.ii).

HELEN *(Troil.)*: the daughter of Zeus and Leda, and the wife of Menelaus. Her abduction to Troy by Paris is the cause of the war. We hear that she is the 'mortal Venus, the heart-blood of beauty, love's invisible soul' (III.i). When she appears she is a flirt, who thinks of little else but love. Diomedes' bitter assessment of her role in the war is borne out by the play:

> She's bitter to her country: hear me Paris,
> For every false drop in her bawdy veins,
> A Grecian's life hath sunk: for every scruple
> Of her contaminated carrion weight,
> A Troyan hath been slain. Since she could speak,

She hath not given so many good words breath,
As for her, Greeks and Troyans suffer'd death.
(IV.i)

HELENA *(All'sW.)*: the orphan daughter of a famous doctor, now a gentlewoman under the protection of the Countess of Rousillon. She goes to Paris and offers to cure the mortally ill King with a remedy she has inherited from her father; she is allowed to try, with death as her reward if she fails, and the choice of a husband from any of the bachelors at court if she succeeds. She succeeds, and chooses Bertram; he unwillingly accepts her, and quickly abandons her, leaving her a cruel letter. She leaves Rousillon secretly and goes to Florence disguised as a pilgrim; she sees Bertram with the army (III.v). She finds that Bertram claims to love Diana Capilet, and persuades her widowed mother to allow her to replace Diana in bed (Bertram had scornfully told her that he would accept her if she could get a ring from his finger and conceive his child). Bertram remains unaware that he has spent the night with his wife. When Helena's death is announced to him, he remains unmoved. At the end, in the presence of the King, a pregnant Helena appears and produces Bertram's ring; Bertram acknowledges her as his wife.

For Coleridge she was Shakespeare's 'loveliest character'; Hazlitt admired her: 'She is placed in circumstances of the most critical kind, and has to court her husband both as a virgin and a wife: yet the most scrupulous nicety of female modesty is not once violated. There is not one thought or action that ought to bring a blush into her cheeks, or that for a moment lessens her in our esteem.' This perhaps suggests that she is more insipid than she really is: the intensity of her passion for Bertram is the mainspring of the play.

HELENA *(MND.)*: an Athenian maid in love with Demetrius, who loves Hermia. She follows Demetrius when he pursues Hermia into the wood (II.i); she finds Lysander asleep, and under the influence of Puck's love-charm he falls in love with her when he wakes up. Owing to Puck's muddled magic, the same thing happens to Demetrius. With both men claiming to love her she becomes suspicious, and suspects that they have contrived a joke at her expense. In the end she awakes to find that Demetrius alone loves her, while Lysander is united with Hermia (IV.i).

HELENUS *(Troil.)*: a priest, son of Priam, King of Troy. He takes part in the debate on Helen, and agrees

above Helena *(All's Well that Ends Well)* by J. W. Wright and B. Eyles *(left)*; *A Midsummer Night's*

Dream: Helena and Hermia, by Sir Edward J. Poynter *(right)*.

with Hector that Helen should be given up; he is fiercely rebuked by Troilus, who tells him 'You fur your gloves with reason' (II.ii).

HELICANUS *(Per.)*: an old lord of Tyre who Pericles leaves to govern in his place while he goes to Tarsus. Because of Pericles' long absence it is suggested that he should take over the throne, but he refuses, and insists that the search for Pericles is continued. In the Epilogue Gower calls him 'A figure of truth, of faith, of loyalty'.

HENRY BOLINGBROKE, DUKE OF HERE-FORD (later Henry IV) *(R.II; 1&2 H.IV)*: in *Richard II* as Bolingbroke, he accuses Mowbray before Richard of being a traitor. A judicial combat between him and Mowbray is arranged by, and then stopped by the King, who condemns Bolingbroke to exile for ten years (later reduced to six), and makes him take an oath never to plot against the King or to be reconciled to Mowbray (I.iii). He goes to Brittany, and returns with an army to claim the patrimony that Richard had appropriated on the death of his father John of Gaunt. He tells Richard that he will lay down his arms if his exile is repealed and his patrimony restored, and professes loyalty. When he hears from

York that Richard will abdicate, he ascends the throne. He commits Richard to the Tower, where he is murdered by Pierce of Exton who is seeking to please the new King. Bolingbroke, now Henry IV, plans a crusade to Jerusalem to purge his guilt.

In *1 Henry IV* he is contemplating his crusade when he hears of the successes of the rebellion led by Hotspur (I.i). He criticizes his son Hal for his loose living, but, impressed by his contrition, he gives him command against the rebels. At the Battle of Shrewsbury Henry is overcome by Douglas, and is only saved by the intervention of Hal. After the battle Henry condemns all the rebels (except Douglas) to death.

In *2 Henry IV* Henry's conscience still troubles him: his nights are sleepless, and he longs to go to the Holy Land. Even the defeat of the rebels in the North does not calm his spirit. While he is asleep, Hal enters the room and takes the crown, and contemplates it; Henry awakes and thinks his son has anticipated his death, and is angry (IV.v). Hal explains his conduct, and his father forgives him; the two are reconciled, and Hal accepts his father's advice. Henry still wants to die in Jerusalem: when he feels that he is dying, he asks to be taken to the Jerusalem Chamber, where he dies.

Bolingbroke is Shakespeare's Machiavellian King, the master of dissimulation for political ends. Early on in *Richard II*, the King says he had:

> Observ'd his courtship of the common people;
> How he did seem to dive into their hearts
> With humble and familiar courtesy;
> What reverence he did throw away on slaves,
> Wooing poor craftsmen with the craft of smiles
> And patient underbearing of his fortune,
> As 'twere to banish their affects with him.

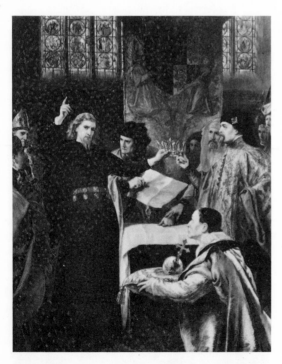

above Richard II: the deposition scene (IV.i). Richard resigns the crown to Henry Bolingbroke. A painting by Sir J. Gilbert *(left).* Henry Bolingbroke (1367–1413)

receives the dukes of Exeter and Surrey at Chester. From an early French history of the reign of Richard II *(right).*

Off goes his bonnet to an oyster-wench;
A brace of draymen bid God speed him well
And had the tribute of his supple knee,
With 'Thanks, my countrymen, my loving friends.'
(I.iv)

Enlistment of the common people was one of Machiavelli's basic precepts for the would-be ruler.

In the *Henry IV* plays, Bolingbroke, now Henry IV, is haunted by his usurpation:

God knows, my son,
By what bypaths and indirect crook'd ways
I met this crown; and I myself know well
How troublesome it sat upon my head.
(2 H.IV, IV.v)

His usurpation, and the murder of the legitimate king, has brought instability to the realm and despair to him. He sees that his guilt may be purged by his son – but, in a characteristic moment, reminds him that he will need some strategy to help him:

... Therefore, my Harry,
Be it thy course to busy giddy minds
With foreign quarrels; that action, hence borne out,
May waste the memory of the former days.
(2 H.IV, IV.v)

The first part of *Henry IV* was probably written in the later part of 1596, with the second part following shortly afterwards in early 1597.

HENRY, EARL OF RICHMOND (later Henry VII) *(3 H.VI; R.III)*: in *3 Henry VI* he appears as a youth. Henry VI predicts that this 'pretty lad' will wear a crown and 'prove our country's bliss' ((IV.vi).

In *Richard III* he is in Brittany, where he is joined by Dorset and the Bishop of Ely. He sets sail for England, and lands in Wales. He plans to fight at Bosworth field; he is encouraged by the ghosts of Richard's victims, who appear to him in his sleep. He kills Richard in the battle, and has the crown placed on his head by Derby. He prays for peace under the united Roses (v.v).

According to Holinshed, he was 'so formed and decorated with all gifts and lineaments of nature, that he seemed more an angelicall creature, than a terrestriall personage'.

HENRY, PRINCE (afterwards Henry III) *(John)*: he appears in the last scene (v.vii), and is present at his father's death; Salisbury proclaims him king, and appears to see in him someone who will redeem the failures of his father:

... for you are born
To set a form upon that indigest
Which he hath left so shapeless, and so rude. (v.vii)

HENRY, PRINCE OF WALES (later Henry v)

Henry v (1387–1422), King of England.

(1 & 2 H.IV; H.V; 1 H.VI): in *1 Henry IV* he appears as the Prince of Wales, and is known as Hal to his friends. With Poins he plans a joke on Falstaff (I.ii), but reflects that he will shortly throw off his 'loose behaviour' and 'show more goodly'. He and Poins attack Falstaff and his fellow robbers and carry off their booty (II.ii). He reveals his trick to Falstaff, and then attacks him in the role of his father (III.ii). He is himself admonished by his father, and he promises to reform; he is given command against Hotspur's rebels. He meets and kills Hotspur at the Battle of Shrewsbury, and rescues the King from Douglas.

In *2 Henry IV* Hal is with Poins planning another joke at Falstaff's expense when he hears that the King is at Westminster, and feels 'much to blame'; he leaves the tavern. He is watching at his father's bedside and, believing him dead, takes the crown. His father wakes and rebukes him, but he explains that his motives were innocent (IV.v). After his father's death, as Henry v, he is accosted by Falstaff during the coronation procession: he banishes the fat knight from his presence, and commits him to the custody of the Chief Justice.

In *Henry V* Henry's reformed character is praised by the Archbishop of Canterbury (I.i), who then

Henry V, his Queen and his family. A French engraving
by Grignion, after a manuscript painting.

persuades him to claim his rights in France. He sends
a defiant reply, declaring war, to the Dauphin's
insulting message and present of tennis balls (II.ii).
At Southampton Henry condemns Scroop, Grey and
Cambridge to death for plotting against his life. At
Harfleur he inspires his men to further attacks with
the famous speech 'Once more unto the breach . . .'
(III.i). In the English camp on the night before Agincourt Henry disguises himself and passes among his
troops; he is troubled by the weight of kingly responsibility. Before the battle he inspires his army with
a stirring speech (IV.vi); after the battle he orders all
the French prisoners killed. He meets the French
court at Troyes, and arranges a treaty; he woos
Princess Katharine, to whom he is formally betrothed
as part of the peace agreement.

In *1 Henry VI,* the play opens with the funeral of
Henry V (I.i).

We first hear of Hal in *Richard II,* when Bolingbroke
asks after his 'unthrifty son'. We first see him in
1 Henry IV, in the underworld of the tavern. From the
outset, his seriousness is established. His intentions
are deliberate and calculated:

I know you all, and will awhile uphold
The unyoked humour of your idleness.
Yet herein I will imitate the sun,
Who doth permit the base contagious clouds
To smother up his beauty from the world,
Than when he please again to be himself,
Being wanted he may be more wondered at
By breaking through the foul and ugly mists
Of vapours that did seem to strangle him . . .

So when this loose behaviour I throw off,
And pay the debt I never promised,
By how much better than my word I am,
By so much shall I falsify men's hopes,
And like bright metal on a sulten ground,
My reformation glittering o'er my fault,

a good king. When he banishes Falstaff, Hal is the perfect king, if not the perfect man – he cannot be both. And we may perhaps excuse him further, for the Fleet was the prison where Elizabeth constantly sent courtiers and ladies who had incurred her displeasure, and it could be that for an Elizabethan audience

above Lewis Waller as Henry v *(left)*; Laurence Olivier as Henry v in the 1944 film of Shakespeare's *Henry V* which was also directed by Olivier *(right)*.

Shall show more goodly, and attract more eyes,
Than that which hath no foil to set it off.
(1 H.IV, I.ii)

For this deliberate deception Hal has been branded a hypocrite; but this speech is obviously not intended as a piece of self-revelation so much as an explanation to the audience of what is really going on. There is no doubt that Hal's attitude towards Falstaff is consistent throughout. Falstaff simply does not attend to the mordant comments that are mixed with Hal's jokes; and in the mock trial, when Falstaff asks if Hal will banish him, he receives a chilling reply: 'I do, I will.' Hal is seen as a prig for his treatment of Falstaff, but Falstaff (as the side of his character exposed in *2 Henry IV* indicates) represents the anarchy and vice that have to be rejected in favour of the rule of law under

Falstaff's punishment was not utterly dishonourable.

At the end of *2 Henry IV*, and in *Henry V*, Hal is the God-chosen king celebrated by the Tudor historians, the 'mirror of all Christian kings'. For Hall, 'He was the blazing comet and apparent lantern in his days; he was a mirror of Christendom and the glory of his country; he was the flower of kings past, and a glass to them that should succeed. No Emperor in magnanimity ever him excelled.'

This is essentially Shakespeare's view, though Hazlitt found Shakespeare's Henry suggestive of 'an amiable monster', and Yeats of 'some handsome spirited horse'. But though we may not find him attractive, Henry has the essential features of the ideal medieval king (as did the historical Henry for his contemporaries); and to say that Henry represents

Shakespeare's ideal king is not the same as saying he represents his ideal man. Henry is aware, as is Shakespeare, of the limitations set upon his humanity by the crown. He cannot be like other men:

> Upon the king – let us our lives, our souls,
> Our debts, our careful wives,
> Our children, and our sins, lay on the king.
> We must bear all. O hard condition,
> Twin-born with greatness, subject to the breath
> Of every fool, whose sense no more can feel
> But his own wringing. What infinite heart's-ease
> Must kings neglect, that private men enjoy.
> *(H.V*, IV.i*)*

Henry V (1387–1422) was born at Monmouth, the eldest son of Henry IV by Mary de Bohun. He ascended the throne in 1413, at the age of twenty-six. When his father was banished in 1398, he remained in England, and attended Richard II, who took him on his expedition to Ireland, and knighted him there. After his father's succession he spent six years campaigning against Glendower's Welsh rebels. From 1404 until 1409 he governed in the name of his father, who was ill. Whether his youthful follies were anything like those of popular tradition is not known; what does seem certain is that the time he spent on the battlefield or in the council chamber precluded an idle youth of the kind we see him indulging in in Shakespeare's plays.

The details Shakespeare gives of Henry's career are substantially accurate. In the case of the notorious killing of the prisoners at Agincourt, however, history offers some mitigating evidence. At this stage of the battle Henry was worried by a report that a fresh French force had attacked the English rear, and ordered the prisoners killed before he discovered that the force was in fact a band of peasants out for plunder.

The reference to the Earl of Essex's campaign in Ireland in the Prologue enables *Henry V* to be dated reasonably accurately as having been written in 1599. Shakespeare's sources were the chronicles of Holinshed and Hall, and an old play *The Famous Victories of Henry V*, which scholars now see as a degraded version of an even earlier play.

HENRY VI *(1, 2 & 3 H.VI)*: in *1 Henry VI* with 'sighs and tears' he asks his uncles Gloucester and Beaufort to be at peace with one another; he creates Richard Plantagenet Duke of York (III.i). He is crowned at Paris; he banishes Fastolfe *(q.v.)*; he hears that the Duke of Burgundy is in revolt, and sends Talbot against him; he asks York and Somerset to end their quarrel, and makes York Regent of France (IV.i). He makes peace with France, and accepts the offer of marriage to the daughter of the Earl of Armagnac (v.i) The Earl of Suffolk tells Henry of the great beauty and virtue of Margaret

of Anjou, and despite Gloucester's protests, he sends Suffolk to France to bring her to England (v.v).

In *2 Henry VI* he welcomes Margaret, his bride, when she arrives with Suffolk; he makes Suffolk a duke (I.i). His new wife soon finds that he is more fit to be a Pope than a king, and he begins to leave affairs of state to her (I.iii). He fails to check the bitter quarrels among his nobles; he hears that the Duchess of Gloucester has been charged with treason (II.i).

below The marriage of Henry VI (1421–71) and Margaret of Anjou on 22 April 1445, from a painting on glass *(top)*; Henry VI, from the painting at Eton College *(bottom)*.

The wedding of Henry VI and Margaret of Anjou, by
an unknown artist. The actual wedding in France took
place with Suffolk acting as proxy for Henry, as in
Shakespeare's play. There was another ceremony when
Margaret arrived in England.

He pronounces sentence on her and her confederates,
and dismisses Gloucester from the Protectorship;
he believes in Gloucester's innocence, but is forced
to accept the evidence of his accusers. He faints when
he is told of Gloucester's death; he suspects Suffolk,
who he now finds abhorrent. When he hears the
people rioting, he promises that Suffolk will be
banished (III.ii). He pardons Cade's rebels when they
surrender. He hears that York has landed with an
army; when he meets York he is assured by him that
he only seeks the overthrow of Somerset. Henry flees
from the battlefield at St Albans to London.

In *3 Henry VI* he enters Parliament with his followers, and finds York seated on the throne. He tries to prove to him that he has a superior claim to the throne, and finally suggests that he should retain the crown during his lifetime, with it reverting to York, or his family, on his death. His three chief followers desert him for being 'a degenerate king', and he is faced by an angry Queen and Prince – the son he has disinherited (I.i). He attempts to reconcile the differences between the Yorkists and the Lancastrians (II.i). At Towton, having been 'chid from the battle' he soliloquizes on the horrors of war, and the superiority of the peaceful life of the peasant. He escapes to Berwick in disguise, but is overheard discussing affairs of state by two keepers: they guess he is the deposed King, and arrest him. He is sent to the Tower, but is released when Edward is defeated at Warwick. He makes Warwick and Clarence Joint Protectors. He predicts that young Henry, Earl of Richmond, will some day be king (IV.vi). He hears of Edward's invasion; he is captured and taken to the Tower, where he is stabbed by Richard of Gloucester (V.vi).

Henry VI (1421–71), was the only son of Henry V. He succeeded to the throne when he was nine months old; a month later, on the death of Charles VI, he was proclaimed King of France. He was crowned at Westminster in 1429, and at Paris in 1430; the Council of Regency did not allow him to share in the government of his realm until 1437. He was soon warned by the Council that he was exercising his power unwisely. Throughout his reign he was beset by the warring factions around his throne. He was prone to mental illness, and had serious attacks in 1453 and 1455 which encouraged York in his attempts on the throne. Henry recovered in 1456, and travelled round the country trying to quell the unrest. After his defeat by Edward, he spent a year wandering the Yorkshire – Lancashire border in disguise before he was captured. Although it was given out that he died 'of pure displeasure and melancholy', it is certain that he died a violent death, and that Gloucester was generally looked upon as the murderer.

Shakespeare's Henry is essentially the man revealed to us by history. He was weak in body and mind, and a prisoner of the ideas of those immediately surrounding him. He was never much more than an instrument, particularly of Margaret, whose energetic campaigning on his behalf kept him on the throne. He was genuinely pious; Hall relates that his face was 'beautiful, in ye which continually was resydent the bountie of mynde wyth whych he was inwardly endued. He dyd abhorre of hys own nature al the vices, as well of the body as of the soule; Besyde thys, pacyence was so radicate in his harte that of all the injuries to him committed (which were no smal

nombre) he never asked vengeance or punishment . . .'

There are many problems and uncertainties surrounding the dating of the *Henry VI* plays. An apparent borrowing from *1 Henry VI* in *The Troublesome Raigne of King John* (printed 1591) suggests a date of 1590 or earlier, with *2 Henry VI* following in 1590–91 and *3 Henry VI* in 1590–92. Some scholars have argued that Parts 2 and 3 were written before Part 1.

Shakespeare's main sources were Holinshed's *Chronicles of England, Scotland and Ireland* (1587) and Hall's *The union of the two noble and illustre femelies of Lancastre and York* (1548). He sacrifices chronology for dramatic effect: for example, he has Joan of Arc taking part in a battle that took place in 1451, when she was martyred in 1431.

HENRY VIII *(H.VIII)*: he hears from Katharine of the 'exactions' imposed by Wolsey; he orders that a pardon be sent to every man who has resisted the 'commission'; he listens to the accusation against Buckingham made by Knyvet, and orders Buckingham arrested (I.ii). He attends Wolsey's banquet and masque, where he is introduced to Anne Bullen (I.iv).

Charles Laughton as Henry VIII in the 1933 production of *Henry VIII* at the Sadler's Wells Theatre.

He says that his conscience is troubled by his marriage to Katharine. He is attracted to Anne Bullen and makes her Marchioness of Pembroke (II.iii). At the meeting of the divorce commissioners at Blackfriars he declares Katharine to be 'the queen of earthly queens', but says that he is forced to divorce her because of the scruples of his conscience. He resolves to be guided by Cranmer (II.iv). Papers revealing Wolsey's avarice fall into Henry's hands: he makes Wolsey read them in his presence, and points out to him how indebted he is to royal favour (III.ii). He gives Cranmer his ring; he hears of the birth of his daughter; when he hears how Cranmer has been insulted by the council, he enters the chamber and berates the members (v.iii). He attends the christening of Elizabeth.

Shakespeare's play deals with a few episodes selected from the period 1520–36. Henry is a godlike presence in the play rather than a character: he represents the exalted view of kingship that was assiduously fostered by the Tudors. We might find an element of mortal weakness in the apparent hypocrisy of his attitude towards Katharine:

above A portrait of Henry VIII, attributed to Holbein *(top)*; a watercolour by F. Lloyds of the masque scene in *Henry VIII* (I.iv), in the production at the Princess's Theatre in 1855 *(bottom)*.

That man i' th' world who shall report he has
A better wife, let him in naught be trusted,
For speaking false in that; thou art alone,
If thy rare qualities, sweet gentleness,
Thy meekness saint-like, wife-like government,
Obeying in commanding, and thy parts
Sovereign and pious else, could speak thee out,
The queen of earthly queens. (II.iv)

But despite this, he has good motives as a king for divorcing her – the most powerful being her failure to produce an heir – and the play is to some extent a celebration of Henry's success in settling the succession by producing Elizabeth.

The play has long been neglected because the Victorian scholar Spedding (in what was until quite recently taken as the definitive account of the play) found it so disorganized and discontinuous that he thought it could only be the work of two authors, Shakespeare and Fletcher, neither of whom knew what the other was up to. What he failed to realize was that *Henry VIII* was a new type of history play, involving the spectacular displays of the masque tradition and a framework that looks back to the morality plays. It has been called a late morality play, centred on the way that the great fall. It is hard to adapt to the expectations of a modern audience. *Henry VIII* was probably written shortly before 29 June 1613, the day on which the Globe Theatre was burned to the ground during a performance of the play. The sources for the play are the chronicles of Hall and Holinshed.

HERBERT, SIR WALTER *(R.III)*: 'a renowned soldier' who is with Richmond at Tamworth and at Bosworth. He has only one line (v.ii).

HERCULES *(LLL.)*: role assumed by Moth. *(q.v.)*

HERMIA *(MND.)*: the daughter of Egeus. Her father commands her to marry Demetrius, but she refuses, despite his warning that the alternative is death or perpetual virginity. She loves Lysander, and runs off into the woods with him. They lie down to rest, and Hermia awakes alone; she meets Demetrius who, under the influence of Puck's charm, falls in love with her. She then comes across Lysander with her friend Helena: he is professing love for her, though she is not responding to his advances. When Hermia approaches Lysander he rejects her harshly; bewildered, she turns on Helena in a rage. She falls asleep, and when she wakes she is more bewildered when she finds Lysander restored to her (IV.i). At the end Theseus overrules Egeus and commands the wedding of Hermia and Lysander.

HERMIONE *(Wint.)*: queen to Leontes. Leontes tells her to ask Polixenes to prolong his stay at the Sicilian court. She goes with Polixenes into the garden, incurring the jealousy of Leontes, who furiously accuses her of unfaithfulness, and commits her to prison. In prison she gives birth to a daughter, Perdita (II.i). She is charged with treason and adultery; she appeals to the oracle of Apollo, which finds her guiltless, but Leontes is unmoved. She falls into a coma, and is believed dead, when she hears of the death of her son. She recovers, and lives secretly in Paulina's house for the next sixteen years. She poses as a statue of herself, and when the repentant Leontes is brought before her, she reveals herself, and is reunited with him and her lost daughter.

Hermione is a noble, patient woman, the symbol of love that endures through misfortune. Hazlitt saw that her character was 'distinguished by its saint-like resignation and patient forbearance'.

HERNE THE HUNTER *(Wiv.)*: role assumed by Falstaff *(q.v.)* (v.v.).

HERO *(Ado)*: daughter to Leonato. Claudio falls in love with her; Don Pedro says he will woo her on his behalf, but disguises himself as Claudio in an attempt to win her for himself (II.i). Don John tells Claudio what is happening, and joins with Borachio in a plot to discredit Hero. At her wedding, Claudio suddenly violently denounces her for unfaithfulness – he thinks he has seen her entertaining another man. She faints, and then protests her innocence to Friar Francis: he and Leonato decide to have it announced that she is dead. The plot against her is revealed, and Claudio is filled with remorse. At the end Hero is presented to Claudio as the new wife selected for him by Leonato; she removes her mask, and is reunited with him.

She is a very quiet heroine, and inevitably suffers by comparison with the lively Beatrice *(q.v.)*.

HIPPOLYTA *(MND.)*: the Queen of the Amazons, who is betrothed to Theseus, who it appears has won her by defeating her in battle (I.i). She is a harsh critic of the Interlude at the end (v.i).

Shakespeare seems to have taken the story of the marriage of Theseus and Hippolyta from Chaucer's *Knight's Tale*. The Renaissance view was that in defeating her and marrying her Theseus forced her to be true to her sex: by re-establishing the proper hierarchical relationship between man and woman he corrected an imbalance in nature. Her mythical past makes her an apt partner for Theseus the legendary hero:

I was with Hercules and Cadmus once
When in a wood of Crete they bayed the bear

above Elizabeth Farren, Countess of Derby, as
Hermione in *The Winter's Tale* in the late eighteenth
century. After a painting by Zoffany *(left)*; Miriam

Clements as Hero in *Much Ado About Nothing* in 1905
(right).

With hounds of Sparta. Never did I hear
Such gallant chiding; for, besides the groves,
The skies, the fountains, every region near
Seemed all one mutual cry. I never heard
So musical a discord, such sweet thunder. (IV.i)

HOBGOBLIN *(Wiv.)*: role assumed by Pistol
(q.v.) (V.v).

HOLOFERNES *(LLL.)*: a pedantic schoolmaster,
who spends his time exercising his erudition with Sir
Nathaniel and Dull. He suggests the 'Pageant of the
Nine Worthies', and appears as Judas Maccabeus;
the audience only allows him to speak one line.

Holofernes is the very essence of pedantry. He
loves words for their own sake, and speaks like a
dictionary:

This is a gift that I have simple: simple, a foolish
extravagant spirit, full of forms, figures, shapes,
objects, ideas, apprehensions, motions, revolutions.
These are begot in the ventricle of memory, nourish'd
in the womb of pia mater, and deliver'd upon the
mellowing of occasion: but the gift is good in those
in whom it is acute, and I am thankful for it. (IV.ii)

Holofernes is an ironic version of what the lords
set out to be: he is a pure bookman, who loves learning
for its own sake. For all his self-engrossment and
superior airs, he is not foolish. And he can find precisely
the right words when he needs them. His final line is
a marvellous rebuke to the lords and ladies who have
been jeering the pageant: 'This is not generous, not
gentle, not humble.'

Holofernes (Paul Curran) and Sir Nathaniel (Charles
Kay) in the National Theatre Company's 1968
production of *Love's Labour's Lost,* directed by
Laurence Olivier.

HORATIO *(Ham.)*: friend to Hamlet. Marcellus
and Barnardo tell him of the ghost, which he observes
for himself; he tells Hamlet. Hamlet tells him of his
conversation with the ghost, and swears him to secrecy.
Hamlet explains to Horatio his plan to expose Claudius
with the play; at the play Horatio becomes convinced
of the King's guilt. On Hamlet's return from England
Horatio greets him, and talks with him in the grave-
yard. He warns Hamlet not to accept Laertes' challenge.
When he sees Hamlet mortally wounded he wants to
kill himself, but Hamlet stops him and delivers his
last injunctions to him.

Horatio is Hamlet's friend and confidant, a com-
posed, temperate figure who has his unreserved
respect:

        . . . dost thou hear,
Since my dear soul was mistress of my choice,
And could of men distinguish, her election
Hath seal'd thee for herself. For thou hast been
As one in suffering all, that suffers nothing.
A man that Fortune's buffets, and rewards
Hath ta'en with equal thanks. And blest are those,
Whose blood and judgement are so well commingled,
That they are not a pipe for Fortune's finger,
To sound what stop she please. Give me that man,
That is not passion's slave, and I will wear him
In my heart's core, ay, in my heart of heart,
As I do thee. (III.ii)
Horatio has the qualities of the Stoic Roman hero
who was so much admired during the Renaissance.

HORNER, THOMAS *(2 H.VI)*: an armourer who is accused of treason by his apprentice Peter Thump (I.iii). Gloucester orders them to resolve their dispute by judicial combat. Peter Thump kills his drunken master, who confesses his guilt before he dies (II.iii).

According to Stow this was William Catur, who fought his servant John David in 1446; Catur's head was set up on London Bridge. The point of the incident in Shakespeare's play is that dissension has spread throughout the realm, even down to the common people.

HORTENSIO *(Shr.)*: a suitor to Bianca. He and his rival Gremio agree to try and get Katharina married off so that Bianca will become available for them to compete for. Hortensio encourages Petruchio to woo Katharina by telling him she has a huge dowry. He disguises himself as a music teacher to Bianca, but is sent to teach Katharina, and returns 'with his head broken'. He attempts to woo Bianca during a music lesson; when he sees that his suit is failing, and Lucentio's prospering, he quickly consoles himself by marrying a rich widow (IV.ii). He believes that Petruchio's example has taught him how to handle her, but at Lucentio's feast he is surprised to find that his wife disdains his authority.

HORTENSIUS *(Tim.)*: the servant of one of Timon's creditors. He and others are sent by their masters to collect their debts from Timon. Hortensius is reluctant to undertake the task because it seems unjust:

I know my lord hath spent of Timon's wealth,
And now ingratitude makes it worse than stealth.
(III.iv).

Timon is enraged, and drives the servants away.

HOST OF AN INN *(Gent.)*: the elderly landlord of Julia's lodgings in Milan. He takes her to find Proteus, and they overhear Proteus wooing Silvia (IV.ii).

HOST OF THE GARTER INN *(Wiv.)*: he accepts Bardolph as his tapster. He eggs on Caius when he is preparing to fight Evans, and then sends the combatants to different meeting-places. They have their revenge by stealing three of his horses. He is very upset, but is cheered up by Fenton, who gives him gold in return for his help in wooing Anne Page (IV.vi).

HOSTESS *(Shr.)*: she appears haranguing Sly for some glasses he has broken in her inn; she goes off to get help, and does not reappear (Induction).

HOSTILIUS *(Tim.)*: the second of the 'three strangers' (the only one named) who appear with

Lucius and tell him of the rumours they have heard: that Timon is short of money, and that Lucullus has refused him a loan. Lucius protests his own readiness to lend money, but when Servilius enters and asks for money for Timon he refuses him with a feeble excuse. Hostilius is amazed at Lucius' ingratitude:

   . . . He ne'er drinks
But Timon's silver treads upon his lips,
And yet, oh see the monstrousness of man,
When he looks out in an ungrateful shape;
He does deny him (in respect of his)
What charitable men afford to beggars. (III.ii)

HOTSPUR (HENRY PERCY) *(R.II; 1 H.IV)*: in *Richard II* he is presented to Bolingbroke by his father, and is with him before Flint Castle (III.iii). He challenges Aumerle (IV.i). He brings news to Bolingbroke of his 'dissolute' and 'desperate' son Prince Henry (V.iii). He brings the Bishop of Carlisle before the King for sentence (V.vi).

In *1 Henry IV* he excuses himself to King Henry for not having delivered up his Scottish prisoners to him; on the King's departure he rages at 'this canker'd Bolingbroke', and vows that he will not hand over the prisoners. When his anger subsides, he listens to the plot outlined by Worcester (I.iii). He exchanges banter with his wife (II.iii). He wrangles with Glendower and Mortimer over a map showing the intended tripartite division of the kingdom; he apologizes to Glendower for laughing at his claims to have supernatural powers (III.i). He hears that the King's forces are advancing and longs to meet the Prince of Wales in battle; he hears that Glendower has been delayed. He sends Worcester as envoy to Henry when he receives his offer of terms; he hears Worcester's false report of the King's reply, and sends Douglas to carry his defiance to Henry: he prepares for battle. In the battle he is killed by Prince Henry; his corpse is stabbed by Falstaff, who carries it off claiming that he has killed him (V.iv).

We have two differing estimates of the fiery, gallant Hotspur: from his widow (who had had to compete strenuously for attention with his horse when he was alive) we hear that:

   . . . He was indeed the glass
Wherein the noble youth did dress themselves.
He had no legs, that practised not his gait;
And speaking thick, which nature made his blemish,
Became the accents of the valiant,
For those that could speak low and tardily
Would turn their own perfection to abuse,
To seem like him. So that in speech, in gait,
In diet, in affections of delight,
In military rules, humours of the blood,
He was the mark and glass, copy and book,
That fashioned others. (*2 H.IV*, II.iii)

above The dispute over the partition of England between Hotspur, Glendower, Mortimer, and Worcester *(1 Henry IV,* II.iii); by Henry Fuseli *(left)*. The

death of Hotspur at the hands of Prince Henry at the Battle of Shrewsbury in 1403. From a painting by Rigaud *(right)*.

Nobody, it seems, could see beyond appearances to the essential man. Hal gives us a better idea of Hotspur:

> I am not yet of Percy's mind, the Hotspur of the North, he that kills me some six or seven dozen of Scots at a breakfast, washes his hands, and says to his wife, fie upon this quiet life, I want work. O my sweet Harry, says she, how many hast thou killed today? Give my roan horse a drench, says he, and answers, some fourteen, an hour after, a trifle, a trifle. *(1 H.IV,* II.iv)

This is the Hotspur we see in the play, a man whose dog is appropriately called 'Lady'. His rather shallow virtues provide a false image of nobility by which Hal temporarily is diminished, at least in the eyes of his father.

In Shakespeare's plays Hotspur and Prince Henry are represented as being approximately the same age; Hotspur was in fact much the older – he was probably older than Bolingbroke.

HUBERT DE BURGH *(John)*: John gives him custody of the young Prince Arthur, and instructs him to murder him. The boy's entreaties touch Hubert, and he does not blind him (which is apparently what the written warrant orders him to do). He hides Arthur, and tells John that he is dead. When he reveals that Arthur is still alive he is wrong, since Arthur has been killed trying to escape.

Hubert de Burgh was a descendant of Charlemagne; he was one of John's most powerful subjects.

HUME, JOHN *(2 H.VI)*: a priest who is bribed by Cardinal Beaufort and Suffolk to undermine the position of the Duchess of Gloucester. He procures Margery Jourdain, a necromancer, to raise a spirit for her to question (I.iv). He is hanged when his part in the plot is discovered.

HUNTINGDON, EARL OF *(H.V)*: after the English victory at Agincourt Henry sends Huntingdon, Exeter, Clarence, Gloucester and Warwick to draw up the terms of peace with the French King (v.ii).

HUNTSMAN, A *(3 H.VI)*: when Edward IV is a prisoner of the Archbishop of York at Middleham Castle he is allowed to hunt in the grounds in the custody of this huntsman. When Edward escapes with the help of Gloucester, Hastings and Stanley, the huntsman, fearing punishment, goes with them (IV.v).

HYMEN *(AYL.)*: the god of marriage in classical mythology. An unspecified character appears in the role of Hymen, and solmnizes the marriages of Rosalind to Orsino, Celia to Oliver, Phebe to Silvius, and Audrey to Touchstone (v.iv).

I

IACHIMO *(Cym.)*: in Rome he disputes with Posthumus over the virtue and merit of Imogen, and wagers ten thousand ducats against Posthumus' diamond ring that he will undermine her honour (I.v). He arrives in Britain with a commendatory letter for Imogen from Posthumus; he asks her if he can store a trunk full of valuables in her room for the night. He conceals himself in the trunk, and emerges at midnight: he steals Posthumus' bracelet from the sleeping Imogen, notes all the contents of the room, and observes a 'mole cinque-spotted' on her breast, before re-entering the trunk (II.ii). Back in Rome, he convinces Posthumus by the evidence he produces that he has won the wager. He commands an invading force of Romans in Britain, and is disarmed by Posthumus in battle, and brought before Cymbeline. He is made to confess, and, because he shows remorse, is forgiven by Posthumus, who tells him to 'live, and deal with others better'.

Iachimo is a Renaissance Machiavel, so that his presence in a play about ancient Britons and Romans is a little surprising; but Shakespeare was not concerned with naturalism in this play. He is a lesser Iago, a cynic who devotes his tough-minded rationality to self-gratification. He is not irredeemable: he is filled with spontaneous admiration for Imogen, and is filled with remorse at having falsely accused her.

IAGO *(Oth.)*: ancient, or ensign, to Othello. *(See OTHELLO.)* By means of a carefully worked-out campaign of deception and insinuation, he persuades Othello that his wife, Desdemona, has become the mistress of his lieutenant, Michael Cassio, and is thus directly responsible for their tragic deaths. Iago also murders his infatuated accomplice Roderigo, after the latter has failed to kill Cassio, and stabs his own wife, Emilia, to death because she has betrayed his secret. After Othello's suicide, the Venetian commissioners decree that Iago should be put to death by torture.

Iago typifies the rancorous outsider, a disappointed 'angry man'. His motives are mixed. Does he really believe (as he once insinuates) that his wife may

Iachimo succeeds in entering Imogen's chamber. Frontispiece to *Cymbeline* in Rowe's 1709 edition of Shakespeare's plays.

formerly have been the General's concubine? Coleridge announced that Iago's behaviour exhibits the 'motive-hunting of a motiveless malignity'; while Hazlitt chose to regard him as an example of 'diseased intellectual activity, with the most perfect indifference to moral good or evil, or rather with a decided preference of the latter, because it . . . gives greater zest to his thought and scope to his actions . . . He is an

Mr Bensley as Iago in an eighteenth-century production of *Othello*.

amateur of tragedy in real life . . .' What he detests about Othello is both his simple-minded, easy-going nobility and his evident superiority; for, although the General calls him 'honest Iago', he does so with a certain hint of patronage, and cannot help showing that he prefers the companionship of the gentlemanly Cassio, whom Iago condemns as an amateur soldier, an 'arithmetician' and a 'counter-caster'. The ancient despises, yet is bound to envy, the personable and well-bred young lieutenant. Iago is an under-dog who possesses wolf-like fangs.

IDEN, ALEXANDER (later Sir) *(2 H.VI)*: a Kentish gentleman who finds Jack Cade hiding in his garden. They fight, and he kills Cade; Iden takes Cade's head to the King and is rewarded with a knighthood and a thousand marks (IV.x; v.i).

Iden is a simple, virtuous figure, representative of honest family life:

This small inheritance my father left me,
Contenteth me, and worth a monarchy.
I seek not to wax great by others' waning,
Or gather wealth, I care not with what envy.

Sufficeth, that I have maintained my state,
And send the poor well pleased from my gate.
(IV.x)

Iden is a small symbol of the orderly existence (ie of existence according to 'degree') that is threatened by the civil wars.

IMOGEN *(Cym.)*: the daughter of Cymbeline. She has married, without her father's permission, 'a poor but worthy gentleman' (Posthumus). He is banished: before they part, she gives him a ring, and he gives her a bracelet. Imogen is lamenting her loss when Iachimo arrives with a letter from Posthumus; she is amazed at the stories Iachimo tells her of her husband's licentious conduct in Rome. She indignantly rejects Iachimo's suggestion that she be revenged on him by behaving similarly herself, but agrees to store a trunk in her room for him. (I.vii). Iachimo hides in the trunk, and emerges from it at midnight: he steals Imogen's bracelet. Imogen rejects Cloten's clumsy wooing. She receives a letter from Posthumus telling her to meet him at Milford Haven; she sets out joyfully, accompanied by Pisanio (III.ii). Pisanio reluctantly gives her the letter he has had from Posthumus accusing her of infidelity and ordering him to kill her; she is overcome with despair, and tells him to carry out his instructions, but he refuses. Pisanio suggests that she disguises herself as a man and presents herself to Lucius, while he tells Posthumus that she is dead; he gives her a drug that is supposed to cure all ills. Cloten sets out in pursuit of her, intent on raping her while wearing Posthumus' clothes (which he has stolen). She wanders into Belarius' cave, and presents herself to him and his two 'sons' as 'Fidele'. She falls sick, and takes the drug, which puts her into a death-like coma. Believing her dead, the brothers lament over her body and strew it with flowers. She wakes, and comes across the headless corpse of Cloten: she thinks it is Posthumus, and faints on top of the body. She is found by Lucius, who takes her for the dead man's attendant. (IV.ii). Cymbeline sees 'Fidele' among the Roman prisoners after the battle, and because he vaguely recognizes her he asks her to choose one prisoner who will be set free. She refuses to name Lucius, and when Cymbeline is puzzled she takes him aside and explains who she is. With Cymbeline's backing she demands that Iachimo explain where he got the ring. He confesses. Imogen springs to Posthumus' side, but he strikes her down, thinking she is a 'scornful page'. Her identity is revealed, and she is restored to her husband, father and long-lost brothers.

For Hazlitt, Imogen was 'perhaps the most tender and the most artless' of all Shakespeare's women. For Swinburne, she was supreme: 'woman above all

Shakespeare's women is Imogen. As in Cleopatra we found the incarnate sex, the woman everlasting, so in Imogen we find half-glorified already the immortal godhead of womanhood.'

This is to make Imogen a little too ethereal: alongside her purity she has an unshakable integrity; like Cordelia, she refuses to deny her feelings in order to

please her father. And her love for Posthumus is remarkable for its sheer intensity:

I would have broke mine eye-strings; cracked them, but
To look upon him, till the dimunition
Of space had pointed him sharp as my needle;
Nay followed him, till he had melted from

G. F. Cooke as Iago in 1800.
From a mezzotint by J. Ward.

The smallness of a gnat, to air; and then
Have turned mine eye, and wept. (I.iii)

INNOGEN *(Ado)*: the Folio stage directions read
'Enter Leonato, governor of Messina, and Innogen his
wife'. She is also present in II.i.

IRAS *(Ant.)*: attendant to Cleopatra. In the last scene
she helps her queen dress in her 'best attires', and vows
that she will never grace a Roman triumph. When
Cleopatra bids her farewell, she falls and dies (v.ii).

It is not clear whether Iras dies of grief, or whether
she is bitten by the asp. Plutarch merely states that she
was found dead at Cleopatra's feet.

IRIS *(Tp.)*: in mythology the messenger of the gods,
a function she performs in the masque of the spirits
when she summons the nymphs and reapers to dance.
She represents purity (IV.i).

ISABEL, QUEEN OF FRANCE *(H.V)*: wife to
Charles VI of France. She prays for God's blessing on
the marriage of her daughter Katharine to Henry (v.ii).

ISABELLA *(Meas.)*: Claudio's sister. She is a novice
in a convent, about to take her final vows; Lucio comes
to her and tells her that her brother has been condemned
to death for fornication, and asks her to intercede for
him with Angelo. Her pleas move the puritanical deputy
in a way that she does not anticipate: he offers to save
Claudio if she will surrender her chastity to him. She is
horrified, the more so when Claudio pleads with her to
submit to Angelo and save him. She meets the disguised
Duke, and he suggests that she arranges to meet Angelo
at night, and that her place in bed is taken by Mariana,
who was once betrothed to Angelo. At the end, Isabella and Mariana appeal for justice to the Duke; he
pretends not to recognize them, and refuses to believe
them until it is revealed that he was the mysterious
Friar Lodowick. Angelo is married to Mariana, but
condemned to immediate execution: Mariana pleads
for him, and begs Isabella for support. Isabella, who
still believes that her brother has been executed, kneels
and asks for mercy for Angelo. The Duke hints at the
end that he will marry Isabella.

Isabella is not a congenial heroine today: she appears
to be a self-righteous prude who is pitiless, self-
absorbed and hypocritical. This is largely because we
have lost the Christian context in which her actions

left Iachimo notes the contents of Imogen's chamber
while she sleeps (*Cymbeline*, II.ii) – an engraving
of 1773 *(top);* Imogen, a nineteenth-century engraving
by J. W. Wright *(bottom)*. *right* Isabella (Lily Brayton)
in *Measure for Measure* (I.iv), 1906 *(top);* Flora
Robson as Isabella in Tyrone Guthrie's 1933 production
of *Measure for Measure* at the Old Vic *(bottom)*

make sense. From the outset, she is marked by a sense of separateness – even the licentious Lucio sets her apart:

> . . . 'tis my familiar sin
> With maids to seem the lapwing, and to jest,
> Tongue far from heart, play with all virgins so.
> I hold you as a thing enskied and sainted,
> By your renouncement, an immortal spirit;
> And to be talked with in sincerity,
> As with a saint. (I.iv)

She wants a stricter restraint than that offered by the votarists of St Clare, which has the reputation of being the strictest women's order in the Roman Catholic church.

Her decision that 'More than our brother is our chastity' is based on Christian principles as they were interpreted during the Renaissance. She is hardly self-indulgent –

> . . . O, were it but my life,
> I'd throw it down for your deliverance
> As frankly as a pin. (III.i)

In the source play *Promos and Cassandra,* Cassandra regards the loss of her chastity as an irreparable destruction of her honour and integrity: chastity was an absolute virtue. Thus Isabella's attitude has a theological sanction; more important in terms of the play, it has the unequivocal praise of the Duke:

> The hand that made you fair hath made you good.
> The goodness that is cheap in beauty makes beauty brief in goodness; but grace, being the soul of your complexion, shall keep the body of it ever fair. (III.i)

Isabella's fault is her lack of humility, the self-righteousness of her revulsion against the weakness of others. Like Angelo, she has to learn the value of humanity: in the end, when she is asked to plead for the man who has murdered her brother and tried to violate her, she is required to show a more than human charity, just as earlier she had shown an almost inhuman saintliness.

Isabella's immediate acceptance of the bed-trick does not brand her as a hypocrite, as some have suggested: it is sanctioned by the Duke, which is an indication that we are to accept it as right. Similarly, the hint at the end that she will marry the Duke is in the spirit of comedy; and it is not necessarily a hypocritical volte-face, since the period of the novitiate is intended to be one in which the novice determines God's intentions for her future. However, although there are grounds for taking a sympathetic view of Isabella, it remains extraordinarily difficult for an actress to make her sympathetic on the stage.

ISIDORE, SERVANT OF *(Tim.)*: his master sends him to collect a debt from Timon. He and the other servants are diverted by Flavius (II.ii).

J

JAMY (JAMES), CAPTAIN *(H.V)*: a Scottish officer in Henry's army. He appears in the company of Macmorris, Fluellen and Gower at the siege of Harfleur (III.ii).

Shakespeare is at pains to indicate the ethnic harmony of Henry's army.

JAQUENETTA *(LLL.)*: a country wench. Don Armado discovers his rival Costard with her in defiance of the King's decree; when Costard is imprisoned, Armado woos her in his pompous manner. At the end Costard claims that she is pregnant by Armado.

JAQUES *(AYL.)*: a melancholic lord attending the banished Duke of Burgundy. A courtier describes how he moralized on a wounded stag (II.i). He tells how he 'met a fool i' the forest', and how he is now 'ambitious for a motley coat' himself, so that he could lash human folly; he compares the world to a stage and describes the 'seven ages of man' (II.vii). He overhears Touchstone's wooing of Audrey, and persuades him not to marry 'under a bush, like a beggar' (III.iii). He meets 'Ganymede', and boasts of his melancholy to him, but is ridiculed for it (IV.i). He decides to join Frederick when he hears that he has 'put on a religious life' (V.iv).

Jaques is representative of the cult of melancholy, and his inability to be happy wherever he is marks him as a malcontent. But the satirist is satirized himself when he encounters the disguised Rosalind.

'Jaques is the only purely contemplative character in Shakespeare. He thinks and does nothing. His whole occupation is to amuse his mind, and he is totally regardless of his body and his fortunes. He is the prince of philosophical idlers.' (Hazlitt)

JESSICA *(Mer.V.)*: the daughter of Shylock. She is in love with Lorenzo. She elopes with him, disguised as a page, taking with her some of her father's money and a casket of valuables. She and Lorenzo look after Belmont in Portia's absence.

She is vivacious and slightly amoral, not a model Jewish daughter.

Jaquenetta (Sheila Reid) and Don Armado (Ronald Pickup) in the 1968 production of *Love's Labour's Lost* by the National Theatre Company.

JEWELLER, A *(Tim.)*: he calls on Timon in the hope of selling him an expensive jewel (I.i).

JOAN PUCELLE (JOAN OF ARC) *(1 H.VI)*: she appears before Charles and tells him of her miraculous call, and proves her power by overcoming him in combat. The Dauphin becomes infatuated by her, but she rejects his advances. She raises the siege of Orleans, and persuades Burgundy to desert the English. She conjures up fiends and offers her body and soul in return for a victory, but the spirits desert her and she is captured by the Duke of York. At her trial she repudiates her father and declares she is descended from kings, and that she is a virgin; when she is sentenced to be burnt she admits that she is with child. She is carried off to execution cursing the English.

Joan of Arc was a country girl who became the

adopting the traditional English view of her as a wicked and impure woman who was in league with the devil. Holinshed records the result of the examination by her English captors of her 'life and beleefe':

Wherein found though a virgin, yet first, shamefullie rejecting hir sex abominablie in acts and apparell, to

Jessica (Jane Lapotaire) and Lorenzo (Malcolm Reid) in the National Theatre Company's 1970 production of *The Merchant of Venice;* directed by Jonathan Miller and designed by Julia Trevelyan Oman, it was set in the Venice of the nineteenth century.

national heroine of France. She heard voices, and encouraged by an ancient prophecy, she presented herself before the Dauphin as the saviour of her country. She was given command of an army, and had a series of military successes: she raised the siege of Orleans in May 1429, and won the Battle of Patay. She was captured at Compiègne on 24 May 1430, by John of Luxembourg, who sold his captive to the Duke of Bedford. She was burnt at the stake as a heretic at Rouen on 30 May 1431.

Shakespeare's Joan is a travesty, but he was merely

have counterfeit mankind, and then, all damnable faithlesse, to be a pernicious instrument to hostilities and bloudshed in divelish witchcraft and sorcerie.

JOHN *(Wiv.)*: a servant to the Fords. Mistress Ford tells him and another servant, Robert, to take the laundry basket containing Falstaff and dump it in a ditch near the river (III.iii). On Falstaff's second visit John and Robert are again told to carry out the basket: they are stopped by Ford, who expects to find Falstaff inside (IV.ii).

above Joan Pucelle, Joan of Arc (1412–31), a
seventeenth-century representation *(left)*; Joan of Arc,
an engraving of 1628 *(right)*.

JOHN, DON, THE BASTARD *(Ado.)*: the bastard
brother of Don Pedro, who admits he is 'a plain dealing
villain' (I.iii). He has been defeated by his brother, and
resolves to be revenged on Claudio, who 'hath all the
glory of my overthrow'; he eagerly falls in with
Borachio's plan to 'misuse the prince, to vex Claudio,
to undo Hero, and kill Leonato' (II.ii). He slanders Hero
to Claudio, and 'proves' her unfaithfulness to him. His
part in the plot is discovered, and he tries to escape, but
is caught and brought back to face 'brave punishments'
devised by Benedick.

Don John is not a strongly characterized villain – he
is one of the lesser descendants of Aaron *(q.v.)*. He
inherits some of the self-revelatory style of homiletic
allegory:

In this, though I cannot be said to be a flattering
honest man, it must not be denied I am a plain-
dealing villain. I am trusted with a muzzle, and
enfranchised with a clog, therefore I have decreed
not to sing in my cage. If I had my mouth, I would
bite. If I had my liberty, I would do my liking. In

the mean time, let me be that I am, and seek not to
alter me. (I.iii)

JOHN, FRIAR *(Rom.)*: Friar Laurence gives him a
letter to deliver to Romeo in Mantua, informing him
that Juliet is alive in the Capulet tomb. The authorities
suspect that Friar John has had contact with the
plague, and prevent him from leaving his house. By the
time he is able to tell Friar Lawrence that he has failed
to deliver the letter, Romeo has already been told that
Juliet is dead.

JOHN, KING *(John)*: he threatens war to the envoy
of Philip of France, and declares that 'abbeys and
priories' will pay for an expedition. He settles the
rival claims of Philip and Robert Faulconbridge, and
knights Philip (I.i). He confronts Philip of France
outside Angiers, and offers peace, but Philip asserts
Arthur's claim to the English throne; he makes an offer
to Arthur, which is also refused, and so he prepares for
battle. The Bastard suggests that John and Philip

should combine to take Angiers; they agree to, and John agrees that his niece Blanche will marry the Dauphin. He offers to make Arthur Duke of Brittany in the hope that this will placate Constance, his mother (III.i). Pandulph, the papal legate, demands to know why John keeps the papal nominee Stephen Langton from the see of Canterbury; John declares that all friends of the Pope shall be his enemies, and is excommunicated by Pandulph. John is furious when Philip of France refuses to side with him against Rome. He gives the young Prince Arthur into Hubert's care; he drops hints to Hubert that he would like to be rid of

Arthur, and is encouraged when Hubert accepts them. At his second coronation his nobles express dissatisfaction at his treatment of Arthur: he says he will hand the boy over to them, but after a word with Hubert, announces that he is dead. The nobles leave in anger. John vows repentance; he is told that Eleanor and Constance are dead, and that the French have landed in England. He sends the Bastard to try and rally the disaffected nobles. He is angry with Hubert until he is told that Arthur is still alive; he tells Hubert to spread the word among the nobles (IV.ii). John makes a submission to the Pope, and receives his crown again from

above The tomb of King John (1166–1216) at Worcester Cathedral; *left* Beerbohm Tree as King John.

Pandulph; he hears that Arthur is now really dead (v.i). He dies in agony, having been poisoned, in the garden of Swinstead Abbey (v.vii).

Shakespeare, though he presents John as a poor king, weak in judgement and over-hasty in action, is kinder to him than most of his contemporaries. As Holinshed wrote:

Verilie, whosoever shall consider the course of the historie written of this prince, he shall find, that he had been little beholden to the writers of that time in which he lived: for scarselie can they afoord him a good word, except when the truth inforceth them to come out with it as it were against their willes.

Shakespeare's John is undistinguished rather than evil in the grand manner of his Richard III; he is not capable of dominating events, but rather lets them govern him.

Various dates are still suggested for the composition of *King John*. On the assumption that it was a re-working of the old play *The Troublesome Raigne of John, King of England* (printed 1591), it has been dated sometime between 1594 and 1597. Some scholars have raised the interesting suggestion that far from being the source of Shakespeare's play, the *Troublesome Raigne* is in fact a 'bad' quarto of it, and they argue for 1590–91 as the date for *King John*.

JOHN OF LANCASTER, PRINCE (later Duke of Bedford) *(1&2 IV; H.V; 1 H.VI)*: in *1 Henry IV* he is at the Battle of Shrewsbury, where he distinguishes himself; afterwards he is sent by the Prince of Wales to deal with the rebels in the North (v.v).

In *2 Henry IV* he captures the rebel leaders by tricking them: he promises to redress their grievances if they disperse their forces, and when they comply he has them arrested and sent to execution as traitors.

In *Henry V* as Duke of Bedford, brother to the King, he is present at Agincourt.

In *1 Henry VI* he is now uncle to the King and Regent of France. He captures Orleans, and then Rouen, where he dies. He is eulogized by Talbot:

A braver soldier never couched lance,
A gentler heart did never sway in court. (III.ii)

Prince John of Lancaster (1389–1435) was the third son of Henry IV. He was made Constable of England in 1413, and was created Duke of Bedford the following year. He was appointed Lieutenant of the realm while Henry V was campaigning in France, and was thus not at Harfleur or Agincourt as in the play. He joined the King in France in 1419; after his brother's death he became Regent of France, and lived in Paris. The advent of Joan of Arc destroyed his hopes of a settled peace; Bedford brought Henry VI to be crowned in Paris in 1431 in the hope of restoring the morale of the people. He died at Rouen in 1435, having seen the cause he had struggled for all his life in ruins.

John has always been overshadowed by his elder brother, but many historians find him the more impressive figure. Handsome and learned, his greatest achievement was to maintain English rule in France against a background of continuing war; as long as he was alive, the situation seemed under control.

Shakespeare's John is a cold Machiavellian figure in *2 Henry IV*; presumably he is intended as a contrast to his brother. In Holinshed it is Westmoreland who treacherously traps the rebels, and not John.

JOHN, SIR, A PRIEST *(R.III)*: he meets Hastings on the way to the Tower, and promises to go to him on the next Sabbath (III.ii).

JOSEPH *(Shr.)*: one of the servants at Petruchio's country house (IV.i).

JOURDAIN, MARGERY (or Margaret) *(2 H.VI)*: a witch who helps the Duchess of Gloucester raise a spirit. She is arrested and sentenced to be burned at Smithfield (II.iii).

She was a real figure, popularly known as the Witch of Eye.

JUDAS MACCABEUS *(LLL.)*: role assumed by Holofernes in the 'Pageant of the Nine Worthies' (v.ii).

JULIA *(Gent.)*: the faithful lover of Proteus. She follows him to Milan disguised as a page (II.vii). She hears that he is courting Silvia, and enters his service as his page 'Sebastian'. She is told to take a ring (her own, that she had given Proteus) to Silvia and exchange it for her portrait. 'Sebastian' describes the neglected Julia to Silvia, and enlists her sympathy. She follows Proteus when he pursues Silvia into the forest; she faints when Valentine offers to yield Silvia to Proteus. When she recovers she produces the two rings, and is reconciled to Proteus.

Julia is ready to give up everything for love:
The more thou dam'st it up, the more it burns.
The current that with gentle murmur glides,
Thou know'st, being stopped, impatiently doth rage;
But when his fair course is not hindered,
He makes sweet music with th'enamelled stones,
Giving a gentle kiss to every sedge
He overtaketh in his pilgrimage;
And so by many winding nooks he strays
With willing sport to the wild ocean.
Then let me go, and hinder not my course.
I'll be as patient as the gentle stream,
And make a pastime of each weary step,
Till the last step have brought me to my love. (II.vii)

JULIET *(Meas.)*: 'beloved by Claudio', she is with child by him, and for this offence he is condemned to death. She acknowledges her share of the guilt to the disguised Duke, but insists that the offence was 'mutually committed' (II.iii). She is restored to Claudio at the end.

JULIET *(Rom.)*: daughter to Capulet. She learns that her parents have approved Paris as her husband (I.iii). She meets the masked Romeo at her father's feast, and falls in love with him (I.v). At her window at night she soliloquizes on her feelings for Romeo, who overhears her from the garden below. They decide on immediate marriage. They are married secretly at Friar Laurence's cell (II.vi). Juliet learns that Romeo has been banished

right A poster for *Twelfth Night* at the Savoy Theatre, showing Viola, designed by Norman Wilkinson of Four Oaks.
overleaf David Garrick as Richard III, painted by Hogarth.

TWELFTH NIGHT

VIOLA

NORMAN WILKINSON
OF
FOUR OAKS

MILES. LITHO. LONDON. W.

left Paul Scofield as the Clown in *The Winter's Tale*, painted by Dame Laura Knight.

above Mrs Patrick Campbell as Juliet in the 1895 production of *Romeo and Juliet* at the Lyceum Theatre.

for killing Tybalt; they spend a last night together.
She learns that her wedding to Paris has been arranged,
and is furiously abused by her father when she refuses
to go through with it. Friar Laurence promises her a
potion that will throw her into a death-like trance for
'two and forty hours'; Romeo is summoned from
Mantua. She drinks the potion, and when she awakes
she finds Romeo lying dead beside her. She stabs
herself.

Juliet is just short of fourteen, but she has 'affections
and warm youthful blood'; and we learn that in Verona
women younger than her 'are made already mothers'.

above Romeo and Juliet – a nineteenth-century
representation by John H. Bacon *(left)*; Ellen Terry as
Juliet *(right)*.

She is lively and vivacious: when she first meets Romeo
she wittily deflates his bookish Petrarchan attitude,
and tells him in exasperation, 'You kiss by th' book.'
In comparison with his rhetorical flights, her speech is
down to earth and direct. Her declaration of love is
straight to the point:

> Dost thou love me? I know thou wilt say ay,
> And I will take thy word; yet if thou swear'st,
> Thou mayst prove false; at lovers' perjuries
> They say Jove laughs. O gentle Romeo,
> If thous dost love, pronounce it faithfully. (II.ii)

When he begins to respond with a 'poetic' vow of love
she cuts him short, and despairs of getting simple
statements from him:

> Well do not swear. Although I joy in thee;
> I have no joy of this contract to-night,
> It is too rash, too unadvised, too sudden,
> Too like the lightning, which doth cease to be
> Ere one can say, it lightens. (II.ii)

The intensity of her love sweeps away these initial
intimations of tragedy, and she loses her worldly
superiority in her devotion to Romeo.

JULIUS CAESAR *(Caes.)*, *see* CAESAR.

Juliet (Olivia Hussey) and Romeo (Leonard Whiting)
in the 1968 film of *Romeo and Juliet* directed by
Franco Zefferelli.

JUNIUS BRUTUS *(Cor.), see* BRUTUS, JUNIUS.

JUNO *(Tp.)*: the queen of the goddesses in Roman
mythology (in Greek mythology, she was Hera). She
appears in the masque of the spirits and, as the goddess
of marriage and fertility, she blesses the betrothal of
Ferdinand and Miranda (IV.i).

JUPITER *(Cym.)*: the supreme Roman god. As
Posthumus lies asleep in his cell, he sees a vision in
which the ghosts of his dead relatives call on Jupiter to
go to his aid. Jupiter appears riding on an eagle, and
angrily dismisses the ghosts, saying 'No care of yours
it is, you know 'tis ours' (v.iv). He promises Posthumus
happiness, and leaves a tablet inscribed with his
prophecy, which the soothsayer Philharmonus later
interprets.

JUSTICE *(Meas.)*: he sits silently by when Pompey,
Froth and Elbow appear before Angelo and Escalus
(II.i). He remarks that 'Lord Angelo is severe'.

K

KATHARINE *(LLL.)*: a lady attending the Princess of France on her visit to the court of Navarre. She falls in love with Dumain. When masked, she is wooed by Longaville who mistakes her for Maria. At the end she promises Dumain that if after a year 'I have much love, I'll give you some'.

KATHARINE OF FRANCE, PRINCESS (afterwards Queen of Henry v) *(H.V)*: the daughter of Charles vi of France. She first appears as the pupil of Lady Alice, who is teaching her English (v.ii). Henry

wants to marry her in order to consolidate the peace with France, and woos and wins her with Alice as interpreter.

Katharine of Valois (1401–37) was the youngest daughter of Charles vi of France. Henry began negotiations for her hand in marriage shortly after his accession, and demanded as her dowry the lost French possessions of the English Norman and Angevin kings. He was refused, and so he went to war and won both bride and territory. He married Katharine in accordance with the Treaty of Troyes in 1421. In December 1421 she gave birth to a son, the future Henry vi. In August

Rosaline (Joan Plowright), the Princess of France (Louise Purnell), Maria (Helen Bourne) and Katharine (Judy Wilson) in the 1968 production of *Love's Labour's Lost* by the National Theatre Company, directed by Laurence Olivier.

1422 she returned from a visit to France as a widow. From 1423 she lived in Baynard's Castle; in 1428 she was secretly married to Owen Tudor, a poor Welsh gentleman, and lived in obscurity until he was imprisoned in 1436. She retired to Bermondsey Abbey, where she died in 1437.

KATHARINE, QUEEN (afterwards Dowager) *(H.VIII)*: she calls Henry's attention to the excessive taxes that Wolsey has been levying (I.i). She hears that she will have scholars 'to argue for her' at the divorce proceedings (II.ii). She pleads her cause in the court with great dignity, and accuses Wolsey of being her enemy (II.iv). She indignantly rejects the suggestion put forward by Wolsey and Campeggio that she should resign her queenhood without a struggle. After the annulment of her marriage she retires to Kimbolton, and falls into a long illness. While asleep she has a vision of six garlanded figures bidding her farewell; when she awakes she receives Capucius and gives him a farewell letter to Henry. She is carried out to die.

Katharine of Aragon (1485–1536) was the daughter of Ferdinand and Isabella of Spain. In 1501 she married

Princess Katharine (Hazel Penwarden) wooed by Henry v (Richard Burton) after the victory at Agincourt. From the production at Stratford in 1951.

Arthur, the eldest son of Henry VII; he died the next year, and she was immediately betrothed to Henry in order to avoid repayment of her large dowry. He married her within two months of his accession. Her two sons both died young; her daughter Mary was her only surviving child. She and Henry lived happily together for twenty years until Henry fell for Anne Boleyn and divorced her. She retired to Ampthill in Bedfordshire, near the monastery at Kimbolton. She died in 1536. Shakespeare has her die before the birth of Elizabeth, which was in 1533.

The nobility and dignity of Shakespeare's Katharine led Samuel Johnson to call her 'the most perfect female character in the whole range of our drama'. The mature dignity of her defence of herself and her role as Henry's wife is reminiscent of Hermione in *The Winter's Tale*:

> I have been to you a true and humble wife,
> At all times to your will conformable;
> Ever in fear to kindle your dislike,
> Yea, subject to your countenance, glad, or sorry,
> As I saw it inclined. When was the hour
> I ever contradicted your desire?
> Or made it not mine too? Or which of your friends
> Have I not strove to love, although I knew
> He were mine enemy? What friend of mine,
> That had to him derived your anger, did I
> Continue in my liking? Nay, gave notice
> He was from thence discharged? Sir, call to mind
> That I have been your wife, in this obedience,
> Upward of twenty years, and have been blessed
> With many children by you. (II.iv)

She does not deserve to fall, but history requires that she does. Shakespeare compensates by investing her and her situation with a pathos that is not found in the chronicle sources. He even exposes Henry to the charge of hypocrisy by having him praise her even as he is divorcing her:

> That man i' th' world who shall report he has
> A better wife, let him in naught be trusted,
> For speaking false in that; thou art alone,
> If thy rare qualities, sweet gentleness,
> Thy meekness saint-like, wife-like government,
> Obeying in commanding, and thy parts
> Sovereign and pious else, could speak thee out,
> The queen of earthly queens. She's noble born;
> And, like her true nobility, she has
> Carried herself towards me. (II.iv)

Her saintliness is confirmed by her vision of the garlanded dancers; it was remarkably daring for Shakespeare to treat her thus in a play that above all celebrated the establishment of the Protestant ascendancy, for she was after all a Spanish Catholic. Her last scene is a carefully organized series of appeals to the pity of the audience, so that she dies with a dignity that approaches the tragic.

KATHARINE MINOLA *(Shr.)*: 'the shrew'. She is the daughter of Baptista Minola; he wants to marry her off, and will not allow her docile sister Bianca to marry until Katharine is off his hands. She spurns all the suitors suggested by her father (I.i). Petruchio hears of her wealth and resolves to marry her and tame her shrewishness (I.ii). He ignores her abuse and assaults, and responds equally aggressively; he announces that they are to be married 'on Sunday' (II.i). After the wedding she is compelled to leave before the bridal banquet and sets out with Petruchio for a journey to his country house; on arrival he sends her to bed with no food (IV.i). Grumio refuses her pleas for food, and Petruchio denies her the cap and gown she has set her heart on with a virtuoso display of petulance. When she leaves for Padua with Petruchio she is thoroughly cowed and subdued; if he tells her to, she will now call the moon the sun (IV.v). At the final banquet she proves her complete wifely obedience, and shows that in this she is now superior to her sister Bianca (v.ii).

From the moment we first see the shrewish Kate bullying her sister there is no doubt that she needs 'taming'. Yet for all her aggressive ill humour, she is not without pathos: we can see how her father's adulation of the quiet beauty of her sister has made her envious and neglected:

> What will you not suffer me? Nay now I see
> She is your treasure, she must have a husband;
> I must dance barefoot on her wedding-day,
> And for your love to her, lead apes in hell.
> Talk not to me, I will go sit and weep,
> Till I can find occasion of revenge. (II.i)

As Petruchio immediately recognizes even before he sees her, her instinctive vitality has been perverted, and it needs to be redirected. Petruchio's first speech catches the implication of her sullen 'They call me Katharine, that do talk of me' and saturates her with attention:

> You lie in faith, for you are called plain Kate,
> And bonny Kate, and sometimes Kate the curst,
> But Kate, the prettiest Kate in Christendom,

below Mary Pickford as Kate and Douglas Fairbanks as Petruchio in the 1929 film version of *The Taming of the Shrew*.

right Elizabeth Taylor as Katharine Minola, the Shrew, in Franco Zefferelli's film version of *The Taming of the Shrew*.

Kate of Kate-Hall, my super-dainty Kate,
For dainties are all Kates, and therefore Kate,
Take this of me, Kate of my consolation –
Hearing thy mildness praised in every town,
Thy virtues spoke of, and thy beauty sounded,
Yet not so deeply as to thee belongs,
Myself am moved to woo thee for my wife. (II.i)

Petruchio's approach is brilliantly successful: the next time we see Kate she is still surly but she is fretting in case Petruchio 'never means to wed where he hath wooed'.

Subsequently Petruchio shows her what she has been like: 'he kills her in her own humour' as one of his servants shrewdly remarks. He is violent and aggressive to everyone except her, whom he treats with the utmost apparent consideration. Though he starves and hectors her 'in reverent care of her', he appears to overdo it when he seems to be turning submission into humiliation by making her call the sun the moon. But she sees the joke, and regains her wit:

Then, God be blessed, it is the blessed sun.

But sun it is not, when you say it is not,

And the moon changes even as you your mind. (IV.v)

Her final speech, in which she instructs her sister on the duties of a virtuous wife, is difficult to accept today, for it seems to reduce Kate to a puppet. But there is no doubt that in Elizabethan terms she and Petruchio have the ideal marriage relationship; and it is worth noting that she ends as she began in the play, berating her sister, only now she is able to take her revenge in a situation that is satisfyingly ironical.

The Taming of the Shrew is of uncertain date, though it is generally accepted that it was written 1592–94. It is not among the plays listed as Shakespeare's by Meres in 1598, and this makes it another candidate for the title *Love's Labours Won,* an unidentified play which is on Meres' list. It was long supposed that the source of the play was *The Taming of a Shrew* (1594), but it is now clear that this play is a corrupt pirated version of Shakespeare's play. The Induction and the shrew story were both familiar in popular tales and folklore; the story of Bianca and her suitors is derived from Ariosto's comedy *I Suppositi,* which was translated by Gascoigne as *The Supposes* (printed 1573).

KEEPER, A *(R.II)*: he brings a meal into Richard's cell at Pomfret Castle. Richard asks him to taste it as he usually does, but he says that Pierce of Exton has commanded him not to. Richard is exasperated and strikes him; he calls for help and the murderers enter.

According to Holinshed, Richard struck the keeper on the head with a carving knife.

below Petruchio harangues the bewildered servants at his country house in *The Taming of the Shrew* (IV.i). From a painting by Sir John Gilbert.

above Frontispiece to *The Taming of the Shrew* in Rowe's 1709 edition of Shakespeare's plays *(left)* ; a song cover for an operatic version of

The Taming of the Shrew by Hermann Goetz (1878) *(right)*.

KEEPER (CLARENCE'S) *(R.III)* : he is Clarence's gaoler. He listens to Clarence's account of his dream, and says that he is frightened by it. He leaves before the murderers enter (I.iv).

KEEPER (DOOR) *(H.VIII)* : under orders, he refuses to admit Cranmer to the council chamber (V.II); he later admits him (V.iii).

KEEPERS, TWO *(3H.VI)* : they are hunting deer when Henry enters in disguise. The first Keeper recognizes him; they declare their allegiance to Edward IV, and lead him away.

According to Holinshed, Henry was recognized by 'one Cantlow'.

KENT, EARL OF *(Lr.)* : a faithful follower of King Lear. He rebukes Lear for his folly in disowning Cordelia, and is banished. He enters Lear's service disguised as 'Caius', a serving man. He trips up Goneril's steward Oswald for insulting the King, and later beats him; Cornwall orders him put in the stocks. He is released on Lear's demand. He follows Lear into the storm, and leads him and the Fool to the hovel. He

takes them on to Dover, where Lear is reunited with Cordelia. After the death of Cordelia, he fails to make the dying Lear recognize him. He is himself a dying man at the end.

Kent is the supremely loyal servant, the honest, plain-spoken counterpart to the fawning courtier or flatterer. He is everything that Oswald is not. Cornwall characterizes him accurately even though he suspects him of deviousness:

. . . he cannot flatter, he,
An honest mind and plain, he must speak truth.
(II.ii)

Like Cordelia, he is untouched by the evil around him, and refuses to compromise with it. During Lear's final agony he speaks on behalf of the audience, his horrified comments allowing some release for their pent-up emotions. His last words are movingly appropriate for a man who has devoted his life to service:

I have a journey, sir, shortly to go;
My master calls me, I must not say no. (V.iii)

The equivalent figure in *The True Chronicle History of King Leir* is the honest Perillus. Kent's role is related to the bluff soldier of stage tradition, the figure that Iago so successfully counterfeits.

L

LABEO *(Caes.)*: an officer in Brutus' army. He appears once during the battle of Philippi, but does not speak (v.iii).

LADIES *(Wint.)*: they encourage Mamillius' chatter; he calls them 'yon crickets', and refuses to believe that one of them has blue eyebrows (II.i).

LADY *(R.II)*: one of the Queen's attendants. While walking in the Duke of York's garden she tries to suggest some amusements to alleviate the Queen's grief. They overhear the Gardener talking to the servants (III.iv).

LADY, (OLD) *(H.VIII)*: lady-in-waiting to Anne Bullen. She is with her when the Lord Chamberlain brings her the news that she has been made Marchioness of Pembroke (II.iii); she takes the news of the birth of Elizabeth to Henry, and is furious at the small gratuity she receives from the King (v.i).

LAERTES *(Ham.)*: the son of Polonius, and brother of Ophelia. He warns her against believing Hamlet's declarations of love. He leaves for France, where Polonius sends Reynaldo to spy on him. He returns to Denmark demanding vengeance for his father's death, and finds his sister mad. He plans Hamlet's death with Claudius. At Ophelia's funeral he protests at her being buried in 'ground unsanctified'; he fights with Hamlet in the grave. In the fencing match with Hamlet he wounds him with the poisoned rapier, but is in turn poisoned by it himself. He confesses his deceit before he dies.

Laertes is a headstrong man of action. His attitude to avenging his father's death is in sharp contrast to Hamlet's:

> How came he dead? I'll not be juggled with.
> To hell allegiance, vows to the blackest devil,
> Conscience and grace to the profoundest pit!
> I dare damnation. To this point I stand,
> That both the worlds I give to negligence,
> Let come what comes, only I'll be revenged
> Most thoroughly for my father. (IV.v)

He is the classic revenger, and as Hamlet recognizes, his counterpart:

> . . . by the image of my cause I see
> The portraiture of his. (v.ii)

But Laertes is not like Hamlet: he is a rather boorish, insensitive figure, not without a streak of evil:

> And, for that purpose, I'll anoint my sword.
> I bought an unction from a mountebank,
> So mortal, that but dip a knife into it,
> Where it draws blood, no cataplasm so rare,
> Collected from all simples that have virtue
> Under the moon, can save the thing from death
> That is but scratched withal. (IV.vii)

Hamlet is not the kind of man who would buy poison just in case he needed it. Laertes is the traditional morally ambivalent revenger, an indication of the role that Hamlet finds himself unable to play.

LAFEU *(All'sW.)*: an old lord. He takes Helena to Paris, and presents her to the King as 'Doctor She'. He quarrels with Parolles, and warns Bertram against him; but when Parolles is exposed, he is considerate to him. At the end, it is he who notices the King's ring on

Rosemary Harris as Ophelia and Derek Jacobi as Laertes in the 1963 production of *Hamlet* by the National Theatre Company.

above Launce (Robert Helpmann) and his dog Crab in the 1956 production of *The Two Gentlemen of Verona* at the Old Vic Theatre *(left)*; Friar Laurence (Campbell Gullan) and Romeo (John Gielgud) in *Romeo and Juliet* at the Regent Theatre in May 1924 *(right)*.

Bertram's finger, thus initiating the denouement (v.ii).

LARTIUS, TITUS *(Cor.)*: a Roman general in the war against the Volscians; he says that he would follow Cominius to the battle even if he had to 'lean upon one crutch and fight with t'other'. After the battle, he is given charge of the prisoners from Corioli, and is left in command of the captured city (i.v).

Plutarch mentions him as 'one of the valiantest men the Romans had at that time'.

LAUNCE *(Gent.)*: 'a clownish servant to Proteus'. He follows his master to Milan. Most of his scenes are comic ones with his dog Crab. He is sent to Silvia with 'a little jewel' of a dog as a present, but he loses it, and sends the incontinent Crab instead.

LAURENCE, FRIAR *(Rom.)*: a Franciscan friar who consents to marry Romeo and Juliet secretly, in the hope that their union will end the feud between the Montagues and the Capulets. He marries the couple in his cell, and keeps Romeo there (iii.ii). Paris tells Friar Laurence that he must be married to Juliet 'on Thursday'; Laurence tells her that he can supply her with a sleeping potion that will make her appear dead for forty-two hours, during which time she will lie in the ancestral vault. In the meantime he sends a message to Romeo in exile – but he does not receive it. He finds Romeo dead in the vault; when Juliet wakes he tells her to seek refuge in 'a sisterhood of holy nuns' (v.iii). At the end, in custody, he explains how the failure of his stratagems led to the tragedy.

Friar Laurence takes it upon himself to solve the crisis caused by the enmity between the two families, and is the unwitting agent of the tragedy. Even so, he does offer a prophetic warning to Romeo:
These violent delights have violent ends,
And in their triumph die; like fire and powder,
Which as they kiss consume. The sweetest honey
Is loathesome in his own deliciousness,
And in the taste confounds the appetite.
Therefore love moderately, long love doth so;
Too swift arrives as tardy as too slow. (ii.vi)

Friar Laurence has a recapitulatory speech at the end, which Johnson did not like: 'It is much to be lamented that the Poet did not conclude the dialogue with the action, and avoid of narrative of events which the audience already knew'. But of course this knowledge is not shared by the other characters on stage: those who have caused the tragedy have to be told of their roles in it, so that Montague and Capulet can see the results of their enmity, and thus be reconciled.

LAVACHE *(All'sW.)*: 'a clown' serving the Countess of Rousillon. He explains why he wants to marry 'Isbel', but after he has been at court awhile he says he 'has no mind to Isbel' (iii.ii). He announces that Bertram has run away; later he announces his return.

He is a typical domestic clown.

LAVINIA *(Tit.)*: the daughter of Titus Andronicus. The new emperor Saturninus claims her as his bride, but she is betrothed to Bassianus, who carries her off and marries her. Tamora's sons Demetrius and Chiron both desire her, and Aaron advises them to rape her. In the wood, Lavinia discovers Tamora with Aaron, and accuses them of adultery; she is carried off by Demetrius and Chiron, who rape her and cut off her tongue and hands. She is discovered in this sorry state by Marcus and brought to Titus. With the aid of young Lucius she directs attention to the tale of Philomel in a copy of Ovid's *Metamorphoses,* and then writes the names of her violators in sand with a stick (IV.i). She helps her father kill Demetrius and Chiron. At the final banquet, her father kills her in order to end her shame.

The 'gentle' Lavinia is not a very amiable heroine, despite her appalling sufferings. She is self-righteously virtuous when she harangues Tamora (II.iii), and she helps her father in his sadistic revenge. While Titus prepares for his grisly banquet she is his mute but

Vivien Leigh as Lavinia in Peter Brook's production of *Titus Andronicus* at Stratford in 1955.

willing helper: she holds a basin to catch the blood when Titus cuts the throats of Demetrius and Chiron, and helps him with his cookery, thus involving herself in sadism as coldly cruel as that by which she lost her tongue and hands.

LAWYER, A *(1H.VI)*: in the Temple garden he plucks a white rose, thus declaring himself a Yorkist and a follower of Plantagenet. (II.iv)

LEAR, KING *(Lr.)*: King of Britain during some primeval period of the island's history, Lear, when he grows old, decides to divide his kingdom between his three daughters, Goneril, Regan and Cordelia. His two elder children loudly profess their love; but Cordelia's protestations, which are far more sincere, fail to satisfy the ill-tempered and demanding patriarch; and he thereupon deprives her of her promised heritage, and banishes his trusted counsellor, Kent, who has ventured to take Cordelia's side. Despite her lack of dowry, however, she is married by the King of France; and, once she has left the country, Regan and Goneril, with the assistance of their no less villainous husbands, Albany and Cornwall, gradually reduce the old man's retinue and agree to shut their doors against him. Lear wanders forth into the storm; and, on a blasted heath, meets another pair of homeless vagrants, Edgar, the legitimate son of Gloucester, whom his bastard half-brother, Edmund, has supplanted, and his companion, the demented Fool. They support the old king in his agony, as afterwards do Kent and Gloucester; but Cornwall puts out the aged Gloucester's eyes. Edgar then leads his blinded father to Dover, and Kent gallantly takes charge of Lear. Meanwhile, Cordelia lands on British soil. She and her miserable father are reconciled; but her troops are presently defeated in battle and Edmund orders that she shall be hanged. Lear enters bearing the body; and, though he imagines that she may still live, 'two extremes of passion, joy and grief', combine to break the old man's heart. Goneril and Regan, now furious enemies, bring about one another's downfall.

As in *Hamlet*, Shakespeare, when he wrote *Lear,* seems to have been working on an earlier drama, *King Leir,* an anonymous drama, produced at the Rose theatre during April 1594. The story had also been told in Holinshed's *Chronicles* (1577) and is referred to in Spenser's *Faerie Queene.* The anonymous play provided a happy ending, and omitted the tragic history of Gloucester. Shelley considered that Shakespeare's *Lear,* performed 'before the Kinges maiestie at Whitehall' on 26 December 1606, was 'the most perfect specimen of the dramatic art'; and Hazlitt declared that it was 'the best of Shakespeare's plays, for it is the one in which he was the most in earnest'. Technically perfect

rule through a display of weakness. Tearing off his clothes, he reveals himself as just such a 'poor, bare, forked animal' as the Fool who bears him company. The atmosphere of the play is dim and cold and gloomy; it has the rugged outlines of an ancient legend; and critics have suggested that Shakespeare's king is a descendant of Lir, the Celtic sea-god, and that his three

above The blinded Gloucester meets Lear in his madness: an eighteenth-century engraving *(left)*;

William Charles Macready as King Lear, in an early nineteenth-century production *(right)*.

it can scarcely claim to be. A high point of the action is the splendid storm-scene, where the terrible confusion of the elements above reflect the cruel conflicts that are being waged on earth; but the simultaneous presence of Lear, Edgar and the Fool – Lear driven mad by his sufferings; Edgar, who is pretending madness to escape the malice of his foes; and the Fool, a natural zany – somewhat weakens its dramatic force. Cordelia would be a more impressive heroine were her behaviour less absurdly tactless; while Goneril and Regan are so unrelievedly malevolent as to be almost indistinguishable.

Few of Shakespeare's tragedies, however, have such strength and depth and majesty. Lear is a man passionately devoted to power, who finds that, once he has lost his throne, his appetite for personal authority becomes a soul-destroying passion. He exhibits the unbridled egotism of harsh, self-centred old age; he is the least heroic of Shakespeare's tragic heroes; and, when he can no longer command through strength, attempts to

daughters represent the winds, Goneril and Regan being the destructive storm-winds, while Cordelia is the gentle western breeze. It is a pagan world that Shakespeare's characters inhabit, uncheered by any hope of salvation or by the reconciling influence of the Christian spirit. Man is born to tears:

Thou must be patient. We came crying hither;
Thou know'st the first time that we smell the air
We wawl and cry. (IV.vi)

And the only consolatory message is delivered by Edgar, who, in the midst of defeat and ruin, addresses the blind, exhausted Gloucester. The old man wishes to die where he stands:

No further, sir; a man may rot even here.
Edg: What, in ill thoughts again? Men must endure
Their going hence, even as their coming hither;
Ripeness is all . . . (v.ii)

Shakespeare seldom hints that he possessed a 'philos-

above King Lear in the hovel during the storm, after the painting by Benjamin West. *below King Lear*: Cordelia is banished by Lear, her father, despite the entreaties of Kent. After a painting by Henry Fuseli. *right* John Gielgud as Lear in the 1940 production of *King Lear* at the Old Vic.

ophy of life'. Perhaps the nearest he ever came to propounding such a philosophy was in Edgar's last three words.

LE BEAU *(AYL.)*: one of Duke Frederick's courtiers. He tells Celia and Rosalind of Charles' triumphs as a wrestler. He warns Orlando that the Duke is ill-disposed towards him, and explains to him which of Celia and Rosalind is the Duke's daughter (I.ii).

Le Beau is verbose and rather slow-witted.

above David Garrick as King Lear *(left)*.

Henry Irving as King Lear in 1892. From a drawing by Bernard Partridge *(right)*.

LE FER, MONSIEUR *(H.V)*: a French soldier captured by Pistol. He offers his captor two hundred crowns to spare his life; Pistol is pleased to accept (IV.iv).

LEGATE, A *(1H.VI)*: a papal legate who accompanies the papal ambassadors to England when they bring the Cardinal's robes for the Bishop of Winchester. Winchester promises him payment 'for clothing me in these brave ornaments'.

LENNOX *(Mac.)*: a Scottish thane in attendance on Duncan. After Duncan's murder he visits his chamber with Macbeth, and he describes how they found the drunken grooms and how Macbeth killed them – an act he apparently approved of. After the murder of Banquo and Macbeth's strange behaviour at the banquet he realizes the truth, and joins the rebels.

LEONARDO *(Mer.V.)*: servant to Bassanio, who is with him when Launcelot Gobbo seeks employment with him (II.ii). He is sent to buy new livery for Gobbo when Bassanio accepts him.

LEONATO *(Ado)*: the governor of Messina, and father of Hero. He consents to the betrothal of Hero and Claudio, in spite of his awareness that Don Pedro wants his daughter. He wants a husband for his niece Beatrice too, and enters Don Pedro's conspiracy to match her with Benedick, though with some doubts, since he fears that if they were married they would 'talk themselves mad' in a week. He at first believes the case against Hero, but is persuaded by Friar Laurence that there is much doubt; he vows that if the slanders prove false he will have vengeance on those who perpetrated them (IV.i). When he becomes convinced of Hero's innocence he challenges Claudio. He insists that Claudio marries Hero's 'cousin' (V.i). He presents Hero, veiled, to Claudio at the ceremony, and when she reveals herself he explains the deception.

In Bandello's *Novella* he is Lionato de' Lionati, a gentleman of Messina.

LEONINE *(Per.)*: servant to Dionyza. She orders him to kill Marina, but just as he is about to do so, he is surprised by pirates and runs away. He thinks that she will not be seen again and that he can safely claim to have killed her. Dionyza poisons him in order to keep the secret (IV.i).

LEONTES *(Wint.)* : the King of Sicilia. Polixenes, his friend since childhood, has been staying at his court for nine months and is now about to leave. Leontes tells him to stay longer, and when he refuses he asks his wife Hermione to persuade him. She does so successfully, and Leontes is irritated that she has succeeded where he has failed. The irritation suddenly swells into violent jealousy as he fancies he sees an undue intimacy between Hermione and Polixenes. He sends them into the garden while he questions his friend Camillo and tells him of his suspicions: by now he is convinced that Hermione and Polixenes are lovers, that Polixenes is the father of the child she is expecting, and he even suspects that his son Mamillius is not his own. Camillo defends Hermione, but can make no impression on Leontes, and is ordered to poison Polixenes (I.ii).

Leontes hears that Polixenes and Camillo have fled together, and feels that his suspicions are confirmed; he orders Hermione to prison, and forbids her to see Mamillius. He sends messengers to the oracle of Apollo to ask it to pronounce on Hermione's faithfulness (II.i). Paulina brings in his newly born child from prison: he flies into a rage and orders it 'consum'd with fire', but relents a little and tells Antigonus to take it and leave it exposed in 'some remote and desert place' (II.iii). At the trial of Hermione Leontes presides, and refuses to accept the verdict of the oracle which declares her blameless. The death of Mamillius is announced to him, and he recognizes the anger of Apollo; Paulina enters with the news that Hermione is dead, and Leontes is overcome with remorse. He lives penitently in deep seclusion for the next sixteen years. His courtiers want him to marry again, but Paulina makes him swear never to do so without her approval. Florizel and Perdita are presented to him, and he hears that Polixenes has also arrived in Sicilia (V.i). Perdita's identity is revealed to him, and he is 'ready to leap out of himself, for joy of his found daughter' (V.ii). He visits the statue of Hermione, and finds that it is Hermione herself; he is joyously reunited with her.

The motivation for Leontes' sudden violent jealousy has long been the subject of critical dispute. It has been suggested that it is not really sudden, that Leontes has been jealous for some time and that he invites Polixenes to stay in order to confirm his suspicions. 'Infection' is Shakespeare's word for what happens to Leontes; he is struck as though by a physical disease:

> ...Too hot, too hot,
> To mingle friendship far, is mingling bloods.
> I have tremor cordis on me; my heart dances,
> But not for joy, not joy. This entertainment

> May a free face put on; derive a liberty
> From heartiness, from bounty, fertile bosom,
> And well become the agent; 't may, I grant.
> But to be paddling palms, and pinching fingers,
> As now they are, and making practised smiles
> As in a looking-glass; and then to sigh, as 'twere
> The mort o' the deer; o, that is entertainment
> My bosom likes not, nor my brows. (I.ii)

In *Pandosto,* Shakespeare's source, Pandosto's jealousy develops relatively slowly; but Shakespeare

Forbes-Robertson as Leontes in *The Winter's Tale* in a late nineteenth-century production.

had already shown a mind being corroded by jealousy in *Othello*. In *The Winter's Tale* Shakespeare seems more concerned with the dramatic effect of Leontes' sudden frenzy than with the psychology of his condition.

LEPIDUS, MARCUS AEMILIUS *(Caes.; Ant.)* : he witnesses the assassination of Caesar. He joins Octavius and becomes the third member of the triumvirate with him and Antony. Octavius thinks him 'a valiant soldier', but according to Antony he is 'a slight unmeritable man'.

In *Antony and Cleopatra* he tries to mediate between Octavius and Antony, and makes excuses for the latter's faults (I.iv). During the negotiations with Pompey he is carried off drunk (II.vii). Later Eros reports that he has been deprived of his position and imprisoned on the orders of Octavius.

He was made Praetor in 49 BC, and Consul with Caesar in 46 BC. In 44 he was made Pontifex Maximus, and went to govern in Gaul and Spain. He was deprived of all power, though not of his title, when he tried to take over Sicily for himself. He died in 13. Shakespeare's Lepidus is weak and ineffective, and totally lacking in integrity; he is an image of political moderation reduced to incompetence.

LEWIS THE DAUPHIN (afterwards Lewis VIII) *(John)*: 'the Dauphin'. He is married to John's niece, Blanch of Spain, but despite her pleas he resolves to take up arms against John, and is persuaded by Pandulph to invade England. He refuses to abandon his attack even when he hears that John has made a submission to Rome, but in the end his expedition is wrecked when the rebel nobles desert him and his supply ships are sunk on the Goodwin Sands (V.v).

The title is inaccurate: it was not until 1364 that the title Dauphin was borne by the eldest son of the King of France. Lewis (1187-1226) is described as 'short, thin, pale-faced, with studious tastes, cold and placid temper, sober and chaste in his life. He left the reputation of a saint, but was also a warrior prince'. In 1215 he received a request from a group of disaffected English barons for aid against John; when twenty-four of them arrived as hostages Lewis invaded England despite the prohibition of the papal legate. After the accession of Henry III in 1216 he was hopelessly defeated, and returned home. He became King in 1223, and continued waging war on the Plantagenets.

The sinking of the Dauphin's supply ships referred to in the play may be a reference to the destruction of a vastly superior French fleet in the English Channel by Hubert de Burgh in 1217; this action was the first great English naval victory.

LEWIS THE DAUPHIN (son of Charles VI) *(H.V)*: he advises that defences be prepared against an English invasion; he boasts of having insulted Henry by sending him tennis balls. He boasts of the coming victory. After the defeat at Agincourt he calls on the French nobles to stab themselves.

He was the eldest son of Charles VI of France. The story of the gift of tennis balls is found in Holinshed, who records that while 'the king laie at Killingworth there came to him from Charles Dolphin of france certeine ambassadors, that brought with them a barrell of Paris balles; which from their maister they presented to him for a token that was taken in very ill part, as sent in scorn, to signifie, that it was more meet for the king to passe the time with such childish exercise, than to attempt any worthie exploit.'

Shakespeare mingles three Dauphins into one during the course of *Henry V*: Lewis died in 1415, shortly after Agincourt, where he was not in fact present; his brother Jean held the title until his death in 1416, when it passed to Charles, afterwards Charles VII.

The Dauphin is presented as the antithesis of Henry: he is all show and vainglory, possessing only the superficial attributes of royalty and none of its substance.

LEWIS, KING OF FRANCE *(3H.VI)*: Lewis XI. He agrees to assist Queen Margaret to reinstate Henry (III.iii). He later agrees to allow his sister-in-law Lady Bona to marry Edward.

Lewis XI of France (1423-83) was the son of Charles VII and Marie of Anjou; he was the first cousin of both Henry VI and Queen Margaret. Before his accession in 1461 he became alienated from his father, but maintained his power by cultivating the support of the towns and their bourgeois classes. In 1470 he helped Margaret and Warwick replace Henry VI on the throne. When Edward IV regained the English throne he entered into a conspiracy with Charles of Burgundy against Lewis; but when Charles died Lewis bought off Edward and carried on with unifying France.

He was a clever but arbitrary ruler. As a man he was very ugly; he wore the meanest clothes, and avoided all ceremony and ostentation.

LIEUTENANT OF AUFIDIUS *(Cor.)*: he warns Aufidius that his authority with his soldiers is being weakened by the growing popularity of Coriolanus, and expresses his regret that Aufidius ever 'join'd in commission with him' (IV.vii).

LIEUTENANT OF THE TOWER *(3H.VI)*: when Henry is released from the Tower, he asks the Lieutenant what his 'due fees' are, and thanks him for his kindness which has made his imprisonment a pleasure (IV.vi). He appears later with Henry and Gloucester on the walls of the Tower, but is dismissed by Gloucester who wants Henry alone in order to murder him (V.vi).

There were two Lieutenants in the period covered. The first was John Tiptoft, who was created Earl of Worcester in 1449. He was a zealous Yorkist, and was appointed Constable of the Tower by Edward IV. He hanged and impaled twenty of Clarence's supporters in 1470, earning himself the title of 'the butcher of England'. He was executed after the flight of Edward IV. He was succeeded by John Sutton, who was his lieutenant.

LIEUTENANT *(2H.VI), see* CAPTAIN (SEA).

LIGARIUS, CAIUS *(Caes.)* : he leaves his sick-bed to join the conspiracy, but is not present at the assassination (II.i; II.ii).

Quintus Ligarius fought with Pompey at Thapsus, and was captured and banished by Caesar. He was pardoned as a result of Cicero's speech (which is still extant) in his defence. He joined the conspirators.

LINCOLN, BISHOP OF *(H.VIII)* : one of the clergy present at the divorce proceedings at Black-friars; he is represented as the first person to suggest the idea of divorce to Henry (II.iv).

John Longland (1476-1547) was confessor to Henry VIII. He was, as Shakespeare says, the initiator of the idea of the divorce, but he later repented it bitterly.

LODOVICO *(Oth.)* : a kinsman of Brabantio. He brings Othello a dispatch from the Venetian senate recalling him from Cyprus; when he enters he is amazed to see Othello strike Desdemona. He finds Cassio lying wounded, and sees Roderigo stabbed by Iago (v.ii); he finds the letters in Roderigo's pocket that reveal Iago's guilt. He orders Othello's arrest, and tells Cassio to assume his authority. At the end he orders the torture of Iago.

Desdemona calls him 'a proper man' (IV.iii), and Emilia says that she knows 'a lady in Venice would have walked barefoot to Palestine for a touch of his nether lip' (IV.iii). When he enters with news from Venice (IV.i) he reminds us of the world beyond Cyprus, and his incredulous question 'Is this the noble Moor?' reminds us of how Othello has changed.

LODOWICK, FRIAR *(Meas.)* : the role assumed by Duke Vincentio when he disguises himself in order to observe the performance of Angelo as deputy. *See* VINCENTIO, DUKE.

LONDON, BISHOP OF *(H.VIII)* : he is on one side of the Queen in the coronation procession (IV.i).

He was John Stokesley (*c.* 1476-1539), chaplain and almoner to Henry VIII. He was made Bishop of London in 1530, and then was sent as 'ambassador to the universities beyond the sea for the kings marriage' (Holinshed).

LONGAVILLE *(LLL.)* : one of the three lords attending the King of Navarre; he readily assents to the oath of asceticism proposed by the King. He falls in love with Maria, and addresses a sonnet to her in which he argues that he has not broken his oath since she is not a woman but a goddess; Berowne cynically comments that the poem is in 'the liver vein, which makes flesh a deity'. When he is disguised as a Muscovite he exchanges banter with the masked Katharine, whom he mistakes for Maria. Maria promises that after a year she will 'change her black gown, for a faithful friend' (v.ii).

Longaville's sonnet, 'Did not the heavenly rhetoric of thine eye', was published in *The Passionate Pilgrim* in 1599.

LORD, A *(Shr.)* : he returns from hunting to find the tinker Sly in a drunken sleep. He orders him to be taken to the best room in his house, and to be told when he wakes that he is a lord who has just recovered from fifteen years of lunacy. He tells a company of players to perform for him that night, and tells his page to pretend to be Sly's wife (Induction I). The lord disguises himself as a servant, and when Sly wakes he tells him that he is a lord, and that his every command will be obeyed (Induction II).

LORD CHIEF JUSTICE *(2H.IV)* : he warns Falstaff that he lives 'in great infamy', and tells him that it is only because of the 'unquiet time' that his part in the Gadshill robbery is not being investigated. Later he orders him to make restitution to Mistress Quickly, and concludes that he is 'a great fool'. He is worried when Henry V assumes the throne, fearing that he is now 'open to all injuries' because of his hostility to Falstaff, and because he had once imprisoned Prince Henry for striking him. Henry confirms his office, and tells him he will be 'a father to [his] youth'; he tells him to enforce the banishment and imprisonment of Falstaff.

He was Sir William Gascoigne (*c.* 1350–1419). He was made Lord Chief Justice in 1400. The story of Henry insulting him and being sent to prison has no historical foundation: it is found in Hall and in Elyot's *Governor* (1531). Hall and Elyot both say that Henry insulted the Lord Chief Justice after one of his servants had been arraigned before him, and that he was imprisoned and banished from the court with the approval of the King. Gascoigne's office was not in fact renewed under Henry V, probably at his own request.

LORD MARSHAL *(R.II)* : he conducts the formalities at the duel between Bolingbroke and Mowbray; when he orders them to begin fighting Richard tells them 'to return back to their chairs again'.

He was Thomas Holland (1374–1400), the 1st Duke of Surrey. He was a devoted follower of Richard II, who created him Earl Marshal in 1398 so that he might officiate at the duel between Bolingbroke and Norfolk. He was deprived of his dukedom in 1399, and at the beginning of 1400 he conspired with his uncle John Holland to seize Henry IV at Windsor, but they were betrayed by Rutland. They fought valiantly, and Thomas Holland escaped to Cirencester where he was beheaded by the local people.

LORD MARSHAL (Duke of Norfolk as) *(H.VIII)*, *see* SURREY, EARL OF.

LORENZO *(Mer. V.)* : a young gentleman, friend to Bassanio. He is in love with Shylock's daughter Jessica. He elopes with her, and they take some of his jewels and ducats (II.vi); Salerio tells them to go to Belmont. They look after Belmont while Portia is in Venice, and they welcome her home.

For Heine, Lorenzo was 'the accomplice of one of the most infamous burglaries'; but this was a result of that writer's misconceived sentimentalization of Shylock. Lorenzo is the man of good sense in the play, the careful user of words. It is he who brings together all the themes of the play at the end with a resonant and beautiful speech:

How sweet the moonlight sleeps upon this bank.
Here will we sit, and let the sounds of music
Creep in our ears. Soft stillness and the night
Become the touches of sweet harmony.
Sit Jessica. Look how the floor of heaven
Is thick inlaid with patens of bright gold.
There's not the smallest orb which thou behold'st
But in his motion like an angel sings,
Still quiring to the young-eyed cherubins;
Such harmony is in immortal souls,
But whilst this muddy vesture of decay
Doth grossly close it in, we cannot hear it (v.i)

LOVEL, LORD ('Sir Thomas') *(R.III)* : with Ratcliffe he takes Hastings into custody (III.iv); he brings in his head to Richard (III.v).

He was Sir Francis Lovel, who was a strong supporter of the claims of Richard Duke of Gloucester after the death of Edward IV. When Richard came to the throne he made Lovel Chamberlain and Chief Butler of England. In 1485 he was sent to Southampton to organize a fleet to prevent Richmond landing, but he failed. Lovel is referred to, along with Ratcliffe and Catesby, in a rhyme which William Collingbourne posted on the door of his parish church, and for which Richard executed him:

The Catte, the Ratte, and Lovel our dogge,
Rulyth all Englande under a Hogge.

Lovel was at Bosworth, but escaped capture, and eventually found his way to Flanders. He returned with Lambert Simnel, and was reported killed at Stoke; it was also said that he was seen trying to swim the River Trent on his horse. It is possible that he escaped to his house at Minster Lovell in Oxfordshire, and lived there for some time in a secret chamber before dying of starvation. In 1708 a secret chamber was discovered in the house, and in it the skeleton of a man seated at a table before books, papers and a pen. The bones, which were said to be Lovel's, crumbled to dust soon after they were exposed to the air.

LOVELL, SIR THOMAS *(H.VIII)* : Chancellor of the Exchequer, and member of the council. Buckingham's surveyor claims that his head was in danger from Buckingham's treason (I.ii). He superintends Wolsey's banquet (I.iv).

He fought with Richmond at Bosworth, and was held in high esteem by Henry VIII, even though he was a Catholic. At the time of the arrest of Buckingham he was Constable of the Tower, with Sir Richard Cholmondeley as his Lieutenant.

LUCE *(Err.)* : a kitchen maid at the house of Antipholus of Ephesus. She refuses to let Antipholus and Dromio of Ephesus into their own house because Antipholus and Dromio of Syracuse (who she has mistaken for them) are already inside (III.i).

LUCENTIO *(Shr.)* : Vincentio's son, and suitor to Bianca, with whom he falls in love at first sight. To gain access to her he disguises himself as 'Cambio', a tutor; in this role he is engaged by Gremio to plead his suit to Bianca under the pretence of teaching her Latin. He woos her for himself, and secretly marries her. He presides at a banquet in his own house, and is amazed when he loses a wager that his wife is more obedient than the previously fractious Katharine.

LUCETTA *(Gent.)* : Julia's waiting woman. She admires Proteus above all her mistress's admirers. She gives her a letter from him which she had been given by Valentine's page; Julia refuses to take it, and when Lucetta presents it to her a second time she tears it up (I.ii). Lucetta tries to discourage Julia from going to Milan, but fails; she is entrusted with the care of Julia's possessions in her absence (II.vii).

LUCIANA *(Err.)* : sister to Adriana. She confuses Antipholus of Syracuse with Adriana's husband Antipholus of Ephesus, and is distressed when he starts making advances to her. She presumably marries him after the errors have been resolved at the end.

LUCIANUS *(Ham.)* : part assumed by one of the Players *(q.v.)*.

LUCILIUS *(Caes.)* : a friend to Brutus and Cassius. Captured at Philippi he declares that he is Brutus, and offers his captors money to kill him. Antony recognizes him, and gives orders for him to be well-treated (v.iv).

Plutarch recounts this episode, and adds that Lucilius remained faithful to Antony.

LUCILIUS *(Tim.)*: one of Timon's servants. He wishes to marry, but the girl's father, an old Athenian *(q.v.)*, objects because he is low-born and poor. Timon offers to give Lucilius money equal to the girl's dowry, and the old man is satisfied, and allows the marriage to go ahead (I.i).

LUCIO *(Meas.)*: a Venetian rake. He meets his friend Claudio who is being taken to prison, and agrees to ask Isabella to intercede with Angelo for him. He explains Claudio's position to Isabella, and takes her to Angelo; when she is pleading with him, he urges her to show more passion. When Pompey is arrested, he refuses to stand bail for him (III.ii). He slanders the Duke to Friar Lodowick (who is in fact the Duke in disguise), claiming that he was a libertine. When this is reported to the Duke at the end, Lucio claims that it was a 'meddling friar' who spoke ill of the Duke; he continues to maintain this even when confronted by 'Friar Lodowick'. When the Duke reveals himself he condemns Lucio to be whipped, but withdraws this punishment and makes him marry a whore that he has wronged.

In the 'Names of the Actors' in the First Folio Lucio is 'a fantastique': that is, an improvident young gallant. He is a witty opportunist, a cynic without integrity or loyalties, who lives by his cunning in the margin between the underworld and respectable society. His vulgarity and honest acceptance of sex make him an attractive character to a modern audience; the judgement of the play is more harsh. He is careless with words, and has no regard for the truth: behind the Duke's condemnation of his slanders at the end lies the biblical injunction 'But I say unto you, that every idle word that men speak, they shall give account thereof in the day of judgment' (Matthew xii: 36). He saves himself from a whipping by his wit: even the Duke cannot fail to be amused by him. But he is punished for his lack of responsibility, for deserting his child and its mother.

LUCIUS *(Caes.)*: a boy servant to Brutus. He twice falls asleep on duty, the second time while singing to Brutus just before the appearance of Caesar's ghost. Brutus is fond of him: before Philippi he says to the sleeping boy 'If I do live, I will be good to thee' (IV.iv).

LUCIUS *(Tim.)*: a lord who flatters Timon, and makes him a present of 'four milk-white horses, trapp'd in silver' (I.ii). He refuses to lend to Timon when he is in need, and even sends a servant to try to collect a debt from him (III.ii).

LUCIUS *(Tim.)*: servant to Lucius above, he is known by his master's name. He applies to Timon for a debt due to his master, but is unable to collect it (III.iv).

LUCIUS *(Tit.)*: the eldest son of Titus Andronicus. He demands that the 'proudest prisoner' from among the captured Goths be sacrificed for his brothers who were killed in the battle (I.ii). He helps Bassianus carry off Lavinia. After the rape and mutilation of his sister he flees to the Goths in order to raise an army against Saturninus. He returns with an army, and captures Aaron, who confesses to him in order to save his child. At Titus' banquet he kills Saturninus; he justifies the deeds of his father, and is proclaimed emperor. He orders Tamora's body thrown to the wild beasts, and that Aaron should be set breast deep in the earth and left to starve.

At the end Lucius heralds a new and more civilized order, though there are elements of his character that suggest that he is hardly suited for the role of moral saviour of Rome. He is a strange mixture of tenderness and cruelty: he is quite callous when Tamora pleads for her son (I.i), yet shows concern for Aaron's illegitimate black child (V.i).

Lucius was traditionally the first of the Christian British kings; he was supposedly (for example, in Foxe's *Book of Martyrs*) descended from Aeneas. It is noteworthy that in the play he apparently changes from the worship of the Roman Gods to being a Christian, for Aaron says he has known him to have a conscience 'with twenty popish tricks and ceremonies'.

LUCIUS, CAIUS *(Cym.)*: the Roman ambassador, and then general of the Roman invasion force. He demands tribute from Cymbeline, and on his refusal to pay declares war on Britain 'in Caesar's name'. He takes 'Fidele' (the disguised Imogen) into his service, and after the Roman defeat and his capture he asks 'him' to choose him as the prisoner to be spared. To his surprise 'Fidele' refuses to plead for his life; but when all is revealed he is pardoned by Cymbeline, who agrees to pay tribute to Rome.

LUCIUS, YOUNG *(Tit.)*: son to Lucius, and grandson to Titus. He fears that Lavinia is mad when she pursues him with books, but discovers that she wants to point out a passage in Ovid to him that reveals the story of her ravishment; Lucius vows to avenge her when he grows up (IV.i). He presents a bundle of arrows with messages wrapped round them to Tamora as Titus instructs him (IV.ii). He shoots arrows in the air for Titus (IV.iii). He laments his grandfather's death at the end.

LUCULLUS *(Tim.)*: an Athenian lord. Timon sends

Flaminius to him to ask for a loan. Lucullus tries to bribe Flaminius to report to Timon that he could not be found, but Flaminius throws the money in his face (III.i). Lucullus is one of those invited to Timon's final 'banquet' (III.iv).

LUCY, SIR WILLIAM *(1H.VI)*: he tells Somerset and York to go to the aid of Talbot; he blames Talbot's death and the consequent English defeat on sedition (IV.iii). He negotiates with the Dauphin for the return of the bodies of Talbot and his son.

This could be either Sir William Lucy of Charlecote (1398–1466), a Yorkist; or the Sir William Lucy who was killed at the Battle of Northampton (1460) at the age of forty.

LYCHORIDA *(Per.)*: Marina's nurse. In the storm she brings the newborn baby to Pericles, and tells him that Thaisa is dead (III.i). She is left to look after Marina when Pericles returns to Tyre (III.iii). Gower reports her death in the Prologue to Act IV.

LYMOGES, DUKE OF AUSTRIA *(John)*: he is welcomed by the Dauphin and Arthur before Angiers, and promises to help Arthur, who forgives him 'Coeur-de-lion's death'. Lymoges wears a lion-skin taken from Coeur-de-lion, which brings him bitter insults and threats from Philip Faulconbridge, the Bastard (II.i). He is denounced by Constance for deserting Arthur's cause; his attempts to justify himself are prevented by Philip's ribald mockery (III.i). Philip kills him in battle, and enters with his head (III.ii).

Shakespeare has confused and combined two historical enemies of Richard Coeur-de-lion. One was Vidomar, Viscount of Lymoges, whose castle Richard was besieging when he received his mortal wound in 1199. The other was Leopold V, 1st Archduke of Austria, who imprisoned Richard on his return from the Third Crusade, and released him on his death-bed. He died in 1195, five years before Richard.

LYSANDER *(MND.)*: he asserts his claim to Hermia in the presence of Theseus, and accuses his rival Demetrius of inconstancy; he laments that 'the course of true love never did run smooth'. He suggests to Hermia that she meets him in the wood that night. In the wood they lie down to sleep; Puck applies magic love-juice to Lysander's eyes, and he awakes and sees Helena, and falls in love with her. She leaves, thinking he is mocking her; Lysander says he hates the sleeping Hermia (II.iii). He continues making passionate protestations of love to Helena, and tells Demetrius that he can have Hermia; when Hermia clings to him he insults her, calling her a dwarf, and saying that he hates her. He leaves to fight with Demetrius, but is led astray by Puck, who applies a counter-charm to his eyes when he sleeps (III.ii). He is woken by the sound of hunting horns, and finds Hermia next to him; he is oblivious of his previous enchantment, and finds his love for her restored (IV.i). He watches the Interlude at the end.

LYSIMACHUS *(Per.)*: the governor of Mytilene. He finds Marina in a brothel: instead of enjoying her as he intended, he is shamed and then regenerated by her virtue, and gives her gold and promises her help. He finds Pericles speechless with grief, and sends for her to arouse him. After the reunion of Pericles and Marina, it is announced that Lysimachus is to marry her.

There is some ambiguity about Lysimachus. He arrives at the brothel in a thoroughly licentious mood, saying 'How now, how a dozen of virginities?' (IV.vi) and eager to 'do the deed of darkness'. Yet when he discovers Marina's purity he says.

Had I brought hither a corrupted mind,
    Thy speech had altered it. (IV.vi)
and later sounds even more hypocritical:
        . . . For me, be you thoughten
    That I came with no ill intent; for to me
    The very doors and windows savour vilely. (IV.vi)

M

MACBETH *(Mac.)*: the historical Macbeth, who had seized the Scottish throne by defeating and slaying his predecessor, King Duncan I, seems to have ruled Scotland with some success for seventeen years, from 1040 to 1057. In Shakespeare's tragedy it is as Duncan's victorious general that we first encounter him. Riding home after a triumphant campaign against a force of Scottish rebels and their Norwegian allies, he and his fellow general Banquo meet three witches on a blasted heath; and the Weird Sisters hail Macbeth as Thane of Cawdor, and Banquo as the progenitor of a line of future sovereigns. Soon afterwards Macbeth learns that his grateful King has indeed recently dubbed him Thane of Cawdor. He describes the witches' prophecy to his wife; and Lady Macbeth, an ambitious and fiercely devoted woman, determines that, when Duncan visits their castle, he 'must be provided for'. Though Macbeth is hesitant – he is the gentler of the two and, originally, the less grasping – he agrees at length to carry out his wife's design and murders the King, while Lady Macbeth contrives to incriminate the royal attendants who have been sleeping in his chamber. Duncan's sons, Malcolm and Donalbain, since they have prudently left the castle, are accused of having planned his death. Macbeth is crowned king and, remembering the rest of the witches' prophecy – that Banquo shall become the sire of monarchs – kills his former associate, but fails to lay hands on Banquo's youthful son, Fleance. Dark suspicions now crowd the usurper's mind; and not only does the ghost of Banquo haunt him, but he begins to suspect and fear his noble liege-lord Macduff. In desperation he seeks the Weird Sisters, who impart a reassuring message: 'none of woman born shall harm Macbeth'; and, until 'Great Birnam wood' shall advance against Dunsinane hill, Macbeth shall remain unconquered. Hearing that Macduff has fled to England, where he has joined Malcolm, Duncan's rightful heir, the King commands that both Lady Macduff and her little boy are to be assassinated. His orders are carried out; but, meanwhile, under the pressure of her hideous imaginings – she believes that her hands are indelibly stained with blood – his wife's sanity has broken down. She kills

herself; and Macbeth prepares for battle, only to learn on the field that the witches have deluded him. The invading army cut branches from Birnam wood, beneath which they march against the stronghold that he occupies at Dunsinane; and Macduff proclaims that he had had an unnatural birth, 'untimely ripp'd' from his mother's womb by some primitive Caesarian operation. Macduff slays the usurper in single combat, and regains the kingdom that Macbeth had stolen.

Shakespeare derived the outlines of his drama from the *Chronicles* of Holinshed, published in 1577; and Holinshed took his account of Scottish history from the *Scotorum Historiae* of Hector Boece, issued half a

Macduff (Mr Alexander) confronts Macbeth (Mr Irving) in a nineteenth-century production of *Macbeth* at the Lyceum Theatre.

century earlier. *Macbeth*, probably written about 1606, seems to have been intended to serve a double purpose. King James I was deeply concerned with witchcraft, and in 1597 had produced a learned treatise on the subject of the black arts. He was also likely, as a direct descendant of Banquo, to appreciate any reference to his ancient Scottish ancestry. Being one of 'the King's

above The two murderers (B. Duffield and W. Alland) with Macbeth (Orson Welles) in the 1949 film of *Macbeth* directed by Welles *(top)*; Mr Henderson as Macbeth, 1778, after George Romney *(bottom)*.
left Drawing of Act III of *Macbeth*, Charles Kean's production at the Princess's Theatre in 1853 *(top)*. Drawing of the banquet scene in the same production *(bottom)*.

Men', Shakespeare, always a diplomatist, was mindful of the sovereign's tastes; but, at the same time, he found the story of Macbeth a particularly congenial theme. All his tragic heroes are somehow cut off from life: Hamlet by a secret sense of failure; Othello and Antony by their overwhelming passions; Lear by his blind egotism, which gradually degenerates into madness; Coriolanus by his inextinguishable pride. None can escape from his self-constructed prison; each is a lonely man, whose feelings of inner solitude grow steadily more and more oppressive.

There is much to recommend Macbeth; he is brave, eloquent and energetic. But no sooner has he committed his first crime than the rapid accumulation of guilt begins to brutalize his character. When his wife dies, he loses his last companion. He is now entirely alone; and he likens his fate to that of one of the wretched animals kept to be baited, and eventually done to death, in an English bear-garden:

They have tied me to a stake; I cannot fly,
But bear-like I must fight the course (v.vii)

– and, at Dunsinane, he is pulled down and perishes.

Before he falls, he has become aware not only of the horror of life, but of its meaningless monotony:

Tomorrow, and tomorrow, and tomorrow,
Creeps in this petty pace from day to day,
To the last syllable of recorded time . . . (v.v)

Macbeth seems as darkly pessimistic as *Othello*, *Lear* or *Hamlet*. The usurper's guilt is a disease that presently infects his whole realm:

Foul whis'prings are abroad: unnatural deeds
Do breed unnatural troubles: infected minds
To their deaf pillows will discharge their secret . . . (v.i)

Many of its images are borrowed from the idea of night;

'the crow makes wing to the rooky wood'; the 'shard-borne beetle' whirs across the shadows; and the fearful traveller hastens towards the inn, glancing back at the last 'streaks of day'. It is surely significant, writes Caroline F. E. Spurgeon, the author of *Shakespeare's Imagery*, 'that there are only two plays in which the word "love" occurs so seldom as in *Macbeth*, and no play in which "fear" occurs so often . . .' Shakespeare's witches, whom Caroline producers, like Sir John Davenant, with the help of many ingenious devices, made a central feature of the play, have ceased to alarm a twentieth-century audience. Far more real nowadays are Macbeth's subjective sufferings – the 'terrible dreams' that pursue him, and his incessant 'torture of the mind'.

MACBETH, LADY *(Mac.)*: herself of royal blood, the grand-daughter through his eldest son of King Kenneth IV of Scotland, Lady Macbeth is described by Holinshed as 'very ambitious, burning in unquenchable desire to have the name of queen'. Macbeth was her second husband; and, as we learn from one of the most terrible speeches that Shakespeare puts into her mouth, during her earlier marriage she had borne a son:

> . . . I have given suck, and know
> How tender 'tis to love the babe that milks me:
> I would, while it was smiling in my face,
> Have pluck'd my nipple from his boneless gums,
> And dash'd the brains out, had I so sworn as you
> Have done to this. (I.vii)

She is also a woman who rages constantly against the limitation of her own sex; and, when she learns that Duncan is to visit her castle, she at once determines that she will overcome any remaining traces of mere womanly weakness:

> . . . Come, you spirits
> That tend on mortal thoughts, unsex me here . . . (I.v)

Macbeth, too, recognizes her masculine character:

> . . . Bring forth men-children only;
> For thy undaunted mettle should compose
> Nothing but males. (I.vii)

In the opening scenes of the tragedy, it is Macbeth who follows, and his wife who leads; and, should he hesitate, she drives him on:

> Macb.   If we should fail?
> Lady M.   We fail!
>   But screw your courage to the sticking-
>   place,
>   And we'll not fail. (I.vii)

Later, she devotes her tremendous courage and energy to supporting her accomplice. She lacks his sense of guilt; and, when Banquo returns to haunt Macbeth, he alone beholds the apparition. Yet the woman collapses before the man. When Macbeth leaves her and prepares to confront his enemies, Lady

above The death of Lady Macbeth, by Dante Gabriel Rossetti *(top)*; Lady Macbeth seizing the daggers from her husband. A painting by Henry Fuseli *(bottom)*.
left Diana Rigg as Lady Macbeth in the 1972 production of *Macbeth* by the National Theatre Company.

Macbeth experiences in sleep some of the 'thick-coming fancies' – the dark projections of 'a mind diseased' – that she has sternly banished from her waking hours. As a somnambulist she relives the murder of Duncan and sees the hands she holds out stained with blood. At Dunsinane Macbeth hears of her suicide; and then, because it deprives him of his last hope, it helps to confirm him in his resolution. Life is 'a tale told by an idiot'; he himself a baited animal:

> I 'gin to be a-weary of the sun,

And wish the estate o' the world were now undone.
Ring the alurum-bell! Blow, wind! come, wreck!
At least we'll die with harness on our back. (v.v)

MACDUFF *(Mac.)*: thane of Fife. He finds Duncan
murdered in Macbeth's castle, and is suspicious. He
refuses to attend Macbeth's coronation feast. The
witches warn Macbeth to 'beware Macduff': but they
reassure him that 'none of woman born shall harm
Macbeth'. Macduff joins Malcolm in England, and it is
there that he hears of the murder of his wife and
children; he vows revenge on Macbeth. He leads the
army to Dunsinane; he meets Macbeth on the battlefield, and tells him that he was 'untimely ripp'd' from
his mother's womb before he kills him. He brings in
Macbeth's head, and hails Malcolm as King.

MACDUFF, LADY *(Mac.)*: wife to Macduff. The
witches warn Macbeth to 'beware Macduff': Macduff
flees to England, but Macbeth has his wife and children
– all 'that trace him in his line' – brutally murdered
(IV.ii).

below Macbeth (IV.ii): Lady Macduff (Maxine Audley)
and her sons (John Rogers and Philip Thomas), in the
1955 production at Stratford *(left)*; Malcolm (Trader

of Scotland, who proclaims him Prince of Cumberland
and heir to the throne. After the murder of his father
Malcolm flees from Macbeth's 'murtherous shaft' to
England (II.iii); his flight throws suspicion on him. He
is joined by Macduff, and they assemble an English
army. At Birnam Wood Malcolm orders his soldiers to
conceal themselves with branches before advancing
on Dunsinane Castle. After the battle, Macduff gives
Malcolm Macbeth's head and proclaims him King.

Historically he was Malcolm Canmore (or
Caenmohr), the surname meaning 'great head'. He was
the elder son of Duncan I of Scotland. According to
Holinshed he fled to Cumberland, and then to the
court of Edward the Confessor to escape the enmity of
Macbeth. After the defeat of Macbeth he was crowned
at Scone in 1057. Subsequently he engaged in incessant
and successful warfare to establish and protect the
independence of his kingdom.

MALVOLIO *(Tw.N.)*: steward to a rich, unmarried
chatelaine, Olivia, whose entourage also includes two
disreputable, but gentlemanly hangers-on, her drunken

Faulkner) and Macduff (Keith Michell) in the 1955
production of *Macbeth* at Stratford *(right)*.

MACDUFF, SON OF *(Mac.)*: he is murdered by
order of Macbeth (IV.ii).

MAECENAS *(Ant.)*: a friend of Octavius who tries to
heal the breach between him and Antony (II.ii). He
finally sides with Octavius.

MALCOLM *(Mac.)*: the elder son of Duncan, King

uncle, Sir Toby Belch, and his friend, Sir Andrew Aguecheek, a foolish pretender to the lady's hand. The steward, a conscientious but humourless person, does his best to instil some kind of domestic order into his employer's ill-run household, thereby antagonizing not only Sir Toby Belch and Sir Andrew but her lively maid, Maria. With the help of a forged message, they persuade Malvolio that he has inspired a secret passion in Olivia's heart, and that, to show that he returns her love, she wishes him to assume a pair of yellow, curiously cross-gartered stockings. Malvolio swallows the bait; and his attitude towards Olivia becomes so odd and so alarming that he is subjected to the primitive shock-treatment reserved for Elizabethan lunatics, cast into a cell 'as dark as ignorance', and obliged to lie upon a bed of straw. Though he is at last released, and Olivia herself admits that 'he hath been most notoriously abused', Malvolio retires to meditate revenge.

Malvolio is at once a broadly comic and a subtly tragic character. 'Sick of self-love', like many of Shakespeare's doomed heroes he is a solitary, self-secluded man; and there is even some resemblance between Malvolio and that bloodthirsty tyrant, King Richard III; for, just as Richard is reduced to admiring his shadow, the steward is observed by Maria 'practising behaviour to his own shadow' in the garden 'this half-hour . . .' Yet, except for his vanity and complacent egotism there is nothing really discreditable about Malvolio's personality. 'He is not essentially ludicrous,' wrote Charles Lamb, '. . . but dignified, consistent, and . . . of a rather over-stretched morality. . . . His bearing is lofty, a little above his station, but probably not much above his deserts . . . . His dialect on all occasions is that of a gentleman and a man of education.' Undoubtedly, he is far superior to the pair of commonplace parasites who manage to engineer his downfall; and in the 'hideous darkness' of his prison he still retains a certain dignity. The 'gentle-man servitor', an educated man attached to a rich employer's household, was a familiar Elizabethan type; and, oddly enough, we have the autobiography of just such a servitor, first published in 1961, that describes a somewhat similar emotional crisis. Thomas Wythorne, too, conceived the idea that the prosperous lady he served was secretly enamoured of him;

below Mr Yates as Malvolio in *Twelfth Night*: an eighteenth-century engraving *(left)*; Malvolio: poster by Norman Wilkinson for the production of *Twelfth Night* at the Savoy Theatre in 1912 *(right)*.

Malvolio and the Countess Olivia. A painting by Maclise.

The Winter's Tale at the Princess's Theatre in 1856, with Charles Kean as Leontes and the eight-year-old Ellen Terry as Mamillius.

whereupon he appeared before her wearing, not yellow stockings, but a sober suit of russet, 'which colour signifieth the wearer to have hope', and a garland of hops, another symbol of hope, wreathed around his hat-brim. Wythorne himself was very soon disillusioned; the lady quickly understood his meaning. 'If you have any hopes of me,' she remarked, *'the suds of soap shall wash your hope'*, as she dismissed him from her presence. *Twelfth Night*, thought to have been written in 1600 or 1601, was performed in the Middle Temple on 2 February 1602.

MAMILLIUS *(Wint.)*: the young son of Leontes and Hermione. When his mother is disgraced he falls ill, and dies; his death is apparently caused by a combination of fear of his jealous father and the absence of his beloved mother. His death is announced during Hermione's trial, just as Leontes has declared Apollo's oracle false; it had affirmed Hermione's innocence, and had prophesied that 'the king shall live without heir if that which is lost, be not found' that is, Perdita.

'Any one but Shakespeare would have sought to make pathetic profit out of the child by the easy means of showing him if but once again as changed and stricken to the death for want of his mother and fear for her and hunger and thirst at his little high heart for the sight and touch of her: Shakespeare only could find a better way, a subtler and deeper chord to strike, by giving us our last glimpse of him as he laughed and chattered with her 'past enduring, to the shameful neglect of those ladies in the natural blueness of whose eyebrows as well as their noses he so stoutly declined to believe.' (Swinburne)

MARCADE *(LLL.)*: a messenger. He arrives with news of the death of the King of France that transforms the whole tone of the play.

The entrance of this silent figure in black is one of the most dramatic in Shakespeare. As soon as he has spoken the courtly games are invalidated, and reality can no longer be ignored. The name Marcade was one of the common forms used for the supposed author of the French *Dance of Death*.

MARK ANTONY *(Caes.)*, see ANTONY.

MARCELLUS *(Ham.)*: a sentry at Elsinore. With Barnado he has twice seen the ghost during the midnight watch. They tell Horatio, who joins them on the third night, when the ghost appears again (I.i); they all go to inform Hamlet. When Hamlet has seen the ghost, he makes Marcellus and Horatio swear to tell no one of what they have seen (I.v).

Marcellus has the famous line 'Something is rotten in the state of Denmark' (I.iv).

MARDIAN *(Ant.)*: a eunuch attending Cleopatra. He is sent by her to tell Antony that she has killed herself (IV.xiii); he gives Antony a graphic description of the supposed event (IV.xiv).

MARGARELON *(Troil.)*: the bastard son of Priam, King of Troy. During the battle he challenges Thersites, who refuses to fight with him, saying 'One bear will not bite another, and wherefore should one bastard?'

MARGARET *(Ado)*: a gentlewoman attending Hero. She is drawn into Borachio's plot against Hero: she is seen in Hero's room by Claudio, and she appears to be accepting the advances of Borachio. Claudio thinks that it is Hero being unfaithful. When Borachio confesses he exonerates Margaret, who was innocent of the plot.

Benedick says her wit 'is as quick as a greyhound's mouth'.

MARGARET PLANTAGENET *(R.III)*: the daugh-

Genevieve Ward as Margaret of Anjou in *Richard III*, at the Lyceum Theatre, 1896.

ter of the Duke of Clarence. Richard marries her off to 'some mean poor gentleman'.

She was the youngest daughter of Clarence, and the last of the Plantagenets; she was famous for her misfortunes. When Richard mentions her marriage (in 1483), she was only ten. She was in fact married around 1491 to Sir Richard Pole in accordance with the wishes of Henry VII. Henry VIII, who described her as the most saintly woman in England, created her Countess of Salisbury in 1513 in an attempt to atone for the treatment of her brother Edward Plantagenet. But her son offended Henry in 1536, and the family was destroyed: her sons were executed, and she was arrested and executed in 1539.

MARGARET, QUEEN *(1, 2 & 3 H.VI; R.III)*: Margaret of Anjou. She becomes the prisoner of Suffolk after the capture of Joan of Arc. He is struck by her beauty, but is unable to marry her because he already has a wife. He plans to make her his paramour by making her 'Henry's queen'; he negotiates with her father, who says he will aprove her marriage to Henry (v.iii) (*See* REIGNIER, DUKE OF). Henry resolves to marry this beautiful princess on the strength of Suffolk's

glowing description of her; Suffolk sees his way clear to rule the realm through her (v.v).

In *2 Henry VI* she is presented to Henry (I.i). As his queen, she says that she finds him more fitted to be Pope than to be King. She is infuriated by the Duke of Gloucester, who derides her poverty, and demands his dismissal (I.iii). At the royal hawking party Henry has to restrain her when she abuses Gloucester; she hears that the Duchess of Gloucester has been accused of witchcraft (II.i). When Gloucester is forced to resign his office, she feels that at last she is a queen (II.iii). She warns Henry against Gloucester, and with Suffolk and Beaufort she plots Gloucester's death. When she see Henry's grief at the news of Gloucester's death she angrily accuses him of caring more for him than for her; she pleads for Suffolk when he is accused of Gloucester's murder, and reveals her love for him, saying that in exile he will take her heart with him (III.ii). She mourns bitterly over Suffolk's head. At St Albans she foresees the defeat and urges Henry to escape with her to London.

In *3 Henry VI* she denounces Henry as a 'timorous wretch' for disinheriting his son, and declares that she will divorce herself from him until this wrong is righted; she departs to join her army (I.i). She captures York at Wakefield, and reviles him, and places a paper crown on his head before she stabs him (I.iv). She welcomes Henry to the city of York, and asks him to knight their son. At Towton, seeing that the battle is lost, she tells Henry to escape (II.v). She goes to France, and obtains a promise of aid from King Lewis; she warns him against consenting to the marriage of Lady Bona to Edward IV. She gladly enlists Warwick's aid when he defects from Edward, and follows him to England (III.iii). She is captured at Tewkesbury, and faints when she sees her son murdered (v.v). She is ransomed by her father, and sent to France.

In *Richard III* she overhears an argument between Richard and Queen Elizabeth; she reveals herself and recites the crimes of the house of York, and curses all its members, especially Richard; she warns Buckingham of his fate (I.iii). Later she joins the Duchess of York and Queen Elizabeth in reciting their woes and cursing Richard, 'hell's black intelligencer'.

Margaret first appears as a beautiful princess who overwhelms Suffolk even as he takes her prisoner:

My hand would free her, but my heart says no.
As plays the sun upon the glassy streams,
Twinkling another counterfeited beam,
So seems this gorgeous beauty to mine eyes.
Fain would I woo her, yet I dare not speak. (*1H.VI*, v.iii).

When she reappears in *2 Henry VI* it is quickly apparent that she is a scheming politician with an iron will, the 'tiger's heart wrapt in a woman's hide'. It has been shown that her character in the second two parts of *Henry VI* has affinities with the characters of Regan and Goneril in *The True Chronicle History of King Leir*. Her most triumphant moment, when she shows herself the 'she-wolf of France', comes when she humiliates her arch-enemy York:

Brave warriors, Clifford and Northumberland,
Come make him stand upon this molehill here,
That raught at mountains with outstretched arms,
Yet parted but the shadow with his hand.
What, was it you that would be England's king?
Was't you that revelled in our parliament,
And made a preachment of your high descent?
Where are your mess of sons, to back you now?
The wanton Edward, and the lusty George?
And where's that valiant crook-back prodigy,
Dicky, your boy, that with his grumbling voice
Was wont to cheer his dad in mutinies?
Or with the rest, where is your darling Rutland?
Look York, I stained this napkin with the blood
That valiant Clifford, with his rapier's point,
Made issue from the bosom of the boy;
And if thine eyes can water for his death,
I give thee this to dry thy cheeks withal.

(3H.VI, I.iv)

Margaret of Anjou (1430–82) was the daughter of René of Anjou. She was betrothed to Henry in 1444 after the Treaty of Tours; she was not captured. She was married at Nancy in 1445, with Suffolk as proxy bridegroom. There was no question of any improper relations with him: he was an old man at the time, and he had his wife with him. His wife became a firm friend of Margaret, and remained so after her husband's death. When Margaret arrived in England she was crowned in Westminster. She identified Henry with the faction that had introduced her to England, and never won the confidence of many people outside that faction. She was politically active, but immature: she was only fifteen at the time of her marriage to Henry. When Suffolk died she transferred her confidence to Beaufort. When Henry became temporarily insane in 1453 York became Protector, and a feud between him and the Queen quickly developed. In the same year she gave birth to Edward, an event which disposed of the possibility of a peaceful succession. In 1455 Henry recovered, and, prompted by Margaret, dismissed York and replaced him with Beaufort. York took up arms and defeated the royal forces at St Albans; Beaufort was killed and York became Protector again. Margaret left Henry and went round the country raising support. Henry was defeated in 1460, and as a result of a settlement with York he disinherited his son. This infuriated Margaret, who went to Scotland. In the meantime the Lancastrians won the Battle of Wakefield, where York was killed: Shakespeare's version of his death by

Margaret's hand is fictional. She marched southward and defeated Warwick at the second Battle of St Albans in 1461. But Warwick joined with the new Duke of York, Edward, who claimed the throne as Edward IV, and together they crushed Margaret's forces at Towton. She fled to Scotland with Henry. She went to Brittany, and then tried an abortive invasion of England in 1462; subsequently she lived obscurely in France for seven years, but when Warwick quarrelled with Edward IV she joined forces with him and followed him to England in 1471. Warwick was killed at Barnet, and Margaret was defeated at Tewkesbury, where her son was killed and she was taken prisoner. She was imprisoned for the next five years, and then in 1475 she was released and exiled to France. She was granted a pension by Louis XI, but it was not paid for long, and she died in great poverty in Anjou in 1482.

Margaret never returned to England after 1475, so her presence in *Richard III* is an anachronism. Her presence in the play is also strange: she is a strange, semi-supernatural figure, Richard's most formidable opponent. Richard even refers to the fact, and says 'Wert thou not banished on pain of death?' (I.iii). She is powerful just because of her ambiguous existence: her eerie curses and incantations have assumed a dreadful potency by the end of the play.

MARIA *(LLL.)*: one of the ladies attending the Princess of France. Longaville falls in love with her. When masked she is wooed by Dumain, who mistakes her for Katharine. She promises to marry Longaville after she has spent a year in mourning with the Princess. (*See* LONGAVILLE.)

MARIA *(Tw.N.)*: a gentlewoman attending Olivia and a 'most excellent devil of wit'. She contrives the plot against Malvolio, writing the love letter in Olivia's hand, and leaving it where he will find it. It is she who suggests to Olivia that Malvolio's strange behaviour can only be accounted for by madness; and it is she who persuades Feste to impersonate Sir Topas and torment Malvolio in prison. It is announced at the end that she has married Sir Toby Belch.

She is small, witty and vivacious; she is able to humiliate Malvolio so effectively because she understands him so well.

MARIANA *(All's W.)*: a neighbour to the Widow of Florence. She warns the widow's daughter Diana to beware of Bertram and Parolles, saying that 'Many a maid hath been seduced by them' (III.v).

MARIANA *(Meas.)*: a Venetian lady who had been betrothed to Angelo, but who was deserted by him when she lost her dowry in a shipwreck. She now leads a

Olivia (Phyllis Neilson-Terry) and Maria (Clare Harris) in *Twelfth Night* at the New Theatre in 1932.

secluded life in 'a moated grange'. At the disguised Duke's suggestion, she consents to take Isabella's place when Angelo visits her at night. When the Duke returns, she tells him of Angelo's duplicity, but the Duke feigns disbelief. When Angelo's guilt is revealed, he commands him to marry Mariana before he is executed. She pleads for his life, and Isabella joins her; he is spared.

The story of the deserted wife seeking her husband in disguise was a commonplace of romance: modern objections to the 'bed-trick' are misplaced. Mariana's contract with Angelo was evidently a public one, unlike that of Claudio and Juliet, so that they were effectively man and wife. And Mariana will not agree to take Isabella's place until Friar Lodowick assures her that it is no sin.

Mariana is a gentle, poignant figure: her lonely life in the 'moated grange' inspired Tennyson's poem *Mariana*. Her pleas for Angelo are simple and moving:

   . . . O my dear lord,
I crave no other, nor no better man.

Similarly later, as she appeals to Isabella against all logic:

Sweet Isabel, do yet but kneel by me,
Hold up your hands, say nothing, I'll speak all.
They say, best men are moulded out of faults;
And, for the most, become much more the better
For being a little bad; so may my husband. (v.i)

Her love for Angelo enables her to see through his cold outside to the confused man within.

Shakespeare divided the Cassandra of *Promos and Cassandra* into two characters, Isabella and Mariana.

MARINA *(Per.)*: the daughter of Pericles and Thaisa.

She is born at sea during a storm; her mother is believed to have died in childbirth. Pericles leaves the baby in the care of Cleon and Dionyza. She grows up and incurs the jealous hatred of Dionyza (III.v). She is about to be murdered by Leonine on Dionyza's orders when she is carried off by pirates. They sell her to a brothel; at Tharsus Cleon and Dionyza erect a monument over her supposed grave (IV.iv). Lysimachus, the governor of Mytilene, visits the brothel in search of a fresh virgin, and is offered Marina: her virtue as she appeals to him changes his intention, and he gives her gold to buy her release. The Pandar and the Bawd are glad to be rid of her since she has been reforming all their customers. She becomes a teacher. When Pericles arrives with a 'distemperature' she revives him with song, and makes herself known to him (v.i). At the temple of Diana at Ephesus she is restored to her mother Thaisa (v.iii).

Marina was one of the favourite heroines of Victorian moralists: even Swinburne was moved by her 'heroic purity'. She is not as fully realized as Imogen, or even Cordelia, yet she is a powerful embodiment of virtue and constancy. Pericles describes her in a brief but profound passage:

   . . . Yet thou dost look,
Like patience, gazing on King's graves, and smiling
Extremity out of act. (v.i)

MARINER, A *(Wint.)*: he lands Antigonus and the infant Perdita on the coast of Bohemia, and is glad to be 'rid of the business'. We hear later that his ship was wrecked and the whole crew lost (v.ii).

MARINERS *(Tp.)*: they man the ship carrying Alonso and his court. After the shipwreck Ariel guides the ship to a safe harbour and sends the mariners to sleep 'all under hatches stowed'. He wakes them at the end for the journey back to Naples.

MARSHAL *(Per.)*: he shows Pericles to the place of honour at the banquet following King Simonides' tournament. Pericles modestly objects but is persuaded by another knight (II.iii).

MARTEXT, SIR OLIVER *(AYL.)*: 'a country curate'. He is about to marry Touchstone and Audrey in the forest when he is stopped by Jaques, who tells them to go to church 'and have a good priest' (III.iii).

MARTIUS, CAIUS *(Cor.)*, see CORIOLANUS.

MARTIUS, YOUNG *(Cor.)*: son to Coriolanus and Virgilia. He accompanies his mother and grandmother to plead with Coriolanus not to destroy Rome (v.iii).

MARTIUS *(Tit.)*: son of Titus Andronicus. He and

his brother Quintus are enticed by Aaron into a pit containing the body of Bassianus : they are discovered there and accused of his murder. They are executed.

MARULLUS *(Caes.)* : a tribune who with his colleague Flavius chides the plebeians for their ingratitude to Pompey's memory, and tells them to go home. He doubts if the images may be disrobed on a festival day (I.i). However we hear later that Marullus and Flavius 'for pulling scarves off Caesar's images, are put to silence' (I.ii).

MASTER (SHIP'S) AND MATE *(2H.VI)* : they are both allotted a prisoner; the master gains a thousand pounds as ransom. The captain is also present. The master would be the navigating officer.

MAYOR OF COVENTRY *(3H.VI)* : he appears at Coventry, where Warwick waits for reinforcements. He does not speak.

MAYOR OF LONDON *(1H.VI)* : he quells a riot in the city between the followers of Gloucester and Beaufort; he asks the King to intervene because the brawls are ruining trade in the city (III.i).

At this date (1425) the Lord Mayor of London was John Coventry.

MAYOR OF LONDON *(H.VIII)* : he is present at the baptism of Princess Elizabeth, and is thanked by the King (v.v).

He was Stephen Pecocke.

MAYOR OF LONDON *(R.III)* : he agrees that Hastings' execution was just, and offers to explain it to the citizens (III.v). In the charade put on by Buckingham to convince the citizens that Richard is devout, he entreats the reluctant Richard to accept the crown (III.vii).

He was Sir Edmund Shaw, a wealthy goldsmith. He was a Yorkist, and was instrumental in persuading the citizens to support Richard.

MAYOR OF ST ALBANS *(2H.VI)* : he is taken in by the impostor Simpcox who claims to have been cured of blindness at St Alban's shrine, and presents him to the King (II.i).

There was in fact no mayor at this date, since the town was not incorporated until the reign of Edward VI. The chief officer of the town was probably a bailiff.

MAYOR OF YORK *(3H.VI)* : he refuses to admit Edward to his city because he has taken an oath of allegiance to King Henry; Edward persuades him to admit him as the Duke of York (IV.vii).

He was Thomas Beverley, who was Mayor for the second time in 1471.

MELUN *(John)* : a French lord who warns the English nobles who have defected to the French that the Dauphin intends to murder them if John is defeated (v.ii; v.iv).

MENAS *(Ant.)* : a notorious pirate. He and Menecrates have helped Pompey gain supremacy at sea (I.iv). He is opposed to the ·peace treaty which Pompey signs at Misenum, and suggests to him that the triumvirs be murdered; Pompey rejects the plan, and tells Menas that he should have done the deed first and then told him about it. Menas, disillusioned by such scruples, resolves to leave Pompey (II.vi; II.vii).

MENECRATES *(Ant.)* : a pirate who has helped Pompey gain supremacy at sea (*see* MENAS).

MENELAUS *(Troil.)* : the King of Sparta, and husband of the abducted Helen. He is one of the Greek commanders at Troy. On the battlefield he meets and wounds Paris, to the delight of Thersites (I.i). He fights with him again later (v.viii).

Shakespeare follows Homer in making Menelaus a man of few words.

MENENIUS AGRIPPA *(Cor.)* : a patrician friend of Coriolanus. He argues with the plebeians, using the fable of the belly to convince them that they need the patricians to govern them and care for them (I.i). He greets Coriolanus warmly, but warns him that he has enemies in Rome. When Coriolanus has to appeal to the plebeians for confirmation as consul, Menenius begs him not to reveal his contempt for them. He is Coriolanus' chief apologist at his 'trial' (III.iii). When he learns that Coriolanus is marching on Rome he takes delight in telling them of their imminent fate. He pleads with Coriolanus to spare the city, but is rebuffed.

He is almost wholly Shakespeare's creation : Plutarch only refers to him as 'one of the pleasantest old men' in the Senate. According to Livy he was 'an eloquent man and dear to the plebeians as being one of themselves by birth'.

MENTIETH *(Mac.)* : a Scottish nobleman who brings his forces to join Malcolm's English troops at Birnam (v.ii; v.iv).

MERCADE *(LLL.), see* MARCADE.

MERCHANT, A *(Err.)* : Angelo the goldsmith is in debt to him; he threatens to have him arrested if he does not pay. Angelo asks Antipholus of Ephesus for payment for the gold chain that he has mistakenly given to Antipholus of Syracuse; when Antipholus of Ephesus indignantly refuses to pay, Angelo and the merchant have him arrested.

MERCHANT, A *(Err.)*: a friend to Antipholus of Syracuse. He warns him of the risks he runs at Ephesus, where Syracusans are proscribed, and gives him a purse which he had been looking after for him (I.ii).

MERCHANT, A *(Tim.)*: in the opening scene the merchant, a poet and a painter are waiting for Timon in an antechamber of his house (I.i).

MERCUTIO *(Rom.)*: a kinsman of the Prince of Verona, and friend of Romeo. He accompanies Romeo on his way to the Capulets' ball, and Romeo's lyrical protestations of love for Rosaline provoke Mercutio to his famous speech on Queen Mab (I.iv). Mercutio and Benvolio meet Romeo in the street later, and Mercutio teases him again, before swapping some bawdy repartee with the Nurse. When Romeo is

An eighteenth-century engraving of Mr Dod in the role of Mercutio in *Romeo and Juliet*.

challenged by Tybalt and refuses to fight him, Mercutio takes his place, and is mortally wounded when Romeo tries to intervene.

Mercutio has attracted the most lavish praise: he has been called the epitome of Renaissance man, Shakespeare's ideal man, a great poet, and an actor's dream. Here is Coleridge on him:

> Mercutio is a man possessing all the elements of a poet: the whole world, as it were, subject to his law of association. Whenever he wishes to impress anything, all things become his servants for the purpose: all things tell the same tale, and sound in unison. This faculty, moreover is combined with the manners and feelings of a perfect gentleman, himself utterly unconscious of his powers.

Even so, he has a function in the play: his tough and bawdy wit shows up the fatuity of Romeo's Petrarchan attitude to love at the outset. His rapid prose contrasts with Romeo's more stolid verse. His supreme passage of verse has a curious tone, with its combination of images of fairy delicacy and of sexual disease:

> Her wagon-spokes made of long spinner's legs;
> The cover, of the wings of grasshoppers;
> Her traces, of the smallest spider web;
> Her collars, of the moonshine's watery beams;
> Her whip of cricket's bone; the lash of film;
> Her wagoner, a small grey-coated gnat,
> Not half so big as a round little worm,
> Pricked from the lazy finger of a maid.
> Her chariot is an empty hazel-nut,
> Made by the joiner squirrel or old grub,
> Time out a mind the fairies' coachmakers.
> And in this state she gallops night by night
> Through lovers' brains, and then they dream of love;
> O'er courtiers' knees, that dream on curtsies straight;
> O'er lawyers' fingers, who straight dream on fees;
> O'er ladies' lips, who straight on kisses dream,
> Which oft the angry Mab with blisters plagues,
> Because their breaths with sweetmeats tainted are.
>
> (I.iv)

His death, accidental and pointless as it is, introduces a note of high seriousness to the play: he focuses it in a celebrated pun: 'Ask for me tomorrow, and you shall find me a grave man'.

Dryden, who seems to have been the first to record the legend that Shakespeare found it necessary to kill Mercutio off, also took a sanguine view of him that is a useful corrective to the more extravagant flights of enthusiasm:

> Shakespear show'd the best of his skill in his Mercutio, and he said himself, that he was forc'd to kill him in the third Act, to prevent being kill'd by him. But, for my part, I cannot find he was so dangerous a person: I see nothing in him but what was so exceeding harmless, that he might have

liv'd to the end of the Play, and dy'd in his bed, without offence to any man.

MESSALA *(Caes.)* : a friend of Brutus and Cassius. He brings them news of the deaths of Portia and Cicero. He sees the body of Cassius, and leaves to tell Brutus (v.iii). He is taken prisoner.

He was Marcus Valerius Messala ; he was pardoned by the triumvirs after Philippi.

METELLUS CIMBER *(Caes.), see* CIMBER.

MICHAEL *(2H.VI)* : a follower of Jack Cade. He brings word that Sir Humphrey Stafford and his brother are approaching with the King's army (IV.ii).

MICHAEL, SIR *(1H.IV)* : an associate of the Archbishop of York, who gives him letters to take to the Lord Marshal and Scroop (IV.iv).

MILAN, DUKE OF *(Gent.)* : the father of Silvia. He intends that she will marry Thurio. Proteus tells him that she is about to elope with Valentine ; he banishes Valentine on pain of death. He tells Proteus that Silvia is pining for Valentine, and asks him to slander Valentine to her and persuade her to marry Thurio. He follows Silvia when she pursues Valentine, and is captured by outlaws ; he is saved by Valentine, and consents to his marriage to Silvia.

MIRANDA *(Tp.)* : Prospero's daughter. She is cast away with him on the island. She is about fifteen. She sees the shipwreck, and is filled with pity for the 'poor souls' until she is reassured by Prospero that they are all safe ; she listens as Prospero relates how they came to be on the island. When Ferdinand enters she thinks he is a spirit, since 'nothing natural I ev'r saw so noble' ; he calls her 'the goddess on whom these airs attend'. He ignores Prospero's anger, and offers to marry her ; Prospero ignores her pleas and casts a spell on him and sets him to menial labour (I.ii). He is hauling logs when Miranda enters and offers to do the work for him ; they declare their love for each other and agree to marry. Prospero accepts Ferdinand as suitable for her, and they watch the spirit masque put on by Ariel to celebrate the betrothal (IV.i). Miranda and Ferdinand are revealed playing chess to the penitent Alonso ; when Miranda sees all the nobles she exclaims, with unconscious irony since Antonio and Sebastian are among them, 'O brave new world that has such people in it !'

She is beauty and innocence, a descendant of the beautiful maiden of fairy tales and folklore.

MONTAGUE *(Rom.)* : the father of Romeo, and head of the House of Montague, which is feuding with the Capulets. He enters during a fight between the adherents of the two houses, and is eager to fight his rival Capulet, but is restrained by his wife (I.i). He worries about his son's melancholy state, but does not understand it until the end when the tragedy is explained. It is only then, Romeo and Juliet both dead, that he is reconciled to Capulet ; he says that he will raise a statue 'in pure gold' to Juliet.

MONTAGUE, LADY *(Rom.)* : the wife of Montague. She stops her aged husband from joining the fight (I.i). Later Montague announces her death due to grief at Romeo's exile (v.iii).

MONTAGUE, MARQUESS OF *(3 H.VI)* : a Yorkist, the younger brother of Warwick the Kingmaker. He shows his sword at St Albans stained with 'the Earl of Wiltshire's blood' (I.i). he is sent to London to raise support, and is placed in command of the Yorkist forces. He objects to Edward's marriage to

Eric Porter as the Duke of Milan in Peter Hall's 1960 production of *The Two Gentlemen of Verona* at the Shakespeare Memorial Theatre, Stratford.

Lady Grey, but says that he will remain loyal (IV.i). But he later enters at Coventry, crying 'Montague, Montague, for Lancaster!' He and his brother are killed at the battle of Barnet; Margaret laments the loss of 'our top-mast'.

He was John Neville (d.1471). After the battle of Barnet the bodies of Montague and his great brother Warwick were exposed to the public view in St Paul's Cathedral, and then buried at the family seat at Bisham Abbey in Berkshire.

Montague seems to have been reluctantly drawn into Warwick's conspiracy against Edward; according to Hall, 'Even as the marques was loth to consent to his unhappie conspiracie, so with a faint heart he shewed himself an enemie unto King Edward; double dissimulation was both the destruction of him and his brathren.'

MONTANO *(Oth.)*: Othello's predecessor as Governor of Cyprus. He is wounded by the drunken Cassio in a brawl (II.iii). In the last scene he disarms Othello and puts him under guard.

In II.i he greets neither Desdemona nor Othello when they enter, yet he apparently remains on stage, since his exit is not provided for.

MONTGOMERY, SIR JOHN *(3H.VI)*: at York he insists that Edward resume the title of king, rather than remain just Duke of York (IV.vii).

He was Sir Thomas Montgomery; his brother John was in fact a Lancastrian who was beheaded by Edward IV. He arrived with his forces at Nottingham (not York) to greet Edward; he is recorded as 'boldlie affirming to him that they would serve no man but a king' (Holinshed). He became a close adviser of Edward, who made him Treasurer of Ireland and Captain of Caernarvon Castle.

MONTJOY *(H.V)*: the title of the chief French herald. He conveys a formal message of defiance to Henry (III.vi). He is sent by the Constable of France to ask Henry what ransom he would offer, since he is bound to be defeated and captured (IV.iii). After the battle he acknowledges defeat, and asks for permission to bury the French dead (VI.vii).

MOONSHINE *(MND.)*: impersonated by Starveling *(q.v.)* in the Interlude.

MOPSA *(Wint.)*: a shepherdess who is in love with the Clown. In the sheep-shearing scene she takes part in the dancing, and sings a song with Dorcas and Autolycus (IV.iii).

MORGAN *(Cym.)*: name assumed by Belarius *(q.v.)*.

MOROCCO, PRINCE OF *(Mer.V.)*: he is 'a tawny Moor all in white', his skin 'the shadowed livery of the burnished sun'. He comes as a suitor to Portia and takes the test of the caskets. He chooses the golden casket, with its inscription 'Who chooseth me shall gain what men desire'; inside he finds a death's head, and a scroll with an inscription:

> All that glistens is not gold,
> Often you have heard that told;
> Many a man his life hath sold

above The Tempest: Miranda and Caliban, by James Ward *(top)*; *The Tempest*: Prospero and Miranda, by F.R. Pickersgill *(bottom)*.

But my outside to behold;
Gilded tombs do worms infold:
Had you been as wise as bold,
Young in limbs, in judgment old,
Your answer had not been inscroll'd,
Fare you well, your suit is cold. (II.vii)

He leaves immediately; Portia is glad, since she does not like his colour.

MORTIMER, EDMUND, EARL OF MARCH *(1H.IV)*: we hear of his capture by Glendower (I.i). Hotspur demands that Henry IV ransom him, but he is refused (I.iii). Mortimer discusses the tripartite division of the kingdom with Hotspur and Glendower; he has trouble communicating with his wife, who speaks only Welsh (III.i).

He was Sir Edmund Mortimer (1373–1409), the second son of Edmund Mortimer the 3rd Earl of March. He was a supporter of Bolingbroke. He fought with Hotspur against Glendower, and was captured by him. He subsequently married his daughter, and became an ally when Glendower joined him and the Percys against King Henry. The famous tripartite division of the kingdom was Mortimer's work. After Shrewsbury Mortimer was driven back to Wales, and finally besieged in Harlech Castle, where he died in 1409.

MORTIMER, EDMUND, EARL OF MARCH *(1H.VI)*: he is 'brought in a chair by two keepers', and speaks of himself as being

Even like a man new-haled from the rack,
So fare my limbs with long imprisonment;
And these grey locks, the pursuivants of death,
Nestor-like aged, in an age of care,
Argue the end of Edmund Mortimer.
These eyes, like lamps whose wasting oil is spent,
Wax dim, as drawing to their exigent;
Weak shoulders, overborne with burthening grief,
And pithless arms, like to a withered vine,
That droops his sapless branches to the ground.
(II.v)

He talks with Richard Plantagenet, and reminds him of the history of his family; he was the nominated heir of Richard II, since he was 'the next by birth and parentage'. Thus he had been kept in confinement, and he warns Richard to be wary of dealing with the 'strong-fixed' house of Lancaster. He is carried out to die (II.v).

Edmund Mortimer (1391–1424) was heir presumptive to the throne. After the accession of Henry IV he was placed under guard at Windsor, and later committed to the custody of Henry, Prince of Wales. An extraordinary friendship developed between these two rival heirs to the throne, and when Henry became

Henry V Mortimer was restored to his title and estates. In return he remained loyal to Henry, despite repeated attempts that were made to persuade him to claim his rights. In 1415 Cambridge *(q.v.)* headed a plot to abduct Mortimer to Wales and proclaim him king as soon as Henry had left for France; Mortimer informed Henry, and the plot was crushed. Mortimer went to France with Henry, and distinguished himself on the battlefield. He was a member of the Council of the Regency after Henry's death, but the jealousy of Humphrey of Gloucester caused him to retire to Ireland (where he was Lieutenant). He died there of the plague in 1424.

Shakespeare's scene is difficult to understand: he apparently confuses this Mortimer with his uncle who appears in *1 Henry IV*. He could also have had in mind Lionel Mortimer, the son of the ally of Hotspur, who was imprisoned in the Tower after his father's death at Harlech in 1409, and who may have died at about this time. The significance of Shakespeare's character is as a reminder of the genuine claims of the house of York.

MORTIMER, LADY *(1H.IV)*: the daughter of Owen Glendower and wife to Mortimer. She speaks only Welsh, which her husband cannot understand (III.i), but he likes the sound of her voice:

. . . thy tongue
Makes Welsh as sweet as ditties highly penned,
Sung by a fair queen in a summer's bower,
With ravishing division to her lute. (III.i)

MORTIMER, SIR HUGH *(3H.VI)*: he and Sir John Mortimer are uncles and followers of York. They are killed at Wakefield (I.ii).

Edward Mortimer, Earl of March, after Northcote.

MORTIMER, SIR JOHN *(3H.VI)*, *see* above.

MORTON *(2H.IV)*: he reports the defeat and death of Hotspur at Shrewsbury to Northumberland (I.i).

MOTH *(LLL.)*: Armado's page. He leads Costard to prison (I.ii), and later releases him. He instructs Armado in the art of love (III.i). He plays the infant Hercules in the Pageant of the Nine Worthies.

MOTH *(MND.)*: a fairy. She is one of those chosen by Titania to attend Bottom.

MOULDY, RALPH *(2H.IV)*: one of the potential recruits found by Justice Shallow for Falstaff, who is to select four from among them to serve in the King's army. Mouldy bribes Bardolph, and is not chosen (III.ii).

MOWBRAY, LORD THOMAS *(2H.IV)*: he joins Scroop's rebellion because he has grievances against Henry. He is treacherously seized by Prince John and sent to execution (IV.ii).

He was the eldest son of Thomas Mowbray, 1st Duke of Norfolk. He was fourteen when his father died, and he was humiliated when he was not advanced to his father's title. He joined the conspiracy of 1403 led by Archbishop Scroop, and was party to the list of grievances presented to Henry IV. He joined Northumberland's revolt in 1405; he objected to accepting Westmorland's terms promising redress of grievances at Skipton Moor, but was persuaded. When he had dismissed his soldiers he was arrested with the other rebels and summarily executed.

The title 'Lord Marshal' by which the Archbishop addresses him (I.iii; IV.i) was hereditary in the family, but it was at this time, as Mowbray complained, a barren title.

MUGS *(1H.IV)*: the name by which the First Carrier is addressed (II.i).

MURDER *(Tit.)*: a character assumed by Demetrius (V.ii) *(q.v.)*.

MURDERERS *(2H.VI)*: they murder the Duke of Gloucester. The first murderer tells Queen Margaret that the deed is done; the second expresses remorse (III.ii).

MURDERERS *(Mac.)*: there are two of them; they are paid by Macbeth to murder Banquo (III.i). They waylay him, and kill him, but his son Fleance escapes. Before the murder they are unexpectedly joined by a third who says he has been sent by Macbeth (III.iii)

J.F. Cathcart as Mowbray in *Richard II* in 1857.

The first murderer reports to Macbeth (III.iv).

The third murderer is something of a puzzle. Because he appears to know the victims and their habits very well it has even been suggested that he is Macbeth in disguise, though this seems unlikely.

MURDERERS *(R.III)*: they murder Clarence. They are given their warrant to visit him and are told not to talk to their victim (I.iii). The second murderer is troubled by 'certain dregs of conscience'. They reason with Clarence, who is stabbed by the first murderer. The second murderer 'repents him' and refuses his reward (I.iv).

The scene of Clarence's murder was adapted by Shakespeare from the scene in the old play *The True Chronicle History of King Leir* in which Goneril and Regan try to murder Leir.

MUSCOVITES *(LLL.)*: characters assumed by Ferdinand *(q.v.)* and his courtiers (V.ii).

MUSTARDSEED *(MND.)*: a fairy. She is one of those chosen by Titania to attend Bottom (III.i).

MUTIUS *(Tit.)*: the youngest son of Titus Andronicus. He is killed by his father for trying to prevent him from following Bassianus, who had claimed Lavinia (I.i).

N

NATHANIEL *(Shr.)* : one of the servants at Petruchio's country house (IV.i).

NATHANIEL, SIR *(LLL.)* : a curate, and a devoted admirer of Holofernes, whose pedantry he imitates. He follows him around with notebook at the ready, waiting to preserve any 'singular and choice epithets'. But the bookish infection is harmless, and beneath it, as Costard movingly points out to the nobles as they jeer at Nathaniel's attempt to play Alexander in the pageant, is a man,

> a foolish mild man ; an honest man, look you, and soon dashed. He is a marvellous good neighbour, faith, and a very good bowler. (v.ii)

NERISSA *(Mer.V.)*: gentlewoman attendant to Portia, and her confidante. She marries Gratiano, and follows Portia to Venice disguised as a lawyer's clerk. While in disguise she obtains a ring from Gratiano, one that he had vowed 'to keep for ever'. At Belmont she accuses Gratiano of having given her ring to a woman, and teases him before revealing the deception.

NESTOR *(Troil.)* : the aged King of Pylos who is one of the Greek commanders at Troy. He supports Ulysses' plan to rouse Achilles by getting Ajax to fight Hector, and helps Ulysses to flatter Ajax (II.iii). He describes Hector's exploits on the battlefield (v.v).

In Homer he was renowned for his wisdom, justice and eloquence. In Shakespeare he is in his dotage ; according to Thersites he is a 'stale old mouse-eaten dry cheese'.

NICANOR *(Cor.)* : a Roman who is serving as a spy for the Volscians. He is on his way to Antium to report when he meets Adrian, a Volscian who had been sent to find him. He tells Adrian of the 'strange insurrections' in Rome, and of Coriolanus' banishment. Adrian tells him that the Volscian army is in a state of readiness (IV.iii).

NICHOLAS *(Shr.)* : one of the servants at Petruchio's country house (IV.i).

NORFOLK, DUCHESS OF *(H.VIII)* : she bears the Queen's train at the coronation of Anne Bullen, wearing 'a coronet of gold, wrought with flowers' (IV.i). She is a godmother to the infant Princess Elizabeth at the christening (v.v).

NORFOLK, DUKE OF *(3H.VI)* : he appears briefly as a Yorkist supporter (I.i ; II.ii). He was John Mowbray, 3rd Duke of Norfolk (1415–61).

NORFOLK, DUKE OF *(R.II)* : he and Bolingbroke accuse each other of treason ; Richard agrees to their fighting a duel (I.i). On the day appointed for the duel Richard changes his mind, and banishes them both, in Norfolk's case for life. His death is reported later.

He was Thomas Mowbray, 1st Duke of Norfolk (*c.* 1366–99). In 1384 he was invested for life with the title of Earl Marshal of England by Richard II. He went with Richard to Ireland in 1394, and helped to arrange his marriage to Isabel of France in 1396. As Captain of Calais he received Gloucester into custody there ; when called on to produce his prisoner he claimed that he had died in prison. Mowbray confided his fears about the King to Bolingbroke, who reported them to Richard. They were both summoned to appear before the parliament at Shrewsbury ; on the way there Mowbray is supposed to have laid an ambush for John of Gaunt. Bolingbroke accused Mowbray of treason, and it was decided that the matter should be resolved by a combat at Coventry. After the combatants had actually entered the lists the duel was stopped by the King, who banished Mowbray for life and Bolingbroke for ten years. Mowbray reached Venice in 1399, and began preparing for a pilgrimage to Palestine, but he died in the same year.

It is not known what part Mowbray played in the death of Gloucester ; according to Holinshed Mowbray tried to save the Duke, thus incurring Richard's dis-

right Sir Nathaniel (Charles Kay), Don Armado (Ronald Pickup), and Holofernes (Paul Curran) in *Love's Labour's Lost* at the Old Vic, National Theatre Company, 1968.

pleasure, since he wanted him dispatched 'with all expedition'.

NORFOLK, DUKE OF *(R.III)* : a faithful supporter of Richard. At Bosworth he and his son the Earl of Surrey 'have the leading of the foot and horse' (v.iii). Norfolk is killed in the battle.

He was John Howard (*c*.1430–85), the 1st Duke of Norfolk in the Howard family. In 1462 he was appointed Constable of Norwich Castle, and was granted several manors that the Earl of Wiltshire was forced to forfeit. He was created Baron Howard by Henry VI in 1470, but he remained faithful to the Yorkists. He supported Gloucester when he came to the throne as Richard III, and was created Duke of Norfolk by him in 1483. He remained faithful to Richard and fought with him at Bosworth, where he led the vanguard with his archers.

NORFOLK, DUKE OF *(R.III), see* SURREY, EARL OF.

NORTHUMBERLAND, EARL OF (Henry Percy) *(R.II; 1&2H.IV)* : he talks with the disaffected nobles about Richard's arbitrary conduct of the Kingdom; he reveals that Bolingbroke has sailed from Brittany, and tells them to go and meet him (II.i). He is proclaimed a traitor. He greets Bolingbroke, and joins him. He bluntly presents the articles of accusation to Richard, and torments him until Bolingbroke restrains him (IV.i). He informs Richard that he is to be committed to Pomfret Castle, and the Queen that she is to be deported to France.

In *1 Henry IV* he promises to join his son Hotspur and his brother Worcester in their rebellion against Bolingbroke (now Henry IV); he feels that the King has been ungrateful to his family. He feigns sickness in order to avoid the battle at Shrewsbury.

In *2 Henry IV* he is at first told that his side has won the battle at Shrewsbury, but is soon disabused and hears of the defeat and the death of Hotspur. He says he will join Scroop's rebellion, but flees to Scotland instead. His defeat by the Sheriff of Yorkshire is announced (IV.iv).

Northumberland is a self-seeker, incapable of consistent loyalty. In Holinshed he is also an evil figure, but there he has some nobility, albeit perverted; in Shakespeare he is simply despicable, seen at his worst when flattering Bolingbroke or persecuting Richard in the deposition scene. Holinshed also shows him to have been a skilful politician in his later years; in *2 Henry IV* he is concerned only with self-preservation.

Henry Percy, 1st earl of Northumberland (1342–1408), received his title from Richard II in 1377. He spent many years campaigning in Scotland. In 1397 he supported Richard's assumption of despotic power, but

was soon disgusted with his arbitrary exercise of it, and refused to accompany him to Ireland. He took a large force to meet Bolingbroke when he landed. Northumberland captured Richard when he returned from Ireland, and received from him the declaration that he was ready to resign the crown. For some time he supported Henry IV, who owed his crown to him; he was again sent to the Scottish border, and crushed the Scots at Homildon Hill. He was given a large part of southern Scotland as a reward, but seems to have been overcome by pride in his power. When Henry denied him money, and refused to ransom Sir Edmund Mortimer from Glendower, Northumberland led the Percys in revolt against the King (in 1403).

After the defeat at Shrewsbury Northumberland submitted, and after a period in captivity he was pardoned and restored to his title and lands. By 1405 he was again in revolt, with Lord Bardolph and Sir William Clifford. The rebels were defeated, and Bardolph and Northumberland fled to France. They returned with an army to Scotland in 1408, and marched south; they were defeated by Sir Thomas Rokesby at Bramham Moor, where Northumberland was killed. His head was displayed on London Bridge.

NORTHUMBERLAND, EARL OF *(3H.VI)* : a supporter of Henry and the Lancastrians. He takes York prisoner at Wakefield (I.iv). Edward pays tribute to his bravery after his death at Towton (v.vii).

2 Henry IV: Lady Percy (Irene Palmer), the Earl of Northumberland (Cecil Trouncer) and Lady Northumberland (Phyllis Hatch) at the Old Vic in 1935.

This was Henry Percy, the 3rd Earl of Northumberland (1421–61), the grandson of Hotspur. The death of his father at St Albans is mentioned in the play (I.i). He succeeded his father in 1455, and in 1460 he defeated and killed the Duke of York at Wakefield. He helped Queen Margaret raise an army and he helped her defeat Warwick at the second battle of St Albans in 1461. He led the vanguard at Towton, where he died sword in hand.

NORTHUMBERLAND, LADY *(2H.IV)*: wife to the Earl of Northumberland. She pleads with her husband to escape to Scotland and not to join Scroop's rebellion (II.iii).

NURSE *(3H.VI)*: she appears carrying the infant Prince Edward, son to Edward IV and Queen Elizabeth (V.vii).

NURSE *(Rom.)*: Juliet's nurse. She is garrulous: she talks of Juliet's infancy (I.iii), and gives her and Romeo information about each other (I.v). She later acts as a go-between for them (II.iv), and tells Juliet to go to Friar Laurence's cell (II.v). She tells Juliet that Romeo has killed Tybalt, and carries messages between the lovers. She advises Juliet to marry Paris (III.v). It is she who finds Juliet apparently dead at the Capulet tomb, and raises the alarm (IV.v).

For Johnson she was 'at once loquacious and secret, obsequious and insolent, trusty and dishonest'. For Coleridge she was a paradigm: 'Let any man conjure up in his mind all the qualities and peculiarities that can possibly belong to a nurse, and he will find them in Shakespeare's picture of the old woman: nothing is omitted.'

NURSE *(Tit.)*: she takes Aaron's bastard child by Tamora to him, and asks him what to do with it. When he finds out that only the Empress, the midwife and herself know of the child's existence, he kills her (IV.iii).

NYM, CORPORAL *(Wiv.; H.V)*: a crony of Falstaff; he is obsessed with 'humours'. Falstaff repudiates him when he refuses such a 'base humour' as delivering a letter to Mistress Ford (I.iii). He promises himself 'the humours of revenge', and with Pistol he tells the husbands of Mistresses Ford and Page of Falstaff's letters to their wives.

In *Henry V* Nym appears as a soldier in Henry's army in France. He is betrothed to Mistress Quickly, but quarrels with her, and she marries Pistol instead. He and Bardolph, 'sworn brothers in filching', are hanged for looting (IV.iv).

The Nym of *The Merry Wives of Windsor* is thought to be a caricature of Ben Jonson, who was famous for

Romeo and Juliet in 1882: Mrs Stirling as the Nurse.

his comedies based on the 'humours' of the characters. Though styled by Pistol 'the Mars of malcontents', he is ineffectual, and little more than a walking joke. In *Henry V* he is a more sinister figure, a reminder of what, beneath the endearing vitality, Falstaff really stood for. Falstaff's page characterizes Nym when he explains that he is sickened by him and his fellow 'swashers' and intends to leave them:

... for Nym, he hath heard, that men of few words are the best men, and therefore he scorns to say his prayers, lest a' should be thought a coward: but his few bad words are match'd with as few good deeds: for a' never broke any man's head but his own, and that was against a post, when he was drunk. (III.ii)

'Nym' meant 'to filch': thus Pistol's pun 'I'll live by Nym, and Nym shall live by me' (*Henry V*, II.i).

NYMPHS *(Tp.)*: these Naiads, water nymphs, are summoned by Juno during the masque that Ariel puts on for Ferdinand and Miranda. They dance with the reapers, symbolizing the union of chastity and virility. Iris describes these 'temperate nymphs':

You Nymphs, call'd Naiads, of the windring brooks, With your sedged crowns and ever-harmless looks, Leave your crisp channels, and on this green land Answer your summons. (IV.i)

O

OATCAKE, HUGH *(Ado)*: a watchman. The first Watchman recommends either him or George Seacoal for the post of constable because 'they can write and read' (III.iii).

OBERON *(MND.)*: the King of the Fairies, Oberon is married to the beautiful Titania. But they have recently fallen out; and, when they meet again by moonlight in a haunted 'wood near Athens', Titania reproaches Oberon both with his casual infidelities and with his insensate passion for Hippolyta,

> . . . the bouncing Amazon,
> Your buskin'd mistress and your warrior love (II.i)

An illustration to *A Midsummer Night's Dream* by Sir Joshua Reynolds.

who is soon to be married to the Athenian ruler, Theseus; while Oberon reminds his Queen of her own velleity for Theseus:

> Didst thou not lead him through the glimmering night
> From Perigenia, whom he ravished?

> And make him with fair Aegle break his faith,
> With Ariadne and Antiopa? (II.i)

Into this mysterious wood stray a quartet of distracted human lovers, Lysander and Hermia who are eloping from the court of the Athenian monarch, pursued by Demetrius, who loves Hermia, and by Helena who loves Demetrius. At the same time, Bottom, a weaver, and his homespun friends, a group of 'rude mechanicals', settle down in a convenient forest glade to rehearse a play, the tragedy of Pyramus and Thisbe, which they hope to be privileged to perform at Theseus' forthcoming marriage feast. The jealous Oberon has already revenged himself on Titania by squeezing a magic juice upon her sleeping eyes that will cause her to become passionately enamoured of the first creature she beholds at the moment of awakening, and later commands his servant Puck to weave a similar spell around Lysander. Puck by a disastrous mistake anoints the eyelids of Demetrius, thus reducing the human lovers to a state of wild confusion. A naturally mischievous spirit, Puck has also planted an ass's head upon the harmless weaver's shoulders; and, when Titania wakes, she first catches sight of Bottom and elects him as her royal favourite. Not until Oberon and Puck have at last removed the spell does she recognize him as the good-natured dolt he is.

A Midsummer Night's Dream appears to have been written to grace a fashionable wedding, possibly that of William, Earl of Derby and Elizabeth Vere, which was solemnized at Greenwich Palace on 26 January 1595, with the Queen among the celebrants. As a native of Warwickshire, brought up near a village that is still reputed to be a centre of the witch-cult, Shakespeare was versed in supernatural lore, and no doubt he had

right A Midsummer Night's Dream : the Old Vic Company. Oberon (Robert Helpmann) and Titania (Moira Shearer).

studied Reginald Scot's treatise, *The Discoverie of Witchcraft,* published eleven years before he wrote the play, which tells the story of how a certain English seaman, visiting a Mediterranean port and entering a woman's house to purchase eggs, had been transformed by her magical arts into the semblance of an ass. Throughout southern England, Robin Goodfellow, otherwise Puck or Pook, was a legendary apparition, a spirit who sometimes assisted his human neighbours, sometimes tormented and deluded them. The name Titania Shakespeare owed to the poems of Ovid; Oberon, to the French medieval romance, *Huon de Bordeaux* in Lord Berner's sixteenth-century version. But this treatment of their characters and attitudes is extremely individual. They are both more and less than human beings; and it is to them, though they are the stuff of dreams, rather than to the human lovers, who remain mere decorative puppets, that he gives many of his finest and most exquisitely melodious speeches. In *A Midsummer Night's Dream*, observed the great Italian critic, Benedetto Croce, 'the quick ardours, the inconstancies, the caprices, the illusions . . . of love . . . become embodied and weave a world of their own', which seems to hover half way between the real and the imaginary. Shakespeare's comedy was often revived during the next hundred years; and, in September 1662, Samuel Pepys attended a performance by the King's company, and dismissed it as 'the most insipid, ridiculous play that ever I saw in my life'.

OCTAVIA *(Ant.)*: the sister of Octavius Caesar. The 'patient Octavia' is married to Antony as part of a political scheme to bind him close to her brother Octavius (II.v); she is devoted to her husband. When she returns from Athens she discovers that Antony has rejoined Cleopatra in Egypt, and is preparing for war against Octavius (III.vi).

The 'patient Octavia' is a rather sad victim of the political intrigues. In Plutarch she remained loyal to Antony even after his death, and brought up his children by Cleopatra.

OCTAVIUS CAESAR *(Caes.; Ant.)*: the son of Julius Caesar's niece. He returns to Rome after the assassination, and joins Antony (III.ii). He helps draw up the list of proscribed men. With Antony he defeats Brutus and Cassius at Philippi. He orders that the body of Brutus be treated with due honour (v.v).

In *Antony and Cleopatra* he, Antony and Lepidus make up the triumvirate ruling Rome and its empire. His relationship with Antony has become strained because of Antony's dalliance in Egypt with Cleopatra, and he readily agrees to the marriage of Antony to his sister Octavia as a way of strengthening the alliance. When Antony leaves Octavia and returns to Egypt,

Octavius arrests Lepidus and deprives him of his power; he tells Octavia of her husband's conduct, and attacks Antony and the Egyptians. He defeats Antony at Actium; he derides Antony's challenge to single combat (IV.i). He defeats Antony again at Alexandria. He laments the dead Antony, and sends a soothing message to Cleopatra; he visits her in the monument and tries to reassure her that she will be well treated (v.ii). At the end the entire empire is in his control.

In *Julius Caesar* Octavius is very much secondary to Antony; in *Antony and Cleopatra* he is a formidable character in his own right. He is political man at his most efficient. Like all Shakespeare's successful politicians, he is deficient in warmth and humanity. Johnson wrote of his 'heartless littleness': this is to diminish him too much, and to diminish Antony and Cleopatra with him. For part of their splendour lies in their defiance of the immense power and authority of Octavius. And on a rational level at least, he is nearly always in the right, and he comes close to being the ideal politician as described by Elizabethan authors.

Octavius became the first emperor of Rome, with the name Augustus, in 27 BC. Sir Thomas Elyot praised

Orsino (Jack Hawkins) and Olivia (Anna Neagle) in an open air production of *Twelfth Night* in Regent's Park in 1934.

him for his 'magnanimity, nobility, tolerance, frugality, and sobriety'.

OLIVER *(AYL.)*: the eldest son of the late Sir Roland de Boys, and brother to Orlando and Jaques. He dislikes and has ill-treated his younger brother Orlando, who has been left in his care. He tells Charles the wrestler to kill Orlando when they fight (I.i). Orlando hears that Oliver is planning to kill him, and runs away. The Duke commands Oliver to find Orlando and to bring him back 'dead or living'. In the forest Orlando saves Oliver from a snake and from a lioness. Oliver repents, settles his estate on Orlando, and marries Celia (v.iv).

OLIVIA *(Tw.N.)*: a wealthy lady of Illyria. She is loved by Duke Orsino, but rejects him and all other suitors, supposedly because she is mourning the death of her father and her uncle. She refuses to receive Orsino's messenger. Later she receives 'Cesario' (the disguised Viola) and consents to hear Orsino's message. When 'Cesario' talks of what she would do if she were in her master's place, Olivia comments 'You might do much'. She rejects Orsino's suit, but gives 'Cesario' an excuse for returning by sending Malvolio after him with a ring which she alleges he left behind (I.v). Olivia finds she has fallen in love with 'Cesario'; when she tells him so, she is scornfully rejected, and he firmly insists that 'no woman' has his heart (III.i). Malvolio comes to woo Olivia, to her amazement: she declares his conduct to be 'very Midsummer madness'. She encounters Sir Toby Belch about to fight Sebastian (who she thinks is 'Cesario'), and stops him; she invites Sebastian to her house (IV.i). She persuades the bemused Sebastian to be betrothed to her before a priest. She meets Cesario and calls him husband: when he does not understand, she accuses him of breaking faith with her, and calls the priest to testify to the betrothal. When Sebastian enters she is amazed at the resemblance between him and 'Cesario'; she accepts the situation and marries Sebastian. She admits that Malvolio has been 'monstrously abused' (v.ii).

Like Orsino, Olivia is self-indulgent in her melancholy, and has to be exposed to an even greater delusion before she realizes what Feste sees clearly, that she has been behaving like a fool. She is a great lady, fully aware of her status and honour: at the inception of her passion for 'Cesario', she is careful to enquire about his parentage.

OPHELIA *(Ham.)*: the daughter of Polonius, and sister to Laertes. She loves Hamlet, whom we hear has wooed her honourably (I.iii), but both her brother and her father tell her not to take him seriously. She tells her father later that Hamlet has visited her in a state of

Hamlet (III.i): Hamlet abuses Ophelia. By Dante Gabriel Rossetti.

apparent madness; she is ordered to arrange it so that she encounters him alone, while Polonius and Claudius listen, unobserved, to their conversation (III.i). Hamlet insults her and womankind in general, and Ophelia concludes that he must be mad. She goes mad herself when she hears that Hamlet has killed her father, and is brought before the King and Queen in a distracted state. It appears that she subsequently drowns herself, though according to Gertrude's account her death was an accident (IV.viii). She is buried in 'ground unsanctified'.

Ophelia, 'the young, the beautiful, the harmless, and the pious' (Johnson) is not a complex figure, yet there is particular poignancy in the way she is manipulated, insulted and finally driven to her death. Two questions have puzzled critics. Does Hamlet love her? And, why does she go mad? Hamlet's letter to her suggests that he loves her: but we note that he never once mentions her in his intimate soliloquies. She certainly loves him, and this is the source of her madness. She appears distracted after the death of her father; but as Thomas Hanmer shrewdly wrote in the eighteenth century, 'It is not often that young women run mad for the loss of their fathers.' She loves Hamlet, and is forbidden to see him; when she does meet him, he appears mad and insults her, and she sees herself the cause of his strange behaviour. Already disturbed by unrequited love, the death of her father is enough to derange her mind completely, and drive her to her ambiguous death:

above Ophelia's madness, from the painting by
Henrietta Rae *(top)* ; Ophelia's death, from the
painting by Millais *(bottom)*.

The death of Ophelia, by Delacroix.

There is a willow grows askant the brook,
That shows his hoar leaves in the glassy stream;
Therewith fantastic garlands did she make
Of crowflowers, nettles, daisies and long purples
That liberal shepherds give a grosser name,
But our cold maid's do dead men's fingers call them.
There on the pendent boughs her coronet weeds
Clamb'ring to hang, an envious sliver broke,
When down her weedy trophies and herself
Fell in the weeping brook. Her clothes spread wide,
And mermaid-like awhile they bore her up,
Which time she chanted snatches of old tunes,
As one incapable of her own distress,
Or like a creature native and indued
Unto that element; but long it could not be
Till that her garments, heavy with their drink,
Pulled the poor wretch from her melodious lay
To muddy death. (IV.vii)

ORLANDO *(AYL.)*: the youngest son of the late Sir Rowland de Boys. He has been ill-treated by his elder brother Oliver, who has denied him an education and has withdrawn his patrimony (I.i). He agrees to fight the King's wrestler Charles; he ignores Rosalind and Celia when they attempt to dissuade him from the fight, and in the event he wins (I.ii). The old Steward Adam persuades him to flee from the malice of Oliver, and together they set out for the Forest of Arden. Orlando interrupts the old Duke's 'banquet' with drawn sword and demands food; he brings in the exhausted Adam (II.vii). In the forest, he hangs verses in praise of Rosalind on the trees, and carves her name on their trunks; he meets Jaques, and then 'Ganymede' (Rosalind) and 'Aliena' (Celia), but does not see through their disguises. 'Ganymede' amuses herself at his expense by getting him to pretend that he is Rosalind while 'he' makes love to 'her'; she explains that this will cure him of his lovesickness. Orlando is wounded by a lion when he rescues his brother Oliver (IV.i). He happily assents to the marriage of Oliver and 'Aliena', and is told by 'Ganymede' that he will marry his Rosalind the next day as well (V.II). When Celia and Rosalind reveal themselves the next day at the wedding ceremony, Orlando cries 'If there be truth in sight, you are my Rosalind!'

Orlando is, as he admits, 'Fortune's 'minion'; he

As You Like It: Orlando and the wrestler, after Maclise.

proceeds cheerfully from one accident or coincidence to the next, rarely trying to shape his own destiny. The corresponding character in Lodge's *Rosalynde* is Rosander.

ORLEANS, BASTARD OF (Dunois) *(1H.VI)*: he announces that he has brought with him a 'holy maid' who will save France, and brings in Joan Pucelle (I.ii). He escapes from Orleans when Talbot attacks (II.i), and is present at Rouen when Burgundy joins Charles (III.iii). He proposes that the bodies of the Talbots be mutilated (IV.vii).

He was John, Count of Dunois (1403–68), the illegitimate son of Louis, Duke of Orleans by Marie d'Engheim, the wife of his chamberlain, Albert, Lord of Cawny. He was a brilliant soldier: he commanded Orleans, and held the town until the arrival of Joan of Arc. He later directed the attacks that she led against the British from the town. He directed a long series of successful campaigns, culminating with his entry into Paris in 1436. He continued to attack the English, and in 1451 took Bordeaux and Bayonne, which the English had held for three hundred years.

ORLEANS, DUKE OF *(H.V)*: before Agincourt he scorns Henry and his 'fat-brain'd followers', and boasts of taking a hundred prisoners; he is himself captured in the battle (IV.viii).

Charles, Duke of Orleans (1391–1465) was cousin and friend to the Dauphin.

ORLEANS, MASTER-GUNNER OF, AND HIS SON *(1H.VI)*: he tells his son that he has discovered the location of a secret window through which the English have been spying on the city, and that he has aimed his cannon at it. He leaves his son watching for the English at the window; when they appear the boy fires a shot himself which kills Salisbury and Gargrave (I.iv).

ORSINO, DUKE (OR COUNT) OF ILLYRIA *(Tw.N.)*: he is a suitor to Olivia, who ignores him; he studiously maintains the melancholy disposition to which this rejection entitles him. Olivia, cultivating her state of mourning with equal intensity, refuses even to receive his messengers. He employs 'Cesario' (the disguised Viola) as his page, and sends him to plead his suit, but is still rejected. Viola falls in love with Orsino, and when he realizes that he cannot have Olivia, he transfers his love to her.

Orsino is another of Shakespeare's self-indulgent lovers who appears to have read all the right books. He is a sentimentalist, who indulges and luxuriates in his delicate, carefully nurtured melancholy. At the outset, he enjoys having a woman who rejects him: he acclaims the 'tyranny of love', and prefers to lie on 'beds of flowers' thinking 'love-thoughts' rather than to do anything.

OSRIC *(Ham.)*: a courtier. He is sent to tell Hamlet that the King has laid a wager on the outcome of a fencing match between him and Laertes. Hamlet derides his affectations and flowery language, but agrees to the match. Osric hands the foils to Hamlet, and acts as umpire; the dying Laertes reveals Claudius' treachery to him. Osric announces the arrival of Fortinbras.

Osric is totally servile, a reflecting surface for the views of others. Hamlet is bitter about him and his kind:

'A did comply with his dug, before 'a sucked it. Thus has he, and many more of the same bevy, that I know the drossy age dotes on, only got the tune of the time, and outward habit of encounter, a kind of yesty collection, which carries them through the most profound and winnowed opinions; and do but blow them to their trial, the bubbles are out. (v.ii)

Osric is the name of the foster-brother of Amleth in the Saxo-Grammaticus story.

OSWALD *(Lr.)*: Goneril's steward. He is impudent to Lear, for which he is tripped up by the loyal Kent (I.iv), who later beats him (II.ii). He is preparing to murder the blind Gloucester when he is killed by Edgar.

His one good quality is his devotion to his mistress; Edgar calls him

. . . a serviceable villain;
As duteous to the vices of thy mistress
As badness would desire. (IV.vi)

It has been suggested that Oswald is Goneril's lover, and that it is he that Edgar, as 'poor Tom', has in mind when he talks of himself as a one-time servingman

that curl'd my hair, wore gloves in my cap, serv'd the lust of my mistress' heart, and did the act of darkness with her; swore as many oaths as I spake words, and broke them in the sweet face of Heaven; one that slept in the contriving of lust, and wak'd to do it.
(III.iv)

OTHELLO *(Oth.)*: a Moorish soldier of fortune in the pay of the Venetian Senate. Though on the Jacobean and Caroline stage, he was often presented as a 'thick-lipped' negro. Othello, we learn, was a native of

'Barbary', or Mauretania, and may therefore perhaps have been a Berber chieftain. He has already done the State distinguished service. At the beginning of the play, his treacherous subordinate, Iago, and Iago's foolish accomplice, Roderigo, awake the respectable senator Brabantio at dead of night with the information, shouted from the darkness beneath his casement, that the foreign general has seduced his daughter. Brabantio then rushes to the council chamber, where the Senate

above Orsino (Cecil Ramage) and Viola (Jean Forbes-Robertson) in *Twelfth Night* at the New Theatre in 1932. *overleaf* Othello relating his adventures to Desdemona and her father.

is in session, and complains that Othello has corrupted and abused his child by means of magic 'spells and medicines'. Othello, however, who accompanies the infuriated parent, explains that he and Desdemona have lately made a secret marriage. Asked whether he has not employed some 'indirect' method to 'subdue and poison this young maid's affections', he replies that it was the stories she heard him tell, when he visited her father's house, of his early hardships and adventures, that had gradually won her heart:

She loved me for the dangers I had pass'd,
And I loved her that she did pity them. (I.iii)

This defence of his conduct, to which Desdemona adds her voice, soon satisfies the friendly Senate. Meanwhile, news has arrived that Venice's hereditary foes are threatening an outpost of her empire – 'The Turk with a most mighty preparation makes for Cyprus' – and thither they despatch Othello. At 'a sea-port in Cyprus' the General and his young wife are rapturously re-united; and Othello feels that he has achieved a climax of happiness that it seems impossible he can ever reach again:

. . . If it were now to die,

above A Moor (Othello) by James Northcote; Mr Kean as Othello *(top right)*; Johnston Forbes-Robertson as Othello *(bottom right)*; Othello (Laurence Olivier) and Desdemona (Maggie Smith) in the film of the National Theatre Company's production of *Othello (far right)*.

'Twere now to be most happy; for I fear,
My soul hath her content so absolute
That not another comfort like to this
Succeeds in unknown fate. (II.i)

But at the same time, Othello's ancient, or ensign, Iago, is still covertly spinning the web that he had begun to weave in Venice. Being bitterly jealous of Michael Cassio, a gay and attractive young Florentine whom Othello has promoted lieutenant over his own more deserving and experienced head, he tricks him into getting drunk on duty. Cassio raises a riot; and when Othello upbraids and dismisses him, Iago persuades Desdemona to plead the unhappy young man's cause. Next, he whispers in his trustful master's ear that between Cassio and Desdemona there may be something more than friendship, finally pointing out that a precious embroidered handkerchief, once given by Othello to his wife, is now in Michael Cassio's hands. Iago's hints at first disturb Othello, then slowly warp his spirit and undermine his judgement. His vague suspicions give rise to savage jealousy, and gnawing jealousy to murderous rage. Henceforward he inhabits a nightmare world, where every thought is lethal and every object is distorted. Entering his wife's chamber he make a hideous pretence that he is crossing the threshold of a brothel, where Emilia, Desdemona's maid

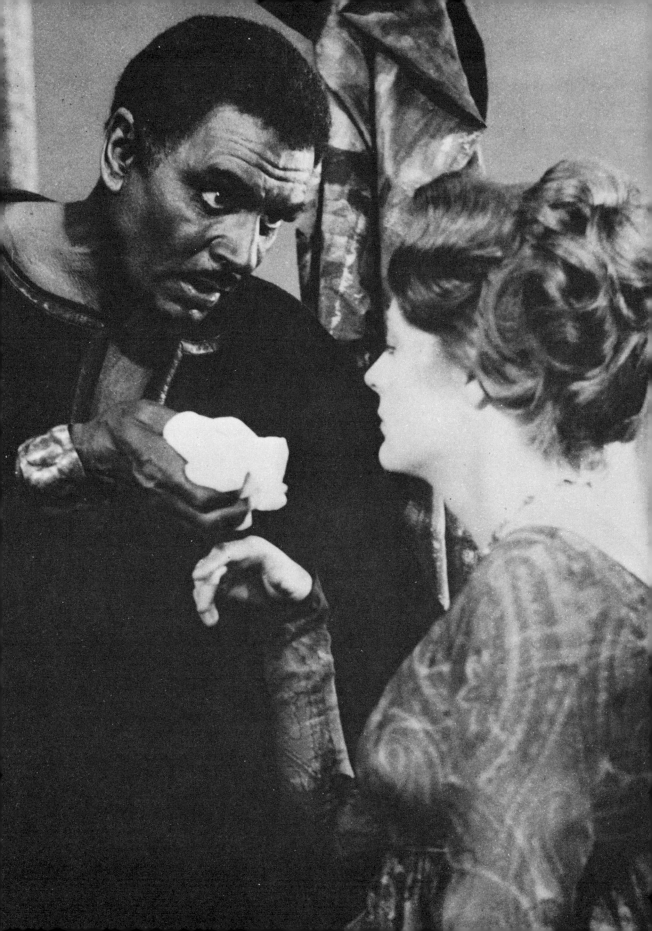

(who is also Iago's deluded wife, and has, in fact, purloined the fatal handkerchief), sits at the receipt of custom. After delivering an impassioned speech of farewell, he suffocates the helpless Desdemona. Soon

Pompey (John Kane) and Mistress Overdone (Eileen Beldon) in the 1970 production of *Measure for Measure* by the Royal Shakespeare Company at Stratford.

afterwards commissioners from Venice arrive. Iago's guilt is laid bare; and Othello is arrested. Snatching a sword that he knows lies hidden in the room, he stabs himself and falls dead.

Othello (for which Shakespeare borrowed the raw materials of his plot from an Italian *novella,* published in Cinthio's *Hecatommithi* nearly forty years earlier) was originally staged at the Banqueting House, Whitehall, on 1 November 1604. It is one of the most moving and subtly constructed of its author's great tragedies. The hero is a deeply poetic personage; 'poetry [a recent critic has suggested] is the element in which he moves; and, whether he speaks of his soldierly past or of his royal parentage beneath a blazing African

sky, the images he evokes…have a powerful incantatory charm. Nothing about him is common or trivial.' Shakespeare's play, which inspired Verdi's almost equally magnificent opera, as another commentator has remarked is planned on somewhat operatic lines; and, whenever the hero makes his appearance, he is accompanied by a melody that belongs to him alone, and commands a hush and clears a space around him. The clue to Othello's tragedy is his essential innocence and his romantic unpreparedness. Surprised by love, he is later surprised by jealousy. All his life a gallant foreign adventurer, he has seen comparatively little of the modern European world, with its dark intrigues and sordid passions; whereas Iago is a crafty, unscrupulous worldling, who 'knows his price', doggedly pursues his own interests and has deliberately rejected every moral value, believing 'good' and 'evil' to be relative terms, and love at best a fashionable delusion.

OUTLAWS *(Gent.)*: three bandits who have been banished from Milan. They waylay Valentine and Speed, and ask Valentine to join them as leader of their band, which they say contains several banished gentlemen. Valentine agrees to their offer,

Provided that you do no outrages,
On silly women or poor passengers. (IV.i)

At the end Valentine persuades the Duke to pardon them all (V.iii).

OVERDONE, MISTRESS *(Meas.)*: 'a bawd of eleven years continuance'. She deplores the ruin of her trade by Angelo's strict enforcement of the old law against immorality; she is committed to prison by Escalus (III.ii).

She has had nine husbands, and was 'Overdone by the last'. Despite her trade, she has a warm streak of humanity: we hear that she has been looking after Lucio's bastard child by Kate Keepdown for over a year (III.ii).

OXFORD, EARL OF *(3H.VI; R.III)*: a supporter of the Queen and the Lancastrian cause. His father and elder brother had been executed by Edward IV. He joins the Queen at Tewkesbury, where he is captured (V.iv).

In *Richard III* he is with Richmond at Bosworth; he speaks only two lines (V.ii).

He was John de Vere, 13th Earl of Oxford (1443–1513). He was imprisoned as a Lancastrian in 1468; he escaped to France after the Battle of Barnet. In 1473 he returned, but was captured and held prisoner in Hammes Castle. In 1477, with Richard III on the throne, he escaped and joined Richmond in France. He landed in England with him, and commanded the right wing of his army at Bosworth. He was rewarded with the office of Lord Chancellor by Richmond as Henry VII.

P

PACORUS *(Ant.)*: the son of Oredes, King of Parthia. He is killed in battle with the Roman army led by Ventidius, and his body is borne in triumph (III.i).

PAGE, A *(All'sW.)*: he interrupts the conversation between Helena and Parolles to announce to the latter that Bertram is calling for him (I.i).

PAGE, A *(H.VIII)*: he is attending Gardiner when he meets Thomas Lovell late one night (v.i).

PAGE, A *(2H.IV)*: the King sends him to fetch the Earls of Surrey and of Warwick (III.i).

PAGE, A *(Meas.)*: Mariana's boy, who is singing the plaintive song 'Take, O, take those lips away, that so sweetly were forsworn' when the Duke enters disguised as a friar. The boy is immediately dismissed (IV.i).

PAGE, A *(R.III)*: he recommends Sir James Tyrell to Richard as a man whom gold might persuade 'unto a close exploit of death'. He is sent to find him (IV.ii).

PAGE, A *(Rom.)*: he accompanies Paris to the tomb of the Capulets and is told to keep watch while his master strews flowers in memory of Juliet. He whistles to warn of the approach of Romeo, and when Paris and Romeo fight he hurries away to call the watch (v.iii).

PAGE, A *(Tim.)*: he is in the service of a courtesan, along with the Fool. He appears with two letters and asks Apemantus to tell him to whom they are addressed as he cannot read (II.ii).

PAGE, ANNE *(Wiv.)*: the daughter of Mistress Page. Her mother wants her to marry Dr Caius, while her father favours Slender. She elopes with Fenton and marries him, and is forgiven by her parents. She leads the band tormenting Falstaff.

PAGE, FALSTAFF'S *(2H.IV; H.V; Wiv.)*: he is put into Falstaff's service by Hal. He reports to his master

Anne Page invites Slender to dinner. A painting by Thomas Duncan.

(I.ii). He is rewarded by Hal for his mockery of Bardolph (II.i). Later he is in attendance (II.iv).

In *Henry V* his title is Boy, but he is presumably the same character. He summons Pistol to see Falstaff who is 'very ill' (II.i). He recalls some of his master's sayings (II.iii). After Falstaff's death he characterizes the 'three swashers', his new masters (III.ii). He interprets between Pistol and his French captive (IV.iv). He is left to guard the baggage at Agincourt, and is killed by the French (IV.vii).

In *The Merry Wives of Windsor* he brings letters to the wives (I.iii). He tells Mistress Ford that Falstaff has arrived at her back door, and assures Mistress Page that Falstaff is unaware of her presence; later, he shows in Mistress Page as though she had just arrived, and when Falstaff panics he helps conceal him in the basket (III.iii).

In *The Merry Wives* he is called Robin.

PAGE, MASTER GEORGE *(Wiv.)*: a gentleman living at Windsor, the father of Anne and William. When Nym tells him of Falstaff's designs on his wife, he is prepared to trust her, and advises the jealous Ford to do

below The Merry Wives of Windsor (III.iii): Falstaff is hidden in the laundry basket. *right The Merry Wives of Windsor* (II.i): Mrs Page and Mrs Ford outside Page's house. Both illustrations are by the Rev. Mathew William Peters.

the same (III.iii). He tells Ford his jealousy is making him behave like a lunatic. At the end he joins in the baiting of Falstaff, but afterwards bids him 'eat a posset' at his house that night. He accepts the marriage of his daughter Anne to Fenton (V.v).

In I.i he is called Thomas.

PAGE, MISTRESS *(Wiv.)*: one of the merry wives; she is called 'Meg' by her husband. She receives one of Falstaff's love letters, and joins with Mistress Ford in planning to humiliate him. She bursts in when Falstaff is with Mistress Ford and says that Frank Ford is nearby; the ladies force Falstaff to escape in a laundry basket. Later they force him to dress up as 'the old woman of Brentford'. Mistress Page devises the plan for baiting Falstaff in Windsor Forest by recalling the old tale of Herne the Hunter.

PAGE, WILLIAM *(Wiv.)*: George Page's young son. Sir Hugh Evans questions him on his Latin (IV.i), and he is one of the boys who pretend to be fairies to fool Falstaff (V.iv).

PAGES *(AYL.)*: two pages who are part of the banished Duke's retinue. Audrey and Touchstone meet them and Audrey asks them to sing. They oblige with 'It was a lover and his lass' (V.iii).

PAINTER, A *(Tim.)*: in the opening scene he is outside Timon's house with a poet and a merchant, all of them waiting for payment from Timon (I.i). Later the poet and the painter, hearing of Timon's hoard of gold, seek him out in his cave (V.i).

The painter may have been suggested to Shakespeare by Plutarch's anecdote telling how Alcibiades 'kept Agatharcus the painter prisoner in his house by force, untill he had painted all his walles within, and when he had done, dyd let him goe and rewarded him very honestly for his paines.'

PANDAR, A *(Per.)*: the owner of a brothel in Mytilene. He is short of girls, and buys Marina from the pirates in the hope that a high-quality virgin will bring back the customers. He plans to sell her virginity to the highest bidder, but she proves quite incorruptible, and even reforms the customers before sending them away. He becomes desperate to be rid of her (IV.ii; IV.vi).

PANDARUS *(Troil.)*: Cressida's uncle. He acts as go-between for her and Troilus: he brings them together and returns to witness their vows of mutual fidelity. He tells Cressida that she is to be exchanged for Antenor (IV.ii). He appears as a commentator throughout the action, and speaks the epilogue.

He is genial, but degenerate; a voyeur, but a harmless one. He controls the love affair between Troilus and Cressida, as Troilus realizes: 'I cannot come to Cressid but by Pandar'. But his presence brings its distinctive tone to their love affair, surrounded as he is with the ambience of the brothel.

In Homer Pandarus is a brutal warrior, a great archer who wounds Menelaus before being killed by Diomedes. He first appears as a companion of Troilus in Boccaccio's *Filostrato,* where he is a chivalrous knight and a faithful friend.

It is in Chaucer that he first appears as a go-between, a kindly uncle-figure to the lovers. But for the Elizabethans his name was used for a pimp or procurer just as Cressida's name stood for whore.

The discrepancies in Pandarus' role in the play suggest that the text that has come down to us is partly a revised version of an earlier play that was possibly presented on Revels Night (when bawdiness was expected) at one of the Inns of Court. Pandarus is dismissed twice by Troilus with the same words:

Hence, broker, lackey, ignomy and shame

Pursue thy life, and live aye with thy name. (v.iv; v.x) Pandarus' Epilogue has long been thought to be an addition. It has been suggested that it would be offensive on the public stage, and that thus it provides further evidence of a coterie audience:

As many as be here of Pandar's hall,
Your eyes, half out, weep out at Pandar's fall;
Or if you cannot weep, give yet some groans,
Though not for me, yet for your aching bones.
Brethren and sisters of the hold-door trade,
Some two months my will shall here be made.
It should be now but that my fear is this,
Some galled goose of Winchester would hiss.
Till then I'll sweat, and seek about for eases;
And at that time bequeath you my diseases. (v.x)

PANDULPH, CARDINAL *(John)*: in France he pronounces the ban against John for contumacy (III.i). He advises Lewis how the death of Arthur is to his advantage (III.iv). He receives the crown from John and hands it back by favour of the Pope (v.i). He tells Lewis that John 'hath reconciled himself to Rome', and tells the Dauphin not to invade England (v.ii).

He first came to England in 1211 to negotiate with John for the installation of Stephen Langton as Archbishop of Canterbury; when John refused to agree to it, Pandulph pronounced sentence of excommunication on him. In May 1213 he returned, and at Dover he received the submission of John to Rome. He then worked to stop the threatened French invasion. In 1215 he was with John at Runnymede, and excommunicated the barons who made him sign the Magna Carta. John rewarded him with the bishopric of Norwich. Henry III found Pandulph arrogant, and in 1221 engineered his recall to Rome. He died in 1226, and his body was brought to Norwich for burial.

PANTHINO *(Gent.)*: servant to Antonio. He advises his master to send his son Proteus to serve the Duke of Milan. He accompanies Proteus and Launce to the ship (II.ii; II.iii).

PARIS *(Rom.)*: a young nobleman whose betrothal to Juliet has been arranged by her father. She rejects him, despite the Nurse's eulogy of him (I.iii). He is killed by Romeo when taking flowers to Juliet's tomb.

PARIS *(Troil.)*: second son of Priam and Hecuba. His abduction of Helen, the wife of Menelaus, was the cause of the Trojan War. He fights with Menelaus, and is wounded by him (I.i); he fights with him again during the battle at the end.

PARIS, GOVERNOR OF *(1H.VI)*: he is present at the coronation of Henry in Paris, and is ordered by

Lafeu (Brewster Mason) and Parolles (Clive Swift) in the Royal Shakespeare Company's 1967 production of *All's Well that Ends Well.*

Gloucester to take an oath of fealty (IV.i).

He was John of Luxemburg, appointed by the Duke of Bedford when Paris was captured.

PAROLLES *(All's W.)*: a follower of Bertram, who he urges to leave France and go to the wars. His cowardice is exposed when he is captured and blindfolded, apparently by enemies: they speak to him in gibberish, and he offers to betray 'all the secrets of our camp' in return for his freedom (IV.i). He is then brought before the lords, and utters any slander that he thinks will please the enemy. When he is allowed to see, he discovers that he has been in the hands of the officers and nobles of his own army all along. He bounces back by saying 'Who cannot be crushed with a plot?' (IV.ii).

PATCH-BREECH *(Per.)*: one of the three fishermen who find Pericles on the beach at Pentapolis where he has been washed ashore (II.i).

PATIENCE *(H.VIII)*: Katharine's lady-in-waiting who attends her as she lies dying. Katharine has dictated to her the letter that she asks Capucius to take to the King (IV.ii).

PATROCLUS *(Troil.)*: one of the Greek commanders, and close friend of Achilles. He amuses Achilles with his mimicry of the other Greek leaders as they idle away the time in their tent; Patroclus has been trying to persuade Achilles to take up arms again, but to no effect. It is only when he is killed in battle by Hector that Achilles' wrath is aroused (v.v).

In Homer's *Iliad*, 'god-like' Patroclus takes the field wearing Achilles' armour in an attempt to inspire the Greeks, and is killed by Hector.

PAULINA *(Wint.)*: the wife of Antigonus, and lady-in-waiting to Hermione. She vehemently defends Hermione when Leontes accuses her of unchastity (II.iii). She takes him the prison-born Perdita. Her husband is ordered to take the infant to a desert spot and abandon it; he does so but is eaten by a bear. She tells Leontes of Hermione's death (III.ii). Sixteen years

The Winter's Tale (II.i): a design for Charles Kean's production at the Princess's Theatre in 1856.

later she makes Leontes promise that he will not marry again without her approval. She shows him Hermione's statue, which turns out to have been replaced by Hermione herself. After the reunion of Leontes with his family, Paulina prepares to mourn her own husband in seclusion, but Leontes persuades her to marry Camillo. These two worthy and honest characters are well suited.

PEASEBLOSSOM *(MND.)*: a fairy. She is one of those chosen by Titania to attend Bottom (III.i; IV.i), together with Cobweb.

PEDANT *(Shr.)*: he is frightened by Tranio into impersonating Vincentio, the father of Lucentio. In this role he consents to the marriage of Lucentio and Bianca. When the real Vincentio arrives the Pedant tries briefly to maintain his role, but runs away when he is exposed (v.i). He is presumably forgiven, for he is present at the final banquet.

PEDRO, DON, PRINCE OF ARAGON *(Ado)*: he has defeated his bastard brother Don John, and is now apparently reconciled to him. Together they visit Leonato at Messina; Don Pedro woos Hero on Claudio's behalf, and resolves to match Beatrice and Benedick – 'one of Hercules' labours'. He supports Claudio when he charges Hero with unfaithfulness, thinking that there is 'very full proof' of the accusation against her (v.i). When the truth is exposed he offers to make amends for his mistake.

PEMBROKE, EARL OF *(John)*: he disapproves of John's submission to the Pope, and accuses him of Arthur's murder; he defects to the Dauphin when he invades England. He returns to John when he discovers that the Dauphin plans to murder the English nobles if he defeats John.

He was William Marshal (d.1219). He in fact remained loyal to John; his son joined the Dauphin, and it is possibly him that Shakespeare intended here.

PERCY, LADY *(1&2H.IV)*: wife to Hotspur, and sister of Mortimer. Though her name is Elizabeth, she is always called 'Kate' by her husband. She playfully entreats Hotspur to tell her what 'heavy business' he has in hand, but he refuses, though he says that he trusts her. She follows him to Wales, where they join Mortimer and Glendower. At Glendower's castle Hotspur chides her for her ladylike manner of swearing; she refuses to sing for him.

In *2 Henry IV* she pleads with her father-in-law Northumberland after the death of Hotspur not to go to war in support of the rebellion in which he had failed to support his son (II.iii).

Programme cover for *The Winter's Tale* at the Savoy Theatre in 1912.

PERCY, THOMAS, EARL OF WORCESTER *(1H.IV)*: in an angry confrontation between the Percy family and Henry, Worcester reminds the King that the Percy family put him on the throne; Henry dismisses him for being 'too bold and peremptory' (I.iii). He excuses his part in the rebellion on the grounds that Henry had broken faith with his loyal supporters (v.i). He is sent to talk with Henry at Shrewsbury before the battle. When he returns he does not inform Hotspur of Henry's 'liberal kind offer', but instead says that Henry will show no mercy, and that Hal has challenged Hotspur to single combat (v.ii). He is taken prisoner and executed.

He was Thomas Percy (1344–1403). He served in France from 1369 to 1373, and accompanied the poet Chaucer on his mission to Flanders in 1377. He was appointed steward of Richard II's household, and in 1397 he was created Earl of Worcester. He joined Bolingbroke when he landed, and served him when Henry IV for four years; he then became a bitter enemy of the King, and joined Hotspur's rebellion. His misrepresentation of Henry's peace proposals has

Perdita and Florizel; a painting by Charles Robert Leslie.

never been adequately accounted for: the reasons Shakespeare gives him are quite plausible ones.

PERDITA *(Wint.)*: Hermione has been cast off by her consort, Leontes, King of Sicilia, who is convinced that she has become the mistress of his former friend, Polixenes, King of Bohemia, and gives birth to a daughter, whom Leontes believes to be her lover's child. The baby is then exposed; but a shepherd finds her in the lonely place where she has been abandoned by her father's servants, and rears her at his own cottage. She is named Perdita, 'the lost girl'; and she grows up blithe and beautiful. When Perdita is sixteen, she meets the handsome Florizel, son of King Polixenes. He proposes marriage; his father forbids the match; and the lovers then elope to the kingdom of Leontes. There the Sicilian monarch learns that Perdita is, in fact, his true-born offspring; and Hermione, though her faithful gentlewoman, 'the grave and good Paulina', has previously announced her death, is discovered living in Paulina's house. Polixenes and Leontes renew their friendship; and preparations are made for the marriage of Perdita and Florizel.

Performed at Whitehall on 1 January 1611, *The Winter's Tale* belongs to Shakespeare's second group of comedies, and exhibits the changing tastes of the Jacobean audience, which, seated at its ease in a weather-proof, candle-lit playhouse, demanded elaborate masques and ingenious scenic shows. Thus *The Winter's Tale* provides an attractive transformation scene, where Hermione (whom Paulina has concealed for the last sixteen years) is restored to her friends under the guise of a statue that, when its custodian draws a half-transparent veil, gradually comes to life. The famous stage direction, *Exit, pursued by a bear,* may perhaps indicate that a tame bear, well known to the audience, was somehow brought on to the stage. Shakespeare derived the raw materials of his play from a popular novel, *Pandosto, or The Triumph of Time,* published in 1588 by his old adversary Robert Greene. It has a fairytale atmosphere; and the story teems with picturesque improbabilities. What carries it along is its exquisite lyricism: the beauty of Perdita's speeches and the gaiety and charm of the ditties sung by the strolling

The Winter's Tale (IV.iv): Perdita and Florizel welcome Polixenes to the shepherd's cottage. From the painting by Francis Wheatley.

pedlar, Autolycus. This is indeed 'the golden world'; and the heroine herself is the personification of grace and youthful freshness, born, she says, beneath a dancing star. Like most of Shakespeare's contemporaries, she loves the rhythms of the dance and passionately delights in flowers:

> ... Daffodils,
> That come before the swallow dares, and take
> The winds of March with beauty; violets dim,
> But sweeter than the lids of Juno's eyes, pale
> > primroses,
> That die unmarried ere they can behold
> Bright Phoebus in his strength ... (IV.iv)

Yet Perdita is no mere countrified innocent; she is a sensuous, warm-blooded girl, not afraid to admit that she longs for a flowery bank where she can 'lie and play' within her lover's arms.

PERICLES, PRINCE OF TYRE *(Per.)*: he seeks the daughter of Antiochus in marriage, but when he solves the riddle that he is set he exposes the incestuous relationship Antiochus has with his daughter, and flees

to save his life (I.i). He goes to Tharsus, where he relieves a famine. He is shipwrecked on the coast of Pentapolis (II.i); his armour is saved by some fishermen, and he puts it on and appears in the lists at King Simonides' tournament. Pericles is the victor, and is persuaded to reveal his name (II.iii). Simonides, after testing his courage, gives him his daughter Thaisa as his wife. He hears that he must return to Tyre if he is to succeed to the throne; on the voyage back his daughter Marina is born during a storm, but Thaisa appears to have died in childbirth. Pericles decides to return to Tharsus, where he leaves the infant Marina in the care of Cleon and Dionyza; he vows not to cut his hair until his daughter is married (III.iii). He returns to Tyre. Years later he arrives at Mytilene in a coma, and is revived by Marina's song; he is joyfully reunited with his daughter. Just as he is falling asleep he has a vision of the Goddess Diana telling him to go to Ephesus (v.ii). On arrival there he finds Thaisa in the temple of Diana, and is restored to her (v.iii).

Pericles, Prince of Tyre did not appear in the First Folio. It appeared as a Quarto in 1609, under Shakespeare's name, though it was acted before May 1608, when it appeared in the Stationer's Register. The authenticity of the play has always been suspect, and it has long been argued that it was the result of a collaboration in which Shakespeare hastily revised a play first written by another author (John Day being the most likely candidate). Some scholars argue that

above Pericles (Ian Richardson) and Thaisa (Susan Fleetwood) in the 1969 production of *Pericles* by the Royal Shakespeare Company *(left)*; frontispiece to

Pericles, from Rowe's 1709 edition of Shakespeare's plays *(right).*

the text we have is a badly corrupted one which has been damaged by bad reporting by compositors. Certainly the first two acts are unlike anything else in Shakespeare; but there is no reason why we should not see the peculiarities of the play as Shakespearian experiments in a new manner with new material.

The plot derives from the story of Apollonius of Tyre, which was popular all over Europe during the Middle Ages. Shakespeare probably took his version of it from Gower's *Confessio Amantis;* he also used the poet himself in *Pericles.* His other main source was probably Laurence Twine's *The Patterne of Painefull Adventures* (1576). The prose romance *The Painfull Adventures of Pericles, Prince of Tyre* (1608) by George Wilkins was largely based on Twine's work (which had recently been republished) and a *Pericles* play, which was almost certainly Shakespeare's.

PETER *(Rom.)*: the servant of Juliet's nurse. In IV.v he sings 'When griping grief', which is part of a song written by Richard Edwardes. The part was played by

Will Kempe, the chief clown in Shakespeare's company at this time.

PETER *(Shr.)*: one of the servants at Petruchio's country house (IV.i).

PETER, FRIAR *(Meas.)*: a monk who assists the Duke in his scheme to expose Angelo. He takes Mariana and Isabella to a place where the Duke will see them when he enters the city (IV.vi). He defends 'Friar Lodowick' against Lucio's slanders (V.i).

PETER OF POMFRET *(John)*: a prophet. John has him hanged when he predicts that he will surrender his crown before the next Ascension Day (IV.ii). The prophecy is fulfilled to some extent when England becomes a papal fief (V.i).

According to Holinshed he was 'in great reputation with the common people' for his predictions, and staked his life on John losing his kingdom on Ascension

2 Henry VI: Mr Baddeley as Peter Thump, a fictitious print published in 1786.

Day 1213. When the day passed 'without any other notable damage unto King John' Peter was dragged behind horses through the streets of Wareham and then hanged, along with his innocent son. As John admits in Shakespeare's play, there was some truth in his prophecy, for it was on Ascension Day that John did homage to the Pope for his kingdom.

PETITIONERS *(2H.VI)*: these commoners present their suits to Gloucester. Margaret, angry at this further indication of the Protector's power, tears up their petitions (I.iii).

PETO *(1&2H.IV)*: one of Falstaff's cronies. He takes part in the robbery at Gadshill. He later tells the Prince how they tried to disguise their cowardice, and explains how Falstaff hacked his sword with his dagger to make it look as though it had been used (II.iv).

In *2 Henry IV* he is now 'an attendant on Prince Henry'; presumably this is an indication of his relative honesty. He brings news of the rebellion to the Prince, and tells Falstaff that he has

      . . . met, and overtook a dozen captains,
   Bare-headed, sweating, knocking at the taverns,
   And asking every one for Sir John Falstaff. (II.iv)

PETRUCHIO *(Rom.)*: he is a follower of the Capulets. He is at their feast, and is with Tybalt when he kills Mercutio and is killed by Romeo. (III.i).

PETRUCHIO *(Shr.)*: a gentleman of Verona. He arrives at Padua looking for a wealthy wife. He hears of the shrewish Katharine and her large dowry and immediately resolves to woo and tame her (I.ii). He presents himself to her father and ascertains the exact amount of her dowry; on his first encounter with her he ignores her raillery and says he finds her 'passing courteous'. He tells her father she is 'modest as the dove' and fixes the wedding day, ignoring her furious protests (II.i). On the wedding day Petruchio arrives on a broken-down old horse, and dressed in shabby, ill-fitting clothes; he behaves madly during the ceremony (*see* GREMIO), and insists that he and Katharine set out for the country before the wedding banquet (III.ii). After a hectic journey they arrive at Petruchio's country house, and he immediately berates the servants, insisting that the meat is overcooked, and refusing to allow the starving Katharine to have any food (IV.i). He makes her thank him for serving her with food the next day, and he rejects the clothes that he has ordered for her, though she longs to have them. They set off for Padua, but not before he has persuaded her to call the sun the moon, and the old Vincentio a young maiden (IV.v). At Lucentio's feast Petruchio sets a test of obedience for the new wives. Katharine alone shows her submission, and Petruchio wins the wager, while the other husbands are left to ponder who has really married the shrew (V.ii).

Petruchio is boastful, arrogant, sure of himself; when asked if he means to woo the 'wild-cat' Katharine he replies:

   Why came I hither but to that intent?
   Think you a little din can daunt mine ears?
   Have I not in my time heard lions roar?
   Have I not heard the sea, puffed up with winds,
   Rage like an angry boar chafed with sweat?
   Have I not heard great ordinance in the field,
   And heaven's artillery thunder in the skies?
   Have I not in a pitched battle heard
   Loud 'larums, neighing steeds, and trumpets' clang?
   And do you tell me of a woman's tongue,
   That gives not half so great a blow to hear
   As will a chestnut in a farmer's fire?
   Tush, tush! Fear boys with bugs. (I.ii)

For all his swaggering aggressiveness, Petruchio is not insensitive; he is aware of the roughness of his necessary treatment, and is even worried by it.

   Ay, and amid this hurly I intend
   That all is done in reverent care of her;
   And in conclusion, she shall watch all night,
   And if she chance to nod, I'll rail and brawl,

And with the clamour keep her still awake.
This is a way to kill a wife with kindness,
And thus I'll curb her mad and headstrong humour.
He that knows better how to tame a shrew,
Now let him speak, 'tis charity to shew. (IV.i)

After his virtuoso performance with the tailor, Petruchio explains the point of his antics:

Our purses shall be proud, our garments poor;
For 'tis the mind that makes the body rich.
And as the sun breaks through the darkest clouds,
So honour peereth in the meanest habit.
What, is the jay more precious than the lark,
Because his feathers are more beautiful?
Or is the adder better than the eel,
Because his painted skin contents the eye? (IV.iii)

Katharine has been warped by envy of her 'beautiful' sister; Petruchio directs her to a proper valuation of her own worth. It is understanding that he brings to her, and not subjugation. Once the 'raging war' between them is over there is a sense of complicity and perfect harmony between them.

'Petruchio is a madman in his senses, a very honest fellow, who hardly speaks a word of truth, and succeeds in all his tricks and impostures. He acts his accustomed character to the life, with the most fantastical extra-vagance, with complete presence of mind, with untired animal spirits, and without a particle of ill-humour from beginning to end.' (Hazlitt)

PHEBE *(AYL.)*: a shepherdess. She is loved by Silvius, but rejects him. She falls in love with 'Ganymede' (Rosalind in disguise), and cruelly employs Silvius to carry a love letter to 'him'. She promises to marry Silvius if it ever happens that she refuses Ganymede, as of course she does when Rosalind reveals herself.

PHILARIO *(Cym.)*: a friend of Posthumus' father. Posthumus visits him in Rome. Philario welcomes him, and is his host during his banishment; he vainly tries to dissuade Posthumus and Iachimo from their wager on Imogen's fidelity (I.iv). He is convinced by Iachimo's evidence of his alleged triumph (II.iv).

PHILARMONUS (a soothsayer) *(Cym.)*: he interprets, favourably for Rome, Lucius' vision from the gods (IV.ii), and later, Posthumus' mystic 'label' (V.v).

PHILEMON *(Per.)*: Cerimon's servant. He is ordered by his master to take care of the victims of the shipwreck (III.ii).

below Michael Williams as Petruchio in the 1967 production of *The Taming of the Shrew* by the Royal Shakespeare Company *(left)*; Phoebe (Richard Kay) and Silvius (John McEnery) in the all-male version of *As You Like It* produced by Clifford Williams, by the National Theatre Company in 1967 *(right)*.

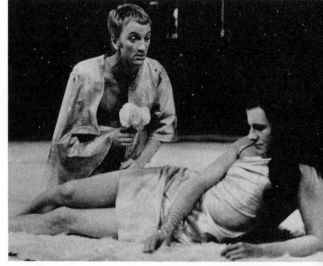

PHILIP *(Shr.)*: one of the servants at Petruchio's country house (IV.i).

PHILIP, KING OF FRANCE *(John)*: he goes to war against John in support of Arthur's claim to the English throne, but they agree to form an alliance by marrying

above Pisanio and Imogen, after a painting by John Hoppner *(left);* Pisanio (Mark Dignam) and the Queen (Joan Miller) in Peter Hall's 1957 production of

Cymbeline at the Shakespeare Memorial Theatre, Stratford *(right).*

the Dauphin to John's niece, Blanch of Spain (II.i). But hostilities are re-opened when John refuses to accept the demands made by Pandulph, the papal legate (III.i). Philip is defeated by the English.

He was Philip II of France (1165–1223), known as Philip Augustus. He joined Coeur-de-lion on the Third Crusade, but on the way to the Holy Land they quarrelled, and Philip returned to France and intrigued against Richard with his brother John. Philip offered the Emperor Henry VI of Germany a large sum to keep Richard in captivity when he imprisoned him on his way back from the crusade. When Richard was released he defeated Philip at Fréteval in 1194. John signed a treaty with Philip in 1200, but in 1202 war broke out again; by 1208 Philip had regained most of the English possessions in France. Philip was a remarkable soldier and a considerable statesman who did much to build up the French monarchy despite the opposition of the great barons.

PHILO *(Ant.)*: a friend to Antony. In the opening scene he describes Antony's total devotion to Cleopatra, and warns Demetrius that Antony is not himself (I.i).

PHILOSTRATE *(MND.)*: the Master of the Revels at Theseus' court. Theseus orders him to arrange the festivities for his wedding to Hippolyta (I.i). After the wedding feast Philostrate gives Theseus a list of entertainments from which Theseus chooses 'Pyramus and Thisbe' against his advice (v.i).

PHILOTUS *(Tim.)*: the servant of one of Timon's creditors. He is sent to Timon to collect his master's debt; when Timon sees him and the others he flies into a rage and drives them off (III.iv).

PHRYNIA *(Tim.)*: one of two prostitutes who appear with Alcibiades when he visits Timon in his cave. Timon abuses them both, and they encourage him, since his insults are accompanied by gold (IV.iii).

PIERCE OF EXTON, SIR *(R.II)*: he overhears Henry say that he wishes that Richard were dead, and murders him at Pontefract Castle. He hopes for Henry's thanks, but is angrily dismissed:

> They love not poison that do poison need,
> Nor do I thee; though I did wish him dead,
> I hate the murderer, love him murdered.
> The guilt of conscience take thou for thy labour,
> But neither my good word, nor princely favour;
> With Cain go wander through the shade of night,
> And never show thy head by day nor light. (v.vi)

According to Holinshed, 'King Henry, on a day at his table, sore sighing said, "Have I no faithful friend which will deliver me of him whose life will be my death, and whose death will be the preservation of my life?".' Pierce was probably a relation of Sir Nicholas Exton, the Mayor of London in 1395, a violent opponent of Richard II.

PILCH *(Per.)*: one of three fishermen who find Pericles on the beach at Pentapolis where he has been washed ashore (II.i).

PINCH *(Err.)*: a schoolmaster and mountebank conjuror. He finds Antipholus and Dromio of Ephesus to be insane, and orders them to be bound and put in a dark room (IV.iv).

PINDARUS *(Caes.)*: a slave captured by Cassius in Parthia and taken into his service. At Philippi, he tells Cassius that Titinius has been captured; Cassius offers him his freedom if he will kill him. He does so, and runs away (V.iii).

PIRATES *(Per.)*: they surprise Leonine as he is about to murder Marina. He runs away and they take her to Mytilene and sell her to the brothel (IV.ii).

PISANIO *(Cym.)*: Posthumus' servant, whom he leaves behind in Imogen's service when he is banished. He receives Posthumus' letter alleging that Imogen has been unfaithful and telling him to kill her. He persuades her to adopt the disguise of a boy and thus to serve Lucius as a page. Pisanio offers to serve Cloten, and brings him the suit of Posthumus' clothes in which he is killed. Pisanio reveals the identity of 'Fidele' at the end.

Like Kent in *King Lear*, Pisanio is the honest, devoted servant who is prepared to disobey when he thinks it right to do so.

PISTOL *(2H.IV; Wiv.; H.V)*: an associate of Falstaff, his 'ancient' (ensign). He brings Falstaff the news of the death of Henry IV, and welcomes 'these pleasant days'. He is taken with Falstaff to the Fleet Prison after Henry V rejects them all.

In *The Merry Wives of Windsor* Falstaff dismisses him when he refuses to act as a go-between; for revenge he tells Ford that Falstaff is in love with his wife. He takes part in the baiting of Falstaff in Windsor Forest.

In *Henry V* he is now Mistress Quickly's husband and the host of the Boar's Head tavern. He goes to France, along with Bardolph and Nym, as a member of Henry's army. He insults Fluellen, who beats him and forces him to eat a leek (v.i). He resolves to leave France – 'to England will I steal, and there I'll steal'.

Falstaff's boy says that Pistol 'hath a killing tongue, and a quiet sword; by the means whereof, a' breaks words, and keeps whole weapons' (*Henry V*, III.ii). He is a braggart, a 'roaring boy', whose extravagant language and violent demeanour conceal a dedicated coward. The boy has more to say of him later:

I did never know so full a voice issue from so empty a heart: but the saying is true, The empty vessel makes the greatest sound. Bardolph and Nym had ten times more valour, than this roaring devil i' th' old play, that every one may pare his nails with a wooden dagger, and they are both hanged, and so would this be, if he durst steal any thing adventurously. (*Henry V*, IV.iv)

PLANTAGENET, ARTHUR *(John)*, see ARTHUR.

PLANTAGENET, EDMUND *(3H.VI)*, see RUTLAND.

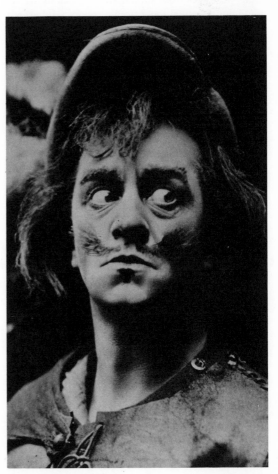

Henry V: William Mollison as Pistol in a production of March 1905.

PLANTAGENET, EDWARD (afterwards Edward IV) *(2H.VI)*, *see* EDWARD.

PLANTAGENET, EDWARD, DUKE OF AUMERLE *(R.II)*, *see* AUMERLE.

PLANTAGENET, EDWARD, PRINCE OF WALES *(3H.VI)*, *see* EDWARD.

PLANTAGENET, EDWARD (son of Duke of Clarence) *(R.III)*: he appears once with his sister Margaret (II.ii).

He was Edward, Earl of Warwick (1475–99), the elder son of George, Duke of Clarence. He was brought up by his aunt Anne, Duchess of Gloucester. When Richard III lost his only son, he thought of naming Edward as his heir, but changed his mind and had him shut up in close confinement in Sheriff Hutton Castle. On the accession of Henry VII he was transferred to the Tower, where he remained for the rest of his life. He was totally restricted from normal life, so much so that 'he could not discern a goose from a capon' (Holinshed). Perkin Warbeck was imprisoned with him after his capture; they planned to escape together, but their plan was ludicrously transformed into a conspiracy against Henry VII, and Edward was beheaded in 1499. The reason for his death was political: his existence threatened the much desired undisputed succession.

PLANTAGENET, GEORGE *(3H.VI)*, *see* CLARENCE, DUKE OF.

PLANTAGENET, HENRY, *see* HENRY IV, HENRY V, HENRY VI.

PLANTAGENET, JOHN *(John)*, *see* JOHN, KING.

PLANTAGENET, LADY MARGARET *(R.III)*, *see* MARGARET.

PLANTAGENET, RICHARD *(1H.VI)*, *see* YORK, DUKE OF.

PLANTAGENET, RICHARD (afterwards Richard III) *(3H.VI; R.III)*, *see* RICHARD.

PLANTAGENET, RICHARD, EARL OF CAMBRIDGE *(H.V)*, *see* CAMBRIDGE.

PLAYERS *(Ham.)*: they visit the court of Elsinore, and Hamlet has them perform *The Murder of Gonzago* before Claudius; he has altered the play so that the story is parallel to the ghost's account of the murder of Hamlet's father. Before the performance Hamlet reminds the players of the style of acting he prefers.

When they perform the play Claudius' reaction convinces Hamlet and Horatio of his guilt.

The speech spoken by the first player from the play that 'pleas'd not the million' seems to be a parody of Aeneas' speech in Marlowe's *Dido, Queen of Carthage* (1594). Hamlet's instructions to the players seem superfluous in a play designed for the popular stage, and have been taken to indicate that the full text of the play was written for a university audience.

PLAYERS *(Shr.)*: they offer their services to the lord. He orders them to perform a play for Christopher Sly, who has been convinced that he is a lord. The play that they perform is *The Taming of the Shrew* (Induction).

POET, A *(Tim.)*: in the opening scene he is waiting outside Timon's house; the poet is waiting for payment for verses which he dedicated to Timon (I.i). Later he and the painter, having heard of Timon's hoard of gold, seek him out in his cave; he gives them gold (v.i).

POET, A *(Caes.)*: he forces his way into the tent where Brutus and Cassius are quarrelling and entreats them to be friends. He is thrown out, but his intrusion ends the argument (IV.iii).

POINS, EDWARD (NED) *(1&2 H.IV)*: a friend of Prince Henry. Together they rob Falstaff and his cronies of their loot from the robbery at Gadshill (II.iv). They mock Francis the drawer in the tavern while awaiting the arrival of Falstaff. Poins joins Henry in mocking Falstaff, but they are outwitted by his incomprehensible lies (II.iv).

In *2 Henry IV* Poins suggests that he and Henry disguise themselves as drawers and serve Falstaff in the tavern so they can see him as he really is. They do so, and Poins hears Falstaff's views on why the Prince likes him:

> Because their legs are both of a bigness, and 'a plays at quoits well, and eats conger and fennel, and drinks off candles' ends for flap-dragons, and rides the wild mare with the boys, and jumps upon joint-stools, and swears with a good grace, and wears his boots very smooth, like unto the sign of the Leg, and breeds no bate with telling of discreet stories, and such other gambol faculties 'a has, that show a weak mind and an able body, for the which the Prince admits him. (II.iv)

Prince Henry is no more truly attached to Poins than he is to Falstaff: he refers to him as 'one it pleases me for fault of a better to call my friend' (*2 Henry IV*, II.ii). When Poins mentions Henry's sick father, he gets a typical reply, one that clearly indicates how detached from him and his kind the Prince is:

> By this hand, thou thinkest me as far in the devil's

above 2 Henry IV: Falstaff and his recruits. From an engraving by Nicholson and Sheeres, published in 1850. *overleaf* Sir John Falstaff reviews his ragged regiment (*2 Henry IV*, III.ii). From the painting (1858) by John Gilbert.

book as thou and Falstaff, for obduracy and persistency. Let the end try the man. But I tell thee, my heart bleeds inwardly that my father is so sick, and keeping such vile company as thou art hath in reason taken from me all ostentation of sorrow. (*2 Henry IV*, II.ii)

POLIXENES *(Wint.)*: the King of Bohemia, and long-time friend of Leontes. Leontes suspects him of adultery with his wife Hermione, and becomes intensely jealous; he orders Camillo to poison Polixenes. Camillo tells Polixenes of the danger to his life, and the two men escape to Bohemia. Hermione is imprisoned for her supposed adultery with Polixenes. Sixteen years later we find Polixenes worried by his son Florizel, who is in love with a young shepherdess, Perdita. He refuses to allow them to marry. He visits Perdita and is forced to admit that she is 'the prettiest low-born lass', but he refuses to allow Florizel to meet her again. The lovers flee to Sicily. Polixenes follows them, and in the end discovers that Peridita is Leontes' lost daughter, and blesses the marriage.

POLONIUS *(Ham.)*: the Lord Chamberlain, and father of Ophelia and Laertes. He warns Ophelia against trusting Hamlet's vows of love, and sends Reynaldo to spy on Laertes in Paris. He comes to believe that Hamlet really is in love with Ophelia, and tells Claudius and Gertrude that he has discovered the source of the Prince's madness (II.ii). With Claudius he secretly observes a prearranged interview between Hamlet and Ophelia (III.i). He resolves to overhear Hamlet's conversation with his mother, and with her permission he hides behind an arras in her closet; when he thinks Hamlet is about to attack her he shouts for help, and Hamlet, suspecting the presence of Claudius, runs his sword through the curtain and the figure behind it (III.iv).

Polonius is a busybody, who wants to know everything, and as such is the ideal eyes and ears for Claudius in the court. But he misinterprets almost everything, largely because he feels that his age guarantees the accuracy of his judgement. He is not the foolish prating old dotard that Hamlet sees him as: he has a streak of nasty, calculating cynicism that leads him to spy on his

remains intractable in the face of laws and codes. He has a crushing reply to Escalus when he tells him of the new strict application of the morality laws in Venice: 'Does your worship mean to geld and splay all the youth of the city?' (II.i). He is quite unperturbed by all the serious moralizers.

above Fred Wright, Senior, as Polonius at the Lyric Theatre, 1905 *(left)* ; John Liston as Pompey in

Measure for Measure. From a painting by Samuel de Wilde *(right).*

own son, and to use his daughter as bait in a trap.

POLYDORE *(Cym.)* : name given to Guiderius *(q.v.)* by Belarius when he is pretending to be his father.

POMPEIUS, SEXTUS *(Ant.)* : the son of Pompey the Great, who was defeated by Julius Caesar. He is carrying on his father's war against Rome, and with the aid of the pirates Menas and Menecrates has assembled a powerful navy. He entertains the triumvirs on his galley at Misenum, and signs a treaty with them. Later we hear that the fighting has been renewed and that Pompey has been defeated (III.v).

POMPEY, BUM (Meas.): 'a clowne'. He is a bawd and servant to Mistress Overdone. When charged by Escalus with running a bawdy house he defends himself volubly, and is dismissed with a warning (II.i). Later he is sent to prison, where he is made assistant to Abhorson the hangman. He is pleased to find many of his old customers in prison.

He represents that element of human nature that

POMPEY THE GREAT *(LLL.)* : impersonated by Costard *(q.v.)* in the 'Pageant of the Nine Worthies' (v.ii).

POPILIUS LENA, *(Caes.)* : a senator who Cassius suspects of having discovered the plot to kill Caesar. For a few minutes Cassius and Brutus fear that he will expose them, but he does not (III.i).

PORTER *(H.VIII)* : he and his assistant try, without much success, to control the eager crowds at Westminster at the christening of Princess Elizabeth (v.iv).

PORTER *(1H.VI)* : he is ordered by the Countess of Auvergne to lock the gates behind Talbot when he enters her castle; Talbot avoids the trap by entering with his soldiers (II.iii).

PORTER *(2H.IV)* : gate-keeper at the Earl of Northumberland's castle. He directs Lord Bardolph to the orchard (I.i).

PORTER *(Mac.)*: he is drunk while guarding the door to Macbeth's castle, and delivers his famous soliloquy while Macduff and Lennox hammer on the door in an attempt to get in. When they are inside the porter confesses that he has been 'carousing till the second cock', and explains that drink is 'a great provoker of three things':

> Marry sir, nose-painting, sleep, and urine. Lechery, sir, it provokes, and unprovokes; it provokes the desire, but it takes away the performance. Therefore much drink may be said to be an equivocator with lechery; it makes him, and it mars him; it sets him on and it takes him off; it persuades him, and disheartens him; makes him to stand to, and not stand to; in conclusion, equivocates him in a sleep, and, giving him the lie, leaves him. (II.iii)

The porter's obsessive concern with equivocators is now generally taken to refer to the trial of Father Garnet, who was executed on 26 March 1606.

PORTIA *(Caes.)*: the wife of Brutus. She pleads with him to confide in her because she is worried by his moody silence; she discloses that she has wounded herself as proof of her faithfulness (II.i). He promises to tell her his secret before long. Before the battle at Philippi, Brutus announces that he has heard that her anxiety for him has driven her to suicide (IV.iii).

She was Porcia, the daughter of Cato Uticensis. She was married to Marcus Bibulus before Brutus. It was after the death of Brutus that she committed suicide, supposedly by swallowing live coals, but more probably by suffocation from charcoal fumes.

PORTIA *(Mer.V.)*: a rich heiress. Her father's will obliges her to accept whichever suitor chooses the correct casket out of three, the correct one being the one containing a portrait of her. Of all her suitors she is only interested in one, Bassanio, whom she had met when he came to visit her father (I.ii). She receives the Prince of Morocco and the Prince of Aragon, who both fail the test. Bassanio arrives, and chooses the right casket; she gladly commits herself to him.

> . . . But the full sum of me,
> Is sum of nothing; which to term in gross,
> Is an unlessoned girl, unschooled, unpractised,
> Happy in this, she is not yet so old
> But she may learn: happier than this,
> She is not bred so dull but she can learn;
> Happiest of all, is that her gentle spirit
> Commits itself to yours to be directed,
> As from her lord, her governor, her king.
> Myself, and what is mine, to you and yours
> Is now converted. (III.ii)

She hears of Antonio's plight, and offers to pay his debt; she tells Bassanio to go to the aid of his friend

(III.ii). She leaves with Nerissa for Venice, and explains her plan to help Antonio. In the guise of 'a young doctor of Rome' she defends Antonio in court, and defeats Shylock by insisting that he take his pound of flesh without spilling any blood. She remains in disguise, and begs her own ring from Bassanio as a reward; he

Mrs F.R. Benson as Portia in *The Merchant of Venice.*

reluctantly sends it to her. At Belmont Portia appears as herself, and pretends to be annoyed with Bassanio for parting with her ring. He is amazed when she produces it and explains her deception (V.i).

She and her world of music and beauty are the antithesis of the harsh commercial world of Venice where Shylock thrives. But when the music of her famous plea for mercy fails to move Shylock, she confronts him on his own realistic terms, and invokes the precise letter of the law. When he is defeated Portia appears to forget her earlier plea for mercy, which seems now to have been a stratagem in her argument. There is an element of the high-spirited girl even in the gravity of this scene, for, despite the seriousness of the issue, she has the winning card up her sleeve all the time. Like the trick with Bassanio's ring, her appearance in the court is a kind of game, a practical joke carried off with consummate skill.

above Posthumus and Imogen, drawn and etched by Robert Dudley *(left)*; *The Tempest* at Stratford in 1952:

Prospero (Ralph Richardson) brings about the ship-wreck by his magic *(right)*.

POSTHUMUS LEONATUS *(Cym.)*: a 'poor but worthy gentleman' who is in love with Imogen. The discovery of their secret marriage leads to Posthumus' banishment by Cymbeline. Before they part, Imogen gives Posthumus a diamond ring, and he gives her a bracelet. He goes to Rome, where he is led into wagering the ring against ten thousand ducats that Iachimo cannot destroy Imogen's fidelity. When Iachimo returns from England, Posthumus is persuaded by his evidence that Imogen has been false, and sends a letter to Pisanio ordering him to kill her. When he thinks her dead he is filled with remorse. He returns to England with the Roman army, but finds himself unable to fight against his own people; he decides to fight for them, and disguises himself as a peasant, but is taken for a Roman and thrown into prison. When he hears Iachimo's confession which proves that Imogen was innocent he is thrown into despair, and when Imogen, still disguised as 'Fidele', runs to him, he knocks her down. When she reveals herself, and forgives him, he responds by extending forgiveness to the repentant Iachimo.

POTPAN *(Rom.)*: a serving-man at the house of Capulet. He is named only when another calls him (I.v).

PRAT, MOTHER, OF BRENTFORD *(Wiv.)*: character assumed by Falstaff (IV.ii).

PRIAM *(Troil)*: the King of Troy, and father of Cressida. He asks his sons' advice as to whether Helen should be restored to the Greeks (II.ii). He tries to stop Hector taking the field on the day that he is killed (V.iii). We hear that Hector's death will 'turn Priam to stone' (V.xi).

PRIEST *(Ham.)*: he conducts the service at Ophelia's funeral. Her brother Laertes objects to the brevity of the ceremony, but the priest declares that it is already too much for a probable suicide (V.i).

PRIEST *(Tw.N.)*: he marries Olivia and Sebastian. She thinks she has married 'Cesario' (that is, Sebastian's twin sister Viola in disguise), and later denies marrying Sebastian. The priest is brought forward to confirm that she has (IV.iii; V.i).

PROCULEIUS *(Ant.)*: he is sent by Caesar to capture Cleopatra, who has locked herself inside the monument. He keeps her talking while his soldiers force their way in (v.i; v.ii).

PROSPERO *(Tp.)*: one-time Duke of Milan, Prospero, scholar and student of the magic arts, has been deposed by his brother, Antonio, with the help of an 'inveterate enemy', Alonso, King of Naples. Evidently, Prospero was a man who had disliked power, for whom his 'library was dukedom large enough'. The conspirators had caught him unawares; and he and his only child, his infant daughter, Miranda, were then consigned to a rotten hulk, so unseaworthy that the rats themselves had instinctively deserted it, and thrust out across the open sea. 'Providence divine', however, had at last brought them to a lonely and mysterious island, where the only inhabitants were Caliban, a 'freckled whelp, hag-born', and Ariel, a delicate spirit, imprisoned by Sycorax, before her unlamented death, within the entrails of a riven pine. Prospero had freed Ariel, and made him a favourite servant. Caliban, however, although Prospero had first befriended him and taught him the use of language, had attacked Miranda's virtue, so that Prospero had condemned the brutish creature to become their household slave. Ariel serves his master gladly, and blithely runs his magic errands; the despised and ill-treated Caliban perpetually rages against his state of servitude.

When the play opens, Prospero and Miranda have lived for twelve years on the island. But a storm gathers, a magic tempest deliberately raised by Prospero, and a ship is driven ashore that contains both Antonio and Alonso. The King of Naples is accompanied by his handsome son, Ferdinand, and by various members of his court. Around the whole assemblage, once they have struggled to safety, Prospero proceeds to weave his spells, among his main objects being that Ferdinand and Miranda should fall in love and join Naples and Milan by marriage. Meanwhile, Alonso's own brother, Sebastian, and the machiavellian Antonio decide that they will slay the King; and, at the same time, Caliban, having encountered Stephano and Trinculo, a drunken butler and jester, whom the storm has also cast ashore, persuades them that they should murder Prospero. From his cell the all-seeing magician watches over and controls their actions, kindles a flame of love between Miranda and Ferdinand, and terrifies and bemuses the courtly miscreants by means of the apparitions and 'quaint devices' that Ariel has conjured up. Soon afterwards, having 'austerely punish'd' Ferdinand to test his new-found passion for Miranda, he agrees that they shall wed, and presents a solemn masque, performed by ghostly actors, which is only broken off when he remembers Caliban, his base accomplices, Stephano and Trinculo, and the dastardly plot he has discovered they are hatching. 'Divers spirits, in shape of dogs and hounds . . . Prospero and Ariel setting them

on', then hunt the ignoble plotters from the stage; and the next to be drawn into his enchanted circle is the band of courtly miscreants. There Prospero reveals himself as the injured Duke of Milan, but forgives both his principal enemies on the strict condition that Antonio must restore his dukedom; and to the King,

The Tempest: design for Prospero's cave by John Henderson Grieve (1770–1845) for John Kemble's production, 1789.

who believes that his son has been drowned – they were separated during the tumult of the shipwreck – he brings the joyful news that the Prince is still alive, and shows Ferdinand and Miranda playing chess. His purpose accomplished, Prospero has already decided that he will abandon his occult studies and, 'deeper than did ever plummet sound', will sink his book of supernatural learning. Before he leaves the island, and the company sail home, he gives back Ariel to the elements, there to enjoy a life of heavenly freedom.

The Tempest, written in 1611, was first staged that year on Hallowmas Night, 1 November, "att Whithall before ye Kinges Maiestie'. Shakespeare made use of numerous sources: a series of travel-books, including an account of a stormy voyage to the 'still-vexed Bermoothes' published in 1610, the poems of Ovid and essays of Montaigne, besides Heywood's *Hierarchie of the Blessed Angels,* from which he borrowed the name 'Ariel'. Like *The Winter's Tale, The Tempest* was designed to satisfy the tastes of the early-Jacobean audience, who demanded elaborate masques and sumptuous pageantry; and Robert Johnson, a popular court-musician of the time, probably set Ariel's songs to music. It was this aspect of the play that no doubt most

above Frontispiece to *The Tempest* from Rowe's edition, 1709. *right* Ellen Terry in the part of Lady Macbeth, painted by John Singer Sargent. *overleaf left* Edmund Dulac's poster for *Macbeth* at His Majesty's Theatre, 1911. *overleaf right* Eric Porter as King Lear in the Royal Shakespeare Company's 1968 production.

Shakespeare's **Macbeth**
His Majesty's Theatre

MILES. LITHO. LONDON. W.

MR KEAN AS RICHARD   MR COOPER AS RICHMOND

delighted seventeenth-century theatre-goers; but Victorian critics found a deeper significance in the literary symbolism of Shakespeare's last comedy. True, during 1612 and 1613 he evidently returned to London, where he undertook some further professional work; but now he usually remained at Stratford; and Prospero's magnificent valediction has often been regarded as Shakespeare's own farewell.

If the old magician is an image of the forty-seven-year-old poet, the portrait is a curious one. Though Prospero is a deeply learned man, he is not by any means benevolent. According to Lytton Strachey, he is both 'opinionated and sour'; and, 'there is no character in the play to whom, during some part of it, he is not studiously disagreeable'. Even Ariel quails before Prospero's anger, when he threatens to renew his captivity, pegged within a knotty oak. The sage is also a stern Puritan. Shakespeare himself, as a young man, had been forced into an unwanted marriage; and Prospero menaces the virtuous Ferdinand, should he anticipate the marriage ceremony, with a succession of domestic torments:

> . . . barren hate,
> Sour-eyed disdain and discord shall bestrew
> The union of your bed with weeds so loathly
> That you shall hate it both . . . (IV.i)

Caliban, naturally, is Prospero's chief victim; and that 'savage and deformed Slave' is at once a repellent and a tragic figure, the type of primitive man, who makes use of the so-called 'civilization' that has been imposed on him only to express his hatred of his tyrants:

> You taught me language, and my profit on't
> Is, I know how to curse. (I.ii)

Nor does he lack a sense of poetry. He loves the island that should be his by right:

> Be not afeard; the isle is full o' noises,
> Sounds and sweet airs, that give delight, and hurt not.
> Sometimes a thousand twangling instruments
> Will hum about mine ears; and sometimes voices
> That, if I then had waked after long sleep,
> Will make me sleep again . . . (III.ii)

By comparison, his accomplices, Stephano and Trinculo, are mere vulgar European middle-men, anxious to delude and exploit the innocent savage in their ruthless quest for riches.

Yet Prospero, whatever his shortcomings, is above all else a master-poet. Like *A Midsummer Night's Dream*, *The Tempest* is essentially a dream-play, made up of several different visions. Each of the characters dreams, and each awakes – except perhaps the happy lovers; and Prospero, in lines of unearthly beauty, dismisses the entire universe as, at its best, an 'insubstantial pageant', and men and women themselves as the transitory creatures of some vast illusion:

above Frontispiece to *The Two Gentlemen of Verona* in Rowe's 1709 edition of Shakespeare's plays.

> Our revels now are ended. These our actors,
> As I foretold you, were all spirits and
> Are melted into air, into thin air,
> And, like the baseless fabric of this vision,
> The cloud-capped towers, the gorgeous palaces
> The solemn temples, the great globe itself,
> Yea, all which it inherit, shall dissolve,
> And, like this insubstantial pageant faded,
> Leave not a rack behind: we are such stuff
> As dreams are made on; and our little life
> Is rounded with sleep. (IV.i)

PROTEUS *(Gent.)*: one of the two gentlemen of Verona. At the outset he is in love with Julia. He is ordered to Milan by his father so that he will be 'tried and tutored in the world' (I.iii). On arrival he meets Valentine, an old friend from Verona, and is introduced by him to Silvia. Proteus immediately falls in love with her, and when Valentine confides in him that he is planning to elope with her, he betrays them to her father the Duke (III.vi). Valentine is banished; Proteus undertakes to take a letter from him to the imprisoned Silvia, but at the same time he promises Thurio that he will 'dispraise' Valentine to Silvia and promote his suit. He tries to woo her for himself, but is rejected. He takes Sebastian (Julia in disguise) into his service (IV.iv), and tells 'him' to take a ring (her own) as a present to Silvia. When Proteus hears that Silvia has fled in search of Valentine, he follows her, and rescues her from the outlaws. He is wooing her roughly when he is confronted by Valentine (v.iv), who reproaches him,

and then offers him Silvia. Proteus asks for forgiveness, and when he discovers the presence of Julia, he is reconciled to her.

PROVOST *(Meas.)*: the prison governor. He is sympathetic to Claudio, and laments Angelo's severity. The disguised Duke persuades him to have Barnadine executed instead of Claudio; when Barnadine refuses to be executed, the Provost suggests presenting the head of Ragozine, a pirate who has just died, to Angelo in place of Claudio's head. He later arrests 'Friar Lodo-

below A Midsummer Night's Dream: Puck and the Fairies by Richard Dadd, engraved by W.M. Lizars.

right Oberon (Alan Howard) and Puck (John Kane) in Peter Brook's widely acclaimed production of *A Midsummer Night's Dream* at Stratford in 1970.

wick' on the evidence of Lucio's slanders. When he reveals himself the Duke promises the Provost promotion for his 'care and secrecy'.

PUBLIUS *(Caes.)*: an elderly senator. He escorts Caesar to the senate on the day of the assassination (II.ii). Afterwards he is 'quite confounded with this mutiny', but he is sent to tell the people that the conspirators mean them no harm (III.i).

PUBLIUS *(Tit.)*: the son of Marcus Andronicus. He

A woodcut of Robin Goodfellow, prefixed to the *Mad Pranks of Robin Goodfellow* (1628).

helps his uncle Titus shoot arrows bearing messages for the gods (IV.iii). With Caius and Valentine he binds Demetrius and Chiron (V.ii).

PUCK *(MND.)*: a fairy in the service of Oberon. He gaily admits to being 'a shrewd and knavish sprite' (II.i). He is sent by Oberon to fetch the flower 'love-in-idleness', and is told to apply its juice to the eyes of a youth 'in Athenian garments'. He administers the charm to the sleeping Lysander (II.iii). He provides Bottom with an ass's head, and scatters the 'mechanicals' with strange sounds. He enjoys the confusion brought about by his blunders. He is ordered by Oberon to produce a fog, and to lead the rival lovers astray within it by imitating their voices, and then to apply a counter-charm to Lysander's eyes. Puck speaks the epilogue of the play.

> Puck is a very English fairy, Robin Goodfellow:
> I am that merry wanderer of the night.
> I jest to Oberon and make him smile
> When I a fat and bean-fed horse beguile,
> Neighing in likeness of a filly foal.
> And sometimes lurk I in a gossip's bowl,
> In very likeness of a roasted crab,
> And when she drinks, against her lips I bob
> And on her withered dewlap pour the ale.
> The wisest aunt, telling the saddest tale,
> Sometime for three-foot stool mistaketh me,
> Then I slip from her bum, down topples she,
> And 'tailor' cries, and falls into a cough,
> And then the whole quire hold their hips and laugh,
> And waxen in their mirth, and neeze, and swear
> A merrier was never wasted there. (II.i)

Yet this homely, colloquial 'shrewd and knavish sprite' who delights in mischief is also a cosmic power, and can

> . . . put a girdle round the earth
> In forty minutes. (II.i)

The identification of Puck with Hobgoblin, or Robin Goodfellow, seems to be an arbitrary link by Shakespeare with the folklore current in his time. 'Puck' (or 'pouke', 'pouk', 'puke') was originally a generic term for a mischievous spirit. (*See* OBERON.)

PURSUIVANT *(R.III)*: Hastings meets the Pursuivant on his way to the Tower and stops to talk to him. It is evident from their conversation that Hastings has no idea of what Gloucester has in store for him.

Q

QUEEN OF BRITAIN *(Cym.)*: wife to Cymbeline, and mother of Cloten by a former marriage. She wants to see Cloten married to Imogen so as to secure the throne for him. When her plan fails, and Imogen marries Posthumus, she tries to poison them both. She rejoices when it appears that Imogen has gone 'to death or to dishonour' (III.v). When she finds that her plans have failed she goes mad, and dies 'with horror', confessing that she had planned to kill Cymbeline, and repenting only that 'the evils she hatched were not effected' (v.v). But such were her beauty and charm, Cymbeline says, that 'It had been vicious/To have mistrusted her' (v.v).

QUEEN, RICHARD II'S *(R.II)*: she overhears the gardeners talking of the deposition of Richard (III.iv). She greets Richard on his way to the Tower, and learns that she must 'away to France' (v.i).

She was Isabel of Valois, daughter of Charles VI of France. She was married to Richard in 1396 when she was less than seven; it was from her friends and relatives that Richard acquired his French tastes. She was only twelve at the time of Richard's deposition, and she never saw him again after he left for Ireland. After the accession of Henry IV she was confined near Reading and was not allowed to see her husband; she was not told of his death until sometime afterwards. After her return to France Henry tried to get her hand for his son the Prince of Wales, but her family refused to acknowledge his succession. In 1400 she married her cousin Charles, Count of Angoulême; she died during childbirth in 1409.

QUICKLY, MISTRESS *(1H.IV; H.V; Wiv.)*: the hostess of a tavern in Eastcheap. She is present when Falstaff impersonates the King. He insists that he has had a ring stolen in her tavern. Later it turns out that Falstaff owes her money: she appeals to Hal to help her to get it, and accuses Falstaff of slandering the Prince (III.iii).

In *2 Henry IV* she is now a widow, and says that Falstaff has promised to marry her. She tries to have

him arrested for debt, but he cajoles her into withdrawing the action and lending him more money (II.iv). She bids Falstaff farewell when he leaves for Gloucester, and adds that she has known him for twenty-nine years. We hear that she and Doll Tearsheet have been imprisoned as a consequence of a fatal brawl in her tavern (v.iv).

In *The Merry Wives of Windsor* she is Dr Caius' housekeeper, his 'nurse, or his dry nurse, or his cook, or his laundry, his washer and his wringer'. She helps impartially all the suitors to Anne Page, and is used by the merry wives to carry messages to Falstaff. Pistol decides to marry her. During the baiting of Falstaff in the last scene she plays the Fairy Queen.

In *Henry V* she is now wife to Pistol. She describes the manner of Falstaff's death (*see* FALSTAFF), and bids farewell to Pistol when he leaves for France. When in France, Pistol says: 'News I have that my Doll is dead i'th' Spital of a malady of France.' It has been suggested that Nell (Quickly's name) was intended here for 'Doll', or that this speech is a remnant of an earlier draft of the play which included Falstaff, who was associated with Doll Tearsheet.

The Mistress Quickly in *The Merry Wives* is not entirely consistent with the Mistress Quickly of the history plays, although her character is essentially the same. In *The Merry Wives* she is at first unknown to Falstaff.

She is the *lena* of Italian comedy, the bawd with a heart of gold; love and kindness are the only virtues she understands.

QUINCE, PETER *(MND.)*: a carpenter. He produces the 'Interlude', though he is continually troubled by Bottom's attempts to usurp his position. In the performance he speaks the Prologue 'like a child on a recorder; a sound, but not in government'.

QUINTUS *(Tit.)*: one of Titus' sons. With his brother Martius he falls into a pit containing the body of Bassianus (II.iv). They are discovered there and accused of murdering him. They are executed.

R

RAFE *(Shr.)*: one of the servants at Petruchio's country house (IV.i).

RAGOZINE *(Meas.)*: a pirate who has died in prison. Only his head makes an appearance: the Provost presents it to Angelo and tells him that it is Claudio's (IV.iii).

RAMBURES *(H.V)*: a lord, master of the crossbows in the French army at Agincourt. He boasts with the Dauphin before the battle (III.vii; IV.ii), during which he is killed (IV.viii).

RAPE *(Tit.)*: character assumed by Chiron (v.ii) *(q.v.)*.

RATCLIFFE, SIR RICHARD *(R.III)*: a follower of Richard. He leads Rivers, Grey and Vaughan to execution at Pomfret; he is told to supervise the beheading of Hastings (III.iv). He rouses Richard at dawn on the day of the battle at Bosworth, and reassures him that the ghosts he has seen were only shadows and not to be feared (v.iii). He is killed during the battle.

He was Richard's chief adviser. He was knighted by Edward IV at Tewkesbury. On Richard's orders he seized and executed Hastings in 1483. He was the 'ratte' of Collingbourne's rhyme (*see* LOVEL). According to Sir Thomas More he was 'a man, having experience of the world, a shrewd wit, short and rude in speech, rough and boisterous of behaviour, as far from pity as from all fear of God'.

He was not in London at the time of the council in iii.iv; on that day he was at Pontefract (Pomfret) Castle disposing of Rivers, Grey and Vaughan. This slight historical problem is sometimes solved by giving his speech in this scene to Catesby.

REAPERS *(Tp.)*: they are spirits summoned by Iris at Juno's command to dance with the Naiads as part of the masque celebrating the bethrothal of Ferdinand and Miranda:

You sunburn'd sicklemen, of August weary,
Come hither from the furrow, and be merry:

Make holiday; your rye-straw hats put on,
And these fresh nymphs encounter every one
In country footing. (VI.i)

REBECK, HUGH *(Rom.)*: one of the musicians engaged to play at Juliet's wedding to Paris. He is aptly named: a rebec was a stringed instrument, an early form of fiddle. (IV.v).

REGAN *(Lr.)*: the second daughter of King Lear, and wife to the Duke of Cornwall. She is given a third of the kingdom after she has skilfully flattered her father (I.i). When she arrives at Gloucester's castle she complains of the 'riotous knights' in Lear's train. She suggests that Kent should be kept in the stocks all night for assaulting Goneril's messenger. She supports Goneril against Lear, and ignores his appeal to her; she says that she will let him into the castle, but not one of his followers. When her husband blinds Gloucester she eggs him on, and eagerly insists that both his eyes be removed (III.vii). She kills the servant who tries to save Gloucester by stabbing Cornwall; she turns Gloucester out of his own castle 'to smell his way to Dover'. She tries to get the letter that Goneril has written to Edmund from Oswald: she claims Edmund for herself, but fears that her widowed sister has an advantage over her. She tells Oswald to kill her sister if he gets the chance, but she is herself poisoned by the jealous Goneril.

She is more coldly callous than Goneril. Goneril's rampant sensuality is behind her desire for Edmund; Regan seems attracted by him more as a fellow evil spirit.

REIGNIER, DUKE OF ANJOU, KING OF NAPLES *(1H.VI)*: he enters Orleans in triumph with Joan of Arc. When Suffolk captures his daughter Margaret he consents to her betrothal to Henry VI provided that he is left to enjoy Maine and Anjou in peace.

He was René, 1st Duke of Anjou (1409–80). After the marriage of his daughter he gradually retired from public affairs and devoted his time to literature and the arts.

REVENGE *(Tit.)*: character assumed by Tamora (v.ii) *(q.v.)*.

REYNALDO *(Ham.)*: Polonius' servant. Polonius sends him to Paris with money for Laertes, and gives him detailed instructions as to how he should spy on him (II.i).

RICHARD II *(R.II)*: King of England. He hears of the accusations made by Hereford against Mowbray, and wonders if they are made out of malice or of loyalty to him; after hearing their mutual accusations, and failing to compose the quarrel, he appoints the time and place for a judicial combat between them (I.i). He presides over the lists at Coventry, and abruptly stops the combat just as it is about to begin. He declares, after taking advice, that in the interests of civil peace Mowbray is banished for life, and Hereford (Bolingbroke) for ten years. Bolingbroke's exile is reduced to six years when Richard sees the 'sad aspect' of his aged father John of Gaunt (I.iii). Richard confides to Aumerle his fears of Bolingbroke before he leaves on an expedition to Ireland. On the way he visits Gaunt on his death-bed, and angrily rejects his warnings; as soon as he is dead he announces that he will seize all his possessions. He appoints York Regent during his absence

in Ireland (II.i). He returns and lands in Wales to face Bolingbroke, and learns that his Welsh army has deserted him; he learns that his favourites Bushy, Bagot and Greene have been executed, and that the revolt is widespread. He despairs, and takes refuge in Flint Castle (III.ii). When Bolingbroke and Northumberland visit him with their demands, he warns them of heaven's vengeance. He descends to meet Bolingbroke in 'the base court', and admits that he is in his power, and proposes that they set out for London together (III.iii). Richard is brought before Parliament in Westminster Hall, and resigns his crown to Bolingbroke; he calls for a mirror to see if the loss of his title has changed him outwardly, and dashes the 'flattering glass' to the ground. He is taken to the Tower (IV.i). On the way there he meets his Queen, and advises her to return to France and forget him; he warns Northumberland that before long Bolingbroke will turn against him (v.i). He is imprisoned at Pomfret Castle, where he is infuriated when the groom describes how Bolingbroke rode his horse 'roan Barbary' on his coronation day; he is killed by Pierce of Exton after a struggle (v.v). His body is brought to Bolingbroke (v.vi).

In *1 Henry IV*, Bolingbroke tells his son Hal of Richard, the king whose throne he took:

The skipping King, he ambled up and down

below Beerbohm Tree as Richard II *(left)*; Alec Guinness as Richard II *(right)*.

The entry into London of Richard II and Bolingbroke
by James T. Eglinton.

With shallow jesters, and rash bavin wits,
Soon kindled, and soon burnt, carded his state,
Mingled his royalty with capering fools,
Had his great name profaned with their scorns,
And gave his countenance, against his name,
To laugh at gibing boys, and stand the push
Of every beardless vain comparative;
Grew a companion to the common streets,
Enfeoffed himself to popularity,
That being daily swallowed by men's eyes,
They surfeited with honey, and began
To loathe the taste of sweetness, whereof a little
More than a little is by much too much.
So when he had occasion to be seen,
He was but as the cuckoo is in June,
Heard, not regarded; seen, but with such eyes
As sick and blunted with community
Afford no extraordinary gaze,
Such as is bent on sun-like majesty
When it shines seldom in admiring eyes. (III.ii)

The Richard that we see at the opening of *Richard II* is very different from this: he is no 'skipping King', but a true king, whose authority is not in doubt. He is magisterial and efficient, and speaks with the strong rhetoric of a ruler:

We were not born to sue, but to command,
Which since we cannot do, to make you friends,
Be ready, as your lives shall answer it,
At Coventry, upon St Lambert's day.
There shall your swords and lances arbitrate
The swelling difference of your settled hate.
Since we cannot atone you, we shall see
Justice design the victor's chivalry.
Lord Marshal, command our officers at arms
Be ready to direct these home alarms. (I.i)

The first we see of his deficiencies is when he hears that John of Gaunt is dying:

Now put it, God, in the physician's mind,
To help him to his grave immediately.
The lining of his coffers shall make coats
To deck our soldiers for these Irish wars.
Come gentlemen, let's all go visit him,
Pray God we may make haste, and come too late.
(I.iv)

The impression of cold wilfulness is confirmed when Richard rejects the advice of his good and honest advisers; and we have already heard from the dying Gaunt of the chaos in the realm due to Richard's misgovernment.

When he returns from Ireland Richard finds himself impotent in the face of Bolingbroke's power, and in the rest of the play we watch his vain struggle to come to terms with the loss of the power that he had exercised so arbitrarily. He has been accused of lapsing into self-indulgent eloquence during the last half of the play, of substituting words for deeds. But the self-conscious expressiveness is Shakespeare's way of showing us Richard the man, and his feelings as he is stripped of everything. Despite his weakness, his is a moving personal tragedy; in the deposition scene he disrupts the public formality by insisting on his own loss of identity that accompanies the loss of his crown. He is defeated, but he has a moral victory, one that is most conspicuous in his superb ironic inversion of the coronation rites:

> I give this heavy weight from off my head,
> And this unwieldy sceptre from my hand,
> The pride of kingly sway from out my heart.
> With mine own tears I wash away my balm,
> With mine own hands I give away my crown,
> With mine own tongue deny my sacred state,
> With mine own breath release all duteous oaths.
> All pomp and majesty I do foreswear;
> My manors, rents, revenues I forego;
> My acts, decrees, and statutes I deny.
> God pardon all oaths that are broke to me.
> God keep all vows unbroke are made to thee.
> Make me, that nothing have, with nothing grieved,
> And thou with all be pleased, that hast all achieved.
> Long mayst thou live in Richard's seat to sit,
> And soon lie Richard in an earthy pit. (IV.i)

Richard, though an incompetent king, ends as an admirable man.

Richard II (1367–1400) was born at Bordeaux, the younger son of Edward the Black Prince by his cousin Joan Holland. He succeeded to the throne in 1377. He married Anne of Bohemia in 1382; she died in 1394, and he married the young Isabella of France in 1396. This marriage damaged his popularity, which had already been undermined by the Duke of Gloucester. In 1397 Richard arrested Gloucester, Arundel and Warwick, three enemies who had already threatened to depose him in 1389. When Bolingbroke accused Mowbray of treason, Richard banished both of them. By now he was ruling despotically, and he instituted forced loans and fines to pay for his love of pomp and ceremony. He was recalled from his expedition to Ireland by the news that Bolingbroke had landed; he was deserted by his army, and surrendered at Flint Castle. Bolingbroke

took him to the Tower, and received his resignation of the crown. When Bolingbroke was crowned as Henry IV, he sent Richard as a prisoner to Pontefract Castle. He died there early in 1400; the official version was that he starved himself to death. Others said that he was starved by his keepers; Shakespeare follows the tradition that he was murdered by Pierce of Exton.

Richard was an intelligent, sensitive man, a connoisseur of art, literature and music; he is supposed to have invented the handkerchief. It is true, as Shakespeare's play shows, that his character deteriorated in his later years, and that by the end of his reign he was ruling with arbitrary wilfulness. According to Holinshed, he was not without his virtues: 'He was prodigall, ambitious, and much given to the pleasure of the bodie. He kept the greatest port, and maintained the most plentifull house that ever any king in England did either before his time or since.'

The generally accepted date for *Richard II* is 1595. Shakespeare's main source was Holinshed's *Chronicles,* possibly supplemented by the anonymous play *Woodstock* and Daniel's poem *The First Foure Bookes of the civile warres* (1595).

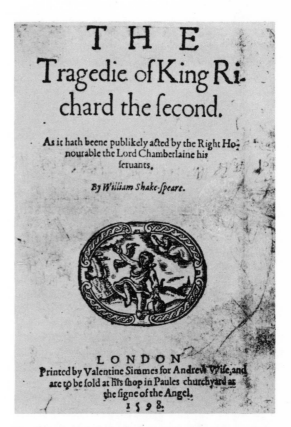

The first work of Shakespeare bearing his name on the title page: *Richard II*, 1598.

On 7 February 1601, the day before the Earl of Essex's abortive rebellion, some of his supporters paid for a performance of a *Richard II* play, almost certainly Shakespeare's, by the Lord Chamberlain's Men at the Globe Theatre. Presumably the politically contentious deposition scene was included; this scene did not appear in the first printed versions of the play. It was first printed in 1608; even now it may not be shown in Ethiopia.

RICHARD III *(1,2&3H.VI; R.III)*: the historical personage whose fortunes Shakespeare began to trace (possibly with the help of several collaborators) in the three parts of *Henry VI,* and whose tragic story he rounded off in the play that bears his name, lived from 1452 to 1485, and seized the English throne in 1483. During the lifetime of his elder brother, Edward IV, he appears to have done him loyal service; but, on the King's death, he himself aspired to the crown, disputed the legitimacy of Edward's two young sons and, later, may have been responsible for their assassination in the Tower. A contemporary, or near-contemporary portrait of Richard shows us a stern and somewhat anxious, but by no means unattractive face; and it is sometimes suggested that, at least during the earlier stages of his career, he may have been as much sinned against as sinning. Shakespeare, however, presents him in the guise of the typical Elizabethan 'Machiavel', who hastens to inform the audience he is 'determined to prove a villain', and then embarks on a series of sinister schemes to procure his own advancement. One of the strangest of these (described in *Richard III)* is his macabre courtship of the Lady Anne – the wooing of a fly by a spider – whose betrothed, the Prince of Wales, son of the murdered Henry VI, Richard has himself stabbed. When his brother dies, he decimates the Queen's party, slaying a number of her kinsmen and finally accounting for the little princes. Henry Tudor, Earl of Richmond and leader of the Lancastrians, then lands with an army upon English soil. At Bosworth Richard is defeated and slain; and Richmond, as Henry VII (grandfather of Queen Elizabeth), becomes the founder of the Tudor dynasty.

Henry VI, written about 1591, was the play that established Shakespeare's reputation; and we know that his success exasperated Richard Greene, an envious and disappointed fellow-writer, whose abusive pamphlet, *Greene's Groatsworth of Wit, bought with a million of Repentance*, where he satirizes the upstart 'Shaks-scene' and parodies one of his more melodramatic lines, appeared in September 1592. Shakespeare's earliest historical drama is a rough and immature work; but, although Coleridge, among others, asserted that Shakespeare could not have written the entire play, particularly the opening speech, modern critics are inclined to think that he may well have completed it without assistance. Certainly, in Part 3, Richard of Gloucester's tremendous declamation has the true Shakespearian ring:

> . . . I, – like one lost in a thorny wood,
> That rends the thorns and is rent with the thorns,
> Seeking a way and straying from the way,
> Not knowing how to find the open air,
> But toiling desperately to find it out
> Torment myself to catch the English crown:
> And from that torment I will free myself,
> Or hew my way out with a bloody axe . . .
> I'll drown more sailors than the mermaid shall;
> I'll slay more gazers than the basilisk;
> I'll play the orator as well as Nestor,
> Deceive more slily than Ulysses could,
> And, like a Sinon, take another Troy. (III.ii)

Richard III, also based on Holinshed's *Chronicles,* followed *Henry VI* in 1592 or 1593; and there the dramatist develops and enriches his portrait of a thorough-paced villain, adding some touches of tragic dignity and providing him with far more complex motives. Richard is haunted by the idea of his physical ugliness, yet always fascinated by his own image:

> Why, I, in this weak piping time of peace,

Kemble as Richard III. Drawn by Browne from a portrait by Stewart, engraved by Thornthwaite; published 1786.

Have no delight to pass away the time,
Unless to spy my shadow in the sun. (I.i)

Even as death approaches, he cannot escape from the
conflict between his ineradicable self-love and a
furious self-hatred:

Richard loves Richard; that is, I am I.
Is there a murderer here? No – yes, I am:
Then fly. What, from myself? Great reason why –
Lest I revenge. Myself upon myself?
Alack, I love myself. For any good
That I myself have done unto myself? (v.iii)

The doomed tyrant is as lonely a figure as Hamlet or as
Coriolanus. Like them, he is condemned to perpetual
isolation in the claustrophobic stronghold of the self.

RICHMOND, HENRY, EARL OF (afterwards
Henry VII) *(3H.VI; R.III), see* HENRY TUDOR.

RIVERS, LORD *(3H.VI; R.III)*: he is told by his
sister Queen Elizabeth that Edward IV has been taken
prisoner, and is told to escape while he can.

In *Richard III* he is an adherent of the Queen, and
supports the coronation of the young Edward v.
Richard has him imprisoned at Pomfret Castle, and
he is executed on his orders (III.iii). His ghost appears

above Laurence Olivier as Richard in his 1955 film of
Richard III.

below David Garrick as Richard III *(left)*; Irving as
Richard III in 1877 *(right)*.

above Isa Bowman and Bessie Hatton as the Princes in the Tower in *Richard III (left)*; Lord Rivers, in an

engraving from a late Victorian edition of Shakespeare's plays *(right)*.

to Richard at Bosworth.

He was Anthony Woodville (1442–83). After his sister Elizabeth *(q.v.)* married Edward IV his advancement was rapid. He was intensely disliked by Richard, Duke of Gloucester. When Edward died, Rivers was at Ludlow, acting as guardian to the young Prince of Wales; he set out for London immediately. He learned that Gloucester was at Northampton, and went to meet him. He was cordially received, but the next day was sent on Gloucester's orders to Sheriff Hutton Castle, and then on to Pontefract, where he was beheaded without trial. He was according to Holinshed 'a right honourable man, as valiant of hand as politike in counsell'.

ROBERT *(Wiv.)*: a servant to the Fords. He helps carry the laundry basket (III.iii; IV.ii).

ROBIN *(2H.VI)*: a fellow apprentice with Peter Thump. With two others, Tom and Will, he drinks to Peter's success in his duel with his master Thomas Horner. Peter thinks he will be killed, and bequeathes his apron to Robin (II.iii).

ROBIN *(Wiv.)*: Falstaff's page, presumably the same character as the small page in *2 Henry IV*. He carries Falstaff's love letters to Mistress Page and Mistress Ford. He is sent to serve Mistress Page, and joins in the plot against his master.

ROCHESTER, BISHOP OF *(H.VIII)*: he is present at the divorce proceedings at Blackfriars. He was John Fisher (1459–1535). He was opposed to the divorce, though he is silent during Shakespeare's scene. He was beheaded for refusing to acknowledge Henry as the supreme head of the English church.

RODERIGO *(Oth.)*: 'a gull'd gentleman' who is in love with Desdemona. Prompted by Iago he arouses Brabantio and tells him that Desdemona has eloped with Othello (I.i). Iago urges him to persevere with his suit, and tells him that Desdemona and Cassio are lovers; he persuades him to pick a quarrel with Cassio that night (II.i). He does so, but is beaten by the drunken Cassio. On his second attempt Cassio wounds him, and Iago, to silence him, kills him in the darkness. Letters relating to Iago's plot against Othello are found in his pocket.

ROGERO *(Wint.)*: he enters and tells Autolycus that bonfires have been lit to celebrate the restoration of the King's lost daughter. He listens to the third gentleman's full account of the reunion. In the stage directions he is 'second gentleman' (V.II).

ROMEO *(Rom.)*: Montague's son. He tells Benvolio of his hopeless love for Rosaline (I.i), and decides to attend Capulet's feast in order to see her. At the feast he meets and falls in love with Juliet Capulet, the young daughter of his father's arch-enemy (I.v). He enters the Capulets' garden at night, and overhears Juliet talking to herself about her love for him; they plan marriage (II.ii). Romeo arranges a secret wedding with Friar Laurence, and takes the nurse into his confidence. He and Juliet are married at Friar Laurence's cell (II.vi). He meets Tybalt in the street, and is challenged by him: he refuses to fight with him because he is a relative of Juliet. Mercutio takes up the challenge, and is killed when Romeo's intervention leaves him open to Tybalt's thrust. Romeo is furious, and kills Tybalt (III.i). Juliet hears that Romeo has been banished for his crime; Romeo falls into despair. Friar Laurence advises him to go to Mantua (III.iii). He bids farewell to Juliet (III.v). At Mantua he hears that Juliet is dead; he buys a deadly poison, and hurries back to the Capulets' tomb. He meets Paris there, fights with him and kills him; he drinks the poison and dies beside Juliet just as she recovers from the effects of the drug she has taken.

At first Romeo is a bookish lover, ever ready to indulge in flights of airy rhetoric as he sighs for Rosaline:

Love is a smoke raised with the fume of sighs;
Being purged, a fire sparkling in lovers' eyes;
Being vexed, a sea nourished with lovers' tears.
What is it else? A madness most discreet,
A choking gall, and a preserving sweet. (I.i)

Juliet teases him for his affectations at first, and says 'You kiss by th' book' (I.v). He never entirely frees himself of his lyrical manner, but once he is in love with Juliet the intensity of his passion fills out the previously empty structure.

'Romeo is Hamlet in love. There is the same rich exuberance of passion and sentiment in the one, that there is of thought and sentiment in the other. Both are absent and self-involved, both live out of themselves in a world of imagination. Hamlet is abstracted

Romeo and Juliet: from a painting by Ford Madox Brown.

from everything; Romeo is abstracted from everything but his love, and lost in it. His "frail thoughts dally with faint surmise", and are fashioned out of the suggestions of hope, "the flatteries of sleep". He is himself only in his Juliet; she is his only reality, his heart's true home and idol. The rest of the world is to him a passing dream.' (Hazlitt)

ROSALIND *(AYL.)*: the daughter of the exiled Duke of Burgundy. She hears of the wrestling match between the King's wrestler and Orlando, and tries to dissuade Orlando from what the Duke has told her is an unequal match. She fails, and sees him win the bout; afterwards she discovers that he is the son of an old friend of her father (I.ii). Duke Frederick orders her to leave court within ten days because she is the daughter of the exiled Duke; she and Celia set out for the Forest of Arden to find her father. They travel in disguise, Rosalind as a man, 'Ganymede', and Celia as 'his' sister 'Aliena'. They are tired when they reach the forest; they buy a cottage, pasture and flocks with the help of an

Romeo (Leonard Whiting) and the Friar (Milo O'Shea) in the 1968 film version of *Romeo and Juliet* by Franco Zeffirelli.

old shepherd (II.iv). Rosalind is astonished to find verses addressed to her hanging on the trees, and her name carved on their trunks. Celia tells her that they were put there by Orlando, who is also in the forest. Rosalind decides to remain 'in doublet and hose', and meets Orlando, who does not recognize her. She converses with him like a 'saucy lackey', and tells him that the forest is haunted by a lovesick swain; Orlando confesses that it is him, and 'Ganymede' explains to him that 'love is merely a madness', and tells him to visit 'his' cottage and seek a remedy for it (III.ii). Rosalind is annoyed when he does not come, and Celia says that she doubts his constancy. As 'Ganymede' Rosalind interrupts Silvius' wooing of Phebe, and reproaches her for being so bitter and scornful to him; Phebe falls for 'Ganymede' (III,v). 'Ganymede' banters with Orlando when he arrives late, but when he has gone admits to Celia that she is 'many fathom deep' in love with him (IV.i). Silvius brings 'Ganymede' a love-letter from Phebe. Rosalind hears from Oliver that Orlando has been wounded when rescuing him from a lioness, and she faints when Oliver produces a 'bloody napkin' (IV.iii). She hears of Celia and Oliver's betrothal, and assures Orlando that by magic art she will bring about his marriage to Rosalind at the same time as theirs. She tells Phebe and Silvius that she will resolve all the next day, but warns Phebe that 'he' loves 'no woman' (V.ii). She appears as Ganymede before the Duke, and reminds him of his promise to give his daughter to Orlando if she can be found. She and Celia enter as themselves, and are joyfully greeted by the Duke and Orlando; the weddings proceed.

Rosalind is in disguise for most of the play, and she flaunts and enjoys the freedom it allows her: she is able to deploy her quick wit in a way that she could not properly do in her own person. She is able to mock Orlando at the same time as enjoying being in love with him. She is one of Shakespeare's most attractive heroines.

As You Like It does not appear in Francis Meres' list of Shakespeare's plays in 1598, and so was probably written sometime between that year and 4 August 1600, the date that it was entered in the Stationer's Register. Shakespeare's main source was Thomas Lodge's romance *Rosalynde or Euphues' Golden Legacy* (1590), based on the fourteenth-century *Tale of Gamelyn*.

ROSALINE *(LLL.)*: one of the ladies attending the Princess of France when she visits the court of Navarre. Berowne falls in love with her. She is wooed by the King in mistake for the Princess when the ladies are masked. At the end she imposes a twelve-month penance on Berowne before she will marry him. She reminds him that 'a jest's prosperity lies in the ear of him that hears it', and condemns him to try his wit in a hospital among the 'groaning wretches'.

Berowne describes her as:

A whitely wanton with a velvet brow,

With two pitch-balls stuck in her face for eyes. (III.i)

The witty duels between her and Berowne prefigure those between Beatrice *(q.v.)* and Benedick *(q.v.)*.

above Rosalind in the Forest of Arden; from a painting by Millais *(top)*; Rosalind gives Orlando her chain *(As You Like It,* I.ii). An engraving after John Downman *(bottom). left* Lillie Langtry as Rosalind in *As You Like It* in 1882.

ROSENCRANTZ *(Ham.)*: a courtier at Elsinore, inseparable from Guildenstern, with whom he always appears. The king asks them to investigate the cause of Hamlet's strange behaviour (II.ii). They are ordered to escort Hamlet to England; he discovers that they are carrying sealed orders for his death, and replaces his name with theirs. They go to their deaths in England. (*See* GUILDENSTERN.)

ROSS, LORD *(R.II)* : he is one of those that defect to Bolingbroke when Richard appropriates the Lancaster estates (II.i; II.iii).

He was Lord William de Ross. He was made Lord Treasurer of England under Henry IV, and remained in favour until his death in 1414.

ROSS, THANE OF *(Mac.)* : he brings Duncan the news of Macbeth's victory over Sweno (I.ii). He has his doubts about the murder, and shares his suspicions with Macduff (II.iv). He explains Macduff's flight to Lady Macduff, and justifies it (IV.ii). He escapes to England to join the rebellion against Macbeth, and to bear to Macduff the news of the murder of his family (IV.iii).

below Rosaline (Joan Plowright) and Boyet (Philip Locke) in Laurence Olivier's 1968 production of *Love's Labour's Lost,* by the National Theatre Company.
right Rosaline with the Princess of France (Louise Purnell) in the same production.

ROUSILLON, COUNTESS OF *(All'sW.)* : the mother of Bertram and the guardian of Helena. She consoles Helena when Bertram deserts her (III.ii), and tries to bring them together again. She begs the King to forgive Bertram at the end (V.iii). Shaw said it was 'The most beautiful old woman's part ever written'.

RUGBY, JOHN *(Wiv.)* : servant to Dr Caius, who wants to use him to demonstrate how he will kill Evans, but is prevented (II.iii).

According to Mistress Quickly he is:

An honest, willing, kind fellow, as ever servant shall come in house withal; and I warrant you, no tell-tale, nor no breed-bate. His worst fault is, that he is given to prayer; he is something peevish that way; but nobody but has his fault. . . . (I.iv)

RUMOUR *(2H.IV)* : the presenter of the play; the stage directions read 'Enter Rumour, full of painted tongues'. He explains that his function is

To noise abroad, that Harry Monmouth fell
Under the wrath of noble Hotspur's sword:
And that the King, before Douglas' rage
Stoop'd his anointed head, as low as death.

(Induction)

The figure of Rumour was a common one in Jacobean masques. Johnson complained that here his speech 'is wholly useless, since we are told nothing which the first scene does not clearly and naturally discover'.

RUTLAND, EDMUND, EARL OF *(3H.VI)* : he is murdered by Clifford at the Battle of Wakefield.

He was the second son of Richard Plantagenet, Duke of York. He was ruthlessly killed by Clifford at Wakefield; he was twelve at the time of his death.

S

SAILOR, A *(Oth.)*: he is a messenger sent by a Signior Angelo to tell the Duke of Venice that the Turks are heading for Rhodes. The Duke and the senators guess correctly that this is false information, and that the Turks are making for Cyprus (I.iii).

SAILORS *(Ham.)*: they are members of a pirate crew which attacks Hamlet's ship and takes him prisoner. They arrive at Elsinore with a letter from Hamlet to Horatio, in which he says that they have treated him like 'thieves of mercy'; he instructs Horatio to follow the sailors to where he is immediately (IV.iv).

SAILORS *(Per.)*: during the storm two sailors ask Pericles to cast Thaisa's dead body overboard, since they believe that the storm will not pass until 'the ship be cleared of the dead' (III.i).

ST ASAPH, BISHOP OF *(H.VIII)*: he is one of the clergy present at the divorce proceedings at Blackfriars.

He was Henry Standish. He was court preacher to Henry VIII, and tried in vain to prevent him from deserting the Catholic Church. During the divorce proceedings he was one of the 'doctors of divinitie' chosen by Queen Katharine to present her case.

SALANIO *(Mer.V.)*, see SOLANIO.

SALARINO *(Mer.V.)*: a friend of Antonio and Bassanio. He helps Lorenzo elope with Jessica (II.vi), and meets Antonio when he is under arrest (III.iii).

He, Salerio *(q.v.)* and Solanio *(q.v.)* are near indistinguishable Venetian dandies; their elegant verse creates an atmosphere of sophisticated culture.

SALERIO *(Mer.V.)*: a friend of Gratiano and Bassanio. He brings a letter to Belmont telling Bassanio that Antonio's ships are lost (III.ii). He is present at the court.

He does not appear in the 1637 Quarto, and he is possibly identical with either Solanio or Salarino.

SALISBURY, EARL OF *(H.V; 1H.VI)*: he comes to tell Henry that the French are prepared for battle (IV.iii).

In *1 Henry VI* he is killed by the cannon-ball fired by the son of the Master-gunner of Orleans *(q.v.)* while observing the siege (I.iv).

He was Thomas Montacute (1388–1428), the eldest son of the Earl of Salisbury below. He was not advanced to this father's title until 1421. He went to France with Henry V, and became one of the most famous English captains. After Agincourt he took part in the subsequent campaigns, and was appointed Lieutenant-General of Normandy. He completed the subjugation of Maine and Champagne in 1425. He began his ill-advised siege of Orleans in 1428. While surveying the city from a window of the fort at Tourelles he was killed by a stone cannon-ball. His death was an event of supreme importance in the war, since the English tended to regard it as a mark of God's anger.

SALISBURY, EARL OF *(2&3H.VI)*: he secures the banishment of his enemy Suffolk for his alleged murder of the Duke of Gloucester (III.ii). He sees his enemy Cardinal Beaufort die (III.iii). He joins York and fights at St Albans, where he is rescued three times by Richard Plantagenet, who says that he will not keep out of danger, despite his age. York praises him:

> Old Salisbury, who can report of him,
> That winter lion, who in rage forgets
> Aged contusions, and all brush of time,
> And like a gallant in the brow of youth,
> Repairs him with occasion? This happy day
> Is not itself, nor have we won one foot,
> If Salisbury be lost. (v.iii)

In *3 Henry VI* we hear that he has been brought 'untimely to his death' by the house of York.

He was Richard Neville (1400–60). He came to the title through his marriage to Alice Montacute, the only daughter of Thomas Montacute *(see above)*. He was Chancellor during York's protectorship 1453–55, but when Henry recovered he was dismissed along with York. He joined the Yorkists, and fought for them at St Albans in 1455. He was wounded and taken prisoner at Wakefield, and later beheaded at Pontefract. The reference to his having been brought 'untimely to death' by the house of York is, of course, erroneous.

SALISBURY, EARL OF *(John)* : he protests against John's second coronation, and suspects him of being behind Arthur's death (IV.ii). He discovers Arthur's body, and accuses Hubert of the murder (IV.iii). He joins the Dauphin, but when he hears of his intended treachery he rejoins John. He is present at John's death, and hails Henry III as king.

He was William de Longespée, the natural son of Henry II and (so tradition has it) Rosamund Clifford, the 'fair maid of Kent'. He married the daughter of the Earl of Salisbury, and succeeded to the title. During the period of John's excommunication he was thought to be one of the King's evil counsellors. In 1215 he attacked and destroyed three hundred ships of the French invasion fleet at Damme, and captured a hundred more, averting the danger of invasion. He was on the King's side at Runnymede in 1215; the next year he joined Lewis of France. He returned and served under Henry III, and fought with distinction in the Holy Land.

SALISBURY, EARL OF *(R.II)* : a loyal supporter of Richard. He tries to prevent Richard's Welsh army from dispersing (II.iv). He joins the rebellion against Henry IV, and is captured and executed at Cirencester; his head is sent to London (V.vi).

He was John Montacute. He played a large part in arranging Richard's marriage to Isabel of France, which gained him Richard's favour but made him unpopular with the people. He accompanied Richard to Ireland in 1398, and was arrested at Flint after the royal surrender. Londoners clamoured for his execution, but he was released. He joined the Abbot of Westminster's conspiracy; he was driven in retreat to Cirencester, where the local people seized him and executed him.

SAMPSON *(Rom.)* : servant to Capulet. He and Gregory quarrel with two of Montague's servants and a fight ensues. Escalus declares that the next man to disturb the peace in this way will lose his life (I.i).

SANDYS, LORD *(H.VIII)* : he discusses French fashions and Wolsey's banquet with Sir Thomas Lovell and the Lord Chamberlain (I.iii). He flirts with Anne Bullen and the other ladies at the banquet before the King arrives (I.iv). He attends Buckingham on his way to execution (II.i).

He was Sir William Sandys. He took a leading part in the preparations for the Field of Cloth of Gold. It was he, and not the Earl of Worcester, who was Lord Chamberlain at the time of Wolsey's masque.

SATURNINUS *(Tit.)* : the son of the late emperor of Rome. He is elected emperor by acclamation after Titus has withdrawn his candidature. He wants Lavinia as his empress, but she is claimed by Bassianus, so he takes Tamora, Queen of the Goths, the secret enemy of Titus, in her place. He orders the execution of Titus' sons Quintus and Martius for their supposed murder of Bassianus. He plans to dispose of the mad Titus (IV.iv); he hears that Lucius is marching with the Goths against Rome. He kills Titus after he has killed Tamora and revealed that he has just served her and Saturninus with Chiron and Demetrius baked in pies; he is himself killed by Lucius.

SATYRS *(Wint.)* : twelve herdsmen dressed as satyrs perform at the sheep-shearing (IV.iv). In Greek mythology satyrs represented the elementary spirits of the forest and the mountains. Their appearance would terrify shepherds and travellers. At first they were animalistic, half-goat and half monkey, and noted for their sensuality: later writers describe them as being of boyish appearance, with small pointed horns and pointed ears, and associate them with the pleasures of music and dance.

SAWYER, A *(2H.VI)* : one of the followers of Jack Cade (IV.ii).

SAY, LORD *(2H.VI)* : he is captured by Jack Cade and accused of extortion, of selling the English possessions in France and of corrupting youth by building a grammar school. He and Cromer are beheaded, and their heads carried through the streets on poles (IV.vii).

He was James Fiennes, one of Henry V's captains in the French wars. He became Sheriff of Kent in 1437. He was associated with Suffolk, and was accused with him of being responsible for the surrender of Anjou and Maine. In 1450 he was handed over to Cade's rebels by Lord Scales. Cade 'caused his head to be stricken off, and pitched it on a high pole' (Holinshed), and paraded it through the streets.

SCALES, LORD *(2.HVI)* : he is in command of the Tower during Jack Cade's rebellion. The citizens ask for aid and he sends Matthew Gough to lead them against the rebels (IV.v).

He was Thomas, 7th Baron Scales, a famous soldier. He fought with Henry V and then with Talbot in the French Wars, and probably remained fighting in France until the English possessions were lost. He returned to England and supported Henry VI against the Yorkists. In 1450 he raised a force against Cade's rebels, and led the fight on London Bridge. Ten years later he was commissioned to hold London for Henry VI; he defended the Tower vigorously against York and

Salisbury until he was starved into surrender. He tried to reach sanctuary at Westminster but was recognized by some boatmen, who murdered him.

SCARUS *(Ant.)*: a friend of Antony. He describes Cleopatra's flight at Antium (III.xi). He remains loyal to Antony, and fights so bravely that Cleopatra promises him 'an armour all of gold' (IV.viii).

In Plutarch, the officer who was given the armour is unnamed, and he deserted to Octavius as soon as he received it.

SCHOOLMASTER, ANTONY'S *(Ant.)*: he is sent as ambassador to Octavius by Antony to say that Antony and Cleopatra will surrender if they are allowed to live quietly in Athens. He reports Octavius' refusal to accept the proposal, and Antony sends him off again with a challenge to Octavius to meet him in single combat (III.xii; III.xiii).

SCRIVENER, A *(R.III)*: a professional scribe. He reveals that at Catesby's command he had begun to copy out the proclamation of Hastings' death before the execution had taken place (III.vi).

SCROOP, HENRY, LORD, OF MASHAM *(H.V)*: with Richard Cambridge and Sir Thomas Grey he is bribed by the French to assassinate Henry as he is about to set sail for France. The conspiracy is discovered, and Scroop and his associates are arrested on the quay and sent to execution (II.i).

SCROOP, RICHARD, ARCHBISHOP OF YORK *(1&2H.IV)*: he sends letters to the Percys saying that he will join them against Henry at Shrewsbury (IV.iv).

In *2 Henry IV*, after Shrewsbury, we hear that Scroop now 'turns insurrection to religion', and is offering Henry another challenge (I.i). He says he is rebelling because he thinks the people are disillusioned with Henry and are prepared to honour the memory of Richard (I.iii). He gives Westmorland the schedule of grievances that the rebels have drawn up for Henry. Prince John tricks them into dismissing their forces and they are arrested and executed (IV.iv).

Richard Scrope (1350–1405) was made Archbishop of York in 1398 at the express wish of Richard II, but he accepted the 1399 deposition, and took part in the coronation of Henry IV. He had family ties with the Percys, and his loyalty to the crown was shaken by their revolt. He took up arms himself in 1405, and issued a manifesto declaring that he sought only better government and more justice. He met Westmorland at Skipton Moor with a superior force, and agreed to a conference. Westmorland induced him to dismiss his forces by promising to redress his grievances, and as soon as he

had done so he had him arrested, along with Mowbray, and sent to Pontefract castle. After a hasty trial Scrope and Mowbray were executed at Bishopthorpe.

'The gravitie of his age, his integritie of life, and incomparable learning, with the reverend aspect of his amiable personage, mooved all men to have him in no small estimation." (Holinshed)

SCROOP, SIR STEPHEN *(R.II)*: he tells Richard that Bushy, Green and the Earl of Wiltshire are all dead, and that the Duke of York has joined Bolingbroke (III.ii).

He was the brother of Richard II's favourite the Earl of Wiltshire. He was one of the few nobles to remain faithful to Richard until his surrender at Flint.

He remained in favour with Henry IV, who made him Keeper of Roxburgh Castle, and then Deputy-Lieutenant of Ireland.

SEACOLE, FRANCIS *(Ado.)*, see SEXTON.

SEACOLE, GEORGE *(Ado)*: a member of the watch. He and Hugh Oatcake are the candidates put forward for the office of constable 'for they can write and read' (III.iii).

SEBASTIAN *(Gent)*: name assumed by Julia.

SEBASTIAN *(Tp.)*: the brother of Alonso, King of Naples. He helped Antonio (with whom he is associated throughout the play) to expel Prospero from Milan. On the island he joins Antonio's plot against Alonso and Gonzalo. He is not frightened by Ariel's spirit manifestations – 'But one fiend at a time, I'll fight their legions o'er' (III.iii). He shows neither gratitude nor remorse at the end.

SEBASTIAN *(Tw.N.)*: the twin brother of Viola. He is shipwrecked on the coast of Illyria with Antonio; he laments the loss of his sister, whom he presumes is drowned. He sets out for Orsino's court (II.i). Feste mistakes him for 'Cesario' (Viola in disguise), as does Aguecheek, who challenges him to a duel; Sebastian wounds him. Olivia, who also thinks he is Cesario, takes him to her house (IV.i). He is totally bewildered, but consents to be betrothed to her. He is confronted with Cesario, and is delighted to discover his 'drown'd Viola'.

SECRETARY *(H.VIII)*: two secretaries accompany Cardinal Wolsey on his first appearance (I.i). As the cardinal passes through he asks one of them if Buckingham's surveyor is present. In the second scene Wolsey tells a secretary to see that the letters revoking his commission are sent (I.ii).

Viola (Jean Forbes-Robertson) and Sebastian (Godfrey Kenton) in *Twelfth Night* at the New Theatre in 1932.

SELEUCUS *(Ant.)*: Cleopatra's treasurer. When she asks him if the list of her valuable possessions she has given to Caesar is complete he reluctantly admits that she has kept half of them back (v.ii).

SEMPRONIUS *(Tim.)*: a lord who has often received Timon's 'bounty'. When Timon sends to him for a loan he refuses (III.iii). He is one of those invited to Timon's final 'banquet' (III.vi).

SEMPRONIUS *(Tit.)*: a kinsman of the Andronici. He helps Titus shoot arrows bearing messages for the gods (IV.iii).

SENATORS, ATHENIAN *(Tim)*: some of them appear at Timon's house in the first scene. One of them is the first to realize that Timon's 'bounty' will not last for ever, and sends for the money he is owed (II.i). Three of them reject Alcibiades' appeal, and banish him (III.v). Two of them visit Timon in his cave when Alcibiades is threatening Athens, and beg Timon to return to lead the defence of the city (v.i). Two of them appear on the walls of the city and tell Alcibiades that

they will throw the city open to him if he will restrict his revenge to Timon's enemies (v.iv).

SENATORS, ROMAN *(Caes.)*: they are present at the Senate when the assassination of Caesar takes place (III.i).

SENATORS, ROMAN *(Cor.)*: some of them are present when Caius Marcius is asked to join Cominius in the war against the Volscians (I.i). Some are with him when he is challenged by the tribunes, and they try to calm his fury; they help defend him against the plebeians (III.i).

SENATORS, ROMAN *(Cym.)*: one of them announces that the Emperor has ordered a levy of gentlemen to be carried out for the invasion of Britain (III.vii).

SENATORS, ROMAN *(Tit.)*: some are present to greet the victorious Titus (I.i). Some are present when sentence is passed on Titus' sons (III.i), and some are invited to Titus' banquet (v.iii).

SENATORS, VENETIAN *(Oth.)*: they are members of the court before which Othello and Desdemona appear. Two of them discuss the news from Cyprus (I.iii).

SERGEANT, A BLEEDING *(Mac.)*: he has served under Macbeth and Banquo in the battle against Sweno and the Norwegians. It is his account of Macbeth's courage in the battle that persuades Duncan to make Macbeth Thane of Cawdor (I.ii).

SERGEANT-AT-ARMS *(H.VIII)*: he arrests Buckingham for high treason (I.i).

SERGEANT, FRENCH *(1H.VI)*: he is with the French army at Orleans. He appoints two soldiers to keep watch, but they fall asleep and Talbot is easily able to take the city (II.i).

SERVILIUS *(Tim)*: servant to Timon. He tries to borrow money from Lucius (II.ii), and offers excuses to Timon's creditors (III.iv).

SETON *(Mac.)*: Macbeth's armourer. He arms him for the final battle (v.iii), and brings him the news that Lady Macbeth is dead (v.iv).

SEXTON (FRANCIS SEACOLE) *(Ado.)*: a scribe. He is sent for 'to bring his pen and inkhorn to the gaol'. He makes a transcription of the proceedings during the examination of Borachio and Conrade and takes it to Leonato (IV.ii).

SHADOW, SIMON *(2H.IV)*: he is one of the men chosen by Falstaff from among Shallow's potential recruits for the King's army. As his name suggests, he is a nonentity (III.ii).

SHALLOW, ROBERT *(2H.IV; Wiv.)*: 'a country justice'. He is an old friend of Falstaff, and claims that he was once 'of Clement's Inn'. He supplies Falstaff with a pool of recruits. Falstaff is staying at his house in Gloucestershire when he learns of the accession of Henry v. They both hurry to London, but not before Falstaff has borrowed a thousand pounds from Shallow on the strength of his expectations under the new King. Shallow is with Falstaff when he is rejected and denounced by Henry, and is sent to the Fleet prison with him. He asks in vain for even half of his thousand pounds.

In *The Merry Wives of Windsor* he is now a doddering eighty years old. He threatens to 'make a Star-chamber matter' of Falstaff who has 'beaten my men, killed my deer, and broke open my lodge' (I.i). He tries to help his cousin Slender to win the hand of Anne Page; he even tries doing his wooing for him, but has no success.

Shallow has been identified with Sir William Gardiner, a Justice of the Peace at Southwark. (*See* FALSTAFF.)

SHEPHERD, OLD *(1H.VI)*: the father of Joan Pucelle. He has been searching for her all over France and finally finds her in Anjou, where she is a prisoner under sentence of death. She fiercely denies that he is her father. He is driven to cursing her, and cries 'O burn her, burn her! hanging is too good' (v.iv).

SHEPHERD, OLD *(Wint.)*: he is the reputed father of Perdita. He discovered her as an infant on the beach, and brought her up as his child. Sixteen years later at the sheep-shearing feast he tells Polixenes that 'Doricles' (Florizel) loves Perdita; he joins the hands of the lovers, and is condemned to death by the angry Polixenes. He goes to Sicilia with Florizel, and when he tells his story to Leontes he is made 'a gentleman born' as a reward (v.ii).

SHERIFF, A *(1H.IV)*: he enters with one of the carriers looking for Falstaff, who has been followed to the inn after the robbery. Hal says that he is not there, and promises to produce him the next day if the thief is still being sought (II.iv).

SHERIFF, A *(2H.VI)*: he leads the Duchess of Gloucester away to exile on the Isle of Man (II.iv).

SHERIFF, A *(John)*: he enters and whispers to either Salisbury or Essex (I.i).

The Sheriff of Northampton at the time was Sir Simon de Pateshull.

SHERIFF, A *(R.III)*: he leads the guard that escorts Buckingham to execution (v.i).

SHIP-MASTER *(Tp.)*: he is in command of Alonso's ship. After the wreck, Ariel sends him and his crew to sleep below decks. He wakes them at the end and they find the ship miraculously repaired and ready for the journey to Naples (I.i; v.i).

SHYLOCK *(Mer.V.)*: anxious to assist his friend, Bassanio, a Venetian fortune-hunter who is setting his cap at the beautiful heiress, Portia, chatelaine of Belmont, the merchant Antonio approaches the Jewish usurer, Shylock, explaining that his own wealth is at the moment invested in various mercantile enterprises that have not yet borne fruit. Shylock promises a loan, but on the 'merry' condition that, if Antonio fails to repay it punctually, he should forfeit a whole pound of his living flesh,

> . . . to be cut and taken off

In what part of your body pleaseth me. (I.iii)
Much as he mislikes and distrusts the Jew, whom he has often publicly abused, Antonio accepts this strange proviso, and receives three thousand ducats. Bassanio manages to win his heiress; but soon afterwards Antonio hears that one of his richest ships has run aground, and that Shylock is angrily demanding he should honour the bond that he has signed. Portia, a young woman as accomplished as she is attractive, now assumes a lawyer's robes; and, thus disguised, in a Venetian court of justice, whither Antonio and Shylock have been summoned to appear before the Duke, delivers an ingenious speech for the defence, not only exalting 'the quality of mercy', a virtue that Shylock has made it clear that he will disregard, but insisting that the plaintiff, though undoubtedly entitled to a pound of the defendant's flesh, must not shed a drop of Christian blood and, moreover, must cut off the pound with a most scrupulous exactitude; for

> . . . if the scale do turn

But in the estimation of a hair,

Thou diest, and all thy goods are confiscated. (IV.i)
This plea, to which the Duke assents, utterly confounds Shylock. His suit fails; he is himself threatened with the death penalty; and although his life is spared, the court orders that he should make his submission to the Christian church, and lose a half-share of his great fortune. Meanwhile, the Jew's faithless little daughter, Jessica, besides appropriating all the ready money in her parent's coffers that she can lay her hands on, has stolen away to marry another Venetian gentleman Lorenzo; and, when Shylock dies, his entire wealth,

above An eighteenth-century Shylock: Mr Macklin in the role in 1775 *(left)*; Edmund Kean as Shylock; by Meyer, after Watts *(right)*.

both the amount he has already lost and the moiety he still holds, is to pass into Lorenzo's and Jessica's keeping. The play ends on an exquisitely lyrical note, as the cheerful Christians meet to celebrate their victory amid the moonlit glades of Belmont.

Though Shakespeare borrowed the idea of Shylock's bond from an Italian story, *Il Pecorone,* published during the 1550s, *The Merchant of Venice,* written in 1597, seems to have been largely inspired by a recent political and racial drama. Early in the summer of 1594, the Queen's physician, a learned Portuguese Jew named Dr Lopez, was accused of having had conspiratorial dealings with the Spanish government. The Cecils supported him; but their chief adversary at court, the Earl of Essex (a royal favourite and the close friend of Shakespeare's early patron, Lord Southampton), had decided to make the issue a political trial of strength and, having conducted his own enquiry, had announced that Lopez was a dangerous traitor, and that he had plotted to kill the Queen by poisoning. Despite the Cecils' efforts and Lopez' vehement protests, he was eventually convicted of the crime of high treason and paid the penalty at Tyburn Tree. Beneath the gallows,

he still proclaimed his innocence, and declared that he loved his Queen as dearly as he loved Jesus Christ – a dying speech, we are told, that moved the attendant mob to roars of loud, derisive laughter.

Shakespeare's play, if not deliberately anti-Semitic, certainly exploited the racial prejudices of contemporary theatre-goers. His Shylock is a bloodthirsty Jewish villain. Yet, as Nicholas Rowe, Shakespeare's biographer and first critical editor, would remark in 1709, we are bound to suspect that 'the incomparable character of Shylock . . . was designed tragically by the author'. Many subsequent critics have taken the same view. Shylock, they have felt, is a much more impressive personage than the commonplace antagonists who drag him down, and has a broader mind and a far stronger spirit. 'That he has but one idea,' writes Hazlitt, 'is not true; he has more ideas than any other person in the piece; and if he is intense and inveterate in pursuit of this purpose, he shews the utmost elasticity, vigour and presence of mind, in the means of attaining it.' Shylock bears a special grudge against Antonio, who has persistently insulted him. Yet he speaks not for himself alone, but for his whole persecuted community:

above Macklin, said to be as Shylock. *below* Programme for a command performance of *The Merchant of Venice* at Windsor in 1848.

I am a Jew. Hath not a Jew eyes? hath not a Jew hands, organs, dimensions, senses, affections, passions? fed with the same food, hurt with the same weapons, subject to the same diseases, healed by the same means, warmed and cooled by the same winter and summer, as a Christian is? If you prick us, do we not bleed? if you tickle us, do we not laugh? if you poison us, do we not die? and if you wrong us, shall we not revenge? if we are like you in the rest, we will resemble you in that . . . The villainy you teach me I execute, and it shall go hard but I will better the instruction. (III.i)

During the nineteenth century, a great German-Jewish poet, Heinrich Heine, described how, at Drury Lane Theatre, he had watched a fine performance of the role. Perhaps Shakespeare, he considered, had 'had in mind to create . . . a trained werewolf, a loathsome fabulous monster thirsting for blood, and thereby losing his daughter and his ducats. . . . But the genius of the poet, the universal spirit which inspires him, is always above his individual will'; with the result that the injured Jew rises high above his petty persecutors: the bankrupt Antonio, the fortune-hunting Bassanio, and Lorenzo, the mean accomplice of Jessica's disloyal theft. Like Shakespeare's other tragic heroes, Shylock is a lonely man; but his solitude ennobles him. He stands alone, facing the terrible reality of his position; his antagonists live in a world of gay poetic make-believe.

SICILIUS LEONATUS *(Cym)*: the father of Posthumus, who died before Posthumus was born. He and his dead wife and sons appear in Posthumus' vision (v.iv).

SICINIUS VELUTUS *(Cor.)*: a tribune of the people. He and Junius Brutus, 'the tongues o' the common mouth', are wary of the pride of Caius Marcius (later Coriolanus), and predict that it will inflame the people against him. They persuade the citizens to revoke their consent to Coriolanus' nomination as consul (II.iii). Sicinius is attacked by the enraged Coriolanus, but is rescued by the mob; he tells them to throw Coriolanus from the Tarpeian Rock, but Coriolanus and the patricians hold them at bay (III.i). Sicinius charges Coriolanus with attempting to seize tyrannical power, and pronounces a sentence of perpetual banishment on him (III.iii). He reassures the citizens when he hears that Coriolanus is approaching Rome with a Volscian army, but he asks Menenius to use his influence to stop the advance. (*See* BRUTUS, JUNIUS.)

right Laurence Olivier as Shylock in Jonathan Miller's production of *The Merchant of Venice,* by the National Theatre Company in 1970.

Shylock, Salerio and Solanio *(Merchant of Venice*, III.i).
A watercolour by Sir John Gilbert.

SILENCE *(2H.IV)* : a country justice. He is a cousin to
Shallow, and as his name suggests, the counter to his
garrulity. He says very little until he gets drunk, when
he boasts that he has 'been merry twice and once ere now'
before he is carried off to bed (v.iii).

SILIUS *(Ant.)* : an officer in the Roman army commanded by Ventidius. He wants to pursue the fleeing
Parthians, but Ventidius points out that a too dramatic
victory might offend Antony (III.i).

SILVIA *(Gent.)* : the daughter of the Duke of Milan.
She is loved by Valentine and Thurio, and later Proteus.
When Proteus arrives in Milan she accepts him as her
'new servant' (II.iv); he falls in love with her, even
though he knows it means losing both Julia and
Valentine. She intends to elope with Valentine, but
their plan is betrayed by Proteus to her father, who
banishes Valentine. She becomes melancholy, and pours
scorn on Proteus for his faithlessness to Julia when he
appeals to her (IV.ii). She refuses to accept his ring

because she knows it came from the 'poor lady Julia'.
She sets out for a rendezvous with Valentine accompanied by Sir Eglamour (v.i). She is captured by outlaws, and rescued by Proteus, who appears to be about
to rape her when Valentine enters. When Proteus
repents, and accepts Julia, Valentine and Silvia are
granted permission to marry by the Duke.

SILVIUS *(AYL.)* : a shepherd. He is in love with
Phebe, who is indifferent to him, and who falls in love
with 'Ganymede' (Rosalind in disguise) at first sight.
When Rosalind reveals herself, Silvius is accepted by
Phebe (v.iv).

SIMONIDES *(Per.)* : the King of Pentapolis, and
father of Thaisa. He crowns Pericles the victor at his
tournament (II.iii). He then insults him and calls him a
traitor in order to test his love for Thaisa before he
allows him to marry her (II.v).

SIMPCOX, SAUNDER, AND HIS WIFE *(2H.VI)* :

Silvia is rescued from the advance of Proteus by
Valentine *(The Two Gentlemen of Verona,* v.iv).
From a painting by Maria Angelica Kauffman.

he claims to have been cured of blindness at the shrine
of St Albans. Gloucester exposes him as an impostor,
and also reveals his lameness as a sham when he has
him whipped and he runs away. His wife admits that
they did it 'for pure need' (II.i).

SIMPLE, PETER *(Wiv.)*: Slender's servant. Evans
sends him with a letter to Mistress Quickly asking for
her help with Slender's suit to Anne Page (I.ii). He blurts
out that Slender is in love with Anne to Dr Caius, who
sends him back with a challenge to Evans. He consults
'the wise woman of Brentford' on Slender's behalf,
and receives oracular answers from the disguised
Falstaff.

SIWARD, EARL OF NORTHUMBERLAND
(Mac.): the uncle of Malcolm. He leads the English
forces sent by Edward the Confessor to help Malcolm
and Macduff against Macbeth (v.iv).

SIWARD, YOUNG *(Mac.)*: son of the above. He is
killed in the battle by Macbeth, who has become
convinced that no man of woman born can kill him
(v.vii).

SLENDER, ABRAHAM *(Wiv.)*: Shallow's cousin.
Shallow suggests that he woos Anne Page, but Slender is
so incapable that Evans and Shallow have to try to do
his wooing for him. He even tells Anne that if it were
up to him he would not bother. But her father approves
of him and arranges for them to elope during the baiting
of Falstaff in Windsor Forest. Anne elopes with Fenton
instead, while Slender runs off with a fairy who turns
out to be a 'great lubberly boy'.

He is an imbecile gull, a stock figure in Elizabethan
drama. He has 'but a little whey-face, with a little yellow
beard' (I.iv).

He has been identified with William Wayte, who on
29 November 1596 craved sureties of the peace against
Shakespeare, Francis Langley, lessee of the Swan
Theatre, and others.

SLY, CHRISTOPHER *(Shr.)*: 'a drunken tinker' who appears in the Induction. He falls into a drunken sleep, and a lord decides for a joke to persuade him when he wakes that he is really a rich lord who has been temporarily insane. He awakes in a rich room, with fine clothes on, and with a wife in attendance. He is told that he has been away from her bed for fifteen years, and immediately he wants to make restitution for this, and says 'Madam undress you, and come now to bed'. He is diverted (his 'wife' is a page dressed as a woman) by a play; he is told that this 'pleasant comedy' will prevent a recurrence of his illness. The play is *The Taming of the Shrew*; by the end of the first scene Sly is falling asleep and wishing that it was over.

Before he is convinced he is a lord, Sly is very sure of his identity:

Am I not Christopher Sly, old Sly's son of Burton-heath, by birth a pedlar, by education a card-maker, by transmutation a bear-herd, and now by present profession a tinker? Ask Marian Hacket the fat ale-wife of Wincot, if she know me not. If she say I am not fourteen pence on the score for sheer ale, score me up for the lying'st knave in Christendom.

(Induction II)

Oscar Asche (1871–1936) as Christopher Sly in *The Taming of the Shrew*.

In Sly we see the outline of Falstaff.

SMITH THE WEAVER *(2H.VI)*: a follower of Jack Cade. He does not believe Cade's claim to be a Mortimer, and interrupts his speech explaining his noble lineage with sarcastic comments (IV.ii).

SNARE *(2H.IV)*: an officer who assists Fang in the arrest of Falstaff when Mistress Quickly arraigns him for debt (II.i).

SNOUT, TOM *(MND.)*: a tinker. Quince allots him the part of Pyramus' father in the *Interlude*. He ends up playing the wall. After his speech in this role Theseus comments 'It is the wittiest partition that I ever heard discourse.'

SNUG *(MND.)*: a joiner. He is allotted the part of the lion in the *Interlude*, for though slow-witted he 'roars well'. Bottom makes him announce that he is not a real lion before he roars so that he will not frighten the ladies.

SOLANIO *(Mer.V.)*: a friend of Antonio and Bassanio. He tries to comfort Antonio when he finds him melancholy (I.i). He describes Shylock's anguish at the loss of his ducats and his daughter (II.viii).

SOLINUS *(Err.)*: the Duke of Ephesus. He sentences Egeon to death, because as a result of a trade war Syracusans are now proscribed in Ephesus and vice versa. Egeon is given one day to raise a thousand marks' ransom; Solinus says that under the law this is all he can do for him. When the errors are resolved at the end he pardons him.

SOMERSET, DUKE OF *(2H.VI)*: he is appointed Regent in France (I.iii). He later announces that France is 'all lost': he is taunted for his failure by York, who demands his removal (III.i). York's attacks on him are averted when he is committed to the Tower (IV.ix). With Queen Margaret he attempts to arrest York, but fails (v.i). He is killed at St Albans by Richard Plantagenet (v.ii).

He was Edmund Beaufort. In his youth he excelled as a military commander, but in later life success deserted him, and he presided over the loss of the English possessions and power in France. After he had been forced to surrender Rouen and six other strongholds he returned to England. Henry sent him to France again, and he was forced to surrender at Caen. He returned again, and invaded Gascony, but the death of Talbot at Chatillon ended his hopes. When York became Protector he committed Somerset to the Tower; when Henry was restored to the throne he was appointed Captain of Calais. He was defeated and killed by York at the first battle of St Albans in 1455. His was the first noble blood spilled in the Wars of the Roses.

SOMERSET, DUKE OF *(3H.VI)*: he joins Warwick because he disapproves of the King's marriage to Lady Grey (IV.i). He is given custody of Edward IV (IV.iii). He is taken prisoner at Tewkesbury and beheaded (v.v).

He was Henry Beaufort, 3rd Duke of Somerset (1436–1464). He was regarded as the great hope of the Lancastrians. After submitting to Edward IV in 1462 he enjoyed the King's favour until 1464, when he joined Margaret at Hexham, where he was taken prisoner and executed.

Shakespeare confuses him with Edmund Beaufort, 4th Duke of Somerset (*c*.1438–71), who became Duke on the death of his brother in 1464. He fought for the Lancastrians at Tewkesbury in 1471, and was captured and beheaded on the orders of Edward.

Shakespeare's confusion is seen in *3 Henry VI*, (IV.i) when Edmund appears at the invitation of Edward, since it was Henry who was in favour with the King at the time.

SOMERVILE, SIR JOHN *(3H.VI)*: a Lancastrian adherent who reports to Warwick in Coventry that Clarence and his troops are due in about two hours (v.i).

SON THAT HAS KILLED HIS FATHER *(3H.VI)*, *see* FATHER THAT HAS KILLED HIS SON.

SOOTHSAYER *(Ant.)*: 'A soothsayer or astronomer of Egypt'. He reads the hands of Charmian and Iras (I.ii). He warns Antony that his 'demon' or 'angel' (that is, presiding spirit) will always be overpowered by Octavius Caesar's when they are together.

SOOTHSAYER *(Caes.)*: he warns Julius Caesar to 'beware the Ides of March' (I.ii). He warns Portia of his fears for Caesar, and before the assassination he reminds Caesar that the Ides of March are come and not yet gone (III.i).

SOOTHSAYER *(Cym.)*, *see* PHILARMONUS.

SOUNDPOST, JAMES *(Rom.)*: one of the musicians engaged to play at Juliet's wedding to Paris. A soundpost is a small peg of wood which supports the belly of a violin and connects it to the back (IV.v).

SOUTHWELL, JOHN *(2H.VI)*: a priest who is arrested while conjuring up a spirit for the Duchess of Gloucester (I.iv). He is condemned to be hanged (II.iii).

He was a priest of St Stephen's, Westminster. He was not executed, but died in the Tower.

SPANISH GENTLEMAN *(Cym.)*: he is present when Iachimo and Posthumus make their wager on the virtue of Imogen. He does not speak (I.v).

SPEED *(Gent.)*: 'a clownish servant to Valentine'. He accompanies his master to Milan; he explains to him 'the special marks' of being in love, and warns him that Proteus is in love with Silvia (II.i). He falls into the hands of the outlaws with Valentine, and he advises him to join them (IV.i).

He is a conventional bantering clown; he is at his best in his comic interchanges with Launce.

SPIRITS *(Tp.)*: in the shape of hounds they chase Caliban, Stephano and Trinculo (IV.i).

STAFFORD, EDWARD *(H.VIII)*, *see* BUCKINGHAM, DUKE OF.

STAFFORD, HENRY *(R.III)*, *see* BUCKINGHAM, DUKE OF.

STAFFORD, HUMPHREY *(2H.VI)*, *see* BUCKINGHAM, DUKE OF.

STAFFORD, LORD *(3H.VI)*: a Yorkist who is ordered by Edward to levy men in preparation for war (IV.i).

He was Sir Humphrey Stafford (1439–69). He fought for Edward IV at Towton, and was knighted on the field. He was created Lord Stafford in 1464. He defected from Edward later, but was captured in Somerset and executed in Bridgwater in 1469.

STAFFORD, SIR HUMPHREY *(2H.VI)*: he and his brother William lead the King's troops against Jack Cade's rebels at Blackheath. They are both killed in the battle, and Cade puts on Sir Humphrey's armour (IV.iii).

STAFFORD, WILLIAM *(2H.VI)*: brother of Sir Humphrey Stafford *(q.v.)*.

STANLEY, SIR JOHN *(2H.VI)*: a gentleman who escorts the Duchess of Gloucester to her banishment on the Isle of Man (II.iv).

He was in fact Sir Thomas Stanley.

STANLEY, SIR WILLIAM *(3H.VI; R.III)*: he helps Edward to escape from Middleham Castle (IV.v). In *Richard III* he is mentioned as one of the nobles who have turned against the King (IV.v).

The story of him helping Edward to escape comes from the Chronicles and is not found elsewhere. Richard III did his best to keep his support, but he joined Richmond; it was his arrival at Bosworth with three thousand 'tall men of Cheshire' that turned the battle against Richard. Stanley later joined Perkin Warbeck's conspiracy, and was accused of high treason and beheaded in 1495.

STARVELING, ROBIN *(MND.)*: a tailor. Quince gives him the part of Thisbe's mother in the *Interlude*. A timid man, he is worried by the killing and the roaring of the lion. He ends up playing Moonshine, but is forced to give up his speech by the jibes of the audience (V.i).

STEPHANO *(Mer.V.)*: a servant to Portia. He is sent by her to Belmont to warn Jessica and Lorenzo that she will soon be returning from Venice (V.i).

STEPHANO *(Tp.)*: a drunken butler. He and Trinculo find Caliban. Stephano gives him alcoholic drink, which leads Caliban to worship him. He accepts Caliban's suggestion that they should murder Prospero so that he could become king of the island (III.ii). Prospero diverts him by hanging 'glistering apparel' in front of his cave, and then drives him and Trinculo and Caliban away with spirits 'in shape of dogs'.

STEWARD *(All'sW.)*: the Countess of Rousillon's steward. He tells the countess that Helena loves Bertram (I.iii). He reads Helena's farewell message to her, and is told to write to Bertram and tell him of Helena's flight (III.iv). He is called Rinaldo in the First Folio.

STEWARD *(Wint.)*: Paulina's steward. He is the third gentleman, who relates the story of the reunion of Leontes and Perdita (V.ii).

STRATO *(Caes.)*: one of Brutus' men. After the defeat at Philippi he holds Brutus' sword for him to run on to. Octavius takes him into his service (V.v).

SUFFOLK, DUKE OF *(H.VIII)*: a warrant for his arrest is issued (I.i).

He was Sir Henry Pole, Baron Montacute (c.1492–1538). He was executed for treason, but his arrest took place eighteen years before his execution.

SUFFOLK, EARL OF *(H.V)*: he does not appear, but his death at Agincourt is described by the Duke of Exeter:

Suffolk first died, and York all haggled over
Comes to him, where in gore he lay insteep'd,

And takes him by the beard, kisses the gashes
That bloodily did yawn upon his face.
And cries aloud; Tarry my cousin Suffolk,
My soul shall thine keep company to heaven:
Tarry, sweet soul, for mine, then fly abreast:
As in this glorious and well-foughten field
We kept together in our chivalry. (IV.vi)

He was Michael de la Pole, 3rd Earl of Suffolk (1394–1415). He was noted for his bravery before his death at Agincourt.

SUFFOLK, EARL OF (later Duke of) *(1&2H.VI)*: he plucks a red rose in the Temple Garden to indicate his opposition to Richard Plantagenet (II.iv). At Angiers he captures Margaret of Anjou, and wavers between wooing her for himself and offering her to Henry. Because he is already married he decides on the latter course, intending to make her his mistress. He guarantees her father Reignier the provinces of Anjou and Maine. While escorting Margaret to England he reflects that he will 'rule both her, the King, and realm'.

In *2 Henry VI* he is made the Duke of Suffolk as a reward for arranging the King's marriage (I.i). He schemes the disgrace of the Duchess of Gloucester and the murder of the Duke of Gloucester; he is accused by Warwick of having knowledge of the murder, and is banished by the horrified Henry (III.ii). He bids Margaret a passionate farewell. He is captured at sea off the coast of Kent and is dragged away and beheaded by Walter Whitmore (IV.i).

Suffolk's passion for Margaret is unhistorical, but it is this that gives Shakespeare's otherwise fairly conventional villain an added dimension. He is driven to seek power by his rampant will:

Faith, I have been a truant in the law,
And never yet could frame my will to it;
And therefore frame the law unto my will. (II.iv)

As a lover he is almost a different character. His farewell to Margaret when he is banished has a poignancy that momentarily associates him with the heroes of romance:

If I depart from thee, I cannot live,
And in thy sight to die, what were it else
But like a pleasant slumber in thy lap?
Here I could breathe my soul into the air,
As mild and gentle as the cradle-babe,
Dying with mother's dug between its lips;
Where, from thy sight, I should be raging mad
And cry out for thee to close up mine eyes.
To have thee with thy lips to stop my mouth;
So shouldst thou either turn my flying soul,
Or I should breathe it so into thy body,
And then it lived in sweet Elysium.
From thee to die, were torture more than death.
(III.ii)

He was William de la Pole (1396–1450), 4th Earl and 1st Duke of Suffolk. He succeeded in bringing about Henry VI's marriage to Margaret of Anjou in the face of the opposition of his powerful rival the Duke of Gloucester. He did not take Margaret prisoner as in Shakespeare, and the marriage negotiations took place fourteen years after the capture of Joan of Arc. He was not Margaret's lover; he was thirty-four years older than she was, and his wife, Alice Chaucer, accompanied him to France when he went as Henry's proxy. After the marriage Suffolk became Henry's supreme counsellor, and was made Duke of Suffolk in 1448. He became unpopular in the country for having agreed to the cession of Anjou and Maine to France. He was accused of being implicated in the death of his enemy the Duke of Gloucester, and was committed to the Tower, and then banished for five years. He was captured and killed at sea off Dover, perhaps at the instigation of the Duke of York.

SUGARSOP *(Shr.)*: one of the servants at Petruchio's country house (IV.i).

SURREY, DUKE OF *(R.II), see* LORD MARSHAL.

SURREY, EARL OF *(2H.IV)*: he is summoned before the King with Warwick, but does not speak (III.i).

He was Thomas Fitzalan, 11th Earl of Arundel and Surrey (1381–1415).

SURREY, EARL OF *(R.III; H.VIII)*: he fights with Richard at Bosworth (V.iii).

In *Henry VIII* he was an eye-witness to the Field of the Cloth of Gold, which he describes (I.i). He dislikes Wolsey, and warns Buckingham against him; he gloats over Wolsey's downfall (II.ii).

Shakespeare has combined father and son in one character. Thomas Howard (1443–1524) was with Richmond at Bosworth. He later became an implacable enemy of Wolsey, and did everything he could to turn Henry VIII against him. His son, Henry Howard (who would have held the title during most of *Henry VIII*), was the famous soldier, poet and scholar. He was only thirteen when he became Earl of Surrey in 1524.

SURVEYOR, DUKE OF BUCKINGHAM'S *(H.VIII)*: having been dismissed from his post he gives evidence against Buckingham, saying that he had heard him plot against the King's life (I.ii).

He was Charles Knevet. He was dismissed from his office, and laid false information against the Duke of Buckingham for revenge.

T

TAILOR, A *(Shr.)* : he delivers a dress that Petruchio has ordered for Katharine, only to be told that it is unacceptable to Petruchio, and treated to a memorable stream of abuse:

> O monstrous arrogance! Thou liest, thou thread, thou thimble,
> Thou yard, three quarters, half-yard, quarter, nail,
> Thou flea, thou nit, thou winter-cricket thou!
> Braved in mine own house with a skein of thread?
> Away thou rag, thou quantity, thou remnant,
> Or I shall so be-mete thee with thy yard,
> As thou shalt think on prating whilst thou livest.
>
> (IV.iii)

He vainly tries to explain that he has carried out his instructions; as he leaves, Hortensio tells him to 'take no unkindness' of Petruchio's 'hasty words', and tells him that he will be paid for the gown the next day.

TALBOT, JOHN, LORD *(1H.VI)* : he is captured at Patay due to the cowardice of Sir John Fastolfe (I.i). He fights with the 'high-minded strumpet' Joan Pucelle, and fears that she is driving back the panic-stricken English by witchcraft (I.v). He drives her and the French out of Rouen (III.ii). He does homage to Henry VI at Paris, and as proof of his loyalty tells him that he has

> . . . reclaimed
> To your obedience fifty fortresses,
> Twelve cities, and seven walled towns of strength,
> Besides five hundred prisoners of esteem . . . (III.iv)

He exposes Fastolfe's cowardice, and tears the Garter from him. He and his son are surrounded near Bordeaux, and because York and Somerset delay in sending help, they are both killed (IV.vi).

Talbot is the hero of the first part of *Henry VI*: according to Thomas Nashe, it was his exploits in the play that made it a popular success with Shakespeare's contemporaries. We first hear of this Titan when his defeat and capture due to the treachery of Fastolfe are described:

> . . . valiant Talbot, above human thought,
> Enacted wonders with his sword and lance.
> Hundreds he sent to hell, and none durst stand him;
> Here, there, and every where enraged he slew.

> The French exclaimed, the devil was in arms,
> All the whole army stood agazed on him. (I.i)

An English soldier scatters the French simply by crying Talbot's name: 'The cry of Talbot serves me for a sword' (II.i). The noble Talbot is pitted against the evil and satanic Joan Pucelle, who has on her side the powers of witchcraft. Talbot is defeated by the dissensions among the English, and his death marks the end of effective English power in France.

He was John Talbot, 1st Earl of Shrewsbury (c.1388–1453). He was imprisoned by Henry V because he was a friend of the Lollard Sir John Oldcastle. From 1419 he fought in France and Ireland; he accompanied the Duke of Bedford to France in 1427, and after a series of brilliant successes was captured and defeated by Joan of Arc at Patay in 1429. He remained captive for four years; he was exchanged for the man who had taken him prisoner, Lord Pouton de Santrailles. He joined the Duke of Burgundy's campaign in north-west France, and again had great success. He was made Steward of Ireland in 1446, but he was recalled to France in 1448 to help Somerset's campaign in Normandy. In 1452 he was sent out to France again, this time as Lieutenant of Aquitaine, and he quickly took Bordeaux. But he was defeated and killed, along with his son, at Castillon in 1453. He was more than sixty at the time of his death, which took place some twenty-two years after the death of Joan of Arc.

Shakespeare ignores chronology and historical accuracy in order to oppose Talbot to Joan – the famous English hero against the symbol of French nationalism. Although Shakespeare has them fight each other, it is unlikely that they ever met. Shakespeare's account of the terror caused by Talbot among the French is supported by Hall: 'This man was to the French people a very scorge and a daily terror; in so much that as his person was fearfull and terrible to his adversaries present, so his name and fame was spitefull and dreadfull to the common people absent; in so much that women in Fraunce to feare their yong children, would cry, "the Talbot commeth, the Talbot commeth!"'

TALBOT, YOUNG *(1H.VI)* : the young son of the

above. He comes to join his father, whom he has not seen for seven years, at Bordeaux. His father tells him to escape for the English are outnumbered, but the boy refuses and dies with his father (IV.vii).

Talbot eulogizes his son's bravery just before he dies himself:

When he perceived me shrink, and on my knee,
His bloody sword he brandished over me,
And like an hungry lion did commence
Rough deeds of rage and stern impatience.
But when my angry guardant stood alone,
Tendering my ruin, and assailed of none,
Dizzy-eyed fury, and great rage of heart,
Suddenly made him from my side to start
Into the clustering battle of the French.
And in that sea of blood my boy did drench
His over-mounting spirit; and there died
My Icarus, my blossom, in his pride. (IV.vii)

TAMORA *(Tit.)*: the Queen of the Goths. She is led captive to Rome by Titus. She pleads for the life of her son Alarbus in vain, and he is sacrificed. Saturninus chooses her as his Empress (I.ii). She joins with Aaron, her lover, in plotting against Titus; Bassianus and Lavinia discover them together, and threaten to inform Saturninus. Tamora tells her sons of the threat, and incites them to take revenge (II.iii). They murder Bassianus and rape and mutilate Lavinia; Tamora and Aaron throw the blame on to the sons of Titus, who are executed for the crime (II.iv). She visits Titus disguised as the figure of Revenge, and asks him to invite Lucius to his banquet; she intends to have him murdered (V.ii). At the banquet she eats pies containing the flesh of her sons, and is then stabbed by Titus (V.iii). Lucius orders her body thrown to the wild beasts.

She is a 'most insatiate and luxurious woman' (V.i), a 'heinous tiger' (V.iii); her disguise as 'Revenge' indicates her dominant passion in the play, for throughout she is 'To villainy and vengeance consecrate'. Unlike Aaron she has a credible motivation, the desire for revenge on Titus, who defeated her and sacrificed her son Alarbus. At the end her body is returned to the world of untrammelled nature that had ruled her life:

No mournful bell shall ring her burial
But throw her forth to beasts and birds to prey,
Her life was beastly and devoid of pity,
And being dead let birds on her take pity. (V.iii)

TAURUS *(Ant.)*: lieutenant-general to Octavius Caesar, in charge of the land forces at Actium. Caesar orders him to wait until the sea-battle has been decided before he attacks Antony's troops (II.viii).

TEARSHEET, DOLL *(2H.IV)*: Falstaff's mistress. His Page describes her as 'a proper gentlewoman' (II.ii).

Lavinia (Vivien Leigh) pleads with Tamora, Queen of the Goths (Maxine Audley) in Peter Brook's 1955 production of *Titus Andronicus* at Stratford.

She drinks 'too much canaries' and quarrels with Pistol; she praises Falstaff for throwing him out. She bids Falstaff a tearful farewell when he is 'going to the wars' (II.iv). She is taken to prison for being the subject of a tavern brawl in which there was 'a man or two lately killed' (V.iv).

Her first appearance ironically follows Lady Percy's eulogy of Hotspur, her late husband. Her few intimate moments with Falstaff reveal the pathos of the old man's situation.

Coleridge suggests that her name was a corruption of 'Tear-street', a street-walker. This would explain Hal's question, 'This Doll Tearsheet should be some road?'.

Jeanne Moreau as Doll Tearsheet in *Chimes at Midnight,* a film directed by Orson Welles based on *1* and *2 Henry IV*.

THAISA *(Per.)*: the daughter of Simonides. She marries Pericles after his victory in the lists in her father's tournament (II.iii). She is believed dead after giving birth to Marina during a storm at sea, and is committed to the waves in a chest (III.i). She is washed ashore at Ephesus, and is revived by the music and arts of Cerimon. When she has recovered she resolves to assume a 'vestal living' at the temple of Diana in Ephesus. Fourteen years later while she is officiating as high priestess there, Pericles and Marina make themselves known to her, and the family is united (v.iii).

THALIARD *(Per.)*: a lord of Antioch. Antiochus pays him to poison Pericles who has guessed that he has an incestuous relationship with his daughter, but Pericles escapes (I.i). Thaliard follows him to Tyre, but by the time he gets there Pericles has left for Tharsus. He presumably gives up the chase at this point, since he does not reappear (I.iii).

THERSITES *(Troil.)*: a scurrilous and foul-mouthed Greek. He rails at Ajax and is beaten by him (II.i); he inveighs against the folly of the Greeks at Troy; Achilles, who has stolen him from Ajax, treats and protects him as a 'licensed man' who can say whatever he likes (II.iii). He gives an account of Ajax to the Greek chiefs (III.iii); he brings Achilles a letter from Hecuba, and reviles Patroclus (v.i). He derides the Greeks during the battle, but is terrified by Hector, who spares him when he describes himself as 'a rascal: a scurvy railing knave; a very filthy rogue' (v.iv). He encounters his fellow bastard Margarelon, and refuses to fight with him.

For Thersites, at Troy 'lechery, lechery, still wars and lechery, nothing else holds fashion' (v.ii); it is his favourite theme.

> Here is such patchery, such juggling, and such knavery: all the argument is a cuckold and a whore, a good quarrel to draw emulations, factions, and bleed to death upon: Now the dry serpigo on the subject, and war and lechery confound all. (II.iii)

Because his cynicism appears attractive today he has been taken as the voice of Shakespeare, as the true hero of the play. But we must not believe all that he says: there is a direct relationship between his deformed body and his repulsive ideas. His prominence is a symptom of the breakdown of order in the Greek camp.

This 'Caliban of demagogic life' (Coleridge) has much in common with Carlo Buffone, the 'black-mouth'd cur' of Ben Jonson's *Every Man out of His Humour* (1599), and with Diogenes in Lyly's *Campaspe*. Thersites is not found in the medieval romances, but comes from Homer, where, in Chapman's translation, he is described as

> A man of tongue, whose ravenlike voice a tuneless jarring kept,
> Who in his ranke mind coppy had of unregarded wordes,
> That rashly and beyond al rule used to oppugne the Lords,
> But what soever came from him was laught at mightilie:
> The filthiest Greeke that ever came to Troy: he had a goggle eye:
> Starcke lame he was of eyther foote: his shoulders were contract,
> Into his breast and crookt withall: his head was shape compact,
> And here and there it had a hayre.

THESEUS *(MND.)*: the Duke of Athens. He asks for revels to be prepared to celebrate his forthcoming wedding to Hippolyta. He hears Egeus' complaint against his daughter Hermia, and tells her to obey her father (I.i). He takes Hippolyta hunting with him, and finds the four lovers lying asleep, and invites them to be married at the same time as himself and Hippolyta; he overrules Egeus and commands that Hermia marry Lysander. He watches the *Interlude*, and orders a fortnight's revels (v.i).

His good sense and reason are reminiscent of an English country squire. He is limited, as his contempt for dreams and fantasies makes clear. His derisive speech on poetry works against his restricted pragmatism even as he speaks it:

> The poet's eye, in a fine frenzy rolling,

Doth glance from heaven to earth, from earth to
heaven.
And as imagination bodies forth
The forms of things unknown, the poet's pen
Turns them to shapes, and gives to airy nothing
A local habitation and a name.
Such tricks hath strong imagination,
That if it would but apprehend some joy,
It comprehends some bringer of that joy.
Or in the night, imagining some fear,
How easy is a bush supposed a bear! (v.i)

Theseus is a man of the day and everyday living. He
knows nothing of the mysteries of the night, and is the
link between the dream and reality.

In mythology he was the son of Aegeus, as well as
being the legendary hero of Attica, and slayer of the
minotaur.

THIDIAS *(Ant.)* : Caesar sends him to use his cunning
to win Cleopatra from Antony. She grants him a private
audience and allows him to kiss her hand, which
infuriates Antony who has him whipped (III.xiii).

THISBE *(MND.)* : part played by Flute in the
Interlude.

THOMAS, FRIAR *(Meas.)* : he helps the Duke when
he seeks concealment in a monastery disguised as Friar
Lodowick (I.iv).

Johnson suggested that he was indentical with Friar
Peter *(q.v.)* ; certainly there is no reason why he should
not be.

THUMP, PETER *(2H.VI)* : servant to Horner *(q.v.)*.
He accuses his master of treason for saying that York
is the rightful King (I.iii). He kills Horner in a duel
fought with sandbags (II.iii).

THURIO *(Gent.)* : the suitor who the Duke favours for
the hand of Silvia, and rival to Valentine. Proteus advises
him to sing beneath her window (IV.ii), and then
persuades him to allow him to woo her on his behalf.
Thurio follows Silvia when she runs away to meet
Valentine ; when he finds her in the forest he claims her,
but backs down quickly when he is threatened by
Valentine (v.iv).

In the Folio 'Names of the Actors' he is 'A Foolish
rival to Valentine'. The Duke calls him 'degenerate and
base' (v.iv).

TIBERIO, SON OF *(Rom.)* : one of the youths who
accompany Romeo to the masque at the Capulets'
house (I.iv; I.v).

TIMANDRA *(Tim.)* : one of Alcibiades' mistresses.

She and Phyrnia appear with him before Timon's cave.
Timon abuses her violently :

Be a whore still, they love thee not that use thee, give
them diseases; leaving with thee their lust. Make use
of thy salt hours, season the slaves for tubs and
baths, bring down rosecheek'd youth to the fubfast,
and the diet. (IV.iii).

When Timon accompanies his insults with gold,
Timandra and Phyrnia encourage him to carry on
(IV.iii).

The two whores seem only to be introduced to give
Timon a chance to revile sex.

TIME (as Chorus) *(Wint.)* : he appears at the beginning
of Act IV to explain that sixteen years have passed, that
Leontes has shut himself up alone with his grief, and
that Perdita has been brought up as a shepherd's
daughter in Bohemia (IV.i).

TIMON OF ATHENS *(Tim.)* : a noble Athenian. He
is surrounded by flatterers and parasites waiting to take
advantage of his well-known generosity (I.i). He presides
at a lavish banquet, where he refuses to accept the
offer of repayment of a loan from Ventidius, saying
that it was a gift ; in a speech he declares 'we are born to
do benefits' ; he watches the 'Masque of the Amazons',
and receives and distributes gifts (I.ii). The servants of
his creditors begin demanding their money: when
Flavius tells him of the desperate state of his finances,
Timon is not worried, for he is sure that his friends will
help him. He send messengers to solicit loans from
them, but none of them oblige (II.ii). He is infuriated by
his clamouring creditors, and pacifies them by inviting
them all to another feast (III.iv). At a mock feast he
abuses his guests violently before driving them out by
hurling dishes at them (III.vi). Disgusted with all
humanity because of the ingratitude shown to him, he
retreats to a cave in the woods where he sits and curses
mankind. While digging for roots he finds a 'store' of
gold ; he decides to use it to corrupt mankind. He gives
some to Alcibiades, and tells him to use it to spread
devastation with his army, and some to his two mistresses, whom he encourages to spread diseases. He is visited
by Apemantus, and they compete with each other in
misanthropy. Timon gives gold to some bandits who
visit him and almost charms them 'from their profession'. Flavius visits his master, and is received as 'the
singly honest man', but Timon tells him to leave in
case he starts cursing him also (IV.iii). Timon talks with
the poet and the painter, who have come because they
have heard of his gold, before driving them off (v.i).
Two senators beg him to return to Athens and lead
the defence of the city against Alcibiades, but he
scornfully refuses (v.ii). We hear of Timon's death, and
his epitaph is read by Alcibiades (v.v).

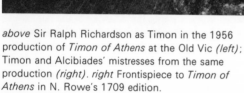

above Sir Ralph Richardson as Timon in the 1956
production of *Timon of Athens* at the Old Vic *(left)*;
Timon and Alcibiades' mistresses from the same
production *(right)*. *right* Frontispiece to *Timon of
Athens* in N. Rowe's 1709 edition.

Timon is not a fully developed character, but rather
an embodiment of two dominant traits. When we first
see him he is a man of 'right noble mind, illustrious
virtue', a generous and liberal idealist, reminiscent of
the personified Hospitality of the morality plays.
When, like Lear, he is a victim of ingratitude, he
becomes a terrifying misanthrope, cursing all humanity:

> ... Matrons, turn incontinent.
> Obedience fail in children. Slaves and fools
> Pluck the grave wrinkled senate from the bench,
> And minister in their steads. To general filths
> Convert o' th' instant green virginity.
> Do't in your parents eyes. Bankrupts, hold fast.
> Rather than render back, out with your knives,
> And cut your trusters' throats. Bound servants,
> steal.
> Large-handed robbers your grave masters are,
> And pill by law. Maid, to thy master's bed,
> Thy mistress is o' th' brothel. Son of sixteen,
> Pluck the lined crutch from thy old limping sire,
> With it beat out his brains. Piety, and fear,
> Religion to the gods, peace, justice, truth,
> Domestic awe, night-rest, and neighbourhood,

above Kemble as Timon : a fictitious engraving
published in 1785 *(left)* ; *A Midsummer Night's*

Dream : Oberon and Titania, engraved by J. C.
Edwards from a painting by H. Howard *(right)*.

Instruction, manners, mysteries, and trades,
Degrees, observances, customs, and laws,
Decline to your confounding contraries,
And yet confusion live. (IV.i)

In a passage that understandably attracted Karl Marx,
Timon turns his fury on to the corrupting power of gold :

That much of this will make black white; foul, fair;
Wrong, right; base, noble; old, young; coward,
valiant;
Ha, you gods! Why this? What, this, you gods? Why
this?
Will lug your priests and servants from your sides;
Pluck stout men's pillows from below their heads.
This yellow slave
Will knit and break religions, bless th' accursed,
Make the hoar leprosy adored, place thieves,
And give them title, knee, and approbation,
With senators on the bench. This is it
That makes the wappened widow wed again;
She, whom the spital-house and ulcerous sores
Would cast the gorge at, this embalms and spices
To th' April day again. (IV.iii)

The potential destructive power of the cash nexus has
perhaps never been so powerfully represented.

Timon of Athens was probably written in 1607–08;
it is generally agreed that the text we have is a rough
draft, and that the play is essentially unfinished. Timon
was the son of Echecratides, and lived in Athens during
the fifth century BC. Shakespeare's main source was
Plutarch's *Life of Antony*, where the story of Timon is
briefly told. Timon became a legendary misanthropic
figure through the influence of Lucian's dialogue
Timon, or the Misanthrope, which Shakespeare may
have read in Latin.

TITANIA *(MND.)* : the queen of the fairies. She
accuses Oberon of having 'come from the farthest steep
of India' for the sake of his 'buskin'd mistress' Hippolyta, and says that their dissensions are disturbing
nature and bringing evil to the 'human mortals', She
refuses to give up her 'young squire' to Oberon, and
leaves angrily (II.i). She sleeps, and Oberon applies
magic love-juice to her eyes (II.ii). She awakes and sees
Bottom with his ass's head, and falls in love with him.
She tells her fairies to wait on him, and to lead him to
her bower (III.i). She awakes disenchanted, loathing
Bottom; she ends her quarrel with Oberon, and leaves
happily with him (IV.i). At the end she tells her fairies to
join in blessing the palace of Theseus and those asleep
in it (V.ii). (*See* OBERON.)

TITINIUS *(Caes.)* : a friend of Brutus and Cassius.

269

above Vivien Leigh as Titania *(left)*; Titania (Peggy Ashcroft) and Bottom (Leslie Banks) in *A Midsummer Night's Dream* at the Theatre Royal, Haymarket, in 1945 *(right). below* Oberon (John Gielgud) with Titania in the same production.

At Philippi he is sent by Cassius to ascertain whether certain troops are friendly or hostile; Titinius finds that they are Brutus' troops. Cassius thinks that Titinius has been captured, despairs and kills himself. When Titinius returns he finds Cassius' body, and kills himself with Cassius' sword (v.iii).

In Plutarch Titinius is a centurion in Cassius' army at Philippi.

TITUS *(Tim.)*: the servant to one of Timon's creditors. He and other servants are sent by their masters to collect debts from Timon. When Timon sees them he flies into a rage and drives them away (III.iv).

TOM *(1H.IV)*: an ostler at the inn at Rochester. He does not appear. The two carriers shout to him offstage, abusing him for the time it is taking him to prepare their horses (II.i).

TOM *(2H.VI)*: a fellow apprentice with Peter Thump. Peter thinks he will be killed in his duel with Horner, and gives away all his possesions. Tom gets all the money that he has (II.iii).

TOM, POOR *(Lr.)*: name assumed by Edgar.

above *As You Like It* (v.i): Audrey, Touchstone, and William, by T. H. Nicolson. *below As You Like It* (ii.iv):

Rosalind, Celia and Touchstone in the Forest of Arden, from a painting by Millais.

TOPAS, SIR *(Tw.N.)*: role assumed by Feste (iv.ii).

TOUCHSTONE *(AYL.)*: Duke Frederick's court Fool. He accompanies Celia and Rosalind into the Forest of Arden, and shares their hardships. He discusses the relative merits of court and country life with Corin (iii.ii). He meets and courts Audrey, a country girl who he admits is 'an ill-favoured thing'; he bemuses and flouts her former lover, the rustic William, with a torrent of extravagant threats (v.i).

Touchstone is a wise fool, the representative of reality and common sense in the unreal world of the Forest of Arden. He is at his best as a parodist of courtly manners, as when he recalls his quarrel with a courtier over 'the seventh cause':

> I did dislike the cut of a certain courtier's beard. He sent me word, if I said his beard was not cut well, he was in the mind it was. This is called the Retort Courteous. If I sent him word again, it was not well cut, he would send me word he cut it to please himself. This is called the Quip Modest. If again, it was not well cut, he disabled my judgement. This is called the Reply Churlish. If again, it was not well cut, he would answer I spake not true. This is called the Reproof Valiant. If again, it was not well cut, he would say

above Mr King as Touchstone in 1774 *(left)* ; Cressida and Pandarus watch Troilus ride by *(Troilus and*

Cressida, I.ii). An engraving by Charles Warren from a painting by Thomas Kirk *(right)*.

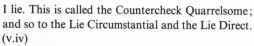

I lie. This is called the Countercheck Quarrelsome; and so to the Lie Circumstantial and the Lie Direct. (V.iv)

Touchstone finds consolation for the loss of these courtly diversions in the rustic Audrey, who he takes to satisfy his desires:

As the ox hath his bow, sir, the horse his curb, and the falcon her bells, so man hath his desires; and as the pigeons bill, so wedlock would be nibbling. (III.iii)

This kind of worldly honesty is demeaning; although Touchstone has the fool's licence to comment on the other characters and their follies, he is not a centre of moral wisdom as his name has sometimes been taken to imply. His reduction of love to animal desire shows the limitations of his wit, especially when we compare it with the sophisticated analysis conducted by Rosalind.

There is no equivalent character in Lodge's *Rosalynde*. It is thought that Touchstone was the first part Shakespeare wrote for Robert Armin, who replaced Will Kempe as the chief comedy actor in the Lord Chamberlain's Men around 1599.

TRANIO *(Shr.)* : Lucentio's servant. He impersonates his master so that Lucentio can woo Bianca in disguise as a tutor. As Lucentio he announces his intention of wooing Bianca so as to draw the attention of his master's rivals (I.ii). Tranio gets Baptista's permission to marry Bianca; he gets the Pedant to pretend to be Lucentio's father (IV.ii). When Lucentio's real father (Vincentio) arrives he places him under arrest as a 'mad knave', but when Lucentio acknowledges him as his father Tranio runs away. He is at the banquet at the end.

He is a shrewd figure, a servant who is wiser than his master.

TRAVERS *(2H.IV)* : a servant to Northumberland. He brings the true news of the defeat at Shrewsbury and the death of Hotspur (I.i).

TREBONIUS *(Caes.)* : one of the conspirators. He agrees with Brutus when he says that Mark Antony should not be killed along with Caesar (II.i). He leads Antony away from the Senate at the time of the assassination, and reports later that he has 'fled to his house amazed'.

In Plutarch's account it is Decius Brutus Albinus who

Tressel

engages Antony in conversation outside the Senate House at the time the assassination is taking place.

TRESSEL *(R.III)*: a gentleman attending Lady Anne. He does not speak (I.ii).

TRIBUNE *(Tit.)*: one represents the people when the imperial succession is being determined, and says that the people will accept whoever Titus nominates as Emperor (I.i). He is present at the gruesome banquet at the end, but does not speak (V.iii).

TRIBUNES *(Cym.)*: they are told by two senators that they are to levy men for Lucius' invasion of England (III.vii).

TRINCULO *(Tp.)*: a jester in the service of the King of Naples. He meets Caliban when drunk, and together they hide under Caliban's cloak, where they are found by Stephano. The three of them plot to kill Prospero, but they are led by Ariel into a 'filthy-mantled pool', and then chased off by spirit hounds. Prospero forgives them all at the end.

TROILUS *(Troil.)*: son of King Priam, Troilus loves Cressida, whose father, Chalchas, leaves her behind in Troy, when he deserts the city for the Grecian camp. Her uncle, Pandarus, encourages their love affair; but, when the Greeks and Trojans agree to an exchange of prisoners, she quits Troy and almost immediately becomes the mistress of the handsome Diomedes. Troilus, distraught and disillusioned, proclaims he will exact vengeance:

> Fly not, for shouldst thou take the river Styx,
> I could swim after. (V.iv)

Diomedes, nevertheless, escapes him; and Pandarus, the unscrupulous 'broker-lackey', rounds off the last scene with his cynical verdict upon the folly and falsity of human passions. (*See* CRESSIDA.)

TUBAL *(Mer.V.)*: a wealthy Jewish friend of Shylock. Shylock says he might have to turn to him to borrow the balance of the three thousand ducat loan to Antonio (I.iii). Later Tubal enters with both bad and good news for Shylock: he tells him that his daughter is spending the money that she stole from her father, and also that another of Antonio's ships has been reported sunk; Shylock is horrified and then delighted (III.i).

TUTOR, RUTLAND'S *(3H.VI)*: a priest in charge of the young Earl of Rutland. When Clifford comes to murder the boy the priest pleads for his life, but is dragged away by soldiers (I.iii).

TYBALT *(Rom.)*: nephew to Lady Capulet. He joins

Costume design for Tybalt, by Randolph Schwabe.

in the street brawl between the rival houses and fights with Benvolio (I.i). He protests against Romeo's presence at Capulet's feast, and picks a quarrel with him (I.v). Later he challenges him, but Romeo refuses to fight him because he is related to Juliet; Mercutio takes up the challenge, and is killed. Romeo is roused and kills Tybalt (III.i).

He is fiery and short-tempered, and reaches for his rapier at the slightest provocation. Mercutio dislikes his fashionable affectations:

> O he's the courageous captain of compliments. He fights as you sing prick-song, keeps time, distance, and proportion; he rests his minim rests, one, two, and the third in your bosom; the very butcher of a silk button, a duellist, a duellist; a gentleman of the very first house, of the first and second cause. Ah the immortal passado, the punto reverso, and hay! (II.iv)

TYRREL, SIR JAMES *(R.III)*: he is recommended to Richard by the page as one who might easily be bribed. He agrees to arrange the murder of the young Edward V and his brother in the Tower; he suborns Dighton and Forrest to murder them, and reports the deaths to Richard (IV.ii; IV.iii).

U

ULYSSES *(Troil.)* : one of the Greek commanders at
Troy. In the Greek council, he points out to his fellow
commanders how the Greek campaign is being weakened by the neglect of 'degree' (a proper hierarchical
ordering); he describes how Achilles spends his time
deriding his fellow Greeks, and sets out his plan for
tricking him into returning to the battle by making him
jealous of Ajax (I.iii). Ulysses and the other Greek
commanders flatter Ajax in order to make Achilles
jealous (II.iii). Ulysses suggests that the Greek commanders pass by Achilles and ostentatiously ignore
him; he talks with Achilles, and warns him that he is
being forgotten while Ajax is being exalted, and tells
him that his love for Polyxena is well known among the
Greeks (III.iii). When Cressida arrives he greets her
with a kiss, but describes her as a wanton (IV.v). With
Troilus, he observes Cressida with Diomedes, and restrains Troilus' rage and grief, which is incomprehensible
to him (V.i). In the battle he announces that Achilles
is arming (V.v).

In his formal speeches at least, Ulysses appears as the
wisest statesman in the Greek camp. His philosophy of
'degree' is the expression of a Renaissance ideal :

> Take but degree away, untune that string,
> And hark what discord follows. Each thing meets
> In mere oppugnancy. The bounded waters
> Should lift their bosoms higher than the shores,
> And make a sop of all this solid globe.
> Strength should be a lord of imbecility,
> And the rude son should strike his father dead.
> Force should be right, or rather right and wrong,
> Between whose endless jar justice resides,
> Should lose their names and so should justice too.
> Then every thing includes itself in power,
> Power into will, will into appetite,
> And appetite, an universal wolf,
> So doubly seconded with will and power,
> Must make perforce an universal prey,
> And last eat up himself. (I.iii)

Ulysses does not consistently adopt this heroic tone: at
other times, notably when he observes Troilus'
reaction to Cressida's unfaithfulness, he is a sardonic
commentator not unlike Thersites. It is when we
compare Ulysses' grandiloquent rhetoric with his
actions in the play that we see the irony in Shakespeare's
presentation of him. His noble views turn out to be
little more than intellectual exercises : the only practical
policy that he formulates is a cheap trick to try to get
Achilles to fight. His is a cold, calculating mind, but an
essentially trivial one. For all his grand theories, his
actions are governed by expediency. His kind of
'policy' is fulfilled in Achilles' murder of Hector.

URSULA *(Ado.)* : a gentlewoman attending Hero. As
instructed, she converses with her mistress on the
merits of Benedick and his great love for Beatrice; they
know that Beatrice can overhear them, and that as a
result she will be convinced that Benedick loves her
(III.i).

URSWICK, SIR CHRISTOPHER *(R.III)* : a priest.
Derby sends him to Richmond with the news that
George Stanley, his son, has been imprisoned by
Richard, and that the Queen has agreed to a marriage
between Richard and Elizabeth of York (IV.v).

He was Christopher Urswick, LLD., a churchman.
He was Richmond's chaplain and confessor; he landed
with him at Milford Haven, and was present at
Bosworth.

VALENTINE *(Gent.)*: one of the 'two gentlemen'. He goes to the court of Milan and there falls in love with the Duke's daughter Silvia (II.i). When he is about to elope with her Proteus betrays them to the Duke, who intends his daughter for Thurio; the Duke banishes Valentine (III.i). Valentine meets a band of outlaws in the forest, and agrees to become their leader, since many of them are gentlemen under sentence of banishment like himself. He comes across Proteus apparently about to rape Silvia, and rescues her. He sees Proteus' remorse, and offers to yield Silvia to him. Thurio enters and claims Silvia, but withdraws when Valentine threatens him. The Duke admires his spirit, and grants him Silvia's hand in marriage.

VALENTINE *(Tit.)*: a kinsman of the Andronici. He helps Titus shoot arrows bearing messages to the gods (IV.iii). Later he helps Caius and Publius bind and gag Demetrius and Chiron (V.ii).

VALENTINE *(Tw.N.)*: a lord attending Orsino. He enters to say that he was not admitted by Olivia, but brings a message from her handmaid to the effect that Olivia intends to remain 'cloistered' in mourning for a year (I.i). Later he tells Cesario (the disguised Viola) how much the Duke favours him (I.iv).

VALERIA *(Cor.)*: Virgilia's talkative friend. She accompanies Volumnia and Virgilia to the Volscian camp when they try to persuade Coriolanus to spare Rome (V.iii).

In Plutarch she is named as the sister of Publius Valerius Publicola; she advised the Roman matrons to ask Coriolanus' mother to go with them to the Volscians to plead with Coriolanus.

VARRIUS *(Ant.)*: a friend to Pompey. He brings him the news that Antony is making for Rome (II.i).

VARRIUS *(Meas.)*: a friend of the Duke's. He is the first to arrive to greet him at the city gates, and is with him when Isabella and Mariana expose the treachery of Angelo. He does not speak (IV.v; V.i).

The complete irrelevance of this character suggests that the text we have is not complete.

VARRO *(Caes.)*: one of Brutus' men. He and Claudius are ordered to sleep in Brutus' tent on the night before the battle at Philippi (IV.iii).

VARRO *(Tim.)*: he is Varro's servant. He is sent by his master to collect a debt from Timon, but fails to do so, since Timon has no money (II.ii; III.iv). In III.iv there are two of Varro's men.

VAUGHAN, SIR THOMAS *(R.III)*: he is led to execution along with Rivers and Grey on the orders of Richard (III.iii). His ghost appears to Richard before the battle at Bosworth (V.iii).

He had been a distinguished Yorkist soldier. His only crime was his loyalty to the late King's successor, for which he was executed.

VAUX *(2H.VI)*: Sir William Vaux. He tells the Queen and Suffolk that Cardinal Beaufort is dying (III.ii).

He was a zealous Lancastrian, attainted by Edward IV in 1461. He was with Queen Margaret at Tewkesbury, where he was killed.

VAUX, SIR NICHOLAS *(H.VIII)*: he leads Buckingham to the place of execution (II.i).

He was the son of the above. Wolsey suspected him of complicity in the supposed treason of Buckingham, but no action was taken against him. 'He was a jolly gentleman, both for camps and courts; a great reveller, good as well in a march as in a masque' (Fuller).

VENICE, DUKE OF *(Mer.V.)*: he presides over the court before which the case between Antonio and Shylock is tried. He pardons Shylock on condition that he surrenders half of his wealth to Antonio and half to the state, becomes a Christian, and makes a will in favour of Jessica and Lorenzo (III.iii).

The Dukes (Doges) of Venice did not in fact preside over the courts after the fourteenth century.

VENICE, DUKE OF *(Oth.)*: he hears Brabantio's accusations against Othello, and when he has heard Othello and Desdemona declare their love for each other he advises Brabantio to accept Othello as his son-in-law. He sends Othello to Cyprus to command the island's defence against the Turks (I.iii).

VENTIDIUS *(Ant.)*: one of Antony's generals. He has routed the Parthian army, but refuses to pursue them in search of greater glory for fear of arousing Antony's jealousy:

> I have done enough. A lower place, note well,
> May make too great an act. For learn this Silius,
> Better to leave undone, than by our deed
> Acquire too high a fame, when him we serve's away.
> Caesar and Antony have ever won
> More in their officer, than person. Sossius,
> One of my place in Syria, his lieutenant,
> For quick accumulation of renown,
> Which he achieved by th' minute, lost his favour.
> Who does i' th' wars more than his captain can,
> Becomes his captain's captain; and ambition,
> The soldier's virtue, rather makes choice of loss
> Than gain which darkens him.
> I could do more to do Antonius good,
> But 'twould offend him; and in his offence
> Should my performance perish. (III.i)

Ventidius' words are a sharp satire on the whole great Roman military edifice as embodied in Caesar and Antony, and they make us aware that Antony's status as a commander is not so important as it first appeared.

VENTIDIUS *(Tim.)*: he is imprisoned for debt. Timon pays his debts and has him released (I.i). He becomes very rich and offers to repay the loan, but Timon insists that it was a gift (I.ii). When Timon is in desperate need and appeals to Ventidius for the same sum, he is refused (III.iii).

VENTIDIUS, SERVANT OF *(Tim.)*: he tells Timon that his master is imprisoned for debt, and is sent to tell him that Timon will pay the debt and have him released (I.i).

VERGES *(Ado.)*: a headborough or petty constable, who, in spite of Dogberry's interruptions manages to inform Leonato that the watch have arrested 'two arrant knaves' (III.v). He helps in the examination of Conrade and Borachio (IV.ii).

Verges was the provincial pronunciation of 'verjuice', the acid juice of the crab-apple.

VERNON *(1H.VI)*: he suggests that the dispute between the Earl of Somerset and Richard Plantagenet he decided by the respective numbers of red and white

below Valentine forgives Proteus after saving Silvia from him. *The Two Gentlemen of Verona,* by William Holman Hunt (1851).

roses plucked by their supporters present in the Temple Garden. He himself plucks a white rose, indicating his support for Richard Plantagenet and the Yorkists (II.iv). Later he quarrels with the Lancastrian Basset, and wants to meet him in single combat, but is refused permission by the King.

He was Sir Richard Vernon; he was Speaker of the House of Commons in the Leicester Parliament.

VERNON, SIR RICHARD *(1H.IV)*: he joins Hotspur's rebellion, and suggests postponing the battle for a day (IV.iii). He acquiesces in Worcester's decision not to tell Hotspur of the King's generous offer of peace (V.ii). He is taken prisoner during the battle at Shrewsbury and is executed for treason (V.v).

He was Sir Richard Vernon, of Shipbrook in Cheshire, a man of considerable power in the north of England. He joined Hotspur's rebellion, and was

below Duke Vincentio (Sebastian Shaw) and Isabella (Estelle Kohler) in *Measure for Measure* (left); Kemble as Vincentio in *Measure for Measure*, by an unknown artist *(right)*.

captured at Shrewsbury and beheaded 'Upon the mondaie following' (Holinshed).

VINCENTIO *(Meas.)*: the Duke of Vienna. He says he is going to Poland, and hands over his power to his deputy Angelo, whom he tells to enforce the laws against immorality which have been allowed to lapse. He does not leave Vienna, but stays disguised as Friar Lodowick in order to observe what happens. When Angelo offers to save Claudio's life only if his sister Isabella gives herself to him, the Duke devises a way to save both his life and her honour: he arranges for Mariana *(q.v.)* to take Isabella's place on the night of her assignation with Angelo, and for a dead pirate's head to be presented to Angelo as Claudio's head. He then sends letters to Angelo saying that he is returning to Vienna and wishes to be met at the gates of the city. He arrives, and Mariana and Isabella implore him to

give them justice against Angelo; he at first pretends to disbelieve them, and encourages Angelo to think that he is safe. When he reveals himself he makes Angelo marry Mariana, and then sends him to execution. He only reprieves him when Isabella joins Mariana in asking for mercy for him. He condemns Lucio to be whipped for slandering him, but relents and only insists that Lucio marries the woman whom he has deserted along with his child. The Duke implies that he will marry Isabella.

Escalus says that the Duke is 'one that above all other strifes, contended especially to know himself', and that he is 'a gentleman of all temperance' who has been 'a scholar, a statesman, and a soldier'. He has been seen as an enigmatic figure, even as a hypocrite, because of his machinations while in disguise. But we should see him above all else as a stage duke, the necessary *deus ex machina* who keeps the tragic potential of the plot under control so that we can focus more clearly on the moral issues raised by it. He is also an allegorical figure: his morality is that of Christ, and he is the supreme arbiter of value within the play. He derives partly from the old folktales of the sovereign in disguise mixing with his people; and he can also reasonably be associated with James I. James took his responsibilities as ruler very seriously, and even published a book on the responsibilities of a king, *Basilicon Doron,* in 1603. Many of the qualities that he praises in this book are to be found in Shakespeare's Duke Vincentio, who wants to show Vienna the problems of good government by demonstrating them. *Measure for Measure* was acted at court on 26 December 1604, and it is probable that it was then a fairly new play. Shakespeare's sources were George Whetstone's play *Promos and Cassandra* (1578), and Cinthio's collection of stories *Hecatomiithi*, from which he also took the story of *Othello*.

VINCENTIO *(Shr.)*: an old gentleman of Pisa, father to Lucentio. He meets Petruchio on the road to Padua, and is baffled when he presents him to Katharine as a young maiden; he is told that his son Lucentio has married Bianca (IV.v). When he arrives at Lucentio's house he is accused of being an impostor by the Pedant, and is on the point of being imprisoned when Lucentio arrives and greets him as his father (V.i).

VINTNER *(1H.IV)*: he enters and tells the bemused Francis to be more attentive to his guests, and tells Hal and Poins that Falstaff and his cronies are outside (II.iv).

VIOLA *(Tw.N.)*: the twin sister of Sebastian. She is shipwrecked off the coast of Illyria; she lands safely, and is assured by the Captain that her brother is safe. She hears the story of Orsino's love for Olivia, and decides to go and serve disguised as a page (I.ii). As 'Cesario' she is taken into the Duke's service, and is sent to convey his love to Olivia; she admits that 'Who e'er I woo, myself would be his wife' (I.iv). She gets access to Olivia, and gives an eloquent account of Orsino's

Frontispiece to *Measure for Measure* in Rowe's 1709 edition of Shakespeare's plays.

passion, and goes on to add what 'he' would do in his master's place (I.v). Malvolio gives 'him' a ring from Olivia: Viola realizes that Olivia has fallen in love with 'Cesario' (II.ii). As Cesario, she tells Orlando that she loves someone older than herself, meaning him; she is given a jewel to take to Olivia (II.iv). When she attempts to deliver it and Orsino's message to Olivia she is stopped by Olivia's declaration of love for her as 'Cesario'; 'he' replies that he will give his heart to 'no woman' (II.i). She continues to rebuff Olivia's approaches; she is told by Sir Toby that there is a knight who demands to fight 'Cesario'; she reluctantly prepares to fight Aguecheek, but is interrupted by the arrival of Antonio, who thinks that 'Cesario' is Sebastian. He is amazed when 'he' disclaims all knowledge of him (III.iv). 'Cesario' is claimed by Olivia as her betrothed husband, and produces the priest who performed the ceremony. Viola is saved by the entrance of Sebastian, and hesitantly admits her disguise; she finds that Orsino loves her in her true character (V.i).

Viola is vital, sensitive and considerate; it is her energy that transforms the passivity of Orsino and Olivia.

above Viola (Jean Forbes-Robertson) fights with Sir Andrew (Norman Forbes) in *Twelfth Night* at the New Theatre in 1932 *(top)* ; Julia Marlowe as Viola, 1907 *(bottom)* ; Mrs Hopkins as Volumnia : a fictitious print published 1776 in Bell's Edition of Shakespeare *(right)*.

VIOLENTA *(All's W.)* : she accompanies the Widow of Florence, Diana and Mariana, but does not speak (III.v).

VIRGILIA *(Cor.)* : Coriolanus' wife. She vows not to leave her house until he returns from the wars (I.iii). She welcomes him when he returns, and he calls her 'My gracious silence' (II.i). Later she helps Volumnia persuade him to spare Rome (v.iii).

She is quiet, almost timid, quite unlike the stern Roman matron Volumnia. Whereas Volumnia proudly displays Coriolanus' wounds, Virgilia weeps over them.

VOLTEMAND *(Ham.)* : a courtier at Elsinore. He is sent by Claudius as ambassador, with Cornelius, to the King of Norway to tell him of the Danish concern

about the threatened invasion by his nephew Fortinbras (I.ii). They return later to say that Fortinbras has been persuaded to march against Poland (II.i).

VOLUMNIA *(Cor.)* : Coriolanus' mother. She greets him with his new name 'Coriolanus' when he returns victorious from the war against the Volscians (II.i). She persuades him to conceal his contempt for the plebeians until after they have ratified him as consul (III.ii). She despises them as much as he does. It is she who finally persuades him to spare Rome (v.iii).

Volumnia has made her son what he is; she is obsessed with the harsh Roman military values to the exclusion of natural human feeling:

If my son were my husband, I should freelier rejoice in that absence wherein he won honour, than in the embracements of his bed, where he would show most love. When yet he was but tender-bodied, and the only son of my womb; when youth with comeliness plucked all gaze his way; when for a day of kings' entreaties, a mother should not sell him an hour from her beholding; I considering how honour would become such a person, that it was no better than picture-like to hang by the wall, if renown made it not stir, was pleased to let him seek danger where he was like to find fame. To a cruel war I sent him, from whence he returned, his brows bound with oak. I tell thee daughter, I sprang not more in joy at first hearing he was a man-child, than now in first seeing he had proved himself a man. (I.iii)

VOLUMNIUS *(Caes.)*: one of Brutus' men, and an old school-fellow of his. After the defeat at Philippi Brutus asks Volumnius to kill him, but he refuses and runs away to escape capture by Antony and Octavius (v.v).

Margaret Tyzack as Volumnia in the 1972 production of *Coriolanus* by the Royal Shakespeare Company.

W

WALTER *(Shr.)*: one of the servants at Petruchio's country house (IV.i).

WARDERS *(1H.VI)*: they are guards at the Tower gates. They refuse to admit Gloucester and his men (I.iii).

WART, THOMAS *(2H.IV)*: he is one of the potential recruits found by Justice Shallow, and one of those selected by Falstaff to serve in the King's army (III.ii)

WARWICK, EARL OF *(2H.IV; H.V; 1H.VI)*: he assures King Henry that Glendower is dead, and listens to his views on the turmoil in the realm (III.i). Later he defends Prince Henry's frivolous conduct, and assures the King that when the time comes he will 'cast off his followers' (IV.iii).

In *Henry V* he is present at Agincourt. He intervenes in the quarrel between Williams and Fluellen (IV.viii).

In *Henry VI* he plucks a white rose in the Temple Garden, and predicts the Wars of the Roses (I.i). He helps Richard Plantagenet recover his title of Duke of York by petitioning the King (III.i). He is present at the examination of Joan Pucelle, and is one of those who insist she be burnt (v.iv).

He was Richard Beauchamp (1381–1439). He succeeded his father as Earl of Warwick in 1401. He was a great warrior; he almost captured the elusive Owen Glendower after defeating his rebels, and went on to fight with Henry IV at Shrewsbury. In 1408 he went on a pilgrimage to the Holy Land, and became famous for his chivalry in the lists of France on his way there. In 1415 he went with Henry V to France; he and Clarence were sent back to England with the spoils and prisoners after the siege of Harfleur, and he was not at Agincourt. He returned to France and arranged the truce that preceded the Treaty of Troyes. Henry V bequeathed the care and education of his young son to Warwick, who became a member of the Council of the Regency after Henry's death. He returned to France, and in 1431 he captured the illustrious Pouton de Santrailles, the knight who had captured Talbot; the two distinguished prisoners were exchanged. In 1437 he was appointed

Lieutenant of France and Normandy; he remained in France until his death at Rouen in 1439.

WARWICK, EARL OF *(2&3H.VI)*: a Yorkist. He sheds tears when he hears of the loss of Anjou and Maine, and vows to win the latter back from France (I.i). He quarrels with Somerset (I.iii); he listens to York's claim to the throne, and is convinced that it is just (II.ii). Henry tells him to inspect the body of Gloucester, and he returns and reports that Gloucester has undoubtedly been murdered; he is challenged by Suffolk, and is later accused by him of having attacked him 'with the men of Bury' (III.ii). Warwick and Clifford exchange threats (v.i), and at St Albans Warwick calls for Clifford to fight him, but York claims priority (v.ii). He rejoices in the victory 'won by famous York' (v.iii).

In *3 Henry VI* he hails Richard, Duke of York, as the rightful king, and leads him to the throne; he takes part in the ensuing debate when Henry arrives, and agrees to the proposal that Henry should reign for life (I.i). Warwick announces the Yorkist defeat at St Albans (II.i), but says that he will raise more soldiers to attack the Queen and the Lancastrians. He is derided by the Queen as 'long-tongued Warwick' who fled at St Albans (II.ii). At Towton Warwick kills his horse to show he has no intention of leaving the field; in the battle he 'rages like a chafed bull' (II.iv). He proposes seeking the Lady Bona's hand for Edward, and presents the proposal to her on Edward's behalf; he is amazed and furious when he learns that Edward has married Lady Grey. He renounces him, and vows to be revenged; he joins Henry VI. He seizes Edward in his tent near Coventry, and removes his crown (IV.iii). Warwick and Clarence are made joint Protectors of the realm by Henry. From the walls of Coventry Warwick defies Edward, who has invaded from France. At the Battle of Barnet he is mortally wounded, and dies as he hears of the Lancastrian defeat (v.ii).

He was Richard Neville (1428–71), who after his death became known as the 'King-maker'. He succeeded to the vast Warwick estates in 1449 as a result of his marriage to Anne Beauchamp, the only daughter and heiress of Richard Beauchamp. He supported Richard, Duke of York, when he claimed the regency. He became a popular hero in England through his exploits in the Channel, which included a very successful attack on a Spanish fleet at Calais. He was briefly in control of Henry VI after he captured him at Northampton in 1460, but Margaret recaptured him at the second battle of St Albans in 1461. Warwick then joined Edward Duke of York and helped him become King as Edward IV by defeating the Lancastrians at Towton. Warwick was the real ruler of England during the first three years of Edward's reign. He was offended by Edward's marriage to Lady Grey, and withdrew from court, and went to Calais. He returned and captured Edward near Coventry, but the King escaped from Middleham Castle, and defeated Warwick at Stamford in 1470. He escaped to France, where he and Lewis XI conceived a plan to restore Henry VI. With great difficulty Warwick and Queen Margaret were reconciled, and Warwick invaded England. Edward fled, and Henry was removed from the Tower and restored to the throne, with Warwick and Clarence as joint Protectors of the realm. Edward returned with an invasion force; Clarence defected from Warwick, who was defeated and killed at Barnet in 1471.

John Palmer as the Earl of Warwick in *3 Henry VI*; a fictitious print published in 1786.

Warwick was an energetic opportunist; he was romanticized by Bulwer Lytton in his novel *The Last of the Barons* as 'a man who stood colossal amidst the iron images of the age, the greatest and the last of the old Norman chivalry; kinglier in the pride, in state, in possessions, and in renown than the king himself'. For the chronicler Hall he was 'not onely a man of marvelous qualities and facundious facions but also from his youth, by a certayn practice or naturall inclinacion, so set them forward, with witte and gentle demeanour, to all persons of high and lowe degre, that among all sortes of people he obteyned great love, much favour, and more credence.'

WESTMINSTER, ABBOT OF *(R.II)*: Richard is put in his charge until his trial (IV.i). He plots to murder Henry with the Bishop of Carlisle and Aumerle, but when the plot is exposed he dies 'with clog of conscience and sour melancholy' (V.vi).

He was William de Colchester (*d*.1420). He was one of the commissioners sent to the Tower to receive Richard's resignation of the crown. The story of his conspiracy against Henry IV, and of his subsequent death of palsy brought on by fear, was taken by Shakespeare from the Chronicles; it has no historical foundation. One of the conspirators, Carlisle, was in fact placed under the Abbot of Westminster's care.

WESTMORLAND, EARL OF *(1&2H.IV; H.V)*: a supporter of Henry IV. He sets out against Douglas (III.ii). At the end he is sent to oppose Northumberland and Scrope (V.v).

In *2 Henry IV* he meets the rebels, and invites them to meet Prince John and talk (IV.i). He pledges peace with Scrope and Mowbray, and pretends to dismiss John's troops. As soon as he hears that the rebel forces have disbanded, he and John treacherously arrest the leaders and send them to execution (IV.ii).

In *Henry V* he is at Agincourt. He longs for ten thousand more men, and when he says so he provokes Henry's St Crispin speech (IV.iii).

He was Ralph Neville (1364–1425); he became Earl of Westmorland in 1397. He was one of the first nobles to join Bolingbroke when he landed. He fought against the Percys at Shrewsbury in 1403, and afterwards was sent against Northumberland, who surrendered to him in 1404. When Scrope rebelled in 1405 Westmorland met his forces at Skipton Moor with a much inferior army; he arranged a conference with Scrope and Mowbray to discuss their grievances. He persuaded them that he was sympathetic to their demands, and they agreed to dismiss their troops. As soon as they had done so Westmorland had them arrested and taken to Pontefract, and later executed.

Westmorland's most famous speech in Shakespeare

Westmorland with King Henry v *(Henry V,* IV.iii).

is probably his appeal for more men before Agincourt; he was not in fact in France at the time, since Henry had left him behind to guard the Scottish marches.

WESTMORLAND, EARL OF *(3H.VI)*: a supporter of Henry VI. He loses faith in him when York is made heir to the throne (I.i).

He was Ralph Neville, 2nd Earl of Westmorland. The scene is unhistorical: Westmorland remained aloof from both parties during the Wars of the Roses.

WHITMORE, WALTER *(2H.VI)*: he is given the Duke of Suffolk as a prize, and refuses to accept ransom for him. Suffolk is startled to hear that his captor's name is Walter, since it had been predicted that he would die by 'water'. Whitmore leads Suffolk away, and returns with his body.

Nothing is known of Whitmore: it is possible that he was one of the Whitmores of Shropshire and Cheshire.

WIDOW, A *(Shr.)*: Hortensio marries her when he finds he has lost Bianca to Lucentio (IV.v). At Lucentio's banquet she loses her husband a wager when she does come obediently when he calls (v.ii).

WIDOW OF FLORENCE *(All'sW.)*: the mother of Diana Capilet. She gives lodging to Helena, who promises her gold and a dowry for her daughter in return for her help in winning back Bertram.

WILL *(2H.VI)*: a fellow apprentice with Peter Thump. Peter expects to be killed in his duel with Horner, and gives away all his possessions. Will gets his hammer (II.iii).

WILLIAM *(AYL.)*: a country bumpkin. He is in love with Audrey, whom he loses to the superior wit of Touchstone. He does not seem perturbed by this misfortune (v.i).

WILLIAMS, MICHAEL *(H.V)*: an English soldier with Henry's army in France. He argues with the disguised King on the night before Agincourt; they exchange gloves, and Williams promises to strike the man who claims the glove he will wear in his cap (IV.i). The King gives Fluellen Williams' glove, and tells him that it belongs to the Duke of Alençon. Williams strikes him, and calls him a traitor. The King appears and explains his joke, and gives Williams a gloveful of crowns.

WILLOUGHBY, LORD *(R.II)*: he deserts Richard and joins the rebel nobles after Richard confiscates John of Gaunt's lands (II.i). He joins Bolingbroke near Berkeley (II.iii).

He was Baron William de Eresby (*d.*1409).

WINCHESTER, BISHOP OF *(2H.VI)*, *see* BEAUFORT, HENRY.

WINCHESTER, BISHOP OF *(H.VIII)*, *see* GARDINER, STEPHEN.

WITCHES, THREE *(Mac.)*: they plan to meet Macbeth 'ere set of sun' (I.i). They hail Macbeth as Thane of Glamis and Cawdor, and 'king hereafter', and they hail Banquo as the father of a line of kings (I.iii). Later they are rebuked by Hecate for acting without her authority (III.v); with her they brew a 'hell-broth', and show Macbeth apparitions (IV.i).

The reference to 'the master o' the Tiger' in (I.iii) is probably a reference to Sir Edward Michelbourne's ship of that name which arrived in England on 27 June 1606 after a calamitous voyage of 567 days ('sev'nights, nine times nine'). This suggests that Shakespeare was working on Macbeth during the summer of 1606.

WOLSEY, CARDINAL *(H.VIII)*: he helps bring about the downfall of Buckingham, and tells Katharine to accede to the divorce (III.i). He insists that Henry shall not marry Anne Bullen. Papers which show that he has been extorting money, and a letter to the Pope 'against the King' are intercepted and given to the King; Henry confronts him with them and dismisses him from his office (III.vii). He dies, and Katharine, who had seen him as her enemy, asks Griffith to remind her of his goodness:

> Though from an humble stock, undoubtedly
> Was fashioned to much honour from his cradle.
> He was a scholar, and a ripe and good one;
> Exceeding wise, fair-spoken, and persuading;
> Lofty and sour to them that loved him not,
> But to those men that sought him sweet as summer.
> And though he were unsatisfied in getting,
> Which was a sin, yet in bestowing, madam,
> He was most princely; ever witness for him
> Those twins of learning he raised in you,
> Ipswich and Oxford, one of which fell with him,
> Unwilling to outlive the good that did it;

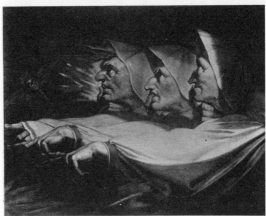

above **The Three Witches** by Decamps *(top)*; *The Weird Sisters* by Henry Fuseli *(bottom)*; *left* J. H. Barnes as Williams in *Henry V*.

> The other, though unfinished, yet so famous,
> So excellent in art, and still so rising,
> That Christendom shall ever speak his virtue.
> His overthrow heaped happiness upon him;
> For then, and not till then, he felt himself,
> And found the blessedness of being little.
> And to add greater honours to his age
> Than man could give him, he died, fearing God.
>
> (IV.ii)

Wolsey is a great and commanding figure, but we see little of the man beneath the public persona. He has some magnificent rhetorical declamations, but says very little that reveals the complexity of the thoughts and emotions behind his obvious surface motives.

Charles Kean as Wolsey in *Henry VIII*.

Cardinal Wolsey (1471–1530) helped to organize the meeting on the Field of the Cloth of Gold in 1520, and was Henry's trusted adviser up to the time of the divorce. At first Wolsey supported Henry's claims, but he fell from favour for apparently delaying the proceedings; the delay was really due to Cardinal Campeggio. His fall was sudden: a bill of indictment was prepared against him, and his property was confiscated, in 1529. The next year he was arrested at Cawood on a charge of high treason which was based on the false testimony of his Italian physician Dr Augustine. He was on his way to London to attend his trial when he died.

Wolsey was not ruined by accidentally giving the King an inventory of his private wealth: the man who did this was Thomas Ruthall, Bishop of Durham (in 1423). It was in fact Wolsey who suggested to Henry that he should confiscate Ruthall's vast wealth.

WOODVILLE, LIEUTENANT OF THE TOWER *(1H.VI)*: acting on orders from the Bishop of Winchester, he refuses to open the gates of the Tower to Gloucester and his men (I.iii).

He was Lord Woodville of the Mote; he was in fact Constable of the Tower.

Y

YORICK (skull of) *(Ham.)*: he was the King's jester in Hamlet's youth. Hamlet sees the gravediggers unearth his skull as they prepare Ophelia's grave. This provokes his famous meditation:

> Alas poor Yorick! I knew him Horatio, a fellow of infinite jest, of most excellent fancy; he hath borne me on his back a thousand times, and now how abhorred in my imagination it is – my gorge rises at it. Here hung those lips that I have kissed I know not how oft. Where be your gibes now? Your gambols, your songs, your flashes of merriment, that were wont to set the table on a roar? Not one now to mock your own grinning? Quite chop-fallen? Now get you to my lady's chamber, and tell her, let her paint an inch thick, to this favour she must come. Make her laugh at that. (v.i)

YORK, ARCHBISHOP OF *(R.II), see* SCROOP, RICHARD.

YORK, ARCHBISHOP OF *(R.III)*: he resigns his seal of office to Queen Elizabeth when he learns that her brothers Earl Rivers and Lord Grey have been imprisoned by Gloucester and Buckingham: he conducts her and the young Duke of York to sanctuary (II.iv).

He was Thomas Rotherham (1423–1500). He was temporarily imprisoned by Richard III for supporting Queen Elizabeth and her sons; he was released after Richard's coronation, and withdrew from public affairs.

YORK, DUCHESS OF *(R.III)*: she mourns the death of Edward IV and Clarence, and goes into sanctuary with Queen Elizabeth and the young Duke of York (II.iv). She is refused entry to the Tower to see the Princes (IV.i); she curses Richard, saying 'Bloody thou art, bloody will be thy end' (IV.iv).

She was Cicely Neville (1438–95). She married Richard Plantagenet, Duke of York, and became the mother of two kings, Edward IV and Richard III.

YORK, DUKE OF *(R.III)*: the second son of Edward IV, and one of the 'Princes in the Tower'. He is taken to sanctuary by the Queen, who hears his life is in danger (II.iv). He banters precociously with his uncle Richard of Gloucester (III.i). He and his brother are murdered by Dighton and Forrest in the Tower (IV.iii).

YORK, DUKE OF, RICHARD PLANTAGENET *(1,2&3H.VI)*: as Richard Plantagenet he tells his supporters in the Temple Garden to pluck a white rose; he quarrels with Somerset who says he is a mere 'yeoman' since his father was attainted (II.iv). He visits the dying Mortimer *(q.v.)* in the Tower and learns of the true reason for his father's execution (II.v). He is restored to the title Duke of York (III.i), and is made Regent in France (IV.i). He refuses to aid the Talbots, and blames their deaths on Somerset's delay (IV.iii). He fights with Joan Pucelle, and insults her when she is taken prisoner (v.iii). At her trial he sentences her to be burnt; he grudgingly confirms the truce with Charles of France (v.iv).

In *2 Henry VI* he is dismayed when he hears the terms of Henry VI's marriage with Margaret of Anjou, and feels that lands that were rightly his have been ceded; he resolves to bring Henry down, and take the throne, to which he has a good claim (I.i). He discusses his title to the throne with Salisbury and Warwick (II.ii). He accuses Gloucester of treason; he is sent to Ireland as Regent, but plans to use Jack Cade to stir up revolt in his absence (III.i). He leads his army to Blackheath, but disbands it when he is told that Somerset is a prisoner; he is furious when he finds that he has been deceived; he declares openly that he is the rightful king (v.i). At St Albans he defeats the royal forces, and kills Clifford; he sets out for London (v.iii).

In *3 Henry VI* York enters Parliament and seats himself on the throne; he refuses to leave when Henry enters, but finally agrees to allow him the crown for the rest of his life, on the condition that it reverts to the house of York (I.i). At Sandal Castle his three sons persuade him to break his oath; he hears that the Queen's army intends to besiege him in the castle (I.ii). He is taken prisoner, and brought before Margaret, who mocks him by seating him on a molehill and placing a

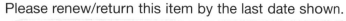

Please renew/return this item by the last date shown.

So that your telephone call is charged at local rate, please call the numbers as set out below:

	From Area codes 01923 or 0208:	From the rest of Herts:
Renewals:	01923 471373	01438 737373
Enquiries:	01923 471333	01438 737333
Minicom:	01923 471599	01438 737599

L32b

Hertfordshire
COUNTY COUNCIL
Community Information

10/12

L32a